Good Blood

A Journey of Healing

Irit Schaffer

For information, contact
MSI Press
1760-F Airline Highway, #203
Hollister, CA 95023

Front cover Photo Lori A. Cheung.
Front cover Photo and Graphic Hendrik Paul
Back Cover Photo of Irit Schaffer by Vaschelle André

Library of Congress Control Number 2016960051

ISBN: 978-1-942891-22-2

To my mom and dad.

~~~~~~~~~

The earth does not belong to man, man belongs to the earth. All things are connected like the blood that unites us all. Man did not weave the web of life, he is merely a strand in it. Whatever he does to the web, he does to himself.

Chief Seattle

Contents

Irit Schaffer

Ackowledgements

I want to thank God and my Guardian Angels, who have always brought me the right people at exactly the right time to help guide me on this amazing journey of *Good Blood*.

I want to thank everyone who appears in the book because it is their contribution that makes this book what it is.

I am grateful to Pam Houston for all that she has done to guide me as a writer. She has been key in helping me with developing *Good Blood*.

I want to give special thanks to Betty Lou Leaver. Her vision, wisdom, and uncanny ability to always guide me in the right direction at the appropriate time is part of what has made this process so magical.

Betty introduced me to Mary Ann Raemisch, my editor. Mary Ann understood the vision of the book, and she always asked the right questions to get me to probe deeper and allow the wisdom and deeper truth to show itself. Awesome, amazing, and a commitment to excellence is how I would describe Mary Ann.

Thank you to:

- Carl Leaver for the cover and so much more on the publishing side;

- Dr. John Upledger for being an important influence in my journey as a physical therapist and healer;

- Sifu Ko Wong, my Chi Kung teacher for over 20 years, and his influence on my understanding of the power of chi;

- Eric Otto for being my spiritual advisor and for being such a powerful intuitive mind, body, and spirit coach, helping me understand myself and my gifts.

- Dana Duryea, Hendrik Paul, Kate Stickley, Tami Anderson, and Sally Thresher, who each played an important role in helping the book with their creative ideas and input;

- Patti Evans for being there for me in physical therapy school; and

- Edna, Ryan, Marc, Mike, Zachary, Jacob, Ben, Alex, Madison, Oliver, Noah, Michelle, Robyn, and Christine, for their love and support.

To my healers, friends, relatives, and clients, a big thank you.

Author Note

People ask me when I began my journey with Good Blood, and my answer is always the same "when I was born." I laugh when I say it, but it is true. As a child in Montréal, I would curl up next to my dad and beg to hear the stories of his childhood, his family, and his incredible war experiences.

"Dad, tell me again how you had the bullets taken out without pain medicine and you didn't even cry. Dad, tell me again how you healed."

"Dad, tell me again," was my favorite line.

With my mom, it was different. It was forbidden to talk to her about the holocaust for fear that she would faint, and I was always afraid she wouldn't come to. Yet, as a child, I did know three things about her war experience, and those three things made a deep impact on me:

- She had exit papers to leave, but she stayed to help her parents.

- A Christian family hid her and her parents, and it was a Jew who informed on them.

- Her father gave her a gold chain when they went into hiding which she kept hidden in a compartment in her shoe. On the day of liberation, she took it out of her shoe and put it around her neck and never took it off again. It was her most important possession and she wouldn't trade it for any amount of money.

However, it took my mom 50 years to share her actual experiences.

I used a strategy on her that my mom had used on me all my life to get her to open up: guilt. "How would your grandkids and great grandkids feel if you were the only one who did not share?" I said over and over again until she finally agreed.

My parent's stories of survival had an impact on everything in my life. The stories sparked my never-ending quest to learn more about the healing powers within us, the resiliency of the human body and spirit, and our ability to overcome and transcend. That is a major theme in this book, following me from my youth and days as a physical education teacher to my life as a healer with a Master's of Science degree in physical therapy.

When I was in physical therapy school, another key event in my journey took place. I was injured and suffered debilitating pain. I was told I would just have to "live with it" even though no one knew what was causing the excruciating pain.

It was my dad's experiences and his innate ability to heal that kept me believing that I would recover and that the impossible was possible. It was then that the idea hit me like a lightning bolt. I had to write a book about healing and get his story down. And so was planted the Good Blood seed.

I decided to travel to Europe to meet the family I knew and loved through all my childhood stories. Their kindness, warmth, and love is something I will always cherish.

The most amazing thing is that none of them had ever uttered a word about any of their wartime experiences, even to each other, until I visited. When they spoke to me, though, they opened up. They all said in unison, "We are doing this for Zoli [my dad]."

They shared not only what happened to them but also how they managed to maintain hope. They shared what had allowed them to continue to believe in the good of mankind in spite of all that they had endured.

My upbringing instilled in me beliefs that allow me to be in constant wonderment of how we heal. It has influenced my ability as a physical therapist to help people on their healing journey. In my book, you will meet clients who have been my amazing teachers of possibility.

~~~~~~~~~~

Fast forward to 2014. In September of 2014, my mom became ill, and I flew to Montreal to be with her. She wanted me to have her gold chain.

On December 31, a week after she passed away, I put on the chain because I was heading back to San Francisco the following day. The chain felt like an incredibly heavy weight. It belonged in a museum and not on me.

On January 2, I felt for the chain—and it wasn't there. My mom had had it for 70 years, through all that she went through, and in two days, I had lost it. The chain, the reminder of unconditional love and light was nowhere to be found. My mom's neighbor, Muriel, who was like family to my mom, checked my mom's old apartment, as did Julie her caregiver, with no results. I was devastated beyond words. I had sleepless nights and could not share any of this with any family members. All I could do was focus on letting go of how bad I felt about losing my mom's most important possession. It represented the miracles of her survival. I kept saying to myself, "there must be a reason for this."

Three weeks later I received an email from Muriel. The night before, it suddenly occurred to Muriel to ask Julie to check and see if, by chance, the gold chain was in the carpet runner I had given Julie. It was still rolled up because Julie hadn't had time to bring it to the cleaners before putting it in her home. Miraculously, the gold chain was found. It is the gold chain on the cover of this book. The gold chain is the reminder to me of the miracles of my parents' experiences: that hope is always possible, that we are not alone, and that there is a light that always shines. It is now in a safe place, and I will never wear it again.

All these stories are true. It is the truth that I remember and the truth as others relayed it to me. Some of the names, places, and addresses have been changed.

The many voices of knowing in the book have inspired me. I look forward to you, the reader, meeting and getting to know the people who belong to the voices, and I believe they will touch you, too, in a special way.

Welcome to Good Blood: A Journey of Healing.
Irit Schaffer

Irit Schaffer

Foreword
by Arjia Rinpoche

I was enjoying the sun rays shining through the giant red wood trees after a stormy winter day in Mill Valley when my dear friend Naomi walked up the stone steps with an attractive lady. She introduced her as Irit. Right after our introduction, Irit and I got into a long conversation about our backgrounds. Suddenly I found myself in memory lane feeling as if I were right back in Tibet in the 1950s. But then quickly I realized I was still in Mill Valley -- just telling my story. Both Irit and I felt deeply connected, and from that moment on, we were able to develop a close friendship because we had shared our memories. Even though, we were from different cultures, we had faced similar challenges in life.

When I was a small boy in Tibet, I had been wrenched from my secure monastery during the Religious Reform Movement of the 1950s and made to divest myself of my monastic robes and attend a Chinese school. Later during the Cultural Revolution, I had been made to work in a forced labor camp for more than a decade. During this time, I had personally witnessed the imprisonment and death of my closest friends and relatives. Only my Buddhist teachings and the close companionship of my uncle and other relatives and friends had allowed me the courage and forbearance to still lead a peaceful and happy life.

Irit grew up in a family that had been victims of the Holocaust. Both of her parents and other close relatives had been forcibly taken from their homes, jammed into cattle cars, and suffered in notorious Nazi camps, including the Bergen Belsen Death Camp in Germany. Although they were close-mouthed about their experiences, Irit had managed to have each parent relate to her some of the horrors they had gone through. Touched deeply by their sufferings, Irit had found comfort in the example of her beloved father who explained to her how closely connected everyone is and that our true purpose and happiness in life is in giving to others. He taught her that always "from something bad, good will come." His love and persistent kindness gave her the resources to also lead a peaceful and happy life.

The two of us have much in common.

The title of her book Good Blood: A Journey of Healing reflects my personal practice of warm heartedness and a lifetime path to true inner peace. In this book, Irit skillfully weaves life experiences with her personal philosophy so that her themes of interconnectedness, higher purpose, compassion, and each person's potential for enlightenment embroider a fabric that explains how we can heal ourselves and each other.

Furthermore, Irit Schaffer's artful story telling allows us to understand deeply how suffering can be made to serve a higher purpose. Her father had taken six bullets, but he made it through; instead of showing hatred toward the people who shot him, he practiced forgiveness and gratitude. I was very touched by his action because I recall my uncle teaching us how to practice the six paramitas and the importance of forgiveness and compassion. "Never have a hateful heart."

Good Blood: A Journey of Healing gives hope to all of us in this challenging world who need to feel the magic touch of healing.

Arjia Rinpoche, Director
Tibetan Mongolian Buddhist Cultural Center
Bloomington, Indiana
January 2016

1

1961

The most beautiful thing we can experience is the mysterious.
It is the source of all true art and science.

Albert Einstein

As soon as I looked into his blue eyes, every cell in my body bubbled with joy. Yes, this must be love. I am in love for the first time. His are the bluest eyes I have ever seen. They are like the deep blue of the ocean on a clear and sunny day. My mom is sitting to my left, my sister, Edna, to my right, and I am falling in love.

Ari Ben Canaan is his name. He is in charge of taking a boatload of people to Palestine. The boat, *Exodus,* is filled with Jewish Europeans planning to make their home in the soon to be independent State of Israel.

Unfortunately, the British authorities have detained the boat in Cyprus. They are not allowing *Exodus* to complete its voyage to Palestine, and Ari has to take charge. His confidence is portrayed in his thin and muscular 5'9" frame.

"We can go back, or we can go on a hunger strike," he says, "but before we vote, we must reflect in our hearts."

I close my eyes and can hear everyone starting the most important prayer there is in the Jewish religion, the first prayer that we are taught in first grade, the Shema, the holiest prayer, the holiest song: *"Shema Yisrael*

Adonai Elohanu Adonai Echad." Even Jews who don't speak Hebrew typically know these words.

The first six words of the *Shema* are all I can remember by heart. We learn the whole prayer, but most people typically only remember the first six words. The rest of the prayer does not seem as important, especially to me, because I know about this prayer in ways no one else does, except my sister, of course. The first six words of the *Shema* saved my dad's life.

My eyes go back to Ari's face on the screen. Before I know it, the credits are rolling, and *Exodus* has become my new favorite movie.

This must be what love is, I think again, but, of course, I decide to keep that thought a secret from everyone. Love is not something I am supposed to talk about because I am only nine years old.

~~~~~~~~~

I look out the glass doors of our apartment building. My family and I live in Apartment 4 at 4634 Dupuis Street in Montréal, Québec, Canada. I like coming out onto the foyer and looking at the stars through these glass doors. I feel like the smartest person in the whole world out here, smarter than my mother, smarter than my father, but this is just another secret of mine.

It is 7:30 p.m., and my dad just got home from work. He is a plumber so he often works late. My mom is washing the dishes while my dad is eating the breaded chicken, mashed potatoes, and onions she made for him. It is his favorite. I sit at the table and watch as he wolfs down the food. Dad is the fastest eater in the whole wide world. Edna, my sister, says it is because he was in the war and had nearly nothing to eat for a long time. I bet if there were a fast eating contest, he would win first prize.

I look at my dad's hands. They are so big and always chapped from working outside. The dirt on his hands never seems to disappear. I have seen him try soap after soap but always with the same lack of results.

"Why don't you just wear gloves?" I had once asked.

He laughed and said, "I've tried as many gloves as I have tried soaps. I can't do the job properly with gloves."

I love looking at hands. I'm not sure why, but somehow I feel like I understand things better when I do. My mom's hands, for example, reflect her childhood. Her left pinky is bent permanently, with a big scar from a graft on her palm. She says it is from when she was a little baby. That is one of the only stories from her childhood that she has told me. Her older sister had pushed her, and a pot of hot water fell off of the stove onto her hand

2

and burnt her badly. She went to the hospital for it, but the scar never went away. When I first heard that story, it helped me finally understand why my mom had always yelled at my sister and me so much whenever we got anywhere near the stove. Now, if I could only understand why she yelled at me so much for everything else!

My mom, Alise, is only 5'2", but she has a husky voice from smoking and can yell louder than anyone I know. My dad, Zoli, on the other hand, is a tall man at 6'2", and his voice is always gentle. My mom gets upset easily, so she yells quite a lot. My dad almost never gets upset. Maybe that is why he never raises his voice at us.

We have a television, but we don't watch it much. I am afraid of television shows that are scary. I will only watch them if my Dad is sitting right beside me. Tonight, my dad is sitting beside Edna and me while Elliot Ness and his men look for bad guys, members of the mafia like Al Capone. As the show progresses, one of the mobsters takes out an automatic rifle and begins shooting into a crowd of people on the street.

"Iritka, Ednooka, that was the gun they used on me when I got shot," my dad tells us.

My name is Irit, and my sister's name is Edna, but in Hungarian, grown-ups add -*ka* to the ends of names as a sign of affection. It always makes me feel good inside when my dad calls me "Iritka."

After the show ends, I turn to him and say, "Dad, can you tell me the story of how you got shot again?" I am always begging him to tell me his war stories.

"Iritka, it is late."

"Pleeeaase! I love the story, and there's no school tomorrow."

He sighs, giving in, "Ok. Get into your pajamas, and then I will tell you about it for a little bit."

My dad is the only father in my class who has been shot and who was a prisoner of war during World War II. I am the only one in my class who has these stories to share, and they make me feel special, like part of a super-secret club.

I rush to my side of the bedroom that I share with Edna and quickly put on my pink-and-purple pajamas with daffodils, daisies, and violets. My Aunt Ersie, my dad's sister, sent me these pajamas. My Dad always tells me that she picked them because purple is her favorite color and she loves flowers, especially violets. I grab my *paplan*, the Hungarian word for *down comforter*, and jump onto my dad's big bed—which is actually two beds put together with a headboard. As I snuggle in, I rub the corner of the *paplan* with my index finger to keep myself from sucking my thumb. After my sixth birthday, I decided that when I was seven I would be too old to suck my thumb. So, the next year at Camp Massad where my mom was the cook, I officially became a big girl and stopped, but even now, at nine years old, I'm often tempted.

My dad finally comes in and joins me on the bed.

"Ok, Dad, I'm ready," I say. "Tell me about how you got shot and how the *Shema* prayer saved your life, and how you had the bullets taken out without any medicine and—"

"But you already know the story," my dad chuckles.

"Tell me again!"

I pull the *paplan* over my chin as I cuddle next to my dad and repeat, "I'm ready."

My father begins, "We were in the Hungarian labor camp. It was early afternoon, and the officers were busy eating so they weren't paying attention to us. I told Barna, 'Now is the time to escape to the Russian camp. Do you want to come with me?'"

Barna was my dad's best friend growing up. I have never met him, but from all the stories I've heard, I feel like I know him well. I would love to visit him in Europe, but Dad says I have to wait until I'm older.

"Barna said, 'Zoli, I can't.'"

Barna and I had known each other since we were your age. Now, after all those years, it was time to say goodbye. 'Good luck,' we both said, and we gave each other a hug. There were two other men who did choose to come with me. When the moment came, we ran away as fast as we could. We saw Russians so I put my hands over my head, waving a stick with a light cloth on it. I was trying to show the Russians that I had no guns and wanted to surrender.

A Russian officer stood a few feet away, and his machine gun was pointed right at me. The two other men who had come with me got scared and hid to watch what would unfold. In an attempt to let the officer know that I was not the enemy, I said, '*Tovarash*,' which means *comrades*. 'I am your brother, and I am a Jew.' I could see the man's hand gripping the machine gun, so I said, '*Tovarash*' again, but he pulled the trigger. The two men made it back to camp and told Barna and everyone else that I had waved the flag and then died from many gunshot wounds."

"So what happened next, Dad?"

"Next thing I knew, I was lying on the ground. I must have passed out. I had a dream, and then I woke up to the sound of a group of men standing around me and speaking Russian. I heard one say, 'He is still breathing. Finish him off.'"

"What did you do?"

"Once more I said, 'I am a Jew. I am your brother. If you are a Stalinist and this is what Stalin teaches, then you must teach this to your children by example. You must take the machine gun and shoot me yourself if I am to die.'

The Russian soldier then said, 'Prove you are a Jew.'

I could think of only one prayer, and suddenly I could hear myself saying, '*Shema Yisrael, Adonai Elohanu, Adonai Echad.*' Then, I heard another Russian, who was obviously Jewish, say, 'Only a Jew would know that.'

The officer in charge then said, 'Take the wagon and put him in it.' I remember the sun was so hot it burned into my wounds. There were insects feeding on the bullet holes and on my face, but I could not move my hands to swat them away. I could not even move my fingers. I had no feeling in my arms. I was partially paralyzed so I just closed my eyes."

"Dad, tell me about how they took the bullets out, how they took them out without any medicine and you didn't scream. That's my favorite part."

"OK, Iritka. I told them I didn't want them to give me anything that would make me go to sleep because I knew that if they did, I would never wake up. I told them to take the bullets out without anything. One by one, they came out, and I didn't say a word."

"How could you not scream?"

"I was afraid that if I screamed they would put me to sleep forever, so I had no choice."

"So, tell me about the doctor. What happened after she took the bullets out?"

"I remember the doctor well. She was a Russian Jew, and she told me, 'You are a special man. I cannot believe you survived this and didn't even cry.' I even heard her tell one of the guards, 'We must save this man. He is very important, and he is fluent in many languages, so he can help us.' She made all of that up, but because of her words, they made me an interpreter, which was an easy job compared with many others. Of course, I spoke some Russian and German, but I mostly learned as I went.

The doctor took on the task of feeding me every day. I still could not move my hands, but I was getting stronger. There was little food to eat, but she would steal extra for me. She was a special person who gave with her heart. I will always remember her."

I look up at my dad and see that spark of joy and light that I have always loved.

"After she removed the bullets, my left arm got an infection. They said it was gangrene and wanted to cut it off, but she kept saying, 'Let's wait one more day.' She insisted that it was getting better."

"Were you afraid they would cut it off?"

"Iritka, at that point, I didn't care."

"How long before you were better?"

"About six months. The doctor, she saved me."

"If your arm was gangrenous, how did you get better?"

"I have good blood."

"Do I have good blood?"

Dad laughs, but before he can respond, my mom's voice cuts through the air, "Irit, time to go to bed!" Mom always talks in that loud voice when she wants us to do something right away, but I am so wrapped up in the story that I try to argue.

"But Mom, Dad didn't finish the story," I say. "I still want to hear about how he played that game of chess that saved his men in the Russian camp."

"Irit, go to bed now. Do you want to give me a heart attack?" She says at the top of her lungs.

My mom always says, "Do you want to give me a heart attack?" or "You'll give me a nervous breakdown" when I don't do what she wants. It scares me because I take it literally, but my sister always tells me she really doesn't mean it.

"Mom, there is no school tomorrow."

"Iritka, don't get your mother upset," my dad says, finally joining in the argument.

"But it's not fair!"

"Iritka, just ignore the yelling. She can't help it," he says.

"But Dad …"

"Don't get your mom upset. Now give me a kiss, and go to bed." I know from his tone that the fight is over and I have lost so I concede.

"I love you, Dad."

"I love you, too."

As my head sinks into my pillow, I think of that machine gun one last time, the one like the gangsters used in *The Untouchables with Elliot Ness*. Every time I get a splinter and Mom takes it out, I try not to scream, to be like my dad, but I can't help it. I always cry.

When I injured my ankle last year while playing boys catch girls, it hurt incredibly badly every night. The doctor hadn't read the x-rays right so he sent me home with nothing more than an ace bandage. Every day I would tell myself, "Be like your dad. Don't cry." But I cried, anyway.

Finally, the phone rang the next Saturday morning, and before anyone could answer, I announced to the room that it was going to be the hospital calling to say that they had made a mistake. I *had* broken my ankle.

When my mom picked up the phone, I was right; it was the hospital. After that, I knew I wasn't as strong as my dad when it came to pain, but I had something in me that just knew things about my body that others couldn't. Maybe that is a part of the good blood thing my dad talks about. I hope it is at least.

I am never clear on what exactly "good blood" means. It makes me wonder how the body heals. How is it possible that my dad did not scream when he had six bullets taken out of him? How is it possible that he healed from a gangrenous arm that was supposed to be removed? I think of the *Shema*, the six words, "Hear, O Israel, the Lord is our God, the Lord is one," as I drift off. Before I know it, my eyes are opening, and it is morning again.

Breakfast is ready. This morning, it is freshly squeezed orange juice and two eggs, sunny side up, with rye toast. Mom has already buttered the toast for me so I dive right in.

During the week, Mom makes lunch for a Jewish organization called Hillel at McGill University. Mom lived on a big farm when she was growing up, and that's how she learned to cook. She is the best cook ever, and she does everything from scratch. I especially love holidays because that is when she makes at least four desserts. My favorite is her custard éclairs with chocolate.

"Where's Dad?" I ask.

"He had to leave early because of the weather. Some pipes burst. It was before six."

"Does that mean he left while it was still dark?"

"Eat your breakfast, Irit."

I dunk my bread into the yellow part of the eggs, *yummy,* and then I turn to my sister, who is across the table from me. "Dad didn't eat good food for over seven years. Can you believe that, Edna? How comes he eats so fast?

"Because of the war," Edna tells me for the umpteenth time. That is my family's go-to answer whenever my parents act in a way I can't understand.

"But Edna, it's not the war anymore, and he still eats so fast. I don't get it."

"I don't know," she responds indifferently.

"Mom, in the war, did you ever have good food?"

"Irit," my mom responds, raising her voice in Hungarian, "don't be stupid. Don't ask such stupid questions." My mom always gets upset when I ask her questions about the war.

"But Mom," I answer in English. I know she won't talk about it, but I keep asking just in case.

"I told you, don't talk about the war."

"But Mom, Dad said—"

"Iritka, if you keep talking like this you will give me a heart attack."

"But Mom—"

"Stop talking about such stupid things. Do you want me to have a nervous breakdown?"

I suddenly want to put my hands over my ears and scream. My stomach squeezes in, and my chest starts pounding. I don't know why, but my chest always hurts when my mom talks this loud. It doesn't bother my sister so I don't understand why it bothers me so much. It just does.

~~~~~~~~~

After my dad gets back from fixing the pipes, he takes us ice-skating at Beaver Lake, my favorite park. I always feel as if the lion statues at the entrance of the mountain are saying "hi" to me. The four lions seem so powerful. I like to believe they watch over everyone in the park, protecting us from any harm. Looking at the lions always makes me feel safe.

The outside skating rink here is huge and cold. I decided to wear my favorite red, blue, and purple wool pullover, which Mom knit in only ten days, underneath my jacket to keep me warm. My teacher at school once told me she wants a sweater like mine so I am very proud of it. However, the skates I am wearing are not as impressive. They are big and probably older than me so I fall a lot. Whenever we go skating, my dad refuses to put on skates. He always just watches us from outside the rink, and whenever I get up after falling, which I do a lot, he gives me a vote of approval with his smile.

Later on, I put my galoshes back on, and we head out.

"Dad, look at all this snow," I say. "It wants us to play. The snow will be sad if we don't. Can we build a snowman?"

"OK."

My dad works hard so we don't see him much. It is always nice when he can bring us here even though he just watches as Edna and I play. Every time I look up at him from where I am, he smiles at me. Somehow, it makes everything more fun for me.

When we finally get home, we have hot chocolate, and my sister asks if we can play chess. I watch as she and my dad play.

"Ednooka," my dad says. "Remember, whenever you make a move, you should have your piece protected. That way, if you make a mistake, you will be safe." My dad wins within ten moves.

"Ednooka, you didn't protect your man," he says.

"It seemed like I was winning," Edna protests.

"That was the problem. Don't let anyone know, until it is too late, what you're thinking," my dad advises her.

"And then it will be checkmate, right, Dad?" I say. My dad smiles at me. Every time we play chess my dad tells us how to play more effectively. He taught me to play chess when I was five, before I could even read or write. It's a skill that makes me feel special, especially since none of my friends know how to play. "Are those the moves you made when you played the game for your life?" I ask him. "Can you tell me that story again?" I wonder if he ever tires of the stories. Probably, but I know I never will.

"Well, Iritka," my dad clears his throat and begins the story, "after I escaped to the Russian camp, there was very little food for me and the other men, but we still had to go outside to work. It was freezing cold outside one day, and I knew if we went outside, many of us would die.

I also knew that if we didn't eat, we would starve. So, I thought, *What can I do to get food for us and keep us inside today?*

The Russians liked chess, so I bet the best Russian chess player in the camp that I could beat him. He didn't want to play at first, so I said, 'If you win, you can shoot me, but if you lose, we get extra food and stay inside today.'"

"So, then what happened?"

"He agreed to play, and I beat him. He was mad so he told me I would have to play him again. I agreed, but this time I told him I would beat him in ten moves."

"And then what?"

"I beat him, and once more, he said, 'Let's play one more time.'"

"And you beat him again?" I ask triumphantly.

"Yes, so we didn't go outside that day, and we got some food."

"Did you play him again after that?"

"Yes."

"Did you beat him every time?"

"No. Once in a while I let him win."

"Why?"

"Because that was the smart move."

2

1978

Three things in human life are important.
The first is to be kind.
The second is to be kind.
And the third is to be kind.

Henry James

"Okay, Dad, I'll be over at your place in about thirty minutes," I say before hanging up the phone.

I can't believe it, but I am heading to Czechoslovakia, where both my parents and other relatives had spent a portion of their youth. It feels like only yesterday I had cuddled up next to my dad, saying, "Tell me again about the bullets and the chess game and your family." Now, I will finally meet the people and see the places from those stories.

I look around my room one last time. *Did I forget anything? Passport, visa to enter Prague, American Express travelers checks, hundred dollar bills that Aunt Ersie gave me for Elli, Margit and, Barna? Yep! They're all in my pouch.* I zip up my bag and put it around my neck. Just as I am about to walk out the door, the phone rings again. It is my aunt this time.

"Aunt Ersie, you got me just in time. I'm almost out the door."

I met my Aunt Ersie for the first time when I was too little to remember, but when I was 12, she came to visit again. She was just like my dad had described to me. She was beautiful and kind. She was calm, too, just like my dad and never, ever raised her voice.

For my 16th birthday, she and her husband, my Uncle Jusie, gave me a plane ticket to come visit them in California, and I stayed for a month. Purple, her favorite color, was everywhere. Everything in her bedroom was purple: bed sheets, bed skirts, the duvet cover, the two upholstered chairs, and the lilac drapery over her heavy, velvet, dark purple drapes, and, of course, most of her clothes were purple.

The kitchen had purple placemats and purple flowers on the table. On her front lawn, she planted hydrangeas and lilacs. Lilacs were never supposed to survive in southern California, yet my Aunt Ersie somehow talked them into thriving.

Apparently, when she was eight, Aunt Ersie was bitten by a rabid dog, and she had to travel to Budapest to get the treatment shots. She was so traumatized from the experience that she had sat on the outside steps of the hospital, crying uncontrollably. From out of nowhere, a man showed up by her side and presented her with a bouquet of lilacs and comforted her. From that moment on, purple was her favorite color.

"Do you have all the presents packed that I sent you for the family? Don't forget to give Elli, Margit, and Barna the American money I sent you."

"Aunt Ersie," I say, "Between you and my dad, I have enough money and clothing to open up my own store."

"Good! If we tried to just send them the packages in the mail, they would either get lost or half of the stuff would be seized at the border. The family would get the remainder of what we sent if they were lucky."

"I know, Dad tells me the same thing. Anyway, Aunt Ersie, the clothes you made for everyone look like they come from a fancy boutique. Everyone will be thrilled."

"I keep forgetting, how long will you be there?" my aunt asks me.

"I'll be in Prague for a week, and then I'm off to your home town of Košice. I can't believe I'm finally going to see where you and dad were raised in your early life. You both always talk so much about Ellinani and Margitnani and what it was like when you lived in their home when you were kids. It will be great to finally see them in person.

"After I meet them, I'll be off to Budapest for one week, and then to Israel to meet up with friends from Montréal."

I'm lucky because, as a gym and biology teacher, I get to play every day, learn more about the body, and take the summers off to travel.

"Where are you staying in Budapest?" Aunt Ersie asks.

"I was invited to stay with a few different people, but I decided to stay with Aggie, the captain of the women's Olympic volleyball team," I tell her. I met Aggie a few years ago when I got the best summer job ever, six weeks as interpreter for the Hungarian women's volleyball team at the Montréal Olympics.

I remember sitting on the bench when they competed. They had been so shocked when I started rooting for them while they were playing against Canada, my own country. They told me that if they had done that, they would not have been allowed to play. Hungary was under communist rule, and rooting for another country would seem like disloyalty, bringing about serious repercussions. It would be interesting to see what it is like to travel in a communist country.

"Have you been practicing your Hungarian so you can talk with everyone?" Aunt Ersie asks, pulling me out of my memories.

"A little." Growing up, my mom and dad always spoke Hungarian while my sister and I responded in English. So, while I could easily understand it, my speech needed a little practice. I never really liked speaking Hungarian when I was younger, but now I couldn't be happier because it has opened many doors for me.

"Great! Have a safe trip! Be careful, and don't say anything that can get you in trouble!"

"Don't worry. I'll be fine," I say.

"I love you. Bye."

Be careful. Those words keep ringing in my ears. They keep telling me that I have to be careful with what I say and do because saying the wrong thing can get me into trouble. I am excited about finally visiting all the people and places from my father's stories, but I can't help but feel a little anxious.

~~~~~~~~~

My suitcase feels as though it weighs 60 pounds as I drag it down the stairs to the street by my car. *How am I going to maneuver this 3' x 3' monster into my trunk?* I wonder. I look around and see a man passing by.

"Excuse me," I ask him. "Can you help me put my suitcase in my trunk, please?"

"No problem."

After everything is packed, I smile at the man, thank him, and am on my way. I arrive at my parent's house within 20 minutes. My dad is going to give me a ride to the airport because he wouldn't have it any other way.

I leave my car in the driveway and walk up the fifteen stairs to my parent's door as I have millions of times before.

"Iritka," my dad greets me in his heavy Hungarian accent. "Do you want to eat something before you go or maybe bring something with you? Your mom has food for you to take." I smile. I'm not surprised.

When I graduated college and moved to my own place, my mom didn't talk to me for about a year. What would her friends say? She wondered. Apparently a child moving away from home was something unheard of in her world. Getting married or moving to another city for work or other pressing requirements were the only reasons to leave home. I know she would always ask my dad to make sure I was okay, but she refused to speak to me. She would, however, always prepare food and have my dad bring me food she had prepared for me, and whenever I was sick, she would make me chicken soup, my favorite healing food.

When we first moved to Montréal, my mom worked long days, but no matter how tired she was when she got home, she would prepare food. In Israel, she had promised my dad that once we moved to Canada, our family would always have good, fresh food to eat every day. She would make sure of it. She showed her love through food. That is part of the Jewish European culture, one thing that is always a constant. Maybe it is connected to the war, too, like how my dad eats so fast because he had gone so long without good food.

My mom comes into the kitchen, and as soon as she sees me she starts shrieking in Hungarian, "Your skirt is too short, Irit! You can't go to Prague looking like that."

"Mom, it's a mini skirt. It's supposed to be this length." I say exasperatedly.

"Irit, go change!" she screams. "You can't go like this! You look like a tramp. You will give me a heart attack."

I stare her down stubbornly and say, "I'm 25 years old, Mom, and this is what I want to wear. I'm not changing."

"Why are you yelling at me?" she yells.

"Because you're yelling!" I yell back. It is a vicious cycle.

"I'm not yelling," she screams.

She stomps into her room and slams the door. It is time for me to leave anyway, so I say goodbye just loud enough for her to hear. No response. *I'll miss you, too, mom,* I think to myself bitterly.

I walk down the stairs and try to clear my head. As I climb into my dad's truck, I look at the sign on the right side of it. It says Schaffer Plumbing in big, bold letters. He has had this truck for as long as I can remember. I know he is proud of it.

"Be careful. It's heavy," I warn my dad as he lifts my luggage into the back seat. I shut the passenger door and look up at my parents' red brick duplex. I can see my mom staring out the living room window at us. I feel sad that I am leaving on such a bad note, but, unfortunately, that's pretty typical for us.

When my dad gets into the car, his head is bent slightly downwards, as if he is deep in thought. I'm not sure what he is thinking about—maybe about my fight with my mom. Or, maybe he is still worrying about me going to a communist country.

"Why does she always do that to me?" I blurt out. "Why can't she just once wish me a good trip?"

My dad puckers his lips, pauses, and then looks at me and says, "Ignore it. She can't help it. She went through the war, and she will never be the same."

"But you went through a labor camp, a Russian prisoner of war camp, you got shot, and..."

"Iritka, it was different for me."

"But hell is hell, right? How come you're so different?"

"Let's not talk about it now," he sighs.

I turn the radio to 98.6 FM and hear *Let the Good Times Roll* by the Cars blasting through the speakers. I take that to be a good omen and start singing along as we begin our hour-long drive to Mirabel airport. I can worry about my mom later. Now it is time to go learn more about my family history.

After a few minutes of silence, my dad says, "Be sure to take a lot of pictures with your new camera. I would love to see everyone."

"Dad, I promise. I know how much you love to take pictures, and even though it drives me crazy when you take so many, I'm always grateful when I see the results."

"I hope that the clothes fit Barna. I know he—"

"Dad," I interrupt, "almost half of my suitcase is filled with Aunt Ersie's clothes for everyone, and almost half is full of the clothes you got from the factories: the eight pairs of jeans, the 20 pairs of nylons, the ten blouses and shirts, and who knows how many sweaters. The little space left is for my clothes. There are also the five boxes of liquor chocolates from Mr. Lieberman's store that you gave me. Trust me, there will be something for everyone, including everyone's friends, and probably even their friends' friends for that matter. My only concern is that I fit in enough clothes for myself to get me through the trip."

Eighty percent of all women's clothing factories in Canada are in Montréal, and my dad loves visiting them. He even knows most of the owners by name. Before the war, my dad worked in a clothing store. He actually returned to the same store when he came back to Košice after the war. He often told me proudly that he always knew what would look good on customers and, because of that, most people that walked into the store bought something before they left.

The factory owners in Montréal now let him in as if he were one of their family members because they all know that whenever there is a plumbing emergency, Dad will be there day or night, even on the freezing cold winter nights.

Actually, thanks to my dad, with his connections at all the factories, and me, the girls on the Olympic volleyball team from Hungary would always remember me. My volleyball team was contracted with Adidas, and they got free shoes from the company. Still, I decided to call all of the shoe suppliers because they were all at the Olympics. Thanks to my efforts, my team got free shoes and bags from athletic shoe companies that they weren't even contracted with. I even ended up with five new pairs of gym shoes, a bag, and sweatsuits of my own.

I remember when the Olympic women's volleyball players got all of those jeans and other clothes from the factories, word got around. Hungarian interpreters from other sporting teams called wanting us to help their teams, too. Jeans and other clothing was very expensive back home, and even if you had enough money, there was little selection to choose from, so they weren't happy when I told them it was only for the women's volleyball team.

"I am so happy you will meet everyone. Give everyone a kiss for me. Also, find out if they need anything."

"I wish you were coming with me," I say for the hundredth time.

"Iritka, if I went back, they would lock me in jail and throw away the key."

"You are a Canadian citizen now! It is not the same. They are letting people back into the country."

"We have talked about this before. You don't understand. I can never go back."

We finally get to the airport and park.

"We're here," my dad says. "I'll take your luggage, and you take the bag of cooked food your mom prepared for you for the flight."

As we walk into the airport, the aroma of fried chicken and potato salad makes my mouth water and my stomach grumble. I go to the Czech Air station, and the man behind the counter checks my ticket. I am in seat 18E. Good. 18 is my lucky number because in Hebrew it stands for life. He puts a tag onto my luggage and tells me to have a good trip. *"Dekuji,"* I say. *Thank you* is the only word I know in Czech.

I see the sign for passengers only, and I turn back to my dad to get one last look. He used to be 6'2", but now he is probably only 6'0" because his upper back is rounded from kyphosis. It is one of the constant reminders of the rigors, traumas, and scars of his years.

He is wearing his green khaki pants and a checkered green-and-blue shirt. His signature grey cap is placed over his straight brown hair, which has just a few strands of grey showing through. His hair is very thin and wiry because of the typhus that he had during the war. His hands are big and rough, a result of all the hard work he has done throughout his life. My dad has been working hard since he was five and had to milk his family's cows in the cold of winter. It was probably because he was so used to working hard in his life that he was able to survive and overcome the struggles of the war. Jews from wealthy families were usually not used to the limited means and long, hard, working hours so it was sometimes harder for them to cope and survive. My dad had no such problem.

Dad doesn't have an ounce of fat on him. He has been the same weight since I was a kid. It always made me laugh because every winter all his clients would say, "You put on some weight," because of all the layers he had donned to keep himself warm in the Canadian cold. Then, in the summers, they would say, "you lost weight!" because he had removed the layers. He never told them it was just the clothes. It was our little secret.

I stare into his gentle, dark brown eyes and say, "Dad, thank you for everything, and don't worry about me. I'll be fine."

"Iritka, remember you are going to a communist country. Be careful," he reminds me again as he hugs me, holding on a little too tight.

"Yeah, I know, Dad. I love you."

"I love you, too."

I take the escalator up to the gate, and when I reach the top, I turn around. My dad is still standing in the same spot. I can see the fear in his eyes, the fear that has been there ever since I started planning this trip. I know he was tempted, but he never tried to stop me. What is it that my father is afraid of? What is it that won't let him ever go and visit the family he loves so much?

I know that when the war ended my dad was still a prisoner in Russia. When the Russians were letting out Hungarian prisoners, my dad was considered Czech because that is where he lived before the war. When they were letting out the prisoners from Czechoslovakia, he was told he could not be freed because he was born in Hungary and so he was considered Hungarian. He remained a prisoner for almost three more years after the war. That is probably a big part of why he is so afraid to return, but maybe it goes even deeper than that. Maybe he is right, and I just do not understand.

Suddenly, a flurry of negative thoughts starts swirling through my mind. *What if I never see him again?* Every time I travel somewhere I do this. I am always afraid I will never see him again. I know it's crazy, but I can't get these fears out of my head. As I am thinking this, he waves at me, and I see him smile. Tears start to roll down my face.

~~~~~~~~~~

I sit in the waiting area until I hear the announcer say, "Flight 197 is now boarding." That's me. I put my little carry-on bag in the overhead compartment and the meal my mom prepared for me under the seat in front of me, and with boarding pass in hand, I settle into my seat.

My thoughts wander to my mom. *Why do we always have to fight?* I wonder. I buckle up and try to clear my head by going back to the image of my father standing proudly in the airport terminal. After another 30 minutes of waiting, the plane finally takes off.

I become lost in thought as I peer out the windows at the white and grey clouds. I wonder if Barna will recognize me from the pictures Dad sent him over the years.

Barna is like a brother to my dad. They did everything together when they were little, and their bond was sealed forever when Barna's sister, Elli, married my dad's step-grandfather's son. After the marriage, they all lived together on a farm. I wonder...

"Would you like some beer and nuts?" I hear the stewardess say, bringing me back to reality. I laugh. Only on Czech Air would they offer you beer instead of soda. "Sure, I will have a beer," I say. *Why not?*

I read a few pages of *One Flew over the Cuckoo's Nest*, but my thoughts wander back to Barna. *What are Barna and his wife Jofie like?* I am most curious about what Petr, their son, will be like. He has a two-week leave of absence from the Army and is going to be my personal tour guide for the week. Petr was born in Prague. So, he speaks Czech, but he never learned Hungarian since it is not spoken in Prague. Fortunately, he had to learn English in order to prepare himself for medical school. As soon as Petr finishes his Army stint, he is planning on starting his cardiac surgery residency.

Petr had visited Montréal last year to finally come abroad, meet my dad, and see what life was like in North America. I was away at the University of Oslo for the summer so I couldn't meet him. My dad told me that Petr could have stayed in Montréal as a doctor had he wanted to. It would have been easy for him to defect. He considered it, but when the time came to choose, he went back home because he knew his parents would have been devastated if he left for good.

After what seems like no time at all, I hear the flight attendant say, "Return your seats to their upright position. We're beginning our descent. We will land in Prague in 30 minutes."

My stomach turns into knots. Excitement and fear start to take over. *Irit*, I tell myself, *stop worrying. You will have a good time.*

After the plane lands and I get off, I see police officers everywhere. *Welcome to communism*, I say to myself. *Wow, it looks so dark and dreary.*

There were no checkpoints at the airport in Montréal, but here, I am ushered into a room where I show my passport and am frisked by a female police officer. I get a queasy feeling in my stomach. I'm a little scared. I've never been frisked before. I've only seen it in the movies. Finally, I am moved into another room. Once again, I have to show my passport. A policeman looks at it for a few minutes, checks some papers by his desk, and then asks for my visitor's visa. After he gives me back my passport and visa, he nods at me and directs me to the next officer who is ten feet away. This man has a stern look about him.

"Why you have come to our country?" he asks with a straight face.

"To visit friends of my family," I say nervously.

"Where are you staying?" he asks.

I look into my address book and say, "10 Vernoble Ave."

"How long are you staying?"

Maybe Dad was right about not wanting to visit. These people seem incapable of even a little smile. It makes me anxious. "Two weeks," I answer. "One week here, and five days in Košice."

"Why there?"

"Because that is where I have family." I am suddenly seized with fear that this is a wrong answer. Maybe I should not have said I have family here. I'm concerned that if I say the slightest thing wrong they won't let me enter the country, or worse, they won't let me leave. I start panicking and can see the front page headline in the *Montréal Gazette: Canadian girl detained indefinitely in a Communist country*.

"And you are leaving from Budapest, why are you going there?"

"I have friends in Budapest."

"How is it that you have friends there?"

"I worked for the Olympics in Montréal, and the coach of the team invited me to visit."

"Is that where you are staying?"

"No. I will be staying with one of the players."

I'm tempted to ask him why he is asking all these questions, but I keep quiet. I don't want to get myself into trouble, so I just wait and follow his lead.

"Can I see your passport?" For the fourth time that day, I show my passport. I have never had to show my passport so much in my life. I was in Norway last summer, where going through the immigration was a breeze. I went to England, Switzerland, and Italy with my best friend when I was eighteen, and there, too, we just walked through the checkpoints. In fact, when I travelled to England at that time, the airline was flying a new plane that had two levels, and the rules were lax so I went up the stairs and befriended someone who happened to be a standby copilot. He invited me into the cockpit, and I sat there for almost fifteen minutes marveling at the computerized technology. To my surprise, the computers were running the plane. The pilots didn't even have their hands on the steering wheel. I was like a little kid in this amazing magical wonderland. Standing in front of this stern faced officer, it is hard for me to believe that had ever happened.

"Now, since you are staying almost two weeks, you must buy at least $200.00 worth of Czech currency, and you cannot exchange it for other currency when you leave."

"Fine," I answer. If I don't spend it, I can just give it to Barna. He will have to accept it.

"Tomorrow you must report to the police station by 9:00 a.m." That is another policy of the communist regime everyone had to follow. Apparently, four checkpoints at the airport isn't enough security for all those entering the country so I will register one more time at the police station. At this point, I realize I'd better just follow any and all orders they give.

My dad always says many people don't realize how lucky we are in Canada and America. I'm beginning to see what he means. I can't believe I have to go through all of this just to visit family.

"Now you must go and get your luggage. Another officer will check it."

I grab my bags and head to another counter. That officer asks, "Are you bringing any gifts into the country?"

"Just clothes, sir," I respond. The officer rummages through my clothes, zips up my suitcase, looks up at me, and with a straight face, says,

"You can now enter our country."

I walk through the doors of the airport into a huge crowd of people. I decide to stand off to the side, hoping that Barna finds me. My stomach is in knots, and my heart is beating a million times per minute. *What if they don't recognize me?* I begin to panic, *What if I stand here for hours and get arrested for loitering or something?*

One minute elapses, and before any further panic can set in, I see a man and woman approaching me hurriedly, with smiles stretching from ear to ear.

"Irit?" They ask with confidence. I smile as Barna grabs me and gives me a hug that crushes my entire rib cage. Then Jofie gives me a kiss.

"How was your trip?" they ask in Hungarian. "We are so sorry that Zoli would not come, but we are so happy to meet his daughter."

"Let me take your suitcase," Barna says. I know that we are going to be taking public transportation so I feel guilty about making him carry my bag. It is a good thing he is 5'9" and muscular. I hadn't even managed to lift it into my trunk on my own.

"Dad and Ersie sent many presents. That is why the suitcase is so heavy," I blurt out apologetically in my rough Hungarian.

"Don't worry. I am strong," Barna says, smiling.

Jofie takes my hand and smiles. As she does this, I feel completely at ease. This is my first encounter with her, and yet I feel like I've known her for a lifetime. Dad was right about them. "Let me take your little carry-on bag," she says, wanting to help. She reminds me of my grandmother, my mom's mom, who always fussed over me.

My grandmother, like my mom, never talked about the war. In fact, she rarely talked of her past. Maybe, it was too painful. She came from a family of three sisters and three brothers, and the only one who survived was her brother who moved to Israel after the war. She also lost her son, and every time she sees Edna, she is reminded of him since they apparently look so much alike. She never learned English even after moving to Canada, but she managed with Yiddish, Hungarian, and Slovak. In fact, when she visited her brother in Israel, she had to stay overnight in Paris. She didn't speak the language, but she got probably the only cab driver in France who was fluent in Yiddish. He not only took her to the hotel but also went inside to make sure she would be ok. He then picked her up the next day and helped her with the checkout and also made sure she got her boarding pass.

My grandmother had an endearing smile that made people want to help her, and she always wanted to do things for others. Whenever I came over to her house for meals, she would always ask in advance what I wanted, and there it would be when I sat down to eat. She, too, showed her love through food.

"We have another hour to go before we get home," Barna says, "but Jofie has food waiting for you."

Homemade food ready and waiting for me. Yep, this definitely reminds me of home.

We walk to the subway and take our seats in the crowded compartment; twenty minutes later we reach our stop. We get off, climb the stairs, and start walking. Just when I think we are almost there, we reach a bus stop. Barna sets my bag down and pulls out all three tickets. The bus driver punches them, and we sit. We ride Bus #20 for about 15 minutes and then transfer to Bus #50. It has been a long day, and I am exhausted so I sigh with relief when Barna finally says, "This is our stop. We are one block from home."

The 6-story building they live in was constructed 100 years ago. It doesn't have much character. It feels like someone was given a budget that only allowed for necessities. The building holds about 30 tenants. We have to walk up three flights of stairs to get to the door of the apartment of Barna and Jofie. Thank goodness I am in good shape, or it would have been rough. I can't believe that Barna is still carrying my suitcase as if it weighs only ten pounds.

Jofie turns the key and opens the door. As I walk in, my eyes are immediately drawn to their high ceilings and the chandelier dangling over their dining room table. I take in the intricate, white embroidery on the table and chairs. The needlepoint hanging on the wall is similar to the needle-point picture my mom has in her living room. It is beautiful.

The apartment is a total of 3 ½ rooms, but it seems bigger. The family room is huge, with the dining room and living room combined. There is a sofa and a twin bed in the living room, and as I walk into the kitchen, I notice a cot alongside a wood burning stove and kitchen table. "Why are there beds in all of the rooms?" I ask.

"We have lived here for thirty years. We raised Petr and Katy here. They liked having some space to themselves, so we let them sleep in sepa-rate rooms. The bed you will sleep on is in the living-and-dining-room area. It was Petr's. I love to read so I am keeping the kitchen cot open. I often come into the kitchen before bed, put wood in the stove, and read on the cot until I get tired. That way I don't keep Jofie awake."

I continue my tour by walking up to the big, glass, double doors in the living room. I open them and see a huge queen bed with a dresser and two nightstands, and, just as in all of the other rooms, there is a small cot to the left. This cot must have been Katy's when she was growing up.

"Irit," Barna says, "it is so nice you are here. I only wish Zoli would have come."

"Yeah, I know. I tried to convince him many times, but he would not listen," I say. "Now, let me give you all the presents I brought for you. Here are some jeans, nylons, and chocolates my dad sent. Also, Ersie and Dad wanted me to give you this money." I hand them the $100 bills, and I see Barna and Jofie exchange a look.

"No, we cannot take money," Barna says proudly.

"You have to," I assure him, "or Dad and Ersie will be mad at me. My dad told me, 'Barna is proud and doesn't like to take money because he says he has enough, but don't take *no* for an answer.' Now, let me show you what else Aunt Ersie sent me to give to you," I continue.

I show them the clothes, and Jofie picks up the blue and white dress that was made just for her.

"I will try it on," she says excitedly.

"Isn't it beautiful?" I say.

Barna smiles, "That is our Ersie. She was always so talented. When Zoli and I were in our teens, Zoli would brag that Ersie was the best seamstress in Czechoslovakia. I used to tell him that she was the most beautiful as well." Barna winks at me, and just then, the doorbell rings.

"It is Petr," Jofie says. For some unknown reason, my heart starts thump-ing at about 1000 beats per second, and questions start swirling through my head at lightning speed. *Will he like me? Is his English going to be good enough? What if we don't get along? Is he nice? Is he cute?*

Jofie opens the door, and Petr walks in. He kisses his mom on the cheek, says "hi" to Barna in Czech and finally, takes my hand in his and says, in broken English, "It is so nice finally to meet you."

I look at Petr for the first time. He is six feet tall, with short blond hair, blue eyes, an athletic physique, and a mischievous smile. *Not bad,* I think to myself, *not bad.* I shyly say, "Hi," and there is a slight quiver in my voice.

"I do not speak Hungarian because my parents never taught me," he says. "So, we will have to speak in Czech or English."

"Czech was the language my parents spoke when they did not want us to understand," I tell him, laughing, "so we will have to speak English." Petr smiles back at me as he takes off his uniform jacket. "How come you are in uniform? I thought you had a 2-week leave."

"When I am in an official public place, I need to wear my uniform. There are cameras in many places, and you never know if you are being followed. If they catch you without a uniform, you will get into trouble."

I think of my dad again and his mistrust of all things that represent communism. I'm beginning to better understand where he is coming from.

"Are you hungry? We can eat now," Jofie cuts in.

"Great, I'm very hungry," I say. "Can I help with anything?"

"No! No! No! You talk with Petr and Barna," she insists.

As Jofie prepares everything, Barna asks me to show Petr the presents Zoli sent him. With Barna and Jofie speaking Hungarian and Petr speaking English, I am starting to feel like a ping pong ball going back and forth: English, Hungarian, English, Hungarian. It will be nice when Petr and I head off on our own so I can get a little break.

Before long, Jofie calls us into the kitchen.

"The embroidery on the chair is beautiful," I say as we sit down for dinner.

"Oh, yes, thank you. I did the needlepoint myself," Jofie says.

"My mom does needlepoint, too, but she never taught me," I say. "My mom and dad have a large, 4'x 5' needlepoint that she made hanging in our living room. I always admired her work, but I don't have the patience to learn."

"How many centimeters is that?" Jofie asks.

I had forgotten that they used the metric system here. *Let's see,* I think. *There are 2.54 centimeters in an inch, so that would be ...* I try to do the calculation in my head but quickly give up. "Oh, it is about this big," I say instead, spreading my hands out sideways to the approximate length of the needlepoint.

"Do you like *cholent*?" Jofie asks as she piles some onto my plate.

I smile. I grew up with *cholent*, and it is one of my favorite foods. It is a traditional Jewish stew that is simmered overnight for at least 12 hours and usually served on the Sabbath. My entire plate is covered with a combination of pinto beans, barley, rice, and lamb, the main ingredients found in this dish.

"Ok, there is a lot of food, so eat."

"You have given me enough for two people!" I say.

"Do you want club soda?" Barna asks me. "Press the nozzle on the bottle, and it turns into bubbly water."

"We used to have these sprays on bottles when I was little," I say as I pull the nozzle that makes the water bubble. "Now we can just buy premade soda water, but I always liked this way better."

I dig in and sigh with satisfaction as I eat the last bite of food on my plate. I did it. The food was so good that I didn't even have to struggle to finish it all.

"Irit, you hardly ate. Eat some more," Jofie says.

"I finished the entire portion." I say, laughing. I have heard this many times before with my relatives.

"You need to eat more. You are too skinny."

This sounds so much like something my mother would say to me that I turn to Petr and say, "That must be the Jewish mother mantra." We both laugh, and since Barna and Jofie don't speak English, this joke will be our little secret.

Switching back to Hungarian, I say, "The desserts smell as if they are just coming out of the oven. I want to save room so I can eat those."

"OK, I made chocolate *rugelah* and apple crisps."

Ok, Irit, I say to myself, eat slowly. That was a non-existent concept growing up. I always marveled at how fast my dad ate. I am slow compared to him, but the truth is I, too, eat pretty quickly.

They pile desserts on the center of the table, and they completely disappear within an hour.

At 9:30, Petr gets up to leave. He kisses his mom and dad, and then turns to me. "Irit, I will pick you up tomorrow morning at 8:30. I am going to show you Prague. Make sure you have comfortable shoes. See you tomorrow."

The door closes behind him, and Jofie turns to start making the bed for me in the living room.

"Here is a towel," she says, giving me a hug good night. "We are so happy to have you. Too bad Zoli is not here, too."

"I know," I answer. I'm hearing these words over and over. Yet, each time they say it, I realize more and more how much he is missed and loved. I wish he were here.

"Thank you for everything."

Finally, Barna goes into the kitchen to read, and Jofie goes into her room. It is cold, but as soon as I get underneath the down comforter, my feet start to warm up. This comforter is just like the one I had growing up so it makes me feel right at home. I put my head on the pillow, and the next thing I know it is 3:00 a.m. and I am wide-awake.

It is quiet and dark. I don't want to wake anyone, so I just lay in bed thinking of all that has transpired in the last 24 hours. I am grateful that I can speak Hungarian here even though I always hated having to speak it as a kid. Petr doesn't speak Hungarian because he was born in Prague.

Košice, where Dad and Barna grew up, was Austro-Hungarian until 1918, but then it became a part of Czechoslovakia. From then on, Košice was constantly changing governments.

On June 6th 1919, Košice became part of the Slovak Soviet Republic. Then, it was passed back to Czechoslovakia on July 30th 1919, where it stayed for the next 19 years. In November of 1938, the Vienna Arbitration assigned Košice to Hungary. Finally, in 1945, Košice became part of Czechoslovakia once again. Hungarian is probably spoken in Košice just because of its proximity. Hungary is only 20 km from the border of Košice. Prague, in comparison, is about 667 km from Košice, so no wonder Hungarian is not spoken here.

Thoughts keep swirling in my head until I finally doze off again. The next time I wake up, it is 7:35 a.m. I am still tired, but I am too excited to stay in bed. So, I get up. I'm pleased to discover that Barna is up now, too.

"Do you want to take a bath?" he asks.

I grab my towel and head to the bathroom. There is no shower in their apartment, but there is a huge bathtub that is three feet deep. I'm not used to taking baths because my tub in Montréal is so small, but this bathtub is humungous. I'm sure I will easily get used to it.

The doorbell rings at exactly 8:30 a.m. Petr is right on time, but before we leave, he and I sit down to eat the cream of wheat and *café au lait* that Jofie prepared for us.

"The whipped cream that you make is exactly like my mom's," I say, taking a huge gulp of my coffee mixed with the whipped cream.

"That's because it is part of the Czechoslovakian culture. It is a delicacy that we all grew up with."

"Well, it is absolutely yummy," I say, savoring my last sip.

As we head out the door, Petr looks at me with a mischievous smile, "Irit, let me introduce you to my car. It is a Skoda."

"I've never heard of that brand."

"That is because it is Czech. They wouldn't have it in Canada. Do you know that I had to wait in line for a whole day and night to get this car? It was part of the lottery. If your number is chosen, only then are you eligible to buy the car. When I stood in line, I got so tired that I snuck home in the late evening and slept for five hours. When I got back to my spot, I found out that they had called my number, and since I had left, I wouldn't be eligible for the car. I told them that I had just left to find a bathroom. Fortunately, they believed me, or I wouldn't have the car now."

"You're kidding."

"No, and one more thing, Irit. It is missing something." He grins as if he is hiding some brilliant secret. I can't help but be intrigued.

"Missing? What is it missing?"

"I promise you, you will figure it out soon enough."

He opens the passenger door for me. As I sit down in his grey, midsize four-door sedan, I immediately start looking around for a clue. "No seatbelts," I say. "Is it missing the seatbelts?"

"Well, yes. Those, too, are missing," he laughs.

Petr starts the car, and we head out. We drive one block on the cobble stone streets, and I start to laugh. "I can feel every bump on this road! Where are the shocks?"

"It was too expensive for me to buy a car with shocks. So, I have to do without."

We drive around, and despite the bumpy ride, I feel totally at ease. We sit quietly, side by side, and I don't even feel the need to fill the silence. After we reach our destination, it doesn't take more than a minute for someone to stop me and ask if I am willing to exchange American currency for Czech currency on the black market. Petr says, "Ne," for me, which is *no* in Czech, and we walk away as quickly as possible without drawing attention.

"It is dangerous to make exchanges with those people," he tells me. "You can get ripped off easily. Most of them are cheats who trade with counterfeit money."

"How did they know I was a tourist?" I ask. I don't feel as if I am standing out in the crowd.

"We're speaking English," Petr shrugs nonchalantly.

"Oh, you have a point."

We cross the Charles Bridge, the famous and historic bridge over the Vltava River in Prague, which connects the castle and the city's old town, and two more people stop us, asking to exchange currency. Now it is my turn. "*Ne,*" I say with the utmost confidence. We both laugh as we walk away.

"I am surprised I have only seen a few street artists today. Are there more on weekends?" I ask. Normally, when I have visited European cities, the streets are filled with artists and vendors for the tourists.

"Not really. In 1968, when Alexander Dubcek was in power, he encouraged the arts and the freedom of expression. This place was filled with many different artisans, and we could all feel a renewed optimism and hope back then."

"I read about him in the papers. My dad used to tell me that he would not be in power for long because the Czechs were beginning to taste freedom, and that was not what the communists wanted."

"Dubcek was put into power on January 5, 1968, and then in August of that year, the Russians came in with their tanks. Now we have just a handful of artists, and all of the ones you see have connections with the communist party. That is why they are able to do it."

We see one street artist who specializes in sketches, and Petr asks how much one of the pictures is. "30 korunas," the man says.

"20," Petr bargains.

The artist makes a compromise,"25."

Petr gives him the money, which is equal to approximately one Canadian dollar, and hands me the sketch.

"This is for you," he says. "A souvenir."

It is a black-and-white sketch of the Vltava River, the Charles Bridge, and the fortress. "Thanks!" The sketch is perfect because it is the exact view we can see from where we are standing on the bridge. This stone gothic bridge is 1692 meters, or about 1/3 of a mile. It is one of the must-see attractions in Prague. It is also a perfect place to get a view of Prague and take in the history, with all the statues representing different themes.

What a nice souvenir," I say, grinning from ear to ear.

Petr grabs my hand and looks at me excitedly as he says, "Let me show you more."

We stop at one of the most famous buildings in the old town square. Its gothic, almost 70-meter tower was built in 1364 and houses the oldest clock in Europe, the astronomical clock. Every hour, the bell rings, and 12 apostle sculptures pass by the astronomical dial. We watch as the clock strikes 12. Then, the crowd disperses and we continue our walking tour, visiting fortresses, palaces and castles.

We keep walking and talking. Before we know it, it is 4:00 p.m. "Let's head back home," Petr says. "I'm sure my mom is preparing dinner by now, and I know they will want to see you and hear all about your day. We will eat there, and then, tonight, we will go to the beer garden."

"That sounds great," I say excitedly.

This has been a great day. I find myself hoping it will never come to an end.

When we get to Barna and Jofie's house, Petr pulls me aside before we reach the front door and says, "Come, let me show you something." He takes my hand and leads me to the parking lot at the side of the building where a small black motorcycle is parked.

"Is it yours?" I ask.

"No. It belongs to my dad. This is how my mom and he get around. I am the only one in my family who owns a car. I just wanted to show you a bit about my parents. "

"You know, I once had a boyfriend named Donny who drove a motorcycle, but I never told my father." I laugh as the memory that had been tucked away for so long comes flooding back, "One day, a motorcycle cut us off while we were in my dad's car, and he said, 'Iritka, I am so glad you don't know anyone with a motorcycle because they are very dangerous. Good thing Donny doesn't have one.' I always had the feeling my dad knew Donny had a motorcycle and figured he would use this approach to get me to listen to him."

"It is too bad Zoli did not come. My father would have been so happy."

"I know. It would have been nice." Every time someone says this to me, I feel sad that he isn't here to share this experience. "I bet your dad could have persuaded mine to go on a motorcycle ride with him. That, in itself, would have been worth seeing. I'll have to take a photo of your dad on the bike and send it to him. I could also take a photo with me on it. I'm sure my dad would love that."

We head inside and the smell of food is permeating the room. "I'm so hungry," I say as my mouth starts watering.

"Good. Let's eat," Jofie says.

This time, as I load up my plate, I know better. *Tonight,* I think, *I will try to eat very, very slowly. That way, they won't give me seconds too quickly because, no matter what, they will still think I need to eat more.*

"Irit, you look serious. What are you thinking about?" Petr asks, interrupting my thoughts.

"Oh, nothing, just that I better eat slowly; that way, your parents will only want to give me seconds and not thirds."

Petr shakes his head, laughing, "That's pretty funny, but they will still try to get you to eat more."

We start eating another delicious meal, but I can tell that Petr is eager to finish and continue with our evening. He jumps up the minute dessert is finished and says, "Are you ready? Let's head off to the beer gardens."

I am excited to go, even in his famous, feel-every-bump car.

"I'm sure with my full stomach your car will give me even more of an experience on the cobblestones than it did earlier today," I tease.

Petr chuckles, "I told you. You will go back to Montréal and tell all of your friends that you were in a special car that you could only drive in Prague."

"That is true, Petr! I am very lucky."

~~~~~~~~~

The beer garden here is very similar to the ones I have been to in Montréal. It is smoky and filled with people. The sound system is blaring polka music.

"Do you know how to polka?" Petr asks.

"Sure," I say. "If it's the same as in Montréal."

Petr puts one hand on my shoulder and the other around my waist, supporting and guiding me as we traverse the floor. I smile and look into his eyes as I get swept away with the music.

"You are very good. Where did you learn to dance?" Petr asks.

"We had a class at McGill University when I was studying to become a physical education teacher. Every Friday morning for one semester we did ballroom dancing. I always thought it looked pretty funny, though. We would all be doing Viennese waltzes, tangos, polkas, cha cha's and who knows what else while wearing gym shorts and t-shirts."

"Do you want a beer?" Petr asks.

"Of course."

I look around the room, and I feel I'm back at home. The faces look the same as anywhere else. It is only when someone speaks that I am reminded of where I am.

Petr returns with two beers in hand, and I continue the conversation, "So, where did you learn to dance?" I ask.

"As kids in Prague, all my friends and I had to take lessons."

As the night wears on, we dance polka after polka, and I drink beer after beer.

"Where is the bathroom?" I ask Petr over the loud music.

"Over by the bar, but I will go with you because it costs money."

"You're kidding," I say in astonishment. "Isn't that capitalism?" I thought I had understood the differences between communism and capitalism, but things that I am learning on this trip keep throwing me off.

Petr shrugs his shoulders and gives me a coin for the woman standing watch over the restroom. I give her the money. Then, she hands me a small piece of paper that feels like parchment and opens the bathroom door.

I walk into the stall, and suddenly, I understand what the paper is for. I wonder if it costs more to get more paper. *Welcome to communism,* I say to myself, *where the rules make no sense.*

I leave the stall just as a Viennese waltz comes on. Petr takes my hand, and we start moving across the floor with the one-two-three count of the waltz.

Petr's hands feels secure as we move back and forth, turning right and left, and weaving in and out of people. He brings me closer, and I look up at him, smiling. He winks at me and flashes that mischievous smile that has become so familiar to me so quickly.

The time flies, and it is nearly midnight.

"We should go," he says softly. "We have a busy day tomorrow."

I must have gotten used to riding without shock absorbers because I sit quite comfortably in the Skoda as he drives us back to his parent's place. We get to Barna's flat in no time at all, and I feel a sense of sadness wash over me.

"Why don't you stay longer than one week in Prague?" Petr asks. My heart skips a beat. That was what I was thinking, too. "I have leave for two weeks. I can show you around. Maybe we could go to the country, and then you could go to Košice and Budapest after that."

My head spins as I contemplate this idea. *Maybe I can change my plans,* I think, my heart beating quickly.

"I'll walk you up the stairs," Petr says, and he takes my hand, leading the way. "I'll pick you up tomorrow at 9:00 a.m."

I smile, turn the key Barna gave me in the lock, and let myself in. "Goodnight," I say.

I walk inside and see that Barna is still up, reading in the kitchen. We talk for a few minutes about my day before I close the kitchen door and head off to bed.

The tape of this day keeps playing over and over in my head. It was so great. I can't make up my mind. *Should I stay longer? Should I go as planned? Am I being crazy?*

I think about my dad. Whenever he had a big problem to deal with, he would say, "I'll sleep on it. I always get the best answers in my sleep. So, when I wake up, I will know what to do." It works for him, but I haven't figured out how to make it work for me yet. Tonight I decide I will try once again. *Go to sleep,* I tell myself. *The answer will come to you tomorrow.*

3

1978

Kindness in words creates confidence.
Kindness in thinking creates profoundness.
Kindness in giving creates love.

Lao Tzu

At 5:30 a.m., I wake up, and my head is pounding. A shooting wave of pain goes through my abdomen. Within thirty seconds of waking, I rush to the bathroom. I make it just in time. *Did I upset my stomach? Did anyone else get sick?* I wonder. *Ok, go back to sleep, Irit,* I tell myself.

No sooner do I crawl under the down comforter than the shooting pain sears through my gut again. Almost instantly, I start to feel nauseous, and my hands get clammy. I bolt for the toilet once again, and this time I throw up. *What is going on?* I wonder. *It can't be the food I ate because Barna and Jofie ate everything I did, and they're ok. I would know if they were getting up.* One hour passes, and my back and belly are on fire. As I head to the bathroom for the umpteenth time, I hear footsteps.

Barna's kind Hungarian voice comes through the bathroom door, "Are you alright?"

I'm having trouble thinking of the right words to say in Hungarian. Slowly, I get my wits together and mutter, "I don't feel well." I open the bathroom door and see Barna standing outside with a concerned look on his face.

"What is going on?" he asks.

"I don't know. I hurt everywhere."

He reaches out to touch my face and then says, "Your head is hot. Let me take your temperature."

After a minute, Barna grabs the thermometer from me and reads, "39.5 Celsius."

I sigh with frustration. "Is that a lot?" I ask. "I'm used to Fahrenheit."

"It is a big fever."

"Ok, maybe I just have a little bug, and I'll be better soon," I say, hopefully.

Barna nods and says, "I will make you tea, and when Petr arrives, he'll know what to do because of his medical training."

I see Jofie come out of the bedroom. I feel bad for waking everyone so early.

"Can I make you something?" she asks.

"Just tea," I say, gratefully.

"Do you want a hot water bottle?"

Before I can answer, I have to rush to the bathroom again. For the millionth time that day, I use the cord overhead to flush the toilet. I go into the other room to wash my hands, and as I return to bed, I think, *there can't possibly be anything left in my body*. The pain in my back is not letting up, and the knife-like feeling in my abdomen is getting stronger. My head is spinning, and I'm still nauseous. *This can't be happening to me*, I think, exasperatedly. *This is my vacation! I have never been sick like this in my life.* I'm glad that Petr is a doctor. Maybe he will know what the problem is. I can't imagine what it would be like to get sick in a foreign country if I didn't know anyone. It would be terrifying. As if on cue, I hear the key in the door, which opens to reveal Petr. Before Petr can say anything, Barna rushes to him, and I hear my name. Petr looks over at me.

"Your face looks green," he says.

I give him a weak smile and say, "Thanks! I guess I look as bad as I feel."

"What's wrong?"

"My back, my stomach, my head, everything hurts. I've gone to the bathroom at least six or seven times to throw up."

"I'm sorry that you are feeling so bad," Petr says with concern in his voice.

I look up at him. I have known Petr for only a short period of time. Yet, somehow I feel very close to him.

"Can you lie down?" he asks. "I'll do an exam."

I lay down, and he starts prodding around on my stomach. "Tell me if this hurts," he says.

"Ow!" I shriek as he touches a spot on my right side. "What is going on?"

"Let me check a few more things. Does it hurt here?" He tries another spot, and again my voice rises ten decibels.

"I'll be back in a few minutes. I need to make a phone call."

Don't panic, I say to myself. *You're in good hands.*

Petr comes back into the room and says, "I just got off phone with a doctor."

"Doctor?" I say, unable to hide the fear in my voice. "Why?"

"I think you have appendicitis."

"What? That can't be. Maybe it's just a bug. Appendicitis will spoil my plans! I'm supposed to meet..."

"You have classic symptoms," Petr interrupts. "The doctor can see you in one hour."

There is no letup in the pain as we drive to the doctor's office. Last night I had felt so comfortable in this car even without the shock absorbers, but today I can feel every bump in the road as we go. It hurts too much to talk. We arrive, and it is 1:00 p.m. by the time I enter the doctor's dark office. *It is so spooky in here*, I think as I walk, alone, into the examination room. The doctor walks in behind me, and, in broken English, says, "I do pelvic exam."

"Why a pelvic exam?" I ask.

"To make sure."

"Make sure of what?"

No answer. I feel a sense of dread overwhelm me.

"Now, go on table and put legs here," the surgeon says.

Stirrups? What have I gotten myself into? I am starting to panic. He starts the exam, and I scream as the worst pain yet courses through my body. It feels like he just poked me with a sharp knife.

"Don't be so weak," the doctor says.

Fear is taking over, and I try to think of my dad for comfort. I better not say anything more to the doctor, or he'll make it worse.

"It's not so bad," the doctor says to me in his monotone voice.

He is so cavalier about my pain that, before I can edit my own thoughts, I blurt out, "If you weren't such a butcher, I wouldn't have screamed so much."

The doctor smiles, so I know he probably didn't understand me. At least, I have the language barrier going for me, or that might have caused some trouble. I leave the office, and Petr stays behind a few minutes longer to speak to him.

"I'm sorry, but we have to drive to hospital now. You need to have your appendix removed."

"Petr, he is not doing my surgery," I demand in a panic. "I won't let him." I am getting hysterical.

"He won't," Petr reassures me. "We have to go to Charles Hospital, and the surgeon on call there will do it. I just brought you to this doctor to confirm the diagnosis.

"I can't believe this. Three years ago, I had a grand mal seizure as I was en route to the airport heading to Sweden. Now this!"

"Are you epileptic?"

"No. I just had one seizure. A group of us, participating in a University-sponsored physical education program abroad, stopped for a planned lunch prior to heading for the airport. Unbeknownst to us, the tuna fish salad was laced with cockroach insecticide poisoning, and one by one we suffered grand mal seizures." I remember that experience like it was yesterday. Two days later, the camera crew was at the airport when we arrived again, and my picture ended up appearing in the front page with the headline that read something like *Physical Educators Survive Close Encounter with Death.* Ever since that happened, I have imagined newspaper headlines whenever I'm in high stakes situations.

"Don't worry. You are going to the best hospital in Prague. It is where I was born."

As if that is a good barometer, I think. *I'm about to have surgery in a communist hospital. That's a little bit scarier than being born if you ask me.* I pause and try to calm myself down. *Petr is a doctor.* I remind myself, *he won't let any harm come to me.*

"Stay with me until I'm in the operating room," I beg him. "Remember, I don't speak the language."

"I'm not going anywhere. I'll be with you," he says, taking my hand in his.

"An appendectomy is not too serious. Don't worry."

"But Petr, five years ago, a friend of my parents went in for surgery for a broken arm in Montréal, and he never woke up. Something about the anesthetics killed him." I know this is a rarity and I am being irrational, but I can't help but be concerned. I am about to have surgery in a foreign country. I am terrified.

"Don't worry. You'll be fine. This is the best hospital in Prague," Petr says once again. "Now come on, we have to fill out these papers before surgery."

"I don't speak the language."

"Don't worry. I'll do it for you. Just sign here. This form just says that you cannot leave the country until you pay for the surgery."

"That's incentive enough to pay," I say. "Good thing I have insurance." I had spent so much time trying to assure my dad that there was no way they could keep him in this country, and now here I am, worrying about what might happen to me. I guess I wasn't entirely right in my assertions.

"Alright, Irit, they want you to go with them," Petr tells me, gesturing to a nurse who had just walked into the lobby.

I look up at him and can't bear the thought of moving forward without him. "Can you come in with me? You're a doctor."

Petr speaks to them in Czech for a moment, and the next thing I know we are zipping down the hall together.

I am ushered into a room where I can put on my hospital gown, and Petr helps me get on a gurney. The clock reads 4:25 p.m. Time seems to be moving so slowly and yet so quickly at the same time. The walls of the hospital are grayish white, which matches my glum mood.

This is my second time in a hospital, but it feels like my first. My first time was when I was eight. Esti, my best friend, and I went into the hospital together, her for a tonsillectomy and I for adenoids removal. I remember both of us sitting around and eating as much ice cream and as many popsicles as we wanted after our surgeries. We got the royal treatment. It didn't seem anything like this. I didn't even have pain before that surgery.

The image of my parents' friend with the broken arm comes back to haunt me. *Irit, you're too young to die*, I remind myself. *You will be fine.* I look at Petr and am comforted by the fact that he does not look worried.

A young man walks into the room and introduces himself to me. "I am Dr. Z, and I will be doing your surgery," he says. Even with all of the pain in my stomach, I can't help but notice that he is cute. "I hear you are from Canada. How do you pronounce your name?"

"Ear-eat," I say. "Spelled I-R-I-T. How did you learn to speak English so well?"

"I learned in school, and I have traveled abroad quite a bit."

How is that? I want to say. It took Petr forever to get the visa to come to Montréal for just two weeks. Before I can ask, I hear my dad's voice in the back of my mind. *Don't trust the communists. Don't ask questions.*

"Don't worry," Dr. Z says, misinterpreting the look on my face, "I will give you such a small scar that you will brag to everyone in Montréal about the communist doctor who made the smallest incision ever for appendix surgery. Let's get started. Before you know it, you will be talking to me and laughing."

The nurse puts a mask over my face and tells me to take deep breaths. Suddenly, everything goes dark.

~~~~~~~~~

I can't open my eyes. No matter how hard I try, my eyes stay shut. I can tell that I am lying down, and it feels cold. I try moving my hands, but I can't. *Ok, move your toes,* I command myself. Nothing. *Why can't I even get my toes to move?*

I hear a sound. I can hear people talking, but nothing they are saying makes sense. It isn't English. *I don't understand. What language is that? Where am I?* I try to speak, but no words come out. It feels so cold. I feel trapped. *Come on. Open your eyes. Ask for help. Try to ask for help. Tell them you can't move. Come on.* Still nothing. I am starting to panic. There is no way out. I'm trapped.

Then, out of nowhere, I feel someone touch my hand. This hand feels so warm, almost hot, as it envelops mine. *Someone is holding my hand,* I realize. *Please don't let go,* I want to shout, but, yet again, nothing comes out. The warmth of that touch is so welcoming.

Suddenly, a cold compress is put on my head. It feels so refreshing. I lie there, motionless, trying to squeeze the other person's hand to let them know I am awake, but my hand refuses to cooperate. My eyes and lips are sealed shut like they have been glued. Not even a syllable will escape my lips. I can feel the stranger replacing the compress on my forehead repeatedly. It feels so nice. The comforting hand is still holding onto me, never letting go. My mind finally relaxes, and after what seems like an eternity, my eyes open.

As my eyes start to focus, I see an older woman sitting in front of me. She has light brown eyes and a smile that penetrates every cell of my body. I flex my muscles. I can move again. I look around and finally remember where I am: a hospital in Prague. This woman must be a nurse. I start speaking, but she simply shrugs her shoulders and says something in Czech that I don't understand.

Of course, I think. *She does not speak English.* She looks at me, and I look at her. We both smile.

"*Bolet?*" she asks me.

"Yes." I respond. I had learned the meaning of that word only too well yesterday. *Bolet,* the word for, *it hurts.* The woman stands, and I can see that she is only about 5'2". She looks at me with that warm smile once again and brushes her graying hair out of her eyes.

"I have to pee," I say in a croaky voice. She does not understand me, so I motion to my bladder. I see understanding spread across her sweet face.

She helps me sit up and holds on to my arm as I slowly stand. It still hurts to move, but the stabbing pain in my back is gone. I try to take a step forward, but I am too wobbly to move on my own. With the woman's gentle guidance, I slowly maneuver myself to the commode. I sit, and, after what seems like forever, I am able to pee.

Ok. Get up, I say to myself. Slowly, the woman helps me stand and guides me, with patience and care, back to bed. Who would have thought that in a communist country I would get such good care? As the time passes, she stays with me, never leaving my side. She resumes her rotation of putting compresses on my head and holding my hand, and as I drift off, I dub her my angel.

When I awaken again and glance at the clock, it says 6:05 a.m. She is still sitting by my side, and in our familiar routine, we smile at each other.

Another nurse comes in and takes my temperature and blood pressure. Besides my angel, she is the only other health care person I have seen since waking. This nurse is all business with no emotion. There is no, '*how are you?*' Nothing.

I doze off again once the nurse leaves, and 30 minutes later, I wake up, needing to use the commode again. My helper is by my side. As I get up, I look around the big, rectangular room. There are so many beds in here.

My angel takes my hand and motions for me to take a few steps, but I am hunched over. I cannot straighten up because of the pain. I am afraid to breathe because it hurts, and yet I'm afraid not to breathe because that hurts even more. With each movement, my abdomen feels like it is on fire, but at least the headache and the daggers of pain from the day before are gone. I hold on to her arm as I take one baby step after another. Slowly, I walk around the room and count the beds. Including me, there are 13 people in the room, or at least there are 13 beds. One of the beds is empty, but it seems as though someone occupies it because there is an overnight bag beside it.

I get back into bed after my lap around the room, and everyone applauds. I smile with pride. It's amazing how hard it was to walk. I'm exhausted, and I am filled with awe and joy at the support of the patients. No one knows me or even speaks a language I know, but I feel a sense of camaraderie here. My helper stays by my side, once again, putting compresses on my forehead and holding my hand.

An hour passes, and two orderlies walk in with a gurney. They put it beside the empty bed and call out a name. My angel speaks to them, kisses my hand, and lets go. I watch as the two orderlies follow her to the other side of the room. Suddenly, she puts on a hospital gown and climbs onto the gurney. I freeze.

What? She is a patient? This can't be! As I watch them wheel her away, our eyes connect, and the image is imprinted in my brain. *Where is she going?* I wonder. *When is she coming back? What is wrong with her? Who is she?*

Twenty minutes pass, and I doze off. The entrance of my doctor awakens me. I recognize Dr. Z. He is the only familiar face I have seen since the surgery.

"I kept my word." Dr. Z smiles, "I made you a very small incision, a work of art if I say so myself. How are you feeling?"

"I'm better. Last night, after the surgery, I could hear everything, but I couldn't move. I couldn't speak. I couldn't even open my eyes to see, but the woman they just took away, she was with me all night, helping me."

"You weren't able to move because we gave you anesthetic from the myorelaxans family. It is like curare. It paralyzes you so we can do surgery. Usually people don't wake up until after anesthetic wears off."

Just my luck, I think. I don't completely understand what Dr. Z is saying, but at least I know that it was the drug, whatever he called it, that paralyzed me and not something else.

"The woman they just took away, what is happening with her?"

"She is having surgery in 20 minutes."

"Will she be back in here after her surgery?"

"No, she will be in intensive care," he says with a blank face.

My heart sinks when I hear those words. "What is wrong with her?" I ask, dreading the answer.

"I cannot say, but it is very serious. It will be at least a 6-hour surgery, probably longer."

"Can I visit her in intensive care? I want to see her." I figure that maybe I could sit next to her and hold her hand.

"We'll see. Now, let me check your scar. It looks good. I will come back later to see you."

He leaves, and my thoughts stay on my angel. I can't believe she is a patient. She didn't even know me. Yet, she chose to stay by my side, holding my hand, giving me compresses, and making me feel safe, protected, and loved when there was only darkness and fear around me. There were 13 people in that room. What made her choose me? I will always remember her immense gift. She must have somehow known that I was terribly frightened and desperately needed help.

After a few minutes, Petr walks in with his endearing smile, bringing me back to the present.

"So, you ready to go for a walk in Prague?"

I look at Petr and smile. "Maybe not today, but how about a walk to the bathroom? Where is it?"

"Outside the room. I'll go with you."

"Petr, this won't be easy. My abdomen is hurting so bad. It is hard to walk."

"Just keep breathing."

"Yeah, easier said than done."

I begin my walk, with one hand on Petr for support and the other holding my abdomen. We head into the hallway, and I am shocked by the atmosphere. There are no waste baskets in sight. It seems so bizarre. Papers are just strewn on the floor here. It is quite different from the hospital I remember from my childhood.

We walk at a turtle's pace for what seems like two hours to get to the toilet. Finally, somehow, after what seems like forever, I am back in bed, exhausted.

"I'll see you later," Petr says.

I am so tired all I want to do is sleep, but I muster up enough energy to ask, "Where are your parents?"

"Oh, they will be here during visiting hours this afternoon. Because I am a doctor, I can come now." I hadn't realized he was bending rules for me. Once again, I'm so thankful that I am here with a doctor.

At 12:00, a woman comes into the room and puts trays of food by each of our beds. I remove the lid on mine and look over the food. Mashed potatoes, peas, soup with vegetables, and something that looks foreign to me. I take a bite of the potatoes and almost spit them out. They taste worse than cardboard. I try again with one bite of the peas. They taste like they were frozen, thawed, frozen again, thawed again, and then served. I can't even tell what the other food is, but it is covered in a brown sauce and looks yucky. I can't eat this. People back home complain about hospital food, but I can't imagine it being this bad.

When my dad was recovering from his bullet wounds at that Russian camp, I know this food probably would have seemed phenomenal to him. I think of all his years without sustenance. I try to imagine it and be thankful for the food in front of me, but I still can't bring myself to eat it. *How did he survive?* I wonder. *I can't even eat hospital food.*

My tray is taken away, with most of the food still on it, and replaced with tea. *Yay.* I think. *At least, I will have something warm to soothe my body.* I take a sip and spit it out. It is cold and tastes as if it is days old. Tears roll down my face for the first time since this whole ordeal started, and they won't stop. *They can't even get the tea right,* I think agitatedly to myself.

~~~~~~~~~~

I awaken to a nurse entering the room. She is in the typical white uniform. Her hair is disheveled, and she is sniffling. She smiles as she walks over to my bed, but it seems like one of those pasted on smiles, the kind that tells you to be careful of the person presenting it.

She starts to get a syringe ready. The needle looks about 8" long. As she tips the top of it up, she sniffles. I get a knot in my stomach. Instantly, I feel like I have entered into the story of *One Flew over the Cuckoo's Nest,* and this is Nurse Ratchet coming to life.

"I don't want a needle," I say fearfully.

She smiles again with that unsettling smile and continues her work.

"I guess you don't speak English," I say. She looks at me and does not answer. I take that as a "yes".

She motions for me to turn over so I repeat, "I don't want the needle." I am getting desperate now, so I emphatically shake my head and say, "*Ne.*"

She sneezes, and that only increases my trepidation. *What ever happened to sanitation?* I wonder. *Is that not part of the communist edict?*

We stare at each other for a moment. She has that look, that exact look that my mom always has when there is no room for bargaining. Her stare wins, and I meekly turn over to give her access to my butt. As soon as the needle penetrates, I feel an incredible tightening in my muscles in the surrounding area. I see stars, and I feel the sharpest piercing sensation I have ever felt in my life. It is like my body has been shot to the sky and back. My hands get clammy and after one second of this agony, which feels like an eternity, I can't hold back any longer. I scream.

"What the hell did you just do?" I yell at her, tears in my eyes.

She looks at me with a straight face, sneezes, writes something on my chart, and walks away without saying anything.

Then, as if to save the day, Petr walks in.

"Petr!" I say frantically, "I don't know what she did, but my butt, it is burning. It hurts really badly from the nurse's injection. I saw stars."

"Just your luck," Petr says sympathetically. "She probably hit a nerve. Does it hurt down the leg?"

"No. Just in the butt."

"That's good. She must have just hit a superficial nerve. Don't worry, the pain should be over soon."

I take a deep breath, trying to calm down, and feel a wave of relief as Barna and Jofie walk in with their radiant smiles.

"Irit, it is so good to see you," they both say as first Jofie and then Barna reach over to give me a kiss on the cheek.

"We spoke to your dad," Barna says.

"You called him?" I ask. *Uh oh.* I know my dad will be far too worried about me now. He was already anxious about me being on communist soil.

"No, he called us," Barna says. I look up at him, surprised. "He says he woke up in the middle of the night, worried. He woke your mother up and said, 'We have to call Barna because Irit is in big trouble. I think they put her in jail.' He couldn't get through for the longest time for some reason. He called every 15 minutes, but all he got was a busy tone. He told me he had paced up and down the room a million times. He was afraid that you were in jail, and he was sure it was because of him. When I told him you were in the hospital because you had had your appendix out, he was relieved that he was wrong and it was surgery, not jail."

My dad wasn't entirely wrong. I think to myself. *I felt like a prisoner, a prisoner in my own body.* He, too, was once a prisoner in his own body he had told me. When he had been shot, he couldn't move, and who knows what pain he must have been in. If it hadn't been for his doctor or my angel, we both would have suffered much more.

My days in the hospital pass with the same routine. The nurse does her rounds, the blood pressure, the thermometer, etcetera, and then Dr. Z walks in.

"Irit, how are you?" he says.

"I'm better. Can I visit my friend in ICU?"

"Not today."

"How about tomorrow?"

"We talk tomorrow," he responds before leaving. Today, however, he sticks around a little longer and asks, "I will get a break a little later. Maybe you want to go to doctors' lounge with me?"

"Doctors' lounge? Patients can do that here?" I ask, surprised.

"No, but you are special, and I want to hear about Montréal."

"Montréal, where I live? Why?"

"You see, I will go there this September with a friend who is a doctor here. Maybe you can show me around, or maybe I can stay with you."

You're kidding, I think to myself. *You're my doctor, you're cute, and now you want to stay with me in Montréal?* There is no extra room in my place with my roommates, but maybe he could stay with my parents. Back home it won't matter if he is part of the communist party. In Montréal, my father won't be as worried. I bet he would be happy to help the doctor who helped me. I start laughing because it feels so surreal, but I stop quickly as it causes a sharp pain in my abdomen. Who would have imagined that I would get privileges because the doctor wants my help? Maybe that's how communism works. Anyway, now I know why I am "special," but that's ok. Who else goes to the hospital and then ends up in the doctors' lounge?

"We will talk later about it, but now there is a woman from London, England coming to stay here in this room. She only speaks English. She will need appendix surgery, but she is pregnant so we will wait a few hours and see if somehow maybe the symptoms will abate."

"Another English-speaking woman?" I say, surprised. "Do many English-speaking people come into the hospital?"

He shakes his head. "We never get English people, and yet now, two in one week. We will move the beds so she is near you, and you can be her interpreter."

"Interpreter? But I only know five words in Czech."

"You be her interpreter," he says again. "You can help her because you already had your appendix out, and she can ask you questions.

Before I know it, the beds are arranged, and a 30-year-old English woman is in the bed next to mine.

"I am so glad that you are here and can be my interpreter," she says. "Knowing that you speak English and can help me understand what they want makes me feel much more at ease. Thank you for being such an angel to me.

"No problem!" I smile. *Pretty funny,* I think to myself, *first I get an angel to help me, and now I have become someone else's angel.* All I am doing is reassuring her and comforting her, and yet I know now how important that is. Those little gestures can make such a difference.

"Are you ready to learn a new language?" I ask.

She smiles.

"I'll start by teaching you the five most important words. After all, they're the only words I know." *How crazy,* I think. Since being in Prague, I have been translating Hungarian with Jofie and Barna and English with Petr, and they only spoke to each other in Czech. My head has been spinning from all the languages, and now, I'm a bona fide interpreter. It reminds me of my dad's interpreting experience. Though, of course, the stakes were much higher for him.

The doctor who had saved his life told everyone that he spoke many languages and could help with interpreting. The Russians thought he was fluent in German, and the Germans thought he was fluent in Russian. Since he was the interpreter, no one had a clue that he was learning as he went. Now, with my vocabulary of five words, I find myself doing the same. What I have gone through pales in comparison to what my dad had to endure, yet it makes me feel somehow connected to him and even more appreciative of the strength he must have had. I can't wait to tell my dad about this.

The next day, after the nurse checks all my vitals, Dr. Z comes in, and I see a bouquet with six roses in his hand.

"Irit, this is for you. Happy birthday," he says. He turns to the other patients and says something in Czech. Suddenly, in unison, they all start to sing. I can't understand a word they are saying in Czech, and the tune is different, but I know it is the birthday song. I look around the room, smiling at each person. In a strange way, I feel as if I will miss them.

"How did you know it was my birthday?" I ask.

"It is in your chart." I am touched that he would be thoughtful enough to take note of that and bring me flowers, but there is really only one thing I want for my birthday.

"I leave tomorrow," I say. "Can I visit my friend today?"

Dr. Z shakes his head, "She can have no visitors. Tomorrow, when you leave, we will talk again. Now I must go." He hurries out.

No visitors still? I think. *How are you, my angel friend? I hope you are well. I will make sure they let me see you tomorrow.*

Petr enters the room, singing the happy birthday song in Czech. Once again, the patients join in.

"It is best if you stay one more week here instead of going to Košice," he tells me, as he has every day since I entered the hospital. "I can show you Prague and the countryside for the next seven days, or if you want, my parents could keep you in the house, feed you every 30 minutes, and ask you how you are every ten minutes. Whatever you prefer." He smiles.

I look at Petr, and I have to hold my stomach to keep it from hurting as I start to laugh.

"So, what do you want to do?" he asks.

"I'll stay with your parents," I say, teasingly

Petr looks at me with a silly, dumbfounded expression, and I laugh again. "Ouch, my abdomen. Stop making me laugh!" I take a deep breath to calm my stomach and then say, "Of course, I want to see Prague."

"Remember, there are no shocks in my car. It will hurt."

"Petr, I'm tough. Remember? I'm from Canada."

"What?"

"One of the doctors said I was weak because I was from Canada. I resent that so … well, anyway, it was a joke." We laugh.

I hear the birthday song once more as Jofie and Barna walk in. I laugh as the patients join in yet again.

"This is for your birthday," Jofie says, handing me a bag filled with homemade food. I start digging in the bag and pull all of the items out: roasted chicken with paprika, crispy roasted potatoes, just like I like them, and cucumber salad. It is all just how my mom makes it. My mouth starts to water. *Real food,* I think happily. *Finally.*

"This is the best birthday present I could get. Thank you so much for making this food for me," I say.

"Petr helped. He waited almost two hours in line for the chicken."

"Thank you. I will always remember this."

"This is the least we could do for you," Barna says. "You are Zoli's daughter." *Zoli's daughter,* I repeat to myself. I feel such a deep outpouring of love when they say those two words. For the hundredth time since I arrived, I wish my dad were here.

~~~~~~~~~

The next morning, my eyes open, and I am alert right away. This is my last day in the hospital.

I look around the room, but I stop midway as my eyes glimpse the empty bed where my angel once stayed. I hope they are leaving it empty, waiting for her to return. *Why can't I see her?* I ask myself. That is the question that has been repeating incessantly in my mind for days. Maybe only family is allowed in the ICU, but I have pull. My doctor and I are on a first name basis. I'm arranging for him to stay with my parents in Montréal when he visits, and he himself said he had bent rules for me because I'm "special." He can pull strings.

I can't believe I have been here for seven days. Like a magnet, my eyes are pulled to the chair by the end of my bed. My angel, with her soft brown eyes and graying hair, had sat there for hours, holding my hand, guiding me, and patiently helping me from dusk till dawn. Her eyes and her smile are embedded in my heart and soul.

The nurse comes by my bed and takes my temperature and blood pressure reading one last time. I try asking her about my special helper, but she doesn't understand, so I just close my eyes and remember the very last time the angel squeezed my hand. I remember her letting go and walking back to her bed, where the orderlies waited with the gurney. She had her head slightly down as she took one slow step after another. *Had she been scared? Is she ok now?* I look around, remembering how she had held me by the arm as I walked and how the patients had applauded as I passed by their beds.

The nurse starts walking out the door, but she turns back for something. I instantly flash back to my last moment with the angel at that exact spot. She had looked up as she was being wheeled out. Our eyes had connected, and she had smiled. She had looked at peace. She hadn't seemed afraid. *I will see you again,* I promise as I hold on to that last image of her, *and this time it will be my turn to help you.*

"Irit, where are you?" Dr. Z says, cutting into my daze. "Are you dreaming of what it will be like when you leave the hospital?"

"Oh, I didn't notice you walk in."

He smiles. "Well, I guess the next time I will see you will be in September in Montréal," he says. "Today you leave, but remember, don't carry anything heavy for at least two weeks."

"Good. I'll tell Petr that it's doctor's orders. Then again, Petr would never let me carry my bags, anyway, even if I hadn't had surgery." Dr. Z smiles at me, and I muster up the courage to ask him one last time. "I know it is hard to see visitors in the ICU, but I have to go and thank my angel," I say. "Today must be the day." He has been putting it off, but I can't leave without seeing her.

Dr. Z hesitates, and my heart sinks at the sympathetic expression on his face as he says, "Irit, I am so sorry, but I have not been able to…"

I stop listening. In that instant, I know why I haven't been allowed to visit, why I would never be allowed to visit, and tears start to run down my face.

But … this woman was there for me when all I could feel was fear, I think. I know I can't say goodbye to her now, so instead, I send out a prayer to her in the universe.

You held my hand, and it took the fear away. You put compresses on my forehead, and it made me feel protected. You gave with your heart, and it made me feel loved. You helped me understand the gift of giving in a new way. Through your eyes and your smile, I could feel your unconditional love, and it enriched my life. You are my angel of light, and I will always remember you. Dekuji! [Thanks!]

I close my eyes, and let all the world fall away. I see nothing but her beautiful brown eyes in that instant before she was taken away.

4

1979

My dear friend, clear your mind of "can't."

Samuel Johnson

"Dan, hand over the gun. It's not allowed in school. You know the rules."

"But, I was just about to put it away," Dan pleads.

"You had it in the hallway in full view. I have no choice but to confiscate it. Hand it over," I wait with my hand outstretched.

"Ms. Schaffer, give me one more chance. Pleeease."

"Well," I ponder. "Is it loaded?"

Dan examines his gun and nods in the affirmative.

"OK, hand it over."

Dan looks at me and, with a mischievous laugh, gives me the water gun. "I just bought it yesterday."

I walk away with the fully loaded water gun in my hand and smile. This is the first water gun I have ever taken from a student. I feel bad having to take it away because, of course, it is harmless, but rules are rules. I just feel lucky to teach at this school. There are no gangs or serious drug issues here, and I haven't had to deal with many discipline problems.

The student population at Lemoyne D'Iberville ranges from 7th to 11th graders, which is high school here in Montréal. The students here seem to be pretty accepting of each other's differences, perhaps because the entire region is rich in diverse cultures.

I walk up the stairs and go into the large gym. There are two gyms in the school, one of which is double the size of the other. I walk into my office, which is situated within the large gym, and peruse the teaching plan for my upcoming class. As time passes, I see all 26 of the seventh grade girls in my class wander into the gym and sit on the benches. They have all changed into their gym uniforms, blue shorts or sweatpants with white stripes on the side and blue t-shirts with the Lemoyne D'Iberville emblem on them. The students are sitting quietly and obediently, waiting for their gym teacher, me, to begin class.

I walk out of my office and notice that a lot of the girls are giving me quizzical looks. I look down and realize that the water gun is still in my hand. As I look around at my students, something devious takes hold of me, and without any thought, I aim, pull the trigger and squirt all of the students with room temperature water. It was a one-shot attempt, and the end result is success.

The students start to shriek and laugh, shouting, "You're not allowed to do this" and, "It's against the rules!"

"Well," I say with a smile, "it's against the rules for the students."

"That's not fair," they laugh.

"Who said life was fair?" I smile at them.

The girls dry off, and there is a new sense of joy and excitement in the room. "Ok," I begin, "today is gymnastics. We will begin with forward and backward somersaults, and then we will try to do headstands and handstands. Let's get you into groups of four, and remember, spotting is important."

I walk around the room and observe the students. Everyone is so focused. I feel proud when I see how much they try to help each other out. As I walk, I give instructions. "Keep your knees together for the backward roll!" "Tuck your chin into your chest." "Curl your back." "Push off with your hands." "Finish in a squat."

After about 15 minutes, the more advanced groups move on to headstands and handstands. "Keep your legs straight and feet pointed," I instruct. "Tighten your abs slightly, and when you are in position, look slightly up with your eyes." I can hear the faint echo of the students repeating my instructions to each other as they attempt their moves.

Rhonda, a chubby girl, maybe 20 pounds overweight, is wearing her sweat pants and grinning from ear to ear as she goes through the exercises. When I reach her side of the room, she looks up at me and says gleefully, "That's the first time I've ever done a backwards somersault without any help!" I smile at her. I love how excited students get when they manage to do something they never thought possible.

I look at the clock. It's 2:00 p.m. Class ends in five minutes, so I announce, "Let's wrap up. Be sure to put away the mats you used, and then get changed."

"Can I take a shower?" Susan, one of the more advanced students, asks.

"Sure, Susan, here's a towel, but make it a quick one, okay? Your next class is in 15 minutes." When I was a high school student, I dreaded showers, but they were a mandatory part of PE. It gave me trepidation about gym class as a whole even though I loved physical activity. When I became a teacher, I promised myself that I would never force anyone to take a shower before or after class. I take it as a good sign when the students want to take showers, though. It means they worked up a sweat.

Gymnastics is actually my least favorite class to teach. I always worry that someone will get hurt with all of the flips and tumbles. It's funny, though, because the only real close call I ever had was when I was teaching a four-week unit on cross-country running.

Ellen, an 8ᵗʰ grader who had transferred from another school, had told me at the beginning of the class that it wasn't safe for her to overexert herself running because she had asthma. I told her to run at her own pace and stop if she needed to. Her doctor had cleared her to participate in all physical education activities with no restrictions, and she hadn't had an asthma episode in over a year, so I wasn't too concerned.

During the cross-country unit, everything had been going smoothly, but suddenly, one day, Ellen turned white and began hyperventilating. The students stopped and looked at me as if I would know what to do. All I could think of was my dad. I remember him telling me repeatedly in my youth that he could tell which prisoners would die next in the war, not because they had been the sickest but because they had given up, which he could always see. When I looked at Ellen, it felt like she really believed she would die, and it was causing her body to give up. My heart was racing. I wasn't sure what to do. The class was petrified, and I knew I had to stay calm or things would get worse. Within a few seconds, something happened. All my thoughts gathered together, all my fears disappeared, and a sense of complete calm took over. I knew what to do. Maybe one day I will better understand what allows this survival mode to activate in one person and not another at times like that. Maybe it has to do with the fact that *when you are calm and let go of fear, you can access wisdom that allows you to know exactly what to* do.

"Ok class, Ellen needs all of you to breathe slowly so she can match her breathing with yours. It will help her."

Anna, who was now also hyperventilating out of panic, asked, "Are you sure?"

"Yes, I'm sure," I said with that same knowing calmness.

Within a minute, Ellen's face was not as white. She was still hyperventilating, but she was starting to look better, and within five minutes, everything was back to normal. The class was dismissed, and when I went into my office, I broke down. I was a mess.

Soon after this, Ellen went to see a physician to get evaluated for a new medical clearance to participate in gym class. During the examination, the doctor discovered that Ellen's mom had believed that if Ellen ran more than 10-15 minutes, she would have an asthma attack and die. Of course, because of her mother, Ellen believed this to be true, too. The physician was, thankfully, able to show them that the beliefs they had were false, and he reassured them both that it was safe for Ellen to run.

He told her to start jogging at a slow pace and then build up speed over time. It would be my job to guide her. He said that, eventually, she would be able to run for as long as she wanted. He also reassured the mom that Ellen was healthy and would not die if she overexerted herself. She just had to carry an inhaler in case she ever needed it. She never used it, and by the end of the running curriculum, when the students were asked to run two miles around the school, Ellen was one of the first to finish.

The bell rings, and I walk into the teachers' lounge. I can hear the faculty talking about the parent-teacher conferences being held tonight. There is a buzz of excitement in the room.

I have been a teacher at this school for five years, but I'm still not used to these conferences. I always get anxious butterflies right before they begin. Somehow, I keep expecting some doom or gloom scenario to surface though it never has.

When I graduated from McGill University with a degree in education, specializing in PE, I applied to all four English public school districts available in Montréal. I was hoping I would get at least one offer. However, there was a shortage of teaching positions at the time, so I wasn't very optimistic. Surprisingly, I got all four jobs that I applied for.

When Lemoyne first contacted me, I was drawn in when they told me I would be a coach. The prospect scared me since I had never coached before, but it also excited me. I was always interested in the psychology of sports and what motivates individuals to excel. I wanted to help people become the best they could be through encouragement rather than fear. That was one of the reasons I went into teaching in the first place.

I was also told I would teach Biology for the 8ᵗʰ and 9ᵗʰ graders. The inner workings and mysteries of the body have always fascinated me so I figured that part would be fun, but I had to learn on the fly. I was far from an expert on plants, the animal kingdom, or science projects and labs, which were all part of the curriculum. In the end, I chose this school because I felt it would push me the most.

When I accepted the position, my one, unrelenting fear was that I wouldn't be able to answer students' questions and that I would lose control of the class. It was an irrational fear that, no matter what I did or said, the students would keep doing whatever they wanted and throw things while I stood there with zero control. The physical education part seemed easy; students were supposed to be active and run around in gym. I did not have the same confidence in the class setting.

I told my roommate at the time about my worries, and she had her good friend, Ed, who was in medical school, come over at night to help me prep. Before every big lab day, he would come over, and we would dissect frogs, worms and who knows what else on top of a heavy plastic cover that we placed over my kitchen table.

I realized that my fear was unreasonable, but I could not let it go. Finally, after all this stress, Jason, a ninth grade student, was the only person who came close to making my nightmare a reality. He was always testing me, and he was the leader of the class. I knew that if I lost him, I might lose everyone. One day, Jason, who was sitting in the fourth row, raised his hand with a smirk on his face. He asked me a question, and I went completely blank. I had no clue what the answer was, and I had already forgotten the question.

I could tell by the look in his eyes that he was testing me. He knew I would not know the answer, and there was that tone in his voice that said, 'I'll show you who is in charge.' It seemed as if the students were holding their breath in anticipation. They were so silent you could have heard a pin drop. All eyes were on me. Something in me changed. I was facing my worst fear, and I was no longer afraid. I looked up at the ceiling as if it might hold the answer, and I kept thinking to myself, *What do I need to do now? What should I say?* Suddenly, something inside of me came to the rescue. "That is a really good question," I said to him with the utmost respect. "I don't know the answer, but if you could look it up and share it with all of us in the next class, that would be great."

At that instant, everything changed for me. I could see how proud he felt, perhaps because I had acknowledged his question in a way that was empowering to him. He said he would let us all know the answer in the next class. The students relaxed, following his lead, and from then on, I knew the class would be fine; I would be fine. I knew that I didn't have to be perfect as a teacher, and I didn't have to know all the answers. It was like a weight was lifted from my shoulders. Jason turned out to be one of my favorite students. I always liked the rebel, smart type.

In this same class, on another day of teacher conferences, I avoided what could have been a potential outcry from the parents.

"The chemical that you will use in lab today is toxic," I started off. "So, you cannot bring it close to your nose. DO NOT INHALE IT," I said emphatically, lifting the chemical up to my face to show the class. Suddenly, I couldn't breathe, and I started to turn red, as much from embarrassment as from my lack of breath. I accidentally inhaled while lifting the beaker. Instinct took over immediately, and I fled the classroom, running to the bathroom in the teachers' lounge, which, thank goodness, was only about 20 feet across from me. I turned on the sink and took handful after handful of water in my hands, throwing it on my face. Within one minute, which seemed like an eternity, I could breathe freely once again.

I was so relieved that I could breathe again and that I wasn't going to die of asphyxiation that when I went back to the classroom, it didn't even occur to me to get upset at myself for my mistake, and in a slightly embarrassed but humorous way, I said "Do as I say not as I do." The class laughed, and everything started to run smoothly.

At the end of the class, I had a special treat for the students and I was excited to share this with my students. Ed, who helped me with my lab preparations, had given me a box of cadaver bones to show them. He was in medical school, and each group of four medical students had their own box of bones to learn from, so he lent me his to do a demonstration. I knew none of the students would have seen anything like that before.

"We still have time before the bell rings," I announced to the class as they cleaned up, "and I have a surprise for you."

I grabbed the box full of human bones and pulled out the femur.

"This is the strongest bone in the body. What do you think it is?" I asked.

"The thigh bone," two of the students said in unison.

Next, I pulled out the radius and ulna, the two bones that go from the wrist to the elbow. I could see the students looking at the bones curiously, and I excitedly pulled out the next bone, the humerus.

"What do you think this bone is? I'll give you a clue..."

"Are those bones real?" one of the students interrupted.

"Yes," I announced proudly. "Can you believe how lucky you all are to see these?" A look of trepidation passed over the faces of the students.

"Yuck, human bones," one of the girls in class piped up. "Wait until I tell my parents."

"I can't believe these bones are real. How gross!" another said.

Instantly, fear took over. I started to imagine the barrage of phone calls to the principal and the subsequent reprimands that would come of this. And, of course, it was a few hours before my very first parent teacher interviews. I could see the headlines in the Montreal paper now, *Teacher Suspended for Poor Judgment and Traumatizing Her Students.*

"Come on, guys," I said, trying to play it cool. "Who would give me human bones to show you? I'm just kidding, but they are exact replicas of what real bones look like. I wanted to get your attention, and I did." I smirked at them and knew I made the right choice from the relieved looks on the student's faces. I realized at that moment how important it was to pay attention to my surroundings and not assume that what was exciting and important to me would necessarily have the same meaning for others. If I were steering in the wrong direction with my enthusiasm and excitement, I could always maneuver back on course and I would be fine.

The bell rings, bringing me back to the present. School is out for the day, and now it is time to go home and get ready for this semester's round of parent-teacher conferences. Before I head out, I go into the large gym, to get a few things from my office. The gym is empty, and I take a moment to look around at the walls. There are many banners on display representing past glory, and I just know that many more will be added in the coming years from my teams. I feel so lucky to be paid to help people have fun and play. It never seems like work to me.

Suddenly, a question arises in my head. *"But what if in ten years you don't want to teach? What if in ten years you want to leave Montréal, and do something else? What will you do?*

I love teaching, I tell myself, startled by this thought, but the voice in my head comes back even louder. *What if, in ten years, you don't want to be in Montréal? Remember Canadian winters? Remember the 20 degree below zero weather, the ice and sleet, the daily use of block heaters to warm up your car so it will start, and the two-week flu?*

I try to ignore the voice, but the question comes back louder every time. I've never heard a voice like this before. The only voices I hear are the ones telling me I'm not good enough or I haven't done enough.

What will you do in ten years if you don't want to teach and you want to leave Montréal?

OK, I wonder. *What would I want to do and what would I love to learn? Learning more about the body and the mechanics of healing would be exciting. How has Dad always been able to heal even in the harshest conditions? How does the body work? I was probably the only person in the world who had lost sleep over those questions as a child. Yeah, that is what I want to learn. But what would I be giving up if I did that?* I look around the gym and sigh.

The voice speaks up again, *If you go back to school and learn more about the body and how to help it heal, even if you just go back to teaching, you will have more knowledge. It will make you a better teacher and coach.*

~~~~~~~~~

My school is in Longueil, a suburb about twenty minutes outside of Montréal. In order to get to work each day, I have to go on the Jacques Cartier Bridge, an 11,239' steel truss cantilever bridge crossing the St. Lawrence River. It connects the island of Montréal to the South Shore.

I live on St. Urbain Street, the street that Mordecai Richler's book, *St. Urbain's Horsemen,* is named after. I love the neighborhood. There is a bakery nearby where I can smell the fresh bread they make every morning. Next door to the bakery is a wine and cheese store, where I do taste testing on a regular basis and they know me by name.

Next door to that is the butcher, and then the fish market, but my favorite store is the St. Viater bagel place that is a few blocks away. They have hot poppy seed and sesame bagels 24 hours a day. It has been there since I was a little kid. I always loved going in to watch them make the bagels. They put them on wooden sticks that go into a big oven, and then, a few minutes later, I have a hot poppy seed bagel, crispy and doughy at the same time, melting in my mouth. It is the best bagel place on the planet.

After school today, however, I decide to head to my favorite Greek restaurant, which is two blocks away from my place. It's my dad's favorite, too. I always get two souvlakis, a Greek dish made of grilled lamb, sliced tomatoes, and onions in a pita bread and covered with *tzatziki* sauce, a plain yogurt that has pureed cucumbers, garlic, salt, olive oil and lemon juice. I order, and as the clerk hands me my meal, I have to remind myself to eat slowly. It doesn't work. I'm starving so I wolf down the food. Some things never change, and the speed at which I eat my food is one of them, especially when I'm really hungry.

I head home, shower, change, and am back to school by 7:20 p.m. for the conferences. I'm 15 minutes early, so I go into the teachers' lounge to relax. The room is in chaos. Everyone is there preparing for the onslaught. After a few minutes, I head back to the large gym to wait for the parents in peace. The school has over 700 students, but every year only about 200 parents show up, and only a handful of those end up coming to the gym. In Montréal especially, parents don't consider gym very important. The parent teacher conferences are really just for the basic subjects: math, science, history, etc.

Finally, after I have been waiting around for an hour, a few parents show up, probably as an afterthought, and the evening drags on. At 9:10 p.m., a lady comes into the gym timidly and asks, "Are you Ms. Schaffer?"

"I am," I smile.

"I'm Rhonda's mom, and I want to talk to you about my daughter."

The sense of urgency in her voice makes me nervous. *Ok, this is the one. This lady, dressed in blue corduroys and a white blouse, and holding onto her coat and black purse, she will be the one to take me down.* My body stiffens, waiting.

"Do you realize that my daughter would cry every morning when there was gym last year? She didn't want to go to school on those days."

I freeze, confused, *But Rhonda likes gym*, I think.

"I was beside myself," she says. "Gym was making her so miserable."

Just today she did a backwards somersault! I think, preparing my defense. *She smiled and was so proud!*

"Ms. Schaffer," she says, "last week, Rhonda was sick. It was a gym day, and she cried. She cried because she was going to miss gym!"

My mind goes blank. "Well, I'm glad ..." I say, lamely.

"I don't know what you do, but she can't stop talking about you."

Amazement and relief take hold of me.

"My daughter loves the Lemoyne sweat pants you allow her to wear. She owns three pairs so she can be sure she always has a clean pair for your class," Rhonda's mother continues. "She hates showing her legs because once, when she was in fourth grade, someone made fun of her."

I flash back to the first day of school. Rhonda had come up to me with pleading eyes and said, "Ms. Schaffer, can I please wear sweat pants instead of shorts?" Before I realized what I had done, I had said yes. After five years of teaching, a new rule had emerged from that split-second decision. "Thanks," she said, the sadness in her eyes suddenly lightening. She seemed so excited. I knew I had made the right choice even though I did not fully understand why. Fortunately, the other gym teachers liked the new policy, too, because they thought it was a good idea to give students another choice as long as it was still school clothes, like the sweats with the Lemoyne emblem.

As Rhonda's mom leaves, I try to take in what just happened. Rhonda's fear of being embarrassed had affected her relationship with physical activity. Even if I had been the best teacher on the planet, she would never have embraced physical activity in those gym shorts. It's just like how I felt about showers in school, and I didn't even realize it until today. She had had the limiting belief that she didn't like physical activity. She had "hated" gym, but now I know she loves it. It's interesting how sometimes we don't even realize what the real problem is, and then we make decisions based on beliefs that are not even accurate.

~~~~~~~~~

At 3:30 the next afternoon I have volleyball practice. Everyone gets to the gym and starts to set up the nets. Tracy, one of the team captains, is 5'7", with the wingspan of someone who is 5'10". I made her the setter because she is the best player on the team. Whenever she walks into a room, everyone notices because she has a big presence and is always joking around. She makes everyone laugh. On the other hand, Gale, her co-captain, is probably the fiercest competitor I have ever coached. I chose to pair the two of them because they bring out the best in each other, and their partnership trickles down to the rest of the team.

"Do we have to warm up?" Tracy asks, knowing the obvious, but somehow hoping that this time I would change protocol.

"Tracy, what do you think?" I say, with a devious smile.

"Whenever you have that smile, I know we're in for a tough workout. I take back that question."

I laugh.

"Let's start with stretches. We don't want injuries."

I lead them in my favorite exercise: wall slides. I can go three minutes without quivering so, of course, I always lead the way.

After warm ups, I call out instructions to the students, "Let's pair up in twos and practice volleying. Start with medicine balls, and then move on to basketballs."

"But medicine balls are so heavy. They weigh a ton," Tracy says.

"That's the idea," I say, laughing.

I put a chair by the net and stand on it to serve the ball as they practice digging and setting. They play two on two, then three on three, and then we start to practice serves.

"Gale, give me a number, ten to twenty."

"Ten."

"Alright, when each member of the team gets ten serves over the net in a row, practice will be over."

Nikki, one of the setters, who is usually the calming presence on the team, gets close to ten three times and misses. She is almost in tears by the end, but the other players encourage her. Finally, after about 20 minutes, everyone has managed to get ten over the net. They let out a big yell of relief and start putting away the nets.

Everyone leaves, and I head into my office to grab my coat. "Coach, our bus didn't show up, and it's snowing," one of the students says, coming back into the gym with a small group of girls.

"How many of you are stranded?"

"Just four of us: Nikki, Wendy, Elizabeth, and me."

"Alright, Tracy, give me five minutes, and I'll drive you guys home."

We all head to my Mazda GLC sport. I hate driving in the snow, and being responsible for the student's safety only adds to my stress. Cautiously, I begin the drive.

"Coach, you're driving at about ten miles an hour! Can't you go faster? My mom usually drives at 35 miles per hour, even in snow. She says the winter tires give us good traction so we shouldn't get scared."

"I'm glad for your mom, but you are lucky I'm even going this quickly. You can't even see more than 30 feet away."

As I say this, I lose control for a split second. The car almost goes into the other lane, but I turn the wheel just enough to stay on course. I've had so many close calls and hear about so many accidents that occur from losing control of the wheel that I just can't relax.

My heart is racing, but I start to laugh when I realize that the girls are so calm and trusting that they didn't even seem to notice. Their calmness provides me with the space I need to relax and trust in myself. I feel blessed to have such amazing kids on my team whom I can trust and who, in turn, can trust me.

I look at my students, and I am thrilled that they have become such a close-knit group. Through the team they have learned that, no matter what, whether they play well or not, they are always encouraged and supported, so there can't be failure. Through the team they have learned to push themselves beyond their perceived limits because of their desire to help the team as a whole.

Thirty minutes later, I get to Brossard, another suburb of the South Shore, where all of the girls live. One by one, they are dropped off. I'm relieved everyone got home safe and sound.

Now for the drive home, I think, wearily. It's snowing harder now, and visibility is decreasing. I'm glad the girls are home, at least. I mentally prepare myself and journey onward. I get stuck behind snowplows as they spray salt on the street, and I creep along behind them. This is actually a good thing since I know that the salt will keep me from losing control.

Finally, I reach my house and turn off the ignition. I sigh deeply and sit in my car for ten minutes, reflecting on my day. I smile, thinking of how fortunate I am to have such great students. Then, the question blasts into my head again. *What will you do if you don't want to teach in ten years?* If I ever left Montréal, I would not miss driving in the Montréal winters, nor would I miss the biting cold. I can see my dad's smile light up in front of me. He knows about healing in a way no one else does. Once again, I feel that unrelenting curiosity that has been pestering me since my childhood. *How did he survive such impossible conditions?*

I think back to when I was ski club supervisor during my second year of teaching. It was icy, and four of the senior guys had asked me to ski with them. They were "hot doggers," or better put, "kamikaze skiers," but I was confident I could keep up with them. I was hoping to maybe even one-up them.

"Coach, let's go down this black diamond slope," one of the boys suggested. I looked at the guide and sighed. They *would* choose the most difficult slopes.

I maneuvered one mogul after another, thinking, *I'll show you guys how well I can ski.* Before I knew what hit me, my face was buried in the snow, and my hands and feet were spread-eagled across the entire slope.

Rich and Jeff skied to my rescue, and in the midst of their laughter, asked, "Are you ok? Do you need the ski patrol?"

I was definitely not going to acquiesce to that. I had too much pride, but I knew I needed help getting out of my predicament. I got up and noticed a twinge of pain in my right knee. It felt like it was going to buckle, but fortunately, it didn't.

Not wanting to let on that it was a big deal, I said, "I'm fine, ski on without me."

I gingerly managed to get down the mountain and take off my boots and skis. Then, I waited at the lodge for an hour before meeting everyone back at the bus.

I woke up the next morning, and my knee was badly swollen so I made an appointment to see Terry King, an athletic trainer. I had taken his first aid class on sports-related injuries, and I knew he was an expert on knee injuries. I figured he would be the best person to help me figure out what was wrong with my knee and aid in my recovery.

For about three weeks, I was on a regimen of ice-cold whirlpools, electrical stimulation, and exercise. Even with all of this, I still had pain whenever I put weight on my knee so Terry sent me to an orthopedist that he worked with. This man was the primary doctor for the Montréal Alouettes, our professional football team.

After reading my arthrogram, the doctor said, "You have a torn meniscus, and, unfortunately, there is no blood supply to the meniscus, so it can't heal naturally. You will need to completely remove it through surgery." My heart sank at the thought of surgery, but it seemed as if I had no choice.

I continued seeing Terry for another month, hoping for a change, but with no results. Eventually, he, too, said, "You need surgery."

I set up an appointment, but a few days before my scheduled surgery, I was reading a medical book that explained how the knee menisci are *shock absorbers.* "Without the meniscus," the book had said, "arthritis will eventually set in, and there will be pain. Your activities will be limited." Of course, I would also have a big scar, which would be a constant reminder. In that instant, I knew I would not have surgery. I believed I would heal. *My dad endured six bullets, a gangrenous arm, and starvation to boot,* I told myself. *He made it out in one piece. Why, then, can't a little meniscus in my knee heal?*

The next day, I walked half a block without pain. It was the first time I had been able to do that since the accident. I told myself that if I could walk half a block now, then, eventually, I would be able to go further. I called my doctor to cancel the surgery.

He suggested I reconsider, "because," he reminded me, "the meniscus has no blood supply and can't heal on its own."

"Are you going to retire anytime soon?" I asked.

"Why would you ask me that? I'll be around for at least another ten years," he said, confused.

"Great. I can always call you back if I need the surgery."

He chuckled and said, "When you're ready, call back to reschedule. The meniscus doesn't heal."

He was so sure. He was my doctor and the expert, but it just didn't make sense to me that a little meniscus could not heal. When I walked that half a block without pain, I just knew I would heal completely. I knew that, eventually, I would have no restrictions. There was no doubt in my mind, no fear.

My dad was the first in a long line of people who proved to me the resilience of the human body. I know that the body is capable of more than most people give it credit for. After some time, I realized that the doctor, from all the information he had and all the research he read, believed it to be impossible. It wasn't that he was wrong or a bad doctor at all. I liked him. His knowledge was based on the most up to-date-research at the time. Who would have known then that a few months later they would find a way to do the surgery with tiny incisions so there wouldn't be a huge scar like I had been worried about? Who would have known that years later, with substantiated research, doctors would discover that parts of the meniscus do have a blood supply and thus can heal without surgery.

I made a full recovery and returned to skiing by the next season. I didn't realize it then, but I know now that I had tapped into what my dad had always called "good blood." I had never really understood what he meant by that. In fact, I still don't fully understand, but I do know that *my own belief in my ability to heal was enough to help me make progress.*

What do you want to do, Irit? The voice pops into my mind once more.

Excitement begins to bubble inside of me, and I get out of my car quickly. I can't wait to get inside and start doing some research. I have finally realized what I want. I want to learn more about how the body works and heals. Maybe I will study sports medicine in order to help athletes. Maybe I will study athletic training, maybe physical therapy, or maybe something else.

~~~~~~~~~

The next afternoon, I visit Terry at the University sports rehab center. I'm hoping he can guide me on my educational journey. I tell him what is on my mind, and, upon reflection, he says, "Your best route is physical therapy because it will leave all doors open to you. If I could do it over again, I would have gotten my degree in physical therapy, not athletic training."

"Thanks for the advice," I say.

As I leave his office, I decide to head to the university library. I feel a huge sense of excitement about my new career path. At the library, I check out all of the physical therapy programs available across the country. There are many great programs in Canada and even Montréal, but they are all undergraduate programs, and I believe that a master's degree would open up more doors for me. I keep gravitating back to a school near my aunt Ersie in California. They have a master's level program in science and physical therapy. It would be fun to get a master's degree in this field and be near my aunt.

After a couple of hours, I head to my dad's office to get his opinion. As I think of the empanadas in the Jamaican place underneath my dad's office, my stomach starts to grumble, and I become ravenous. I park my car and head downstairs into the store.

"An empanada, please, with a well done crust."

The employee promptly prepares one for me. I smile as I watch. I am a regular here. It is hard for me to resist stopping in each time I visit my dad. The employee hands me my order, and I bite happily into one of my favorite pies. *That should hold me over until dinner,* I think. I walk up the stairs to my dad's office. Through the large window, I can see my dad sitting at his desk doing paperwork. When he sees me, he gets up to open the door.

"Iritka, it is so nice to see you," he says.

"I'm glad you're still here, Dad. I drove by on the off chance you would be." My dad sits in his office chair and leans back. I sit in the chair beside him. "Guess what I want to do?" I say, both excitedly and a little nervously.

"What?"

"I want to go back to school and get my master's in physical therapy."

My dad juts forward in his seat, concerned. "Why? You have a good job."

"I want to learn more about how we heal."

He puts his hand on his chin and puckers his lips. "But you love teaching."

The phone rings. My dad picks up, and after a beat, I hear him say, "Don't worry, we will come tomorrow and find the problem." He hangs up the phone and looks at me, not saying a word.

After a moment, I break the silence, "Dad, I went to McGill Library and looked up some schools for physical therapy ... schools in the States. That way, if one day I want to move there, I will be able to."

"But you have a good job."

"There are three schools I'm choosing between, and the good news is that one of them is near Aunt Ersie." As soon as I say my Aunt Ersie's name, my dad smiles, and all the tension in the room eases up.

"California? Iritka, that would be great! This weather here is too cold for you. You always get sick, and Ersie will be able to help you."

"Do you think Mom will be okay with the idea of me going to California?" I look out the window, and as if on cue, I see my mom parking my dad's silver Malibu. My mom, who is close to 60, finally took the plunge and got her first driver's license when my dad got his new Malibu almost three months ago. When I learned that she had done it, I was stunned. I think it is amazing how my mother, when she sets her mind to something, doesn't let anything get in her way, though, of course, I would never mention this to her. Our relationship has always been rocky, but I still admire her ability to adapt.

My dad says she learned to drive because, "she needs her independence." According to him, he pushed her into it, but I actually think she pushed him to teach her in the first place. She wanted to prove to herself that she could learn. My mom has always been able to find her way anywhere. She never gets lost. I'm missing that navigational gene. I get lost all the time, but I somehow find my way back.

My mom walks up the stairs with a confidence that tells me how proud she is of her new skill.

"Hi, Mom," I say.

"Iritka. I just went to the fish market and bought lox. Do you want some?"

"Sure," I say. The fish market has the best lox in the city. Then, I add, "Guess what? I think I want to go back to school and get my master's in physical therapy somewhere in the States."

"You have a good job. Why do you want trouble?" She is baffled.

"There is a school near Ersie," my dad says.

"You have a good job. Don't talk such crazy things."

"But what if I want to leave Montréal?"

"Zoli, I need to get an outfit for Katy's wedding. Let's go to a factory on Saturday," my mom tries to change the subject.

"I think California would be good for me."

"You have a good job. Don't talk crazy. I'll go home now to make dinner. Zoli, will you be home at six?" He nods.

"Iritka, you want to come for dinner?" my dad asks. I want to push the topic of school with my mom, but I know it is probably best to just take my dad's lead and not say anything else.

"I can't. I've made plans with my roommate."

My mom leaves, and I watch her drive away before turning back to my dad.

"Dad, it will be expensive, so I'm not sure how I'm going to do it. I paid for my tuition to go to McGill, but it's so much more expensive at this school. Plus the Canadian dollar is only at about 85 cents right now."

"Maybe I'll be able to help with the first year of tuition," Dad says.

"Dad, it's a lot of money. I'll need about $20,000."

"Don't you have any money saved?"

"Yeah, about $20,000 actually, but it will cost about $40,000 for two years just for the tuition, not to mention room and board. I guess I can work and maybe get a scholarship though." I pause, then ask, "Dad, do you think it is a good idea?"

The phone rings right as he opens his mouth to respond. "Mr. Bass, don't worry," Dad says into the telephone receiver, "I will go tomorrow with Joe, and we will find the leak. Joe will fix the problem."

"Why the smile?" I ask as he hangs up the phone with a big grin on his face.

"Mr. Bass says he doesn't know what he would do without me. He has so many apartments, and as soon as he speaks to me he always knows it will be okay."

"So, what do you think about me?" I ask again.

My dad leans forward in his chair, puts his hand on his chin, and pauses for a second before saying, "As long as you are near Ersie, I don't worry. We'll figure out the money."

"What if I don't go to California? What if I go to Boston? Then I will be alone. Would you be okay with that?"

"Remember, if you smile and are in a good mood, you will not be alone for long. Everyone will want to come near you."

"Thanks for the support. It means a lot to me," I say.

"California will be best for you," my dad says. "It will be warm. That is good for you."

"Thanks! I love you, Dad."

"I love you, too."

I head out the door with my mind made up. I will start taking the courses I need to get into Physical Therapy school. It is time for me to delve into the question that has puzzled me throughout my whole life. *How does the body heal?* And not only that but also *How can the mind heal?* How can a simple man be shot six times and have the bullets taken out with no medication and not scream? He somehow not only survived but also transcended his conditions. What is it that allows him to see the good in mankind?

5

1981-1982

Tell me and I forget.
Teach me and I remember.
Involve me and I learn.

Benjamin Franklin

The excitement and exhilaration that always comes with a new beginning is in the air today. There are new faces in the hall, students are walking back and forth, and chatter all around. This is my eighth first day of school at Lemoyne. Every year, I find comfort in all the familiar faces. At the same time, it's always amazing to see the changes that occur in these teenagers.

"Hi, Ms. Schaffer." I hear.

"Hi, John."

"Hi, Coach. How was your summer?"

"Great, Helen." I smile. Her braces are off, and her hair is longer. I almost didn't recognize her.

"Are you ready for us?" Nikki from the volleyball team says teasingly.

"It's great to see you," I respond. I notice a twinkle in her eyes and a maturity I had not seen before.

Bobby, an athletic senior asks, "When do we start training?" He grew about two inches over the summer, and his shoulders have filled out. I can see a new-found confidence in his stride, and I can't wait to see how it will translate into his athletic performance.

"Cross country will start this week."

One person after another stops me in the halls as I head into my office, and I feel a strange sense of sadness come over me. I know this may be my last year. I was accepted at the University of Southern California this year, but I hadn't saved up enough money to go, plus my dad was not yet in a position to help me, either. So, I decided to put it off.

I'll have to reapply because the spot was not guaranteed for the following year, but if they accepted me this year, there is a good chance I will get accepted again. I'll just wait and hope I get the letter in the mail for next year. It's hard to imagine leaving Lemoyne and Québec. It is a big, scary change. I decided I wouldn't tell anyone, not yet anyway, not until I'm 100% sure.

I head into my office as many students come in and out of the gym to talk to me.

"Hey, Ms. Schaffer, did you miss us?"

"Tracy, what do you think?"

"When do we start volleyball?"

"It's cross country first, Nikki."

"Coach are you going to sign us up for the French league?"

"I sure will, Gale, as soon as I get the application."

"Coach, can we help out with the girls' volleyball team again this year?"

"Sure, Jim."

The bell rings, and I feel a pit in my stomach. Eight years, and I still get that same queasy feeling right before I begin class.

I have the seventh graders for homeroom this year. It will be interesting because this is their first year in the school. They are the new kids on the block. It's nice to know that they'll be nervous, too! I wait while the students file in.

"Have a seat on the floor. We'll wait another few minutes in case some students have trouble finding the gym, then we will get started," I announce.

I hear some whispering, but mostly there is silence. Nervous tension fills the room.

"Welcome to Lemoyne D'Iberville High School," I begin. "I'm Ms. Schaffer, and I will be your homeroom teacher this year. I'm glad to meet all of you, and in time, I will know all of your names. It must be tough to come into this big school of 700 students. How many of you are nervous?"

Most of their hands go up, and I hear a collective sigh of relief. They seem happy to admit what's been brewing inside of them.

"We will meet every day for homeroom here. You will have gym twice one week and then three times the next week. Uniforms go on sale at noon today. You have two weeks to buy them. Until then, you can wear your own t-shirts and shorts or sweat pants. If you want to take a shower after class, it is an option."

A hand raises, "You mean we don't have to take a shower?"

"No, it is up to you."

I can hear more sighs of relief.

"I only have three rules that all of you absolutely must follow. Anyone have any idea as to what they are?"

Not a peep is uttered.

"The first rule is to have fun," I can hear some quiet laughter. "The second rule is, if you are not having fun, don't let me see it. Pretend if you have to." Now there are more chuckles. "And the third, most important rule is, never say, 'I can't.' Any of you opposed to these rules?"

No show of hands.

"Raise your hands if you agree to these rules."

One by one the hands rise until it is unanimous. Class ends, and the students file out quickly while new faces enter the gym for my next class. Before I know it, it is lunchtime. I go into my office and start making a sign-up sheet for cross-country running. We start tomorrow at 3:45 p.m. The school year has officially begun.

I get up to put the sign on the bulletin board outside the gym and am intercepted by eight of the twelve volleyball players from last year.

"Hi, you guys. It is so nice to see all of you," I say.

"We came to ask you, if nothing is going on after school today, can we set up the volleyball nets?"

"Actually, today I can't, and tomorrow after school, cross-country training begins. I have the sign-up sheet here so you guys can be the first to sign up."

"Argh! Do we have to?" I look at Tracy, the volleyball team captain whose vertical jump is 27 inches, higher than most of the guys on the male volleyball team.

"Tracy," I respond, "you know you all have to get into shape for volleyball so what better way to start than through cross country?"

"Yeah, but I don't think it is a good idea for me to compete."

"Why?"

"Well I don't want to ruin the reputation of my people."

"What do you mean?" I ask, confused.

"Coach, I can jump, but I can't run. I'll be the slowest black runner in the history of sports," she jokes.

"Sorry, Tracy," I say with a smile, "good try, but that's not a good enough reason. See you all tomorrow after school."

"Tracy, I told you that approach won't work," I hear Gale saying as they head away. I laugh and think of Tracy, one of the most gifted students I have ever taught and coached. I have known her since she was in seventh grade, and this is her final year of high school. I will miss her and the other volleyball players in her graduation year. Then, I remember; I, too, will probably be leaving Lemoyne soon. I will be leaving the country. I get a knot in my stomach.

Just then, Keith walks into the office. He is wearing blue shorts that show off his muscular legs and a curling sweatshirt. Curling is his favorite sport. He has won many events. Brent, Keith, and I are the physical education teachers. We get along, but we have different teaching and coaching expectations so sometimes we have disagreements.

"How has it been going so far, Keith?"

"Pretty good. Nothing eventful to report."

He sits in his chair and starts shuffling through the papers on his desk.

"I have a question," I say before my nerves can get the best of me.

Keith turns his chair to face me.

"Well, you know how for the past three years I have been talking about doing a sports banquet to celebrate the student's participation in sports?"

"Yeah, I remember, but the lunch time presentations are fine," Keith says.

At Lemoyne, our yearly sports banquet usually consists of a lunchtime event that lasts about forty minutes, which was never acceptable to me. I believed the students deserved to be recognized for their athletic accomplishments in a more profound manner, in a way that would be lasting. They deserve something they will cherish.

When I was at a teaching seminar in California, the values placed on sports resonated with me at a deep level. I think the students at Lemoyne deserve better than what we are giving them. When I went into teaching, I wanted to become the physical education teacher and coach that I had never had. After the seminar, I decided to make it a reality. The only problem was, when I came back to Lemoyne, eager and excited, Dr. Cole and the other two gym teachers shot down many of my plans. I wasn't going to let that happen this year.

"Well, there is no reason why we can't have a sports banquet at the end of the year," I persist.

"What we do is fine. I don't see a reason to change anything."

"We can have a dinner, an award presentation, and a dance afterward. We could transform the small gym into a semi-formal ballroom," I say. This is something I had thought about all summer.

"Irit, are you out of your mind? Who do you think will do all this extra work? You know we have enough to deal with as it is, and track and field takes all my time at the end of the year," Keith says.

Brent walks in, wearing his Lemoyne sweatshirt and sweatpants. He has a stocky and muscular build, which is perfect for rugby, his favorite sport.

"You came just in time. Save me. Irit wants us to put together a fancy sports banquet with dinner followed by a dance," Keith says.

Brent looks at me, shakes his head, and says, "That's crazy. It would be way too difficult. I'm not going to put myself out there for that. Giving out awards like we have in the past should suffice. Besides, the price will be too exorbitant for the students to afford."

I am getting more and more anxious because I know if they say no, there is no way I can make this happen, I pretend to keep calm. I am prepared to make my argument because I anticipated their response. "We will raise money," I say slowly and deliberately, trying to keep my composure.

"We?" Keith says. He puts his hands in his sweatshirt pocket and lets out a sigh. "I don't want that extra work."

Brent fidgets in his seat, crosses his hands in front of his chest, and echoes, "Neither do I."

"Guys, for three years I have wanted to do this. The students will do a good part of the work."

"You're kidding!" Keith blurts out, starting to laugh. "We all know that the students say they will help, but then the onus will be on us. It is too much work. I won't be part of it," Keith says.

"Nor will I," Brent echoes.

"No problem. I will be in charge. All I ask is that you both show up."

"Irit, you have no idea what you are getting yourself into, and when the going gets tough, I'll be too busy with track to be able to help," Keith adds.

"Me, too," Brent repeats.

"I will raise the money, and I will be in charge of it all. It will work out. All I ask is that you do what you have done in previous years. I'll do the rest."

"Sure," Keith says, giving in.

"What about you, Brent?"

"I'm fine with that," Brent says.

"Good. I'll go and talk to Dr. Cole."

"You are dreaming. He wouldn't agree last year, why would he change his mind?" Keith asks. He gets up, clipboard in hand, and gives me a look that clearly says, *there is no way you can pull this off.*

"Last year, it was just in the idea phase. This year, I have the game plan of what exactly we are going to do. You'll see, Keith." I walk out of the office, relieved. I got all I needed from them; they agreed to come to the event. That should give me just enough ammunition for Dr. Cole. It will work out. I know it.

I head to Dr. Cole's office. He is the principal of our school, and I have always felt uncomfortable calling him by his first name, Ned.

Dr. Cole stands a little over 6'2", and he looks like an ex-football linebacker. His posture is so erect and stiff that it makes me uneasy. He always seems tightly wound. His face looks like he has had skin problems for many years. Most of all, he doesn't smile much, and that makes me nervous.

I take a deep breath. *Here goes.* Dr. Cole, do you have a few minutes. I'd like to ask you something."

"Sure, I have a few minutes now. Come on in." He shuts the door. I hate when he closes his door. It makes me feel claustrophobic or like I am about to be reprimanded.

I remember when I was in the middle of my third year of teaching, Dr. Cole had called me into his office and closed the door. Then the boom got lowered.

"Irit," he had said as he leaned back in his chair with his arms crossed. "Your teams are doing poorly. Maybe you should be teaching in the elementary schools where you don't really have to coach."

I could feel my blood rushing to my head, and it felt like I was bursting at the seams. "The guys' teams are doing just as poorly, if not worse," I blurted out. "Have you spoken to them?" For some reason, I had always seemed to just rub him the wrong way, and that was when I knew I was right. I know it had nothing to do with sexism or anything like that. He actually had great friendships with other female members of the staff. It was just something about me.

I held my breath as he tapped his fingers on the table, shuffled through his papers as if looking for something to give me, like my exit papers, paused, and then said, "No."

"Well, then why are you singling me out? That's not fair."

He picked up his cup and took a sip before saying, "Just think about it, and if you would like to, then I can make the arrangements with the elementary school."

"No, I'm staying," I said. I could feel myself getting angrier by the second. "Things are already shifting. You'll see."

From that time forward, all of my teams had winning records. I couldn't believe that I had stood up to him the way I did and that I didn't get in trouble for it. From then on, relations between Dr. Cole and I have always been very tense. Sometimes, it seems like he is putting roadblocks in my way just to make me fail.

"Irit," Dr. Cole says, bringing me back into the present. "What can I do for you?"

"Dr. Cole, this year I would like to have a special event for the students. I feel that it would be a great motivator. It would be something for the students to look forward to. We could have an awesome sports banquet, with a dinner and a dance to follow. We could make it something they will always remember and cherish."

"How do you intend to do this?" he says.

"I'll get the students to help, and I'll raise the money."

He looks at me, tapping his fingers on the desk, and proceeds to say, "I think you are setting yourself up for failure. I certainly won't be helping you, and I can't have the school support the cause financially. So, there will be no money allotted for this."

"But last year $800 was allotted out of the physical education budget for the afternoon event, Dr. Cole." I want to scream, but I stay calm.

"Well, I will allot the same amount I did last year, and that will just cover the cost of the trophies."

"That is fine. As long as I get your permission, I will take this project on by myself."

He has such a good poker face that I have no clue what he is thinking. "What about Keith and Brent?" he says.

"They're supportive of the banquet, but they can't put in any extra work. I told them I would be responsible for the entire event."

"How do you expect to do it all?"

"The students will help."

"Good luck to you," he says with a slight laugh, "but I'm sorry to say, the students will be all talk. Close to the event, I will have to tell you, 'I told you so.' It will all blow up in your face. You'll have no choice but to cancel the banquet."

Why do you sound so much like my mom? I think. *You haven't even met her, but you seem to have picked up her it's-not-going-to-work-out mentality.*

"That's fine," I say. "As long as I have your permission."

"Yes, you have my permission."

I walk out of the office. Despite the other teachers' concerns, I know the students are great helpers. We'll pull it off together. My only fear going in had been that Brent and Keith would not agree to the banquet in the first place. Then, it would have been impossible to get approval from Dr. Cole. It's funny. I'm actually glad that I'm completely in charge because I won't have anyone telling me what to do. I can do everything as I envisioned it. I can't hold back my excitement as I walk down the hall. I pump both of my fists in the air. *Yes!* This will be a great year and a great ending to my run at Lemoyne.

I leave the school and head to my dad's office on Victoria Street, and as usual, I walk downstairs to the deli first.

"Do you want one or two empanadas today?" The man behind the counter asks.

"One, please."

"Today it's on the house," he says, winking.

"Oh, thanks!" *Wow, I can't lose today,* I think.

"Your father is always good to us. This is the least we can do."

I take a bite, and it is so yummy. The crust is well done, just like I like it. I take another bite as I climb the ten stairs up to my dad's office.

"Hi, Dad. I'm so glad you're here."

"Iritka, I'm glad you came. How was school today?"

"It was good. My principal gave me permission to have the banquet I was talking to you about. I'm going to do it at the end of the year."

"That's great."

"Well, he won't help in any way, and he doesn't think I'll be able to pull it off. I think that is why he said 'yes.' I think he is hoping I will fail, so he can say, 'I told you so.'"

"Iritka, don't worry. When you smile, you can do anything. The whole world will be on your side."

I look at my dad. He always looks for the positive in any situation. He says it is because he knows that if he had ever given in to the negativity of the war, it would have been the end for him.

"Iritka, what are you thinking? You look so serious," my dad says.

"Oh, nothing."

"I hate when you say 'nothing.'"

"Dad, no one knows I am planning to leave."

"California will be good for you."

"I agree, but I can't help but worry. I can't believe how expensive school is."

"It looks like we will sell the condo we fixed up, so I will be able to help you with the tuition for the first year."

"It is too bad the Canadian dollar is so weak."

"It will work out. You will see," my dad says. He always just seems to know that everything will be ok. It's not like when other people say that just to be encouraging. He never has a doubt. He somehow just always knows.

"Thanks, Dad, I love you."

"Iritka, I love you, too."

~~~~~~~~~~

The days pass; the months pass. Everything is the same, yet nothing is the same. Suddenly, volleyball season is almost over.

"Hi, Irit," Oscar, the vice principal, says. He is about 5'10" and always well dressed. His hair is white, and it gives him a distinguished look. That look is also aided by the fact that everything he wears matches and looks like it has just been ironed though that is probably just the influence of his wife, who is a seamstress.

"Hi, Oscar, thanks for coming to the tournament," I say excitedly. "The students are always happy to see staff members coming to support them."

Tracy runs over to us, volleyball in hand.

"Mr. Adler, did Coach tell you? We won the first two games! We have a break now. Thanks for coming to watch us play."

"I wouldn't miss watching you all play, Tracy."

The volleyball tournament is being held at Centennial High School. This school is over three times the size of ours, and there are over 3,000 students. The gym alone is partitioned off during school days, allowing six classes to go on at the same time. For the tournament, the dividers have been removed, but there are still six games going on all at once. Suddenly, a ball flies right by my feet. I pick it up and throw it back.

"How come Dr. Cole never comes to see us compete?" Tracy asks.

"I don't know, Tracy. You will have to ask him."

Nikki, our other setter, comes up to us with a ball in her hand. She is Asian, slim, and barely 5'4". Despite her height, she has an amazing, soft touch and can get the ball to her teammates easily. She is quiet, the exact opposite of Tracy, which makes them a good setter combination.

"Mr. Adler, thanks for coming," Nikki says excitedly. "We've won all our games so far." Mr. Adler congratulates her, and then she turns to Tracy. "Do you want to practice volleying?" she asks.

Ignoring Nikki, Tracy presses on, "We even went to Dr. Cole's office and invited him to come see us play. He told us he is too busy on Saturdays, but he never came to watch us play soccer, field hockey or cross-country, either, and those weren't on Saturdays. It just seems unfair because I know he went to some of the boys' basketball games. You are the vice principal, and you come to watch us all the time."

Gale comes and joins our circle, saying, "Mr. Adler, too bad we couldn't have a gym this size! The ceiling is so high here that when I return a serve and it goes too high, the ball doesn't hit the beam, so it's not called out. I guess I like the size of our school better, though. I can't imagine having so many students in one school."

"If you stay till the end of the day, we'll give you a piece of our celebration cake. I made it," Nikki says. "We have had these celebration cakes for the last four years, win or lose."

"That is very nice. I've actually heard of your celebration cakes. The boys' volleyball teams are always jealous since their coaches don't have that after-tournament ritual. "

"Yeah, Coach's is the best, but she only makes it for our first tournament. It is a chocolate nut roll cake. We call it chocolate decadence. We have asked for the recipe, but she said it is a family secret passed on from her mom," Nikki says.

"Yeah, after she said that, we asked if we could get her mom's phone number, but Coach wouldn't give that out, either," Tracy adds, laughing.

"I wish I could stay, but I promised my wife I would be home by four."

"Oh, okay. Well, the practice court just emptied. Let's go practice," Nikki says, dragging Tracy off to volley.

"Irit, this team is so good. Congratulations on a great job," the vice principal says as we watch the girls walk away. "I have watched them improve over the last four years, thanks to you. They are amazing. I think they could beat the guys' team." Oscar has been in this country since 1948, yet his heavy German accent is still prominent.

"Yeah, but if, by chance, they played them and won, the guys would be devastated so I won't do it. Well, not until the end of the year at least, and even then I think I would just mix the teams."

"I guess you're right."

Throughout my years at Lemoyne D'Iberville, no matter what he has accomplished, many staff members have not warmed up to Oscar. They say that during the war he was in the SS, but I'm not so sure that is the case. Besides, who knows what his situation was and what he was forced to do. He was a teenager back then, about the same age as the volleyball players on my team, and it was a complicated time, to say the least. Somehow, these rumors have been labeled as the truth even though I am pretty sure they are based on nothing but hearsay. I feel uncomfortable about it. I know that Oscar gets treated unjustly because of it. Some of the teachers share this gossip without backing it up with a story to prove what they are saying.

"I'm really lucky to have such great teams," I continue.

"It's not luck. You have done much to help our school."

Yeah, tell that to Dr. Cole. I think. Out loud I say, "It will be so nice to have the end of the year sports banquet extravaganza to celebrate the student's achievements. You will be there, Oscar, right?"

"I wouldn't miss it for anything. When are you going to do the raffle to raise money?"

"I'm going to start soliciting for prizes on Monday."

"I will be glad to help in any way I can. If you want, I will make signs for you for the raffle and anything else you need. I like using the computer."

"That's great! I'm glad you have a computer. I don't know anyone else who even knows how to use one, let alone who owns one. It must be so expensive," I say, bursting with joy. He is the first person to offer to help, and at the moment, his help is all I need.

"It saves the school a lot of money. You can count on my help. I just have to do it on my own time because Ned does not want me to help on the school's time," Oscar says.

"Why is he so unsupportive? It is a school function, and he is the principal."

"I don't know," Oscar says.

It is now our turn to play again, this time against the Brossard Cougars. Oscar joins us on the bench. We win the toss, and the game begins. Gale aces the first six serves, and we're energized. The other team serves. Gale receives the ball and bumps it accurately to Nikki, who sets it up high and close to Tracy. Tracy jumps in the air, reaches back with her elbow, and is almost over the net as she straightens her arm and spikes the ball, with accelerated force, right into the thigh of the opposing player. Nikki and Tracy high five. Now it's Tracy's serve, and it is 7-0 before we lose serve again.

The game ends, and we win, 15-9. We win the next game, 15-8, and that means we win the match. Mr. Adler congratulates the students.

"You're our good luck charm," they tell him. I can see Mr. Adler's face light up at this.

Our next match is on center court. If we win one out of our next two matches, we will be guaranteed a first place finish. The Boucherville Lions win the first game, 15-13. The next game we win, 16-14. Now it is the third set, and the score is tied. Gale spikes the ball right between two players. The score is now 14-13 in our favor. Our fate is in our own hands at this point. It is still our serve, and it is match point for us.

Okay, Helen, just get it over the net, I think. I can hardly watch as the ball leaves Helen's hand. My heart drops as I watch the ball go smack into the middle of the net.

The other team serves, and it goes to Eileen. She bumps it, but not cleanly. It is a double touch. The referee blows the whistle. The game is tied. On the next serve, the other team aces. It is now 15-14 in their favor, match point for them. The Lions' player serves. The rally goes back and forth. Spikes that seem to be sure winners are saved time and again. Then, finally, a player from the other team is about to spike, and Tracy and Gale go to block. The player tips the ball just over their hands, and the ball is on the floor.

"We were so close," the girls repeat again and again.

"I know, but you played your hearts out, and I am so proud of all of you." I reassure them. "Plus, we still have one more match, so just hang loose for the next 20 minutes. We can't get discouraged. We still have a shot at first place!" Everyone nods, and I can feel a renewed sense of purpose run through the group.

"Helen, I'm curious," I say. "Do you remember what you were thinking about when you were about to serve the ball for the game point?"

"Oh, Coach, I was afraid you were going to ask."

"Why?"

"You have always harped on us to think positively. I know how you always say it is better to say, 'let's get the ball over the net even if it goes out of bounds,' than to say, 'I hope it doesn't hit the net.' You know, that negative way of saying things."

"Yeah."

"Well, you are not going to believe what I was thinking. It was game point, and I got so nervous. We were on the verge of winning it all, and I knew the serve had to go over to give us that chance, and, well, all I could think of was, 'I hope I don't screw up and hit it into the net.'"

I looked at her, put my hand on her shoulder, and say, "Well, when you compete in college, you will now remember how what you think affects how you play."

"You're kidding me, right, Coach? That is something I will always remember. It doesn't just apply to sports."

"Good, then it will serve you. Excuse the pun." We both laugh.

I am the luckiest coach to have all of you as my players, I think to myself. *How did I luck out to get such fun-loving, hard-working girls and such a cohesive team year in and year out?* We have one more match, and we still could come in first place. To me, though, it's like we have already won, regardless of the outcome.

At 5:30, we pack up and head home on the school bus. For the second year in a row, we placed first in our school district.

~~~~~~~~~

I walk into the teachers' lounge on Monday morning, and Dave, a math teacher, greets me enthusiastically, "Congrats, Irit!"

"Thanks, Dave."

"I heard your team came in first."

"How did you hear about it?"

"The students stopped me in the hall to tell me."

"Hey, Irit, congrats on your success!"

"Thanks, Mary. I think I'll go and tell Dr. Cole." Somehow, I always think that the next time I speak to Dr. Cole, he will give me the validation I deserve, but at the very least, I feel strongly that the girls should get that extra recognition.

I walk into the principal's office and say, "Good morning. Can I have a few minutes of your time?"

"Sure, Irit. Come on in."

The door closes. "Dr. Cole, I'm sorry you couldn't come to see us play on Saturday. We came in first place. We will be playing in the regionals."

"Yes, I know. Your volleyball team came in to tell me. Congratulations."

"Thanks! I was wondering if you could make a special announcement over the intercom about our team. It would mean the world to the players, especially coming from you."

"Irit, we can't be giving special preference to your team and not to the other teams. It wouldn't be fair."

"But Dr. Cole, look what they have accomplished, and this was the second year in a row!"

"No. If I did it now, then I would end up having to announce it over the PA system every time a team wins."

"Well, that wouldn't be such a bad idea, would it? It would give them encouragement and make them feel proud. That carries over into their lives, and isn't that what we want to teach them? And for it to come from the principal makes it even more special."

As usual, I walk out of his office with nothing more than his commitment not to commit. My face is red, and my heart is pounding. I decide to head to the vice principal's office instead, knowing he will be there for me.

"Oscar, can I come into your office?" I ask.

"Sure!"

"Can we close the door?"

"Sure, but I thought you didn't like me closing the door," he says. He, unlike Dr. Cole, takes note of things like that. "What's wrong?"

"What is his problem? It's his school," I start ranting.

"What are you talking about?"

"Dr. Cole! I asked him to announce our team's success, and he wouldn't. He has never once come to any of our games. I think this is the least he could do to show his support."

Oscar looks away from me and fidgets with his pen before responding, "I'll help you in any way I can for the banquet. We should start focusing on the raffle soon so I can prepare it." I almost laugh at this. Oscar's attempt to change the subject without even responding to my ranting reminds me of my dad. That is exactly what he always does when I complain about my mom.

Wouldn't you know it! I am teaching in a school with a principal who is my mom and a vice principal who is my dad. When Dr. Cole has an opinion about something, nothing can change his mind. He becomes inflexible. It's like he gets attached to what he believes to be right, and then he loses his ability to see other perspectives. With Oscar, he always sees the positive and offers to help with an open heart. It's like he knows exactly what to say and how to say it in order to reach me so I never get riled by it.

~~~~~~~~~

The day passes, and I head to my dad's office. I park and follow my ritual of heading downstairs first. Terry and Bob are the owners of the shop, and one of them is usually behind the counter. We don't say much, but they are always generous.

"Irit, would you like one or two empanadas?"

"One today, thanks."

I bite into my empanada and head up the stairs. My dad is sitting at his desk, as usual, doing bills.

"Iritka, what's wrong?" he asks. He can always tell when I'm upset.

"No one in this school seems to want to help."

"What do you mean?"

"Actually, it is just the principal I'm really mad at and the two other physical education teachers and maybe not even them. We're just different. We just have different philosophies about teaching and coaching. If I want them to respect me for my way of looking at things, I guess I should do the same for them. It's just … the person who has been most helpful is Oscar Adler, the vice principal, and wouldn't you know it, the other teachers in the school don't even like him."

"Why is that?"

"We're in a school where maybe ten of us, total, are Jews, if that. Out of the ten, three are teachers, including me and one teacher who doesn't actually observe anything."

"I don't understand, Iritka. Why is that an issue?"

"The rumor, Dad, is that Oscar was in the SS in World War II. A few of the teachers say it is hard for them to support someone who was in the SS."

"You never told me about that."

"I didn't believe it so I just ignored it, but I heard the gossip again today in the staff room and wanted to scream. He works so hard. He cares so much, and he is always helping out the students. Everything he has done for the sports banquet has been on his own time, yet the teachers don't take any of this into account. It's so unfair, and it bothers me."

"Where did they hear that from?"

"I have no idea, Dad, but I don't think it's true. Last month, Oscar invited me to his house to have dinner because I had stayed late at work. He and his wife, Elke, welcomed me into their home with open arms. She made dinner and gave me the leftovers to take home so that I would have food for the next day. Their kitchen reminded me of Aunt Ersie's. Everything was in place, with flowers and even a purple tablecloth just like hers. She put out her fine china because I was a special guest. Elke's voice is soft and her eyes kind, and Oscar loves working with the kids. They are both just so great."

The phone rings, and it is my mom. Dad speaks to her for a minute and hangs up.

"Your mom made chicken soup with noodles," he says. "Do you want her to bring it over?"

"No, I only like chicken soup when I feel sick," I say, before turning my attention back to Oscar. "He was only about 15 or 16 at the most, during the war. Anyway, what really bothers me is the way the teachers in our school act."

"Why?"

"Most of them don't stay for extracurricular activities. I rarely get help from any of them, and yet they are upset with Oscar, who helps out so much with school activities and always shows support. They're upset because he is German."

I can't help but wonder from time to time which of those teachers would have been willing to help Jews in the war. I know it seems absurd, but I can't help but wonder. They probably would have been afraid to commit, just like they are now, and then, after the war, they would have been the first to condemn the Germans for the horrible things they did. It seems so hypocritical.

"I don't understand their mentality. Sometimes they are completely wrong, and yet they don't seem to care or feel bad," I say.

"I'm sorry, Iritka, but that is human nature. People always need someone to blame, especially when they are scared. No matter where you go, you will always encounter good and bad. The important thing to remember is that, during the war, there *were* some people who risked their lives to help us."

I nod. "You know Dad, of all the people working at the school, I am the one who could be somewhat justifiably prejudiced because you were in a forced Hungarian labor camp and Mom was in a concentration camp. So, what I don't understand is, if I'm cool with Oscar, then shouldn't everyone else realize that maybe some of their thought processes are off?"

"Many people don't realize that what they are thinking is not true, and then they make assumptions based on what is not true. Also, for some people, it is just easier for them to blame someone else because they need someone to be mad at. But I'm glad that Oscar is helping you and that he is good to you and the students."

The sound of footsteps puts our conversation on hold. Someone is coming up the stairs.

"Open the door," my dad says. "It's the postman." I do, and the postman quickly hands off the mail to me and leaves. My dad, without even looking at any of the envelopes, puts the mail in his drawer.

"Dad, you're not going to open it? How come?"

"I'm putting it in the drawer with the other mail I haven't opened yet."

I stare at him, confused. "Why?"

"Some of them are bills, and others are from plumbing inspectors. I want to be in the right mood when I open them. I will wait until I'm ready, maybe tomorrow when I am not tired. That way, I will make better decisions."

"I do that, too! I can't handle doing things when I'm not in the right mood," I say, happy to learn that I am not alone in this, "but sometimes I wait too long."

"Me, too," he says.

"Dad, are you okay with Oscar being German?" I know the answer, but I just need to hear another person is on my side.

"It is not a person's country, religion, or skin color that matters. It is what is inside a person's heart that is important, Iritka."

The phone rings. It is my mom again. "She wants me to pick up *challah* before I go home," my dad says. "Do you want to come over for dinner?"

"I can't. I have plans. Actually, I should head out. I love you, Dad."

"I love you, too."

I get home and check my own mail. I freeze, and my heart starts pumping fast.

The letter from USC is waiting for me. I'm glad I am in a good space today. Just like my dad, I know it's better to open it now, when I am feeling ready for it.

As I look at the envelope, my hand starts to shake. A gazillion questions start going through my brain in rapid succession. *What am I going to do if I don't get accepted this time? What am I going to do if I do get accepted? What if I won't be able to afford it? What if—* I stop. *Okay, Irit, this is ridiculous, and you know it. Breathe, and open the letter. You will be fine.*

I rip open the seal and pull out the thick, USC parchment.

Ms. Irit Schaffer,
We're glad to inform you that you have been accepted into the physical therapy program at the University of Southern California. Your hard work

and determination have earned you a spot in this very rigorous and highly respected program. You should take pride in this accomplishment.

Your response to the offer of admission and matriculation must be submitted within the next six weeks. It is your responsibility to read and follow the enclosed Final Requirements sheet.

Once you accept this offer, your student ID number will be mailed to you. Our records show that you are classified as an out-of-state student for tuition purposes.

I look forwards to receiving your response to our offer of admission. You can find out more in the enclosing materials, including information on housing and dining, instructions for accepting your offer, and the list of Final Requirements. If we may furnish additional information, please let us know. I wish to extend you a warm welcome and best wishes for your success at the University of Southern California.

Signed,
Dean of Admissions, USC

6

1982

When we do the best that we can,
we never know what miracle is wrought in our life
or in the life of another.

Helen Keller

The bell rings, and I have a few minutes before I have to go back into the gym so I walk downstairs to Oscar's office. Finally, my vision will come to fruition.

In our school and many other Montréal schools, varsity sports don't carry much significance. Practices are only 3-4 hours a week so it is hard to get students to the skill level we desire. Parents rarely attend games, and frequently, when a student has discipline problems in a class or poor grades, after school sports are taken away—the one thing that makes them believe in themselves and, for many, the only success they have ever experienced.

In our school, we do not have cheerleading teams, nor do we give out letters for achievement. We did not even have a school mascot until four years ago—and then only for our volleyball team.

After that seminar in California, I tried actively to make a difference in how the sports I coached were handled at Lemoyne. My teams began having early morning practices and afterschool practices, frequently lasting two hours, 4-5 times per week. The student athletes would find their own way to practice in the mornings and evenings. School buses didn't get to school that early, and they also didn't stay late enough to transport students home. Parents never drove students to practice. Many would have to use public transportation, which took 30-60 minutes depending on where they lived. Yet, the students never complained. They treasured the camaraderie and bonded in a way that was special to them.

My volleyball team began a new tradition when they introduced a team mascot. They dubbed themselves the "Lemoyne Coyotes," and then they all chipped in to buy a 3' stuffed animal coyote. They sewed him a uniform with the blue-and-white Lemoyne colors, and the coyote became an official member of our team. He is at all of our practices and games.

I reach Oscar's office and knock on the door. "Oscar, do you have a minute?" I ask.

"Sure, come in."

"The raffle prizes are in. We have a stereo system, a Montréal Canadiens hockey sweater, along with a letter from my hero Jean Beliveau, a dinner for two at a crêpe restaurant, a Timmy Raines bat from the Montréal Expos, and a $50 gift certificate to Ski Sport. I can't believe we pulled together all of these gifts."

"Those are great! How did you pull it off?"

"Well, we had a connection get us the stereo system, and from there it was smooth sailing. I told the Montréal Canadiens hockey club that we were raising money for a sports banquet and that we already had a stereo system. Once they committed, I called the Montréal Expos and told them about the Montréal Canadians and Jean Beliveau, and once the Expos committed, I called a sports store and told them about everyone else who had already promised donations. Then, I called a second store with the same tactic, and, voilà, prizes.

"Well, I should have the raffle tickets and posters done by Monday. I'll work on it this weekend."

"Thanks for all your support," I say, beaming. "I better get back into the gym. We have badminton practice tonight, and it looks like we will have a strong contingent of players this year."

~~~~~~~~~

On Monday, the raffle tickets go on sale, and the enthusiastic response is overwhelming. Everyone is asking for raffle tickets, and each ticket is $1. Slowly but surely, we are building up money for the banquet.

"Hi, James," I say as a slim, 5'8", Chinese boy in my class approaches me. He is one of my best badminton players, but he is also good in every other sport he plays. He is always so polite to everyone. I think it must be his parents' influence.

"Coach, can I talk with you?" he asks.

"Sure."

"Do you have a restaurant picked out for our banquet yet?"

"I've made some inquiries, but everything so far seems too expensive," I say. The truth is, I probably could have found some cheap caterers if worse came to worse, but I really wanted great food for this great event. With the money from the raffle adding up quickly, it looked like that was now officially possible. "Why are you asking?"

"Well, I spoke to my parents about our raffle and the banquet. They told me to ask you if you would like them to cater the event. We own a Chinese restaurant, and they would give you a good price."

"Are you kidding me?" I can't believe my ears.

"No. My parents said they would be glad to cater the event. Their restaurant is ten blocks away."

"That would be awesome, James. Can I get their number so I can call them? Do they know that there will be almost 200 people?"

"Yeah. That is no problem for them."

"James, this is the best possible news. I could just kiss you." James blushes, and I laugh.

I rush to my office, bursting at the seams as I dial the number. "Mr. Wang, This is Irit Schaffer from Lemoyne D'Iberville High School."

"Oh great! James has been talking non-stop about you, the banquet, and the raffle."

"Is it true that you would be willing to cater our gala event?"

"Yes, absolutely," Mr. Wang says happily.

I can hardly contain my excitement as he and I work out the details. In a few minutes, it is settled. We will have a 7-dish Chinese meal, with beverages included for $20 per person. The restaurant has a reputation for high quality food so I'm thrilled because it was important for me to have great food to match what the whole evening was about. "We will bring the food to the school, and we can provide the dishes and tablecloths as well."

"I can't believe your generosity. Thank you."

I hang up and can't stop myself from letting out a big, "YESSS!" and pumping both my fists into the air.

As the day continues, everywhere I turn, people are asking for more raffle tickets. I put all of the money into an envelope marked, *Sports Banquet*. Oscar and I count the money at the end of each day, and he puts it into a safe with the raffle prizes. Finally, two weeks pass, and almost 5,000 tickets have been sold. This was unbelievable. The students banded together with such enthusiasm and excitement that even most of the teachers have bought tickets. It helps that we have such great prizes. The entire school is now involved.

~~~~~~~~~

"Ms. Schaffer, can I talk with you for a minute?"

I look up from my desk and see Chris, his straight blond hair almost reaching his shoulders. He has a diamond stud in his ear, which I love, and he is wearing a black Motley Crue t-shirt with the words, *Too Fast for Love,* written across it.

"What's up, Chris?"

"I was wondering if you needed music for the banquet and dance. My cousin is in a band, and he said that they can perform at the dance for $300, or they can do it for free if money is a big problem."

"Are they good?"

"They're great."

I look at Chris. He spoke with such excitement and confidence that I just knew it would be perfect. "Well, I'll be glad to pay. Just ask him to write out a contract. Tell him thank you."

"I know a lot about music and sound systems, too. I would love to help out."

"Perfect. Would you like to be in charge of those for the awards?"

"Awesome, Ms. Schaffer."

I smile. "Just curious, Chris, how did you learn so much about sound systems?"

"My dad and uncle are musicians in their spare time so I grew up with it. So did my cousin."

"Chris, you're fabulous."

"Thanks. It's no problem," he says.

~~~~~~~~~

When school gets out that afternoon, Tracy and Gale come into my office.

"Hey, I'm glad you're here," I say. "I wanted to tell you that the two of you will be in charge of decorating the gym and all the tables so make sure you get all your friends to help."

"Don't worry, Coach, we have it under control. Ms. Garvey is going to let us use the art room to prepare, and she is giving us art paper and streamers to use because there were leftover supplies this year. She also said she will help us if we need it. Don't worry about a thing, Coach. That gym will be the nicest ballroom you ever saw."

I beam at them. I am so proud. It's as if a magical presence has taken hold, guiding us every step of the way and making the preparations joyous and effortless. The other gym teachers and Dr. Cole believe that the students are not responsible and will not follow through. Maybe that attitude is the reason why students don't follow through for them. I know from experience how discouraging it is when you know others don't believe in you, but I have always believed in the students. It never occurred to me to doubt them in any way. The only one I tend to doubt is myself. I always think I can do better, no matter how well I do something. It has always been easy for me to access my inner wisdom when helping others, but when it comes to myself, my critical voice seems to have a higher volume, silencing any wisdom that tries to speak up.

I know that when the other gym teachers and Dr. Cole attend the banquet, they will see how wrong they were about the students. Maybe they will realize that when you get so caught up in one way of thinking that you are not open to new ways, you can miss out on magical experiences. I feel so appreciative that my dad has always shown me how beliefs affect outcomes. It's like his talk about good blood; *the more we focus on the positive, the more positive will occur.* Even in the war, my dad always focused on what he *could* do. He didn't waste energy focusing on things he had no control over because it would have taken away from the energy he needed to focus on what he could do, to focus on the positive, and to focus on how to survive. I know he believes that is part of why he survived.

~~~~~~~~~~

Award presentations are in five weeks, and I know I have to make my announcement before then. I will have to let everyone know I am leaving.

I get to the school and park in one of the teacher spots. *I'll tell them today,* I tell myself. I feel nauseous, and I have a pit in my stomach.

I get out of my GLC sport and think, *Ok, Irit, here we go.* I shut my car door. Too late, I realize that the key is still in the ignition, with the engine running. I guess my nerves are affecting me more than I realized. There are about 20 students hanging out in the parking lot. I want to run and hide, but there is nowhere to go.

"Ms. Schaffer, I'm mad at you," I hear. I look around and see Lucy, an eighth grade student who is maybe 4'10". She has dimples and a contagious smile. *Great,* I think, *I just locked my keys in my car, with the engine running, and now a student is upset with me. How can my day get any worse?*

"So, why are you mad at me?" I ask.

"I had a dream about you last night, and in my dream, you made me run around your car 100 times." I laugh, and some of my tension slips away. She *would* tell me about a car dream at the exact moment that I want to run away from my car because I'm so embarrassed.

"And did you?"

"Yeah, that is why I am mad at you. All that work in the dream made me feel really tired when I woke up!"

"Well, Lucy, I'm just glad that even in your dreams you follow my directions." We both laugh.

"Did you lock your keys in your car with the ignition on Ms. Schaffer?" A tall, 6' senior asks, approaching us with four of his buddies behind him.

"I was hoping no one would notice, Dan," I say as my face turns bright red.

"If you get me a coat hanger, I can open the door. I did it for my mom yesterday," he says reassuringly.

"Oh good, I'm not the only one who does this," I say, and within 30 seconds, the door is open. I turn off the engine.

"Thanks, Dan! You're a lifesaver."

"I'm glad I could help you out."

I can see in Dan's face that he is genuinely glad to have helped, and I smile as the four other students high five him. In some strange way, I feel like his helping me made me bond with him even more.

I always feel as if I have to be perfect, and when I mess up for whatever reason, I beat myself up. Yet, for others, I always see mistakes as learning opportunities. I know that whenever I punish myself for something, others probably don't even see it as a mistake, but that doesn't usually help. It always works out, yet it is still hard for me to be okay with showing my vulnerability. Somehow, it doesn't seem safe even though that doesn't make logical sense.

I walk into the teachers' lounge, and Dr. Cole is there.

"Irit," he says. "I'm hearing a lot about the banquet, but remember, when we get closer..."

"Yeah," I interrupt, "I know. I'm taking full responsibility."

I head to class, and the knot in my stomach won't go away. One class after another comes and goes, and I keep quiet. *I will make the announcement tomorrow*, I tell myself for what feels like the hundredth time.

After my last class, I head to my office, and Tracy comes in to talk to me.

"Schaffes," she says, calling me by the nickname she and the other players gave me. "If we come in early tomorrow, can we play volleyball? Everyone on the volleyball team wants to come, and some of the guys."

Perfect, I think. *I will tell them first thing tomorrow, and then I'll go and give Dr. Cole my letter.*

"Okay," I respond. "How about you get here at 7:30 a.m., but before you guys play I would like to talk to all of you."

"Is it about the banquet?"

"No."

"So, what is it?" she says, curiously.

"You'll just have to wait till tomorrow morning," I say.

If I have the guts to do it, that is.

~~~~~~~~~

At 7:30 in the morning, fourteen eager faces are waiting outside my gym door.

"Wow! You're all here," I say, surprised by the turn out.

I open the door and unlock the equipment closet for them. As they set up, I go into my office. It feels like someone has punched me in the stomach. *Irit, just do it*, I tell myself.

After ten minutes, I go into the gym. The nets are set up, and everyone has already changed. I'm impressed.

"You never move this quickly when we have practice."

"Schaffes," Tracy says, "that's because we have to work hard in practice so we do everything we can to delay it. Now it is just a fun game. Do you want to play with us?"

"Nah," I say, my heart pounding. "Actually, before you start, I want to share something with all of you." I look around at the girls and the group of four guys that I like to call the "gym pack rats" because they always want to hang around and help with the girls' team. I've never been sure if they have a crush on some of the girls or if they just don't want to go home and do homework. It's probably a combination of both. I take a deep breath.

"You know, I have known you all since you were in seventh grade. Now you are in eleventh grade, and some of you are heading off to college." I pause. *Why is this so hard for me?* Finally, I spit it out, "Well... I'm moving to Los Angeles, and I'm going back to school, so I won't be back next year."

Complete silence falls over the room. I look at Tracy, the most talkative girl of the bunch, willing her to speak, but she just looks at me with a blank face. I've never seen her look like that before. Nikki looks as if she's about to cry. Gale is staring at me, with her lips puckered, and Jim has put his hands over his chest, his brow furrowed.

"Okay, you guys." I can't stand the silence a moment longer. "I never thought you would be at a loss for words. Say something!" I look from one blank face to another.

"Coach," Tracy starts, "I would have been mad at you if you left last year. At least, you decided to leave after we graduate."

"Yeah," the chorus of students agrees. The ice is broken, but I still can't stand the awkwardness and start babbling.

"I'm going back to school to get my masters in science, and then I'll be a physical therapist. I'll probably work with sports teams."

"But Ms. Schaffer, why? Are you tired of teaching?"

"No, Dan, I love it."

"Then, why are you leaving?"

"I want to learn more about the body and how it heals. I have always been curious, ever since I was a little girl listening to my dad's stories." I decide I better leave it at that because I have never mentioned my dad around the students before. I'm already getting too emotional so, instead, I say, "Hey, you guys, the nets are up. Play volleyball."

While the students play, I watch from the bench and get caught up in memories of my time at the school. Before I know it, the bell rings, bringing me back to reality. "Take down the nets and get changed, everyone. If you get into any trouble with your teachers, I'll take the blame. I lost track of time."

After the students march out, I head to Dr. Cole's office. I'm grateful that he isn't there so I can just leave him the letter.

By lunchtime, the whole school knows I am leaving. Students keep pulling me aside and asking the same question, "Are you tired of us? Why are you leaving?"

Each time, I try to change the subject, saying, "Let's focus on the banquet." Everything for the event keeps falling into place. I'm constantly amazed at how easy it has been. Oscar has been spending hours after work helping out. Keith and Brent have been busy with track as they warned me they would be, and I understand. Plus, with all of the hard work the students and other teachers are putting in, I don't even need their help.

~~~~~~~~~~

"Tomorrow is the big day," I say. "Dad, I'm so nervous."

Every day has passed quickly, bringing me closer to the banquet and closer to the end of my time at the school. The emotions swirling around inside of me are becoming overwhelming. "Dr. Cole won't let us begin setting up until lunch tomorrow, and he won't let me have a substitute teacher cover my classes though he did tell me that if any regular teachers were willing to cover my classes in the afternoon, he would be fine with that. So, I managed to find a couple of people. He also told me that if any students wanted to take off in the afternoon to prepare, they just needed to get permission from their teachers."

My dad opens his mouth as if to respond, but I keep talking. My mind is spinning from excitement. "Tracy and Gale, the two students in charge of decorations, told me not to worry, and Chris and John, who are in charge of the sound system, told me they have everything under control. There are 15 people helping decorate the gym, and the art teacher, Chloe Garvey has been great. She let the students use the art room to prepare and store things for the last couple of weeks. The trophies are locked in our office. There will be 200 student athletes at the banquet. It's amazing how many students participated in at least one varsity sport this year. I also decided to invite students who participated in four or more intramural sports..."

"Iritka, slow down," my dad finally manages to interrupt me.

"Dad, I have wanted to do this for so many years. It's not just a banquet. It is an opportunity for the students to be acknowledged in a way they never have been. In the past few years, I have let the two other gym teachers and Dr. Cole discourage me. I don't understand why I let people talk me out of things that are important to me. Whenever I hear a tone of disapproval, it feels as if a big movie screen has been lowered in front of me, and the screen reads, 'Your idea doesn't count. You don't count. It is not important. It doesn't matter. You don't matter.'"

"Everything will be fine. It will be even better than you imagine. You will see," my dad says.

I look at my father, and his gentle eyes tell me everything I need to hear. *Ignore what they say. It is important. It does matter.*

~~~~~~~~~~

I walk into school the next morning, and I can feel the electricity in the air. I can't focus as I go through the motions for the four classes I have before lunch. Everyone is ready to begin setting up, but the students have to wait until 12 p.m. because those are the rules. I did manage to get my last two classes off because two teachers volunteered to help me out and sub for my classes.

Throughout the day, students keep running up to me with excitement in their eyes.

"I can't wait until the awards presentations, Ms. Schaffer," one of the students says.

"My parents took me shopping, and I have a new dress just for tonight," another student says.

"That's great," I say. "I can't wait, either."

"Ms. Schaffer, may I speak with you?" Jim, one of the pack rat senior athletes who always want to help out with the girls' volleyball team, asks.

"I'm not going to college because I'm not a good student, but I just want to say thank you. These past few years in high school have been the happiest times for me. I have loved playing varsity sports and participating in intramurals. When I'm in the gym and when I help out, I feel so important. I feel I belong. That is the only time in my life I have felt that way. Participating in most of the school sports has been such a blessing for me. Thank you for the banquet. It's a memory I will cherish."

I want to cry as I say, "Thank you for always giving it your all."

As I sit through my last class, I keep looking at the clock. Time seems to have slowed down, but finally, I hear the bell. I'm off to the small gym. Everyone is already busy setting up. Everyone is focused. Music is playing throughout the room as the guys hook up the sound system for the presentations.

"Chris, I'm amazed that you know so much about this equipment," I say.

"It's what I love to do," he responds happily.

"Hey, Coach. Look what we've done," Tracy says, grabbing me by the arm.

She leads me to the entrance of the small gym, where blue and white streamers, the colors of our school, have been hung, inviting guests in.

"Do you like the floral wreaths we have surrounding the candles in the glass globes? Ms. Garvey showed us how to make them. We are going to put them on all of the tables."

"Wow," I say, overwhelmed by how far above and beyond the students have gone.

"Do you like the streamers on top of the stage?" Tracy asks. I look at the top of the stage where I see blue and white streamers twisted together with bows, creating a feeling of grace and elegance.

"We're going to put blue and white streamers on the walls surrounding the sports posters we are hanging up, too," Gale says.

"Isn't it great, Coach? Ms. Garvey said she would be here tonight," Tracy says.

"It looks great. I will be sure to thank her. Now, are you sure you have everything under control? What about this wall over here?" I ask.

"Coach, I think you should get out of the gym. You're too nervous! You're making us nervous." I see affirmative nods from all of the other helpers around me.

"Yeah, you're right. I feel like I'm going 100 miles per minute," I say.

"Don't worry. We have it under control."

~~~~~~~~~~

Back in the teachers' lounge, Dave, a math teacher, is sitting on the couch. He is one of the teachers who volunteered to substitute for me this afternoon. He has helped out with intramural sports throughout the years, and he always offers to help if I need him.

"Irit," Dave says. "How is the setup going? Are you ready for tonight?"

"Yup," I say. "I'm heading home at the bell to get ready for the event. You'll be there tonight, right, Dave?"

"Absolutely, I wouldn't miss it. All the students could talk about in class today was the banquet."

Before I can respond, the door opens. It is Dr. Cole.

"Irit, can you come into my office?"

I walk upstairs with him, past the secretary's desk, and into his office. "Close the door," he says.

Maybe he had a change of heart and will let the school out early, I think. I take a deep breath and close the door.

"Irit, the school is in chaos today," Dr. Cole says sternly, and my heart sinks. "I need you to talk to the students and tell them they need to be quiet in the halls. If they aren't, you will have to wait until after school to get ready."

"But we need the extra three hours," I protest.

"Well, I'm just warning you. There is too much noise in the gym and in the halls, and if it doesn't stop, I will cancel the event."

"What?" I say, stunned.

"You heard me."

I can't believe what he just said. I feel like he just threw a dagger through my heart, and my mind starts racing. *The whole reason for a banquet was to honor the students. It is an evening they will always remember. Don't punish them because you have something against me!* I want to scream at him, but instead, I say, "Okay." I walk out of his office in a daze and head straight to the gym.

"Guys, I need you all to stop what you are doing and listen," I shout so that everyone can hear me. "I need to make an announcement."

"Is Dr. Cole dismissing school early so we can all get ready?" Tracy asks, excitedly. I can't believe I am about to put them through the same thing Dr. Cole just did to me.

"No, Tracy, but you got the name right. Dr. Cole warned me that, unless you are all quiet in the halls and tone it down in here, he will cancel the preparations until after school."

I can see hurt and anger spread over the faces that were so happy just a moment before. Dr. Cole is not like this with others. I know I just rub him the wrong way, and I know I should know better than to take it personally, but of course I do.

"Why won't he help us?" Tracy says, angrily. "Doesn't he realize…"

"Tracy," I interrupt, "I don't understand, either, but it is his school, and it is his rules."

"It's our school," one of the students says, and I hear murmurs of agreement.

"Yeah, I know, but he is in charge, so we have to be silent in the halls."

"Okay, we'll post someone in the hall to make sure," Tracy says, in her take-charge manner. "Coach, when he comes tonight, he will realize that it was all worth it."

"Yeah, maybe," I say. *But I'm not so sure,* I add to myself. *Dr. Cole has never failed to disappoint.*

I look around at the students in the gym as they get back to work. Enthusiasm is pouring out of them, their eyes are glowing with excitement, and their focus and creativity are inspiring. I think of the meeting I had with Dr. Cole at the beginning of the year. 'There is no way the students will come through,' I hear Dr. Cole, Brent and Keith say.

'Just wait and see,' I had said. I was right. I am looking at the students now, and I feel like I am the luckiest teacher in the world. I am lucky to have students like this to teach and to coach year in and year out. I can't believe I'm leaving all this to go back to school. For the first time, I start panicking. *What if I'm making a mistake?*

I walk through the gym doors into the hall. The bell rings, and Brent and Keith offer to hang around and keep the large gym open for the helpers. That way they can shower and change. I'm glad Keith and Brent are offering to help out.

Everything is set. I turn my key in the ignition of my GLC sport and head off to my hair stylist. I had decided to splurge and treat myself to a makeover for all of the hard work I had put into the event.

"Okay, Irit," my hair stylist says, "let's blow dry your hair, and then Ellen will do a makeover for you. It's your special day. We have to make you into the beauty that you are."

One hour later, I get home and put on my red silk dress. I look in the mirror. Usually, as the gym teacher, I am never done up at school. The students won't recognize me with makeup and a dress. *I* can barely recognize me.

~~~~~~~~~

I head back to school and arrive just in time to help with the finishing touches. It is 6:00 p.m., and everything starts in 30 minutes. I walk into the small gym and see 20 tables set up with white tablecloths and beautiful centerpieces. I remember the girls telling me about them, but they are even nicer than I had imagined. Candles are flickering in big glass globes, with flowers surrounding their base. The teachers' table is closest to the door. I head over and set my purse down.

I notice ten posters on the walls around the gym, each portraying a different sport played at Lemoyne. The posters are made of white paper, and their designs have been sketched in pencil and then painted with bright colors. The excitement and pride behind the students' work shows through, and the paint splatters on the posters show how much fun they had putting them together. I smile when I see the volleyball poster. The girls in the poster resemble Tracy and Gale. They are jumping up to block a shot, with their hands reaching over the net. The white-and-blue Lemoyne banner is on the wall, and a sign, saying, *Congratulations Lemoyne D'Iberville Athletes,* is hanging over the stage.

This simple gym has been transformed into a ballroom. There have been dances in this gym before, but it has never been transformed into a ballroom like this before. I can't believe it. I take a deep breath, but I still have butterflies in my stomach as I head off to the large gym at the other end of the school. Keith and Brent are there in suits and ties, chatting.

Tracy is the first to see me, and she squeals, "Hey, Schaffes, you look great. I almost didn't recognize you."

"You mean I don't look great normally?" I joke.

"No, Coach, you always look good, but you have such nice makeup, and you're all dressed up. You look beautiful."

I smile, feeling a little embarrassed.

"Tracy, you look awesome yourself." I respond. I can feel a buzz go through my body, like the electricity in the air has finally hit me.

At 6:30 p.m., the doors open. A year of planning and three years of dreaming have finally come to life. I walk in with Keith and Brent beside me.

"Irit, I'm stunned," Brent says. "The gym looks marvelous."

"I know." I smile proudly.

"Irit, I was wrong. Congratulations."

"So was I," Keith says. "The students went beyond what I thought possible. Congratulations!"

"Thank you, Keith, and thank you, Brent."

The students enter, and the seats fill up quickly. Everyone is dressed up, and they all look so proud. Oscar Adler and his wife, Elke, arrive and join us at the teachers' table. I look around. Chloe, Dave, Paul, Keith, John, Brent and I are at the table, but there is one empty seat. The students had personally invited Dr. Cole, and he had told them that he would be here. But he has not shown up.

The food from Lotus Emperor arrives. When everything is in place, Chris turns on the background music, and the meal begins. Two tables at a time come to the front where all the platters are set up. Everything is running so smoothly, but it is still hard for me to eat because of my excitement. I look around. Laughter and excited chatter fill the room.

When the meal is over at 8:30, the award presentations begin. Keith begins with an introduction. He has always been the emcee for the sports awards. He is so calm and collected when it comes to speaking to large groups. So is Brent, for that matter. They are both naturals with a microphone. Keith is in charge, and Brent is helping out. The first few minutes of public speaking are always awkward for me until I calm down so I'm glad that they wanted to help with this part. Besides, this is what they love to do.

Keith, Brent and I have seats on the stage for the ceremony. The podium is set up in front of us, and two tables full of trophies are to our left. There are trophies for every event, and Chris even put together specific introductory music for each category, just like in the movies.

Cross-country, field hockey, soccer, and basketball fly by, and now it is time for the volleyball awards. The team howls—my team, the team that I have coached for four years. *What a great group of kids.* I think, feeling the emotions of this event wash over me.

After I finish handing out the volleyball awards, Tracy and Gale surprise me with a gift: a blue sweatshirt with a whistle and the words, *Best Coach,* sewed across the top. "Thank you for always believing in us and teaching us to believe in ourselves," they say. I give them hugs and hear applause from the whole room.

Finally, the table is clear. There are no more awards. It is my turn to speak. I stand up and look around the room. It feels so magical. This whole night feels magical. I can see all of the faces focused on me. They are all so attentive. I know everyone in this room by name. I have known some of them for five years. I look at the teachers' table and see Dr. Cole's empty chair.

I adjust the microphone and begin, "I'm standing here today feeling so proud, and I want to thank—" My voice is cut off by the sound of *Chariots of Fire* suddenly blaring through the sound system. One table of students after another gets up and claps, and I can't speak. There is a lump in my throat. Tears start streaming down my face. The standing ovation is ongoing. As the song continues, I look around the room. All eyes are on me. The connection I feel to my students has no boundaries.

The song ends, but the people are still standing, still clapping. The room is filled with such love. It is so magical and moving. I somehow manage to gain my composure enough to get through my speech, thanking Oscar, Jimmy's parents, and everyone else who helped out. Suddenly, the award presentation is officially over, and it is time for the dance.

Once again, the students take charge. They put everything away, fold up the tables, and help the band set up.

As the dance starts up, Tracy approaches me with Gale and a few other students in tow. "Coach," Tracy says, "I will never forget you." We both hug.

"Thank you for everything. Your commitment to excellence and your perseverance will be with me always," Gale says.

One student after another says the same warm words, *"Do you know what an impact you have made on my life?"* *"Why are you leaving?"* I receive one hug after another, and then I begin to dance with the students.

"Ms. Schaffer, I never knew you could move so well. You're pretty cool!" A student shouts over the music, and I laugh. I can feel the smile on my face radiating through my whole body.

~~~~~~~~~~

As I drive home that night, I reflect. I had no idea I had such an impact on the students' lives. I always believed that if I had known more about the techniques of certain sports I coached, my teams would have done better. Somehow, I never felt as if I had done enough.

My voice of wisdom takes over. *You're too hard on yourself! Look at the impact you made, and you had no idea? How different would it have been had you not been so hard on yourself? What if you had realized this whole time that what you were doing was enough? Imagine how much happier you would have been. You believe in your students, and that belief has never wavered. You have shown it through the years, and your students could not have thanked you in a more beautiful way. So, it is time to start believing in yourself the way you do in others.*

I make a vow and I say out loud: "I will start focusing on the positive, rather than on what I'm not doing right."

7

1983

You may encounter many defeats, but you must not be defeated.
In fact, it may be necessary to encounter the defeats,
so you can know who you are, what you can rise from,
how you can still come out of it.

Maya Angelou

As I drive through a puddle that is at least a foot deep, I fear that my car will stall. *Come on GLC, keep going,* I think, willing my car to work. I get through the river of water and breathe a sigh of relief. My car is still running. I park by the school and gladly step out of my car.

I am a student at the University of Southern California in Downey, where they have the Physical Therapy program. It is reputed to be one of the hardest Physical Therapy programs to get into. They say you usually have to apply many times to get in. I consider myself lucky because they accepted me on the first try.

Six of my classmates are gathered at the front of the building. They are trying to shield themselves from the rain while waiting for the doors to open.

"Irit, how are you doing?" my friend Debbie asks.

"I wasn't sure my car was going to make it through all the water."

"Do they have these kinds of rainstorms in Montréal?" "You must be kidding," I say. "It is a lot worse, but our drainage system is better. Water doesn't back up like it does here."

"Did you hear the wind last night?" Tom, another student in our class asks.

"Yeah, I liked it. I felt so safe lying under my down comforter and listening to the wind howling," I say.

"Not me. I'm from Florida, and I couldn't sleep because it reminded me of the hurricanes we have back home."

Finally, someone comes up to the front door with a key and unlocks it for us, and another day of classes begins. It is the third week of my second semester here. In the first semester, we focused a lot on theoretical information. I'm hoping that this semester we will be exposed to more of "hands on" experience. That is how I learn best.

Debbie, as usual, sits at the front of the class. She always takes great notes, for which I'm very grateful because she is my study buddy. I pick a seat in the back row. After everyone gets seated, silence falls, and class begins.

"Good morning, everyone," Beth Grant, my teacher, begins. "Today, we'll go over the research studies that have been done on electrical stimulation."

When I was doing rehab on my injured knee, the therapist used electrical stimulation on my leg to help strengthen the muscles around the knee. Strengthening the muscles that supported the knee was key to healing, she had told me. Electrodes were placed on two points of the muscle and, depending on the current setting, I would experience either a forceful or a gentle muscle contraction. This was cool because when you are injured it is hard to contract the muscle properly; this machine does it for you. It didn't help my problem, but I still liked the concept and knew it could work for other injuries.

One study after another is shown on the overhead projector. Thirty minutes pass. Forty minutes pass. The studies don't seem to have relevance to me. It's not what I had expected at all.

My God, when will this class end? I think. I want to ask for a break so badly, but I refrain while the instructor just keeps going on. She is like the energizer bunny, never stopping. With all the research studies the teacher shows us week after week, it is hard for me to refrain from raising my hand and saying, *Did you ever hear of the research studies that say our brains can only retain 15 minutes of new information at a time before we need a break? There must be over 1000 studies to substantiate that.*

Even though I have been in this class for almost a month now, I just never seem to get used to this barrage of one study after another on the overhead. With the way the instructor is presenting the information, I can't see how it is relevant to patient care.

I look around the room. Why does everyone else look okay with this seemingly pointless barrage of information? I assume it's just I who can't learn this way. I fidget in my seat, and I'm starting to hope that the instructor will notice. *Can't she get the message?* I look at the clock. *What about a break?* I want to yell. *Break*! The electrical stimulation research studies continue.

Suddenly, from out of nowhere, there is a rumbling sound, and the walls start to vibrate. After a few seconds of this, I hear a shout from our teacher, "Get under a doorway!" Everyone scrambles up out of their seats. I follow the group, wondering, *Why the doorway?* The rumbling stops, and out of the confusion I can only hear the words, "earthquake" and "class dismissed." Class was almost over, so by the time we settled down again we wouldn't have had any time, anyway.

This is my first ever earthquake experience, but instead of being scared, I am just relieved. *Wow! Finally, a break,* I think.

The school is only ten minutes from home, and as I drive, I look for aftermath from the earthquake. Nothing along the way seems to have been damaged. The radio newscaster announces that the earthquake was just a small one. No damages or injuries have been reported yet.

I smile as I think back to the snowstorms in Montréal, the negative 20 degree weather, the frozen pipes, frozen streets, and frozen people. That is where I come from. That is what I am used to. If earthquakes and puddles are as bad as it gets in California, I think I can handle it.

I sit in one class after another, day in and day out. Memorize, memorize, memorize. Study, study, study.

I somehow thought when I entered the program that everything I would learn would be exciting and relevant. I'm disappointed because the information is not being conveyed to me in a manner that I can grasp so I am studying to pass a test rather than to understand. Understanding would help me better learn and retain all the information in the long run. Oh, well, maybe it will gel as time goes on.

I walk into my anatomy lab, and the smell of formaldehyde overpowers me. I wish I could wear a mask in this class. Despite the smell, I love learning about the body. I just don't like the cutting part. I have three hours of anatomy lab twice a week from 9-12, and even after such a long class, I am never hungry for my lunch period afterward. The smell in the room ruins my appetite.

The lab takes place in a cold room, with bodies spread out across it. We go to our respective bodies and remove the sheets covering them. My three lab partners and I stand by our body, or, as we have named her, Mrs. Baker. We wanted to give her a name to pay her respect. After all, she gave her body to science so that we could learn.

We were not given any information about her at the beginning of the semester, but we think she was about 70 and that she died of lung cancer. Her lungs are very black, and two lobes on her right lung have been removed. *Mrs. Baker*, I think, as I do every day, *I'm sorry I have to cut into you, but thank you for being our teacher.*

"Can I do the procedure on the shoulder to reveal the rotator cuff?" Matt asks. Matt and Rona love to cut, whereas Karen and I usually prefer to watch. Each day, I tell myself, *you are learning about the body. It's an inside view. Be grateful!* I love what I am learning, but I'm so glad the others always offer to do the cutting.

This class ends, and another one begins entitled, "Practice Management and Ethics." Kate is the instructor. She always tells us about the importance of communication and the proper procedures and protocols for working as a physical therapist. This is one of my easier classes. Much of what she says is common sense to me, and I'm grateful for her teaching approach.

As class goes on, I start to daydream. Suddenly, I hear my name and am once again brought back to attention.

"Sorry, Kate," I say, flustered. "Can you repeat the question?"

~~~~~~~~~

That evening, I get into my Mazda GLC sport and head off to Studio City for dinner at Aunt Elsie's. I call Elsie my "aunt," but she is actually my dad's second cousin. Growing up, we always joked that she was really my mom's cousin because she and my mom were so close.

It takes a little over an hour to get to Aunt Elsie's. Regardless of what day of the week it is, the freeway is always congested in Los Angeles. They should rename the freeway "the congestion." I look at the time. It has already been an hour and 20 minutes. One more exit, and I'll be there. For now, though, traffic is stopped, and my stomach is starting to grumble. Finally, I see cars starting to move about 30 car lengths ahead. *Good,* I think. *I'll be there soon.*

Suddenly, from out of nowhere, I feel a hard jolt and hear the screeching and crunching sound of metal on metal. My head whips backward and then forward.

As I catch my breath, I look behind me. There is a green pickup truck crammed against the back of my car. As I get out of my car slowly, I reach for the back of my neck and begin to massage it. The guy in the pickup truck gets out of his car, too. He is about 6' and looks like a weight lifter.

"Traffic was stopped. What were you doing?" I say.

"It's no big deal, lady." He puts his hand on my bumper, probably checking for damage. "It's just your bumper."

I look at my bumper and then back at him. My bumper is completely crushed in the middle. "Weren't you paying attention?" I ask, angrily. "Traffic was stopped. Can I have your phone and license plate numbers?"

He puts his hands on his hips and says, "Lady, it's no big deal."

"My bumper is smashed in, and my neck hurts," I say, trying to keep calm.

"You're making that up. It's no big deal. It's just a small dent!" he yells loudly.

I watch in awe as he quickly gets back into his green pickup truck. *I can't believe this,* I think. *You just hit me! You just yelled at me! Now you are just going to get back into your green pickup truck?* I'm stuck in my spot. I can't utter a word.

OK, Irit, hurry, I tell myself, snapping back to attention. *Get back in your car, get a pen, and get his license number. DL7 - the first three numbers. Where's my pen?* The traffic starts to move, and I see the truck pass me in my peripheral vision. "Follow him," I hear myself saying. "Get the other numbers."

Of course, just my luck, the traffic is now moving quickly, and the green truck is nowhere to be found. DL7. That is all that I know about the man who hit me. I reach Studio City, and as I exit, my head feels heavy. I finally arrive at 3457 Colfax, and I open the screen door to find Elsie, Jusie, and Ersie sitting in the living room.

"Irit, you're white as a ghost," Aunt Ersie says when she sees me. My aunt, just like my dad, is always warm and comforting. Her tone is extra soothing to my nerves after what just happened.

"You're not going to believe it. I just got in an accident near the Mulholland Drive exit. Traffic was stopped, and the guy behind me just rammed into me. He wasn't paying attention. He got out of his car, yelled at me, and then drove off. I only got part of his license plate number."

"Irit," Uncle Jusie says, "you didn't get his information?"

"I asked him, and he just said it wasn't a big deal and took off. I couldn't believe it."

"How could you have not gotten his license plate number?"

"Uncle Jusie, it all happened so fast. He yelled at me, and I just stood there. I couldn't move."

Uncle Jusie rolls his eyes in disbelief. "Well, that was stupid. Now, if there is a problem, you will have to pay for it."

Uncle Jusie is a very nervous person, and he has no patience. I know he has a good heart, but he doesn't know how to be soothing when you need him to be. He always criticizes Aunt Ersie, too, but she knows how to just ignore it. She says he can't help himself. He is the worst person to be here at this moment. It's like he is just feeding my fear.

I'm churning everything over in my brain. If only I hadn't left when I did from school. If only I had left later. If only I had stayed home. If only I had had a pen or pencil in the car. If only I had yelled back at the guy who hit me with his truck.

"It's no big deal, Irit. You'll be fine," Aunt Elsie chimes in.

"My neck is sore, and it feels stiff," I say, panicking as the pain increases. "I'm having a hard time moving it to the side."

"Well, how much damage did he do to your car?" Aunt Elsie asks.

"The bumper is smashed in."

"Is that all? Stop complaining. You'll be fine," Aunt Elsie says. I'm immediately reminded of the guy in the green truck. *It's no big deal, lady.* I know Aunt Elsie doesn't mean to be hurtful by her comment. It is just her awkward way of trying to help when she knows that something is amiss, a way of avoiding dealing with something negative that she wishes had not happened. She would do the same things with her children, on first blush dismissing their illnesses but deep down being very concerned about them. Her words, though I understand the intent, are nonetheless making me feel worse. I'm starting to wish I had just gone home after the accident.

The conversation keeps swirling on around me, and I feel like I'm in a war zone. I just got hit by a car, and now I'm being pummeled for my stupidity. To make things worse, I keep playing the accident over and over in my head, and with each replay, my neck feels worse.

"Irit, I'm sorry that you got hurt," Aunt Ersie pipes in with her soft manner.

Thank goodness, I think. *Someone who is not telling me I've done something wrong.* She is so like my dad, and I'm grateful she is here to balance out the others.

"Let's eat. You might feel better."

~~~~~~~~~

Later that night, when I am home in bed, my eyes suddenly jerk open. I feel as if a Mac truck has just run over my body. My head is heavy. It is hard to even lift it off the pillow. A shooting pain is going down my left arm, my right arm is asleep, and my tooth is aching. It's only 6 a.m., but thankfully, I can call home because of the 3-hour time difference.

"Mom, hi," I say when she answers. "You're not going to believe it. I got in an accident yesterday."

"Whose fault was it?" my mom asks abruptly. There is no beating around the bush with her.

"I got hit from behind. It was his fault, but he took off."

"What do you mean? Did you get his license number?"

"I only got part of it," I say, bracing myself for my mother's scolding.

"How could you do that? Why didn't you follow him?"

Here is another chorus of what Uncle Jusie kept telling me. He and my mom are not even related, but they often say the same things when I go to them with problems. They were born in the same town in Czechoslovakia, and that is all they really have in common. Yet, somehow their personalities are very similar.

"Is Dad home?" I ask. He is the one I was really calling to talk to.

"No, he just went out. Weren't you paying attention? Is that why you got hit?"

"Mom, I have to go," I say with exasperation and hang up the phone.

My mom's and Uncle Jusie's voices are bouncing around in my brain. If only I had stayed home that night. If only I had gotten that guy's license plate number. If only I had paid attention and looked in the rear view mirror. Then, maybe I could have braced myself. If only I had left five minutes earlier. If only I had yelled back at him. The phrase, *'If only,'* is burning a hole through my heart, making it hard to breathe. *'If only'* is taking me out of time. I can't get comfortable.

Okay, breathe, I tell myself. *This is not helping. You'll be fine. It was only your bumper.*

After an hour, my neck still hurts, and, on top of that, my tooth is starting to ache. *How can this all be from the accident? It was only a fender bender,* I think.

With each passing moment, it feels like the amount of pain in my tooth is increasing, and I have no ability to control it. The pain starts moving into my head. I desperately want to see a doctor, but it is Saturday. I can't get an appointment until Monday at the earliest. *Maybe I should go to the emergency room,* I think, *but what would* they *be able to do?* I take one Tylenol after another and place one ice pack after another on my neck and upper back.

~~~~~~~~~

"What brings you here today?" The dentist asks as I sit in his chair Monday morning. I am supposed to be in class right now, but I couldn't bring myself to wait any longer for an appointment.

"I keep getting a shooting pain in my tooth. It is so sharp it feels like nerve pain."

"When did it start?"

"I was in a car accident on Friday night, and it started right after that."

"Oh! That's just a coincidence," Dr. Jones says. "Your tooth pain can't be related."

I'm stunned. "It started to hurt right after the accident and has gotten progressively worse since."

"Does it make a difference when you eat something hot versus something cold?"

"No, nothing makes a difference. It doesn't matter if I am eating, lying down, walking, or whatever else, I feel the pain. I tried hot and cold compresses on my cheeks. Nothing has helped."

"We'll take x-rays and see what is going on."

Ten minutes later, Dr. Jones comes back into the room with the newly developed x-rays.

"Your teeth look good," he says, "healthy roots, and I don't see any cavities."

"But my tooth hurts," I say. I am starting to get a little frustrated that he is being so cavalier about this.

"If the pain is so bad, we can pull it."

At first, I am shocked by this suggestion, but as another shooting pain moves across my tooth, I ask, "Will it take away the pain?"

"I can't guarantee it. In fact, sometimes when people complain of tooth pain, it gets worse when the tooth is pulled."

I pause. "If there are no guarantees, and you can't find a problem in my x-rays, then why would I want you to pull my tooth?"

I am frustrated now. The dentist has no clue what is wrong with me, and he is just blindly hoping that pulling my tooth might help. I am glad I am entering the healthcare field so I can find ways to actually help people heal instead of just jumping right into procedures based on the premise, "I have nothing else to offer." There has to be a better way to ease my pain. There has to be a cause to my pain, and if more doctors looked for the source of a problem rather than just trying to alleviate the symptoms, then maybe they could actually help me. I don't understand why so many doctors are satisfied to say something has an "unknown etiology," focus on symptom relief, and then just hope the problem will somehow go away with time. This doesn't make sense to me.

As I leave, I hear Dr. Jones say, "If you change your mind, let me know."

I scramble out of his office. *Now what do I do?* I think. The pain throbs once more, and I want to burst out in tears. I had really hoped the dentist would fix everything. I decide to go home and try to sleep instead of going straight back to school.

I wake up a couple hours later just in time to show up for my last class of the day. After class, I head to my teacher Kate's office. She had recommended this dentist for me and let me skip class to go to my appointment this morning so I wanted to check in.

"Irit, how are you doing?" Kate asks.

"My tooth is killing me, and the dentist has no idea why it is hurting. It seriously feels like a knife is going through my tooth and into my skull. I think I'm going to go to the library to see if I can find out anything about this problem on my own."

"If you need my help, let me know."

"Thanks, Kate. I appreciate it."

I get to the library and look up everything I can find on unrelenting tooth pain. I know the body can heal. My mom, my dad, and my relatives have shown me, time and again growing up, how the body can heal. There has got to be an explanation for why this is happening. I keep seeing the word *referred*, which means that pain can come from somewhere other than the tooth itself. My pain must somehow be coming from my neck. Something is causing tightness in the muscles on the right side of my mouth, and somehow, that is affecting my tooth. So, I was right, the pain is from the accident.

I shift and turn in my seat. I think I have all the information I need so I head home and go straight to bed. I'm hoping I'll feel better when I wake up. I look at the clock, and it is only 4:20 p.m.

As I am lying in bed, the pain suddenly intensifies. From out of nowhere, I am experiencing the worst head pain of my life. It feels like a dentist has put a drill to my tooth and is holding it on the nerve. The pain is exploding in my head. My brain is on fire, 1000 on the Richter scale. I'm feeling nauseous. I try Tylenol, but nothing is working. I just lie in bed until I somehow fall asleep out of pure exhaustion.

I open my eyes at 2:30 a.m. The tooth-caused headache is gone, but the cramping in my mouth remains. I take advantage of this moment of relief to study.

Four hours later, I stop and get ready for my day. At 8 a.m., I leave for the donut place, grab a large cup of coffee, and head off to school.

One class after another passes, and I somehow get through the day. Debbie, of course, had taken good notes the day before, and she lets me copy them to make up for the classes I missed. The day runs fairly smoothly. I'm still experiencing a lot of discomfort, but at least the horrible pain from yesterday is gone.

I get home, and at 4:30 p.m., the drill in my head comes on again. The headache is unrelenting. Migraines, I have had. This pain is beyond that. It is unbearable. The nausea is overwhelming, and it is hard to hold down my food.

Every day for two weeks it's the same. When 4:30 p.m. hits, my head explodes with pain. Then, the nausea kicks in, and I rush to the bathroom. Finally, I fall asleep and awaken at 2:30 a.m. with some relief. I study, go to the donut place, ask for a large coffee, and head to school. I think I am starting to go crazy from this cycle of misery.

~~~~~~~~~

I get an MRI, and before he even gets the results, Dr. Goode, my new doctor, hits me with a list of all the possible negative things that could be affecting me.

"I don't want to scare you," he says, "but this pain may be caused by a brain tumor or even an aneurysm."

"No, the pain in my tooth and the headaches coincided with the car accident," I say. *Why will no medical professional listen to me when I say this? It seems like common sense to me,* I think, getting frustrated.

"It doesn't make sense to have this much pain after just a little fender bender."

"But I know it's from the car accident. I read in a book at school that tooth pain can be referred, and—"

"It doesn't make sense," Dr. Goode interrupts.

"Dr. Goode, I don't have a brain tumor. This is from the car accident."

"We need to admit you into the hospital and get the tests done either way, just as a precaution."

After a barrage of tests; a spinal tap, a CT scan, blood tests, and more blood tests, I'm starting to feel worse than I did before I entered the hospital. And, like clockwork, at 4:30 p.m., the drill starts up in my brain.

"Would you like an injection of morphine?" my doctor asks.

I hate needles, but after two weeks of this, I'll take anything for relief. The needle penetrates, and a warm rush runs through my body. Everything is tingling, everything is hot, and the pain disappears. *No wonder people like these drugs*, I think as I fall asleep.

As I expected, none of the tests show anything. I have spent two days in the hospital, and I am leaving with no answers, feeling worse than I did when I entered.

As soon as I get home, the phone rings. It is my dad.

"Hi, Dad."

"How are you doing?" he asks.

"One drug they gave me worked wonders, but I can only have it if I am in the hospital."

"What is it?"

"Morphine. They gave me Percocet and Vicodin for home, though."

"Do they know what is causing the headaches?"

"No, Dad, but I know it's from the car accident. They thought it may be a tumor, but now, after getting a million needle marks and a million tests done on me, they have no clue. I've lost 15 pounds in less than three weeks."

"Your mom wants to fly out and cook for you. Just tell us when."

"That may be a good idea."

My mom, in all the years I lived in Montréal, never once came to visit me in any of my apartments or houses. That would have meant that she approved of my choice of living on my own.

"If it doesn't go away soon, maybe she should come," I say.
**

Over the next week, I get more blood work done and go through more tests. The results never show anything. At this point, whenever I wear short sleeves, it is hard not to notice all the needle marks. I bet when people see me, they think... Well, I'll let them formulate their own opinions. That thought at least makes me laugh.

Monday morning in my anatomy lab, we are studying the Brachial plexus, and, as usual, Matt asks to do the dissection. *I wonder what they would find if they did an autopsy of my brain. That would be kind of nice because then I'd know what was going on and could heal.* I laugh at the absurdity of the thought. Even if they were to find what is wrong, I couldn't exactly heal afterward. There is no coming back from an autopsy.

Class is over. I survived. This was my first day back at school in a week. I've missed a lot, and I am going to need to catch up quickly. I decide to start with Beth Grant, my therapeutic modalities instructor. Who knows how many seemingly irrelevant scientific research studies I'll have to go over? I doubt that I will ever use this endless string of studies as a basis for protocol in my career, but, alas, studying them is a requirement. I knock on her office door.

"Come in. Oh, hello Irit. I heard you were in the hospital. How are you doing?"

"I had every test known to mankind done on me, and nothing. Nobody has any clue why I am having these horrific headaches and this horrific toothache."

"Maybe you will just have to live with it," she says.

As I hear those words, my face turns red, and before I even realize what I'm saying, I shout, "If you have no idea what is causing these headaches or how painful they are, how the hell can you tell me I might have to live with it?"

"I don't want to give you false hope," she says in a calm and sympathetic manner.

False hope? I want to scream. Dr. Goode, at least ten of my classmates, and Beth Grant have now all told me the same thing. I am so tired of hearing that. With all of the research studies she has gone over, how can she just sum up my pain as something I might have to live with? I storm out of her office. I can't even remember what it was she told me I had to do to catch up. I can't believe I yelled at her. She'll probably want to fail me now.

I get home, and at 4:30 p.m., I continue my routine of getting violently ill. *I just may have to live with the pain*, the fear part of me thinks. *Some pains never go away.* One voice after another reverberates in my head. I know I'm just buying into fear, but I can't help it.

My fear of enduring pain is causing a pit in my stomach. It feels like something is gnawing at my sternum. My body can't stay still. The fear won't let me breathe. The fear won't let me move. The fear won't let me think of the joys of my life. The fear has taken away all my possibilities.

I don't want to live like this, I think. *I can't live in fear. I can't live with this pain. This is not a life. Please, God, give me the key to unlocking all this pain and release my fear. God, are you listening?*

Then I think of my dad. "Dad," I say out loud, "if you could heal after all you went through, then there is no reason why my body shouldn't heal, right? The doctors, the teachers, my classmates, they just don't know what they are doing. All they are doing is scaring me. They don't understand that the body *can* heal. Dad, you healed. You have *good blood*; that is what you always tell me. Everyone can have good blood. People just don't know how to use it. I need to learn how to access it. I need to find a doctor who can help me heal. I can't do this alone."

As I lay in bed thinking, an idea hits me like a bolt of lightning, and for the first time since my accident, I feel hope. It is 8:30 p.m. in Montréal, not too late, so I dial my dad's number.

"Hi, Dad. I had to call you."

"Iritka, how are you doing?"

"My headache is horrible, but I keep thinking ... I know that the body can heal. It's like with my knee. No one thought I could heal from that, either, but I did."

"Your voice sounds better," he says. He can always tell how I am feeling by my voice.

"Yeah. Actually, I was lying in bed, and all of a sudden I figured out what I should do."

"What do you mean?"

"Dad, I want to write a book. I want to get your story. People should know what you went through, that way more people will understand that the body *can* heal. After hearing so many people tell me that there may be no way to heal, I just want to show the world that the impossible is not always impossible.

"When I finish school," I say as, for the first time in a long time, I can feel excitement bubbling up inside of me, "I'll come back to Montréal, and we'll put your story on tape. Dad, people don't understand. None of your doctors have ever been able to explain how you healed. Doctors and teachers just tell people that pain is something that they will have to live with. I know better. I know because I have watched you and listened to you, and I want to share that with others."

"I would be honored to have you do that. Plus, you will get better, too, Iritka. You will see, and you can share your own story in your book."

"People need to know about you," I say with enthusiasm.

"I will be very glad to share. Many people, even many doctors, don't truly understand the body. You will be better. You will see," my dad says.

I get off the phone with a renewed sense of excitement about my life. There has to be a solution to this problem. I won't listen to those who tell me I have to live like this forever. They don't even know what is causing the problem so they can't tell me there is no solution.

The body can heal, I say to myself again and again. My body just needs some help, and I just need to find the right people to help me. *Maybe my dad had good blood because he believed he could heal. He did not live in fear, thinking "what if I don't heal." He never gave up. He always looked for the positive. He just knew.*

Yes, I will write a book and learn about healing and transformation in ways that are beyond what the textbooks teach. I will learn the keys to healing.

The idea of the book makes me feel alive and hopeful again. Somehow, I am connecting to a higher power. It is showing me purpose and possibility while everything around me is still telling me differently. Yes, I will keep on course so I can overcome, and I won't let anyone scare me into thinking I can't heal.

~~~~~~~~~

"I know you are using proliferant injections in my neck to build up new tissue and stabilize the joints, but I don't want to do them anymore," I say right off the bat when I walk into Dr. Goode's office the next day. "I feel like they make me worse."

"Actually, Irit," says Dr. Goode, a spark of excitement in his eyes. "I took a course over this past weekend that was taught by an osteopathic doctor, Dr. Lawrence Jones, called Strain Counterstrain. I'd like to try one of his techniques on you. The instructor said it helps headaches. Plus, this is a gentle procedure. There are no injections."

"In that case, I'm game," I say, always wanting relief.

I lie on the table, and Dr. Goode goes to work. He finds a spot on my neck and presses it. It feels like a bad bruise. He fiddles with my neck and then holds onto that painful spot until it no longer feels like a bruise. Suddenly, within one minute, I feel something I have never felt before. It is like a gust of wind escaping my neck.

"Dr. Goode, I feel better," I say in awe. I know one thing for sure. I want to look into the strain counterstrain method more.

That night, 4:30 p.m. comes and goes, and there is no headache and no searing pain for the first time in weeks.

~~~~~~~~~~

"Those horrible headaches are gone," I tell Dr. Goode one week later at my next appointment. "Now, it just feels like I am having ordinary migraines. The nerve pain that kept shooting through my head is gone. This, at least, is tolerable. Though I can't believe I am saying migraines are tolerable."

He checks me out again, but this time he does not find a tender bruise-like point, which is the basis for these techniques. "This was all I could do for you. I can't find any other points to help you with, but I'll give you a prescription for Percocet and Vicodin if you want."

"I already have some from earlier, so no thanks," I say. I'm surprised he is willing to give me more medications. He already helped me more than he will ever know by doing a simple, hands on technique!

~~~~~~~~~~

When I get home and take the Vicodin with some food, I start to feel loopy and sick to my stomach. An hour passes, and the pain is no better. A little voice inside me says, *this is no good for you. Throw out the prescription drugs. You don't need them.*

I head into the bathroom and throw the pills into the toilet. Sure, I am still in pain, but the drugs are making me feel groggy. I can't even think clearly, and thus it made me feel worse.

I go to bed, my head pounding, my jaw tight, and my tooth hurting. I take three Tylenols and feel better. The Tylenol is giving me dark circles under my eyes, but at this point, I don't care. *Remember Irit, you can and will get a lot better.*

I fall asleep, and for the first time ever, I have a lucid dream. I'm dreaming, and I know I'm dreaming.

I'm in Oslo, Norway in the middle of a field. I spent a summer at the University of Oslo the year before I had my appendix out in Prague, so it looks familiar. Suddenly, from afar, I can see a big dog. It is a scary, black dog. Its teeth are jutting out at me, and I am scared.

Now I am seven. I am wearing my pink turtleneck with two white pom-poms near the chest, and I am looking out the window because I am not allowed outside. I am contagious. I have scarlet fever. The dog is outside the window, so I'm glad I'm indoors. I am scared.

Then, somehow, I am in bed again, and it is the present. The big black dog is beside my bed on the floor. I look at the dog, and I say, 'Dog, I'm dreaming. You are not real, but look how scared I am.' My shoulders hurt, my neck hurts, and the pain is getting worse by the second. My heart pounds, and every muscle in my body tightens. 'You are not real, dog,' I say again. 'You are a figment of my imagination in this dream. How can you still affect me so much?'

A thought suddenly occurs to me while I am in the dream. If I can get scared from something that is not real, then why can't I be soothed in the same way? Can I heal if I imagine something healing me?

I look at the ferocious dog as I think this, and before my eyes, the dog starts to change. It transforms into a white, fluffy, big, loving dog. As I see its beauty, my body relaxes completely.

The dog jumps as if it wants to join me in bed, but in midair, the dog transforms once more. The white dog turns into a white light and penetrates my body.

At this moment, I wake up, and my brain can only process one single thought for the rest of the night. *The body can heal itself. Mindsets are the key.*

~~~~~~~~~

A month passes, and as usual, it is a sunny and hot day in Downey. I have an hour break before going back to the grind of schoolwork. My grilled cheese sandwich is in the toaster oven, and my stomach is grumbling.

"Dad, I'm so glad you caught me at home," I say as I pick up the phone. "You're not going to believe what happened in school today. Someone finally figured out the cause for my headaches."

"That's great. Was it one of your teachers?"

"No, a physical therapist from UCLA came and gave a talk on temporamandibular joint disorders (TMJ)."

"What is that?"

"Dad, I have to take my sandwich out of the toaster. Hold on a second." I open the toaster oven door and try to remove the sandwich. I almost burn my hand so I grab my oven mitt and pull the sandwich out, plopping it down on my plate.

"Dad, this teacher was great. She explained how the joints in the jaw could affect the teeth. She said that sometimes TMJ problems are caused by whiplash from car accidents. She had the class do a test to check for misalignment problems in the mouth. I found out that my top teeth and bottom teeth aren't aligned."

"What are you talking about? I don't understand."

"The car accident! It *is* the reason why I have been having all these headache and tooth problems," I say excitedly.

"So, she will help you?"

"Yeah, she'll help, and she gave me the name of a dentist who sees people for problems like mine. The headaches and tooth pain were from the accident. I knew it."

"When are you going to see her?"

"Tomorrow. I am going to see her and the dentist; they are in the same clinic."

I'm so hungry that I can't refrain from taking a bite out of my sandwich while talking.

"Uncle Jusie told me that it was bad that I didn't get that guy's license plate number because now I have to pay for all of these treatments by myself," I say with a mouthful of food.

"Don't worry about that."

"It is just such a relief after all this time to finally find someone who understands. So many people have told me that I have to live with my pain."

"Sometimes, you have to trust your own judgment when it comes to your body. Remember when I went to the doctor and he said he saw something on my lung in an x-ray? He thought maybe it was cancer, and I said no, it was from a broken rib in the war. They did tests anyway, but I knew I was right. They didn't listen. Many times, doctors try to help but don't understand that we know our bodies best."

"Yeah," I laugh, "it was the broken rib. I remember."

"Good. I'm glad you found someone to help. I told you that you would heal. You will get better. You will see. Now, in February, your mom wants to go to Palm Springs for a week. We want to come visit you for ten days, and then maybe you can come with us to Palm Springs."

"Great! I can't wait to see you. I would love to come with you for the weekend."

"Good."

"I have to go back to class."

"Iritka, I love you."

"I love you, too." I hang up the phone and wolf down the rest of my sandwich.

~~~~~~~~~

I head back to school, and the world looks great again because I can see beyond the pain that has been such a big part of my life for so many months. In my Therapeutic Exercise class, Helen, our teacher, leads us through tests and exercises for lower back problems.

"Remember," she says, "most hospitals will not hire you if you have back problems. Working with hospital patients sometimes requires heavy lifting, Hospitals are concerned that if you hurt your back once, you can reinjure it. So, don't let them know if you have a pre-existing condition. Exercise can help with back problems, but the symptoms typically keep coming back. Back problems can also lead to arthritis and disc degeneration disease."

Don't go there, I think. *Don't tell me I have to suffer from more issues beyond this.* I raise my hand.

"Arthritis is inflammation of the joint, right? So, if the inflammation goes away, then doesn't that mean the arthritis is gone? Plus, can't people with disc degeneration be symptom free?"

"The symptoms go away for both of these conditions sometimes, but very often, they come back, so you can't say the problem is gone."

I tune out. I want to throw those two terms, *arthritis* and *disc degeneration,* out of the physical therapy vocabulary, out of the English language for that matter. Those words are enough to scare anyone. *You're projecting doom and gloom*! No one can heal if you put fear into the equation. It just seems so obvious to me, and I know when I become a practicing physical therapist I will do things differently. I will be able to incorporate the positivity that I know has helped me begin to heal.

~~~~~~~~~

Later that night, my study group of five meets.

"How did you like class today?"

"I loved the visiting teacher," I say, excitedly. "She's going to treat me."

"Great! How are you feeling today?" Tracy asks.

"I have a headache, and if I could figure out a way to walk away from my body and leave the pain behind, I would. When I stop hurting, I'll move right back in." Everyone laughs. *It would be cool if I really could do that,* I think, *like in* Star Trek, *"beam me down," "beam me up."*

After two hours, I go back to my place. Debbie and I are next-door neighbors, and the group usually meets at her place so I don't have to travel too far. The meeting went well, and I'm excited about tomorrow. *I have an appointment with someone who finally knows what is causing my problems.* It's amazing how different the healing journey can be when you find some-one who understands the root causes of your pain and has protocols to help you heal. That is the type of physical therapist I will become.

~~~~~~~~~~

"Iritka, how are you?"

"Better," I say, taking my phone and sitting on the comfy, gold velvet recliner Aunt Ersie gave me. My dad's voice is always so comforting to me.

"Every time I ask you how you are, you always say 'better'. You could win an Olympic gold medal for getting better."

"Well, I'm still not where I want to be."

"How will you know when you are good and not just better?"

"When I run again and play tennis."

"Take a picture when you do run, and send it to me."

"That's a deal. Love you."

"Love you, too."

Irit Schaffer

8

1983 - 1984

Everything can be taken from a man but one thing:
the last of the human freedom—to choose one's attitude
in any given set of circumstances, to choose one's own way.
                                                    Viktor E. Frankl

I arrive at LAX, park in the no parking zone, and wait by my car. There is a guy next to me who seems to be in his early thirties. He has dark, curly hair, and he looks like he is in good shape. He's kind of cute. We look at each other.

"Hi," he says. "Are you also waiting for someone to arrive?"

"Yeah," I say. I would assume that anyone standing beside a car in this forbidden area is waiting for a flight to get in, but I keep that to myself.

"Where are you waiting for a flight from?" I ask.

"Montréal."

"You're kidding? So am I. My parents will be here for two weeks."

"I'm waiting for my parents, too. They'll be here for one week." We both laugh.

"Do you live here?" he asks.

"I'm going to school here, USC. What about you?"

"I moved here six years ago."

"It's nice not to have to deal with the Montréal winters, isn't it?" I say.

"That's for sure. I don't miss the shoveling and driving on ice."

A cop motions us to move.

He looks at me, as if considering something, and then asks, "Can I have your phone number? Maybe we can get together for coffee or something."

"Sure!" I write my number down for him and get into my car. *Coffee with him might be nice,* I think. It would be great to connect with someone from home out here.

"Great. I'll call you in a couple of weeks. Oh, by the way, what's your name?"

"Irit," I smile.

As he heads back to his car, I yell after him, "I didn't get your name."

"George."

The cop takes out his ticket board so we both head back into the big loop around the airport. As we make our first lap, he waves at me. He goes around once and stops, but I decide to go around again. This is too bizarre. LAX is a big airport, with flights arriving from all over the world, and I managed to meet someone who is from Montréal and who has parents visiting. It will be interesting to learn more about him if he calls.

Two circles later, I see my mom and dad.

"Hi Mom. Hi Dad. Welcome to LA," I say brightly.

"Iritka, you're too skinny. You should eat more," my mom says.

"Good. You can cook for me," I laugh as my dad loads the luggage into my trunk.

We get to my place, and I open the door.

"Is this the Chesterfield Aunt Ersie got you? It's beautiful," my dad says.

Aunt Ersie had given me her old gold velvet sofa and chair because she bought new furniture. "Yes. The sofa opens up. You can sleep in my bed or on the couch."

"We'll take the Chesterfield."

"Are you sure?"

"The Chesterfield is good."

My mom opens the fridge.

"Irit, there is no food; we'll go shopping in the morning. No wonder you're so skinny. You don't eat."

"I know my fridge is empty. That's why we're going shopping." I say, becoming a little inpatient.

"But that's your problem. You don't make time."

"Okay, Mom. Enough."

"What do you mean, *enough*?" she responds in a raised voice. "You never want to hear this, but you look terrible."

Very few people can rile me up, but my mom is a master. Maybe that's one of the roles of family. They know exactly how to press your buttons. At this point, I know I should keep quiet because when I'm upset and she's upset, nothing good will happen and things seems to just escalate. I try to keep quiet, but I can't help myself. The words blurt out anyway, "Mom, stop."

"Stop? I am just telling you the truth."

"Mom, if you don't have anything nice to say, don't say anything," I say.

"Stop screaming. You will give me a heart attack."

Yeah, I think to myself. *I know what will come next.* By now I should know better than to take things personally because she is just frustrated. I get the feeling that she believes by criticizing me she is helping me, but of course, I get caught up in the trap again, thinking, *this time she'll hear me.* My dad knows better than to say anything. I should take his lead, but I can't.

~~~~~~~~~~

I watch my mom shop. She is an expert at detecting good food. She smells and feels the fruit, always picking the perfectly ripe stuff. "This cantaloupe is sweet," she says as she smells it. "This will be good."

"Mom, how did you learn to be such a great cook?"

"At home. I learned at home."

"You lived on a farm, right? What was it like?" I ask.

"It was a farm."

My mom picks out yellow beans, throwing the ones that don't look good back in the bin.

"Was it a big farm?"

"It was a big farm."

My mom takes an avocado, feels it, and puts it in the basket. She does the same for the tomatoes and peppers. She puts the broccoli in her hand, looks at it, and says, "This looks good." Into the basket it goes.

"What was it like, the farm?" I say, once again trying to get a more detailed answer.

"Stop asking such questions."

"Why? It's interesting."

"It was a big farm, and we worked hard."

"Did you work after you finished high school?"

"I stayed on the farm."

"What was it like?"

"It was good."

"Anything else?"

"Iritka, I don't want to talk now."

"Mom, you never want to talk."

"Why do you want to make trouble?"

"Mom, forget it." I say. This time I know it is time to stop.

Bubby, my grandma, never spoke about her past, either. Almost every Sunday, I would go to lunch at her home, and she would, of course, have awesome meals prepared for me and wouldn't let me help. Just like my mom, she always told me I was too skinny. No matter how many helpings I had, she would tell me to eat more. But from her, I always knew it was a term of endearment. She said it more softly and sweetly than my mom does. If Bubby didn't say anything, I would think something was wrong.

Maybe it is hard to reminisce about something that no longer exists, and maybe it is easier to shut it out. Maybe Mom learned from my grandmother, but I wish, she wouldn't shut me out so much, I say to myself. *People would love to hear. I know I would. I would love to get to know more about her.*

We get home, and my mom starts preparing lunch.

"Do you want help?" I ask, knowing what the answer will be. Growing up, she never wanted help. In many ways, I think cooking is like her meditation and her place of calmness.

"The kitchen is too small," she says

I smile. "Okay. Dad, do you want to go to the mall? I need a pair of sweats for class."

We get in my silver GLC, and I look at my dad.

"Dad, why doesn't Mom like to talk about where she grew up?" I ask for what feels like the thousandth time in my life. "I know it was a good life."

"Yes, it was a good life. They were rich. Everyone knew them."

"So why doesn't Mom like to talk about stuff?"

"I don't know."

"Why is she so critical?"

"Just ignore it."

"Dad, that's what you have said all my life. I can't. Maybe if I could better understand, then it would be easier to ignore it. How come you never say anything when she gets like that?"

"Iritka, you don't understand."

"You're right, I don't understand. It's not right. Help me out here." I put the car in reverse to back out of my spot. Out of the corner of my eye, I notice my dad is puckering his lips and his hand is on his chin.

"Iritka, I don't want to talk about this anymore. One day you will understand."

"Dad!"

"Let's go shopping."

I put the car in gear, and we head off to the mall. Arriving, we park in front of Nordstrom's, and as we walk in, I see a red velour sweat suit that I absolutely love. It is the only one left.

"I'll go try it on, Dad."

I change, and as I come out to show him the sweats, I hear a saleslady ask my dad, "Can I help you?"

"My daughter is trying clothes," he says in his broken English.

"Your accent is different," the saleslady says. "Where are you from?"

"Czechoslovakia."

"How long are you here?"

"Two weeks."

"Only two weeks?"

"Yes."

"You speak English so well."

"Thank you," my dad smiles at her. I come out of the dressing room, wearing the sweat suit. The pants fit perfectly, and the velour material makes it look elegant. Bright red is my color. I always get compliments when I wear it.

"That red outfit is beautiful, Iritka. I'll buy it for you."

"I'll wear it home."

"You have been here only two weeks? Your English is so good," the saleslady repeats. My dad smiles again, a twinkle in his eye.

"Dad, she thinks you just came from Czechoslovakia," I laugh as we exit the store.

"I know," he gives me a mischievous smile. "This is the first time someone told me I speak English well. I liked hearing it. When I first came to Montréal, I remember I needed to get to somewhere. I asked a lady directions in English, and she said, 'Sorry, I don't speak French.' Now this woman tells me I speak good English."

I park on the street half a block from my place.

The aroma coming from my place is probably making everyone in the complex want to come visit. I open the door and am stunned. *How does she do it?* My mom has transformed my kitchen. She made vegetable soup with *nockerly*, *wienerschnitzel*, and mashed potatoes with onions. Now, she is grinding up the nuts for her famous chocolate nut roll cake.

I have always wanted to learn how to cook this meal, but my mom has no patience to teach me. "Use a little bit of this, a little bit of that," is the most I can get from her. She doesn't measure anything. When I try to learn and keep asking questions, she starts yelling. I did learn how to make the nut roll cake several years ago because I somehow managed to ignore her impatience long enough to make it through that lesson.

"What did you buy? Is it what you are wearing?" she asks as we enter the room.

"Yeah, do you like it?"

"It is too small. Get a bigger size," my mom says in her loud voice.

"Mom, it fits, and besides, this is all they had."

"It's too small."

"Mom, I like it." Let it go, I tell myself. I know if it were a size bigger, she would just say it is too big. This is what she always does.

"It is too small," she says again in a raised voice.

For once, I manage to hold my tongue and not take it personally.

I like this outfit! I think stubbornly. *Yes, the lady in red, that's me.*

~~~~~~~~~~

One week later, I am at the Desert Hot Springs with my parents. I like going here, with the mineral baths and the heat. I was born under the sun in Israel. My body loves warmth.

There are many Hungarians here at this time, and my mom has found a few groups of people who get together to play cards. My dad loves chess but not cards. He only ever plays because of my mom. Today, Mom is taking a nap, so Dad and I are by the pool.

"Iritka, I'll never retire," my dad says.

"What do you mean?"

"If I retired and stayed here, like everyone else, for four months in the winter, I'd go crazy."

"What do you mean?" I repeat.

"I don't like sitting in the sun or by the pool for more than 30 minutes, and I don't really like playing cards. I'd be talking all day about nothing and doing nothing."

"But Dad, don't you want to have more time to travel?"

"I like having projects and meeting and helping people. I like doing something all the time."

"Couldn't you do that and still have more time off? You went back to Israel for a month, remember? You were worried that your business would have problems without you. But it was fine, and you had such a good time. Why is it so hard for you to relax?"

"Iritka, you don't understand."

"Well, explain it to me," I say, but at that moment my mom arrives, and he changes the subject.

~~~~~~~~~

The time passes, and I am suddenly at the airport saying goodbye. I watch as my parents walk away. My mom seems completely in charge as my dad follows her. He is always very protective of her.

As I see them walking away, that pit in my stomach comes up again. *Will I see them again?* I can't believe I keep thinking like this. It makes no logical sense. One of my classmates said, "Fear is false evidence appearing real." She's right, but of course, I still go into my old pattern. Maybe one of these days I'll figure out how not to let it get to me.

When I arrive home, the phone rings. "Irit, this is George. Remember me? I met you at the airport."

"Yeah, that's right. You're from Montréal. My parents just left today. What good timing!"

"Actually, you told me how long they would be here, so I kept track," he says. "Did you have a nice time with your parents?"

"Yeah, what about you?"

"Me, too."

"My parents brought me bagels from Montréal," I say as I go the fridge, take out a poppy seed bagel, and put it in the toaster oven. "They are the best."

"St. Viateur bagels?" George asks.

"How did you know?" I say, surprised. "They're my favorites. There are no bagels here like the ones in Montréal."

"I used to live in a neighborhood near that shop, and I got bagels from there all the time."

"I can totally relate," I say. "I used to live near there, too. I would get the hot bagels on a regular basis. I really miss the bagels and the souvlakis that were nearby."

There is an uncomfortable pause, and then I hear him say, "Where did you go to school?"

"McGill. I majored in Physical Education."

"I went to Loyola. I majored in business. So, how was your program?"

"It was fun. I spent a lot of time in the physical education building even after I graduated. I played a lot of squash, almost two hours every day during the winter months, and in the summers I played tennis in the outdoor courts near my house."

"The court is right across the street from Mount Royal, right? That's where I played as well," he says. "Maybe we can play sometime. I'm a member of a tennis club."

"Actually, I'm recovering from an injury, so tennis is out for a bit," I say.

"Oh," he says, pausing awkwardly. "Well, I was wondering, would you like to have dinner and maybe see a movie this Saturday? I can pick you up, and we can go to dinner near your place. Or, you can come to my neighborhood, and we can go out. Or, I can make dinner," he says.

Now I get nervous. For some reason I am just not sure about him even though it has been fun having someone to talk to about Montréal.

Well, I think, *if I drive and things don't work out, I can leave whenever I want.*

I seem to always choose the wrong guys for relationships. If they are super nice, I find fault with them. If they aren't very nice, I hang around. My last relationship lasted almost two years and ended when I moved to California, but it probably shouldn't have lasted beyond the first month. He was definitely in the 'not so nice' category. Somehow, I made excuse after excuse for the not-nice behavior. I kept thinking I could change him, but I couldn't. When I left Montréal, I decided I would start dating only nice guys with whom I could have fun. This guy seems to fit those criteria even though I'm not completely interested so I figure I should give him a shot.

"How about I come over?"

"Will seven be good?"

"Sounds great. What's your address?"

"1126 Ocean Avenue #8, Santa Monica. I hate to be so quick, but I have to do something for work now. So, I'll see you on Saturday, and we'll catch up."

Catch up? We hardly know each other, I think cynically. *Before today, we had met at the airport once and talked briefly while waiting for our parents.* I hang up the phone and try to shake off my uneasy feeling. *Ok. He's from Montréal. He seems nice. He likes playing sports, and he's in good shape. I'll give him a chance.*

~~~~~~~~~

I sit through classes every day and study groups every night. Finally, it's Saturday afternoon. I drive to George's place, take a deep breath, and ring the bell to #8.

George answers the door. He is about 5'9" and has broad shoulders, which, for whatever reason, is a prerequisite for me. He has curly brown hair and a mustache. I don't remember the mustache. I don't like mustaches. Oh, well.

It feels awkward at the beginning so I accept a glass of chardonnay, the great icebreaker. We talk about Montréal since that is what we have in common while Bob Dylan's, "Mr. Tambourine Man," one of my favorites, is playing in the background.

Next, we head to the kitchen where he is preparing chicken Marsala. "Hope you like mushrooms," he comments.

"I love mushrooms," I say, then in a moment of confusion and jumbled nerves, I think of the double meaning—psychedelic experiences—and add, "The food, that is." There is an awkward pause. I feel flustered so I start helping him set the table to distract myself.

We have Caesar salad and chicken Marsala with wild rice for dinner. He has the music on, setting the tone, and we talk on about nothing very important. After dinner, we go to the movie theatre next to his house and watch *An Officer and a Gentleman*. As we watch the movie, he puts his arm around my shoulders. My brain goes into overdrive. This is our first date. I should be thrilled, but I'm not.

"How about coffee or a liqueur at my place before you leave? I know it is almost an hour drive," he offers as we exit the theater.

"Nah. I think I'll head home. I'm tired."

"But it's late. Why don't you stay the night? It is a long way home," he says.

"I can't." *That would be a mistake*, the little voice inside my head tells me.

"How about getting together next week?" he asks.

"I'll call you."

I get onto the freeway, replaying the evening in my head. He is a nice guy, but the x factor is missing. Everything should flow, but it doesn't. I don't trust him, but he didn't do anything to make me feel that way. It's just something in my gut. Well, maybe I don't have to rationalize it. Just honor it. Maybe I'm progressing.

Suddenly, I snap back to reality as I realize that I have taken the wrong exit. I'm in the worst possible neighborhood in LA: Watts. Crime and drug dealing are the norm here. Even in the daytime, it is dangerous to be alone here, and now it is almost 1:00 a.m. In a flash, fear takes over. I lock the doors of my car and speed through a yellow light trying to get back to the highway as quickly as possible.

Just my luck, the light turns red when I am in the middle of the intersection, and I see a police car behind me turn on its lights. I'm so panicked about being in this area that this is the first time in my life I have been happy to see a cop car turn on its lights behind me.

I pull over, and the officer gets out of his car. He is maybe 6'1" and weighs 225 pounds. He comes over, and the first thing I notice is his handlebar mustache. I really don't like moustaches. Before he can even speak, I blurt out, "I'm so excited to see you. I'm lost. I live in Downey. I go to physical therapy school there, and I took the wrong exit. How do I get back?"

He gives me a disapproving look and says, "You ran a red light, and besides, what would a single white woman be doing in this part of town if she didn't have something else in mind?"

His harsh tone cuts through me, putting me on edge. As he towers over me, I notice the gun strapped onto his right hip. The pit in my stomach, which had been alleviated for a brief moment by the prospect of police help, comes back. "Officer, I'm lost. I took the wrong exit. Can you help me by directing me back to my exit?"

"Do you have any drugs?"

"No! I'm just in physical therapy school. I don't even smoke." I can't believe this. How can he possibly think that about me?

"Sure, lady," he says.

Oh no. He is one of the bad cops, the ones you see on TV all the time, I think. I can see tomorrow's headline in the paper: *Canadian Physical Therapy Student's Body Found in Watts, LA. It does not appear to be drug related.*

"Get out of the car now, and give me your driver's license."

"No," I say, fear now escalating inside of me. I look at the officer. His eye sockets are deep and dark, with beady eyes peering out at me, making me feel queasy. He is definitely one of those corrupt officers.

"Get out of the car," he repeats. He has a smug look on his face, with a half-smile that looks arrogant and dangerous. He seems to be enjoying my fear.

I can't get out of my car. I know that for sure. It will be my demise. Once again, headlines flash before my eyes: *Canadian Physical Therapy Student Found in Watts...*

"Here is my driver's license," I say, "but I'm not getting out of the car." My leg starts shaking uncontrollably.

"Do you have drugs on you?" He repeats, peering into my back seat.

I notice his gun again, but I try to keep calm as I respond, "No. I'm lost. Why would I be in this part of LA of my own volition? I'm lost."

"Get out of the car. That is an order."

I start to panic as I see new headlines for the paper: *Canadian Girl Raped and Killed Not Far from Home.*

"I'm not getting out of my car. There is no reason to. I didn't do anything wrong to warrant getting out of my car. I'm in the wrong place. I didn't come here intentionally." My hands are now shaking, and my whole body is on alert.

"Yeah, sure lady, we get that all the time. You may not look like the type, but no one in their right mind would be here at almost 1 a.m."

"That's right. I took the wrong turn."

"Lady, get out of the car, now, or I'll arrest you and take you to the police station."

Yeah, right, I think. I know that as soon as I get out of the car, my fate will be sealed. I will be the talk of all the Montréal papers: *She was a Jewish Physical Therapy student in Downey...*

My brain is swirling as I try to figure out what to do. I suddenly notice that there is another police officer in the car, and I hear myself say, "I want to talk to your partner in the car."

The officer looks at me for a second and says, "Fine."

The younger officer gets out of the car and comes to my door. I see his name on his uniform, Officer Craig. He is maybe 5'10' and well built. He looks like he runs every day. In complete contrast to the first officer, he is young and has a baby face. He's probably new to the job, less corrupt. He looks at me curiously but doesn't seem angry or hostile. He is probably the guy that plays "the good cop."

"I'm sorry, but we need you to get out of your car. We want to search it."

"I didn't do anything wrong," I say with conviction.

He looks at me almost apologetically and says, "I'm sorry, but you *will* have to get out of your car."

At least, his voice is kinder.

"Where I come from," I hear myself saying, "they don't do things like that."

"Where are you from?"

"Montréal, Québec. It's part of Canada."

"So, you speak French?"

"Yeah, I speak a few languages."

"Which ones?"

I am about to say Hebrew, but then I think better of it. I just know that it might get me in further trouble. Instead, I say, "Hungarian."

"Hungarian?" the officer says. "My dad is from Hungary."

"Really?" I immediately sigh and feel more at ease. "Do you speak Hungarian?"

"No, my dad never taught me."

"That's too bad," I say, trying to sway the conversation.

"It is important you get out of the car," he says kindly.

I get out of the car and stand there, facing the two officers. There is something scary about this scene. If something goes wrong, I know how completely defenseless I am here. It's bizarre to think that in the late 1930s through the mid-1940s, a police officer in Europe could stop someone just to see if they were Jewish. It was against the law for Jews to be in parks, public swimming pools, movie theatres, or even on public transportation. They could be beaten and jailed if caught. It was against the law for the Jews to be human. How did my parents survive this kind of abuse day in and day out? They were constantly in this state of fear. They were on alert every second, always having to watch their backs. I could never understand those types of circumstances. Maybe my dad is right, and I don't understand.

After they search the car and run a check on my driver's license, I am told, "You have no record. You are free to go."

I sigh with relief. "How do I get out of this forsaken place?"

"Take a right at the next light. Go two lights, and you will see the sign for the freeway; then, you will see the sign for Downey."

"Thank you," I say to the Hungarian officer. I don't even look at the other.

I take a shower to cleanse the day away and fall into a deep sleep. The next morning, I wake up at 9 a.m. and head off to Dunkin' Donuts for my coffee fix. I walk into the place and freeze. The tyrant police officer is there, eating a chocolate donut and taking a sip of his coffee. Before I can stop myself, I walk toward him and say, "I told you I live here." He just looks at me with a blank face as I walk to the counter.

"Wendy, a large coffee, please," I say.

As I walk out of the shop, sipping my coffee, I realize how lucky I am to be free.

~~~~~~~~~

Several months later, I once again find myself at LAX. This time I am flying to visit my parents. I am going to visit home for ten days. It will be nice just to chill, hang out with friends, eat my mom's yummy food, spend time with my dad, and maybe learn more about his past. After this trip, my final 3-month rotation will start. I am doing my rotation at Parmer. I am one of the two lucky students at USC to get accepted into their 3-month training program. It will be my first exposure to the Parmer system.

This program is world renowned so physical therapists from all over the world apply. The students who are accepted all live in the dorms together so it should be fun. The program will give us advanced training for working with neurological patients. We will learn Proprioceptive Neuromuscular Facilitation techniques, also known as PNF techniques. Then, in January, I'll take my state boards so I can become a licensed physical therapist.

I'm still not sure what my career plans are after I get licensed, but I have decided to take some time to come back to Montréal afterward. I'll have to figure out my next step there.

I try to strike up a conversation with the person beside me on the flight from LAX to Montréal, but he is reading and answers my questions with monosyllabic words. I leaf through the plane magazines and, probably for the first time in my life, read three newspapers cover to cover. The plane finally lands, and I disembark at Dorval airport.

I love this airport. It is so clean. In fact, the whole city is very clean compared to LA. I really do love it here. *Bienvenue*, the sign says to me, well, to me and everyone else who goes through the gate. It feels comforting. *Bienvenue*, the French word for *welcome*.

I see my dad, in his grey cap, checkered shirt, grey pullover, and black pants, waiting for me. I wave.

"Iritka, I'm so happy to see you. How was your flight?"

I love the way he says my name every time we first say hello. The tone of it makes me feel so warm and welcome. I have always felt that way. "The flight was fine."

"How are you?"

I smirk at him as I say, "I'm better," for the hundredth time. We both laugh.

"You must be hungry. Your mother has made food for you."

We get home, and my dad parks his silver Malibu.

"Iritka, you're going to be surprised. Your mother is much better now. She doesn't scream anymore. She doesn't get nervous like before."

I look at my dad, and he has that mischievous smile on his face.

"Okay, Dad, what aren't you telling me?" I ask.

"Now that I take heart medication for the hole they found in my heart, your mom is afraid to scream because she thinks it will make me sick."

I laugh. My dad uses every opportunity to find the positive in things.

A couple of months ago, his doctors had discovered a hole in his heart that they said was from birth. He has had dreams where he couldn't breathe since before I can remember, and he always thought it was from the war. Now the doctors tell him it is from his condition. He never had this problem before the war though so he is sure it is probably a combination of both the trauma of the war and his condition from birth.

"I'm happy they figured it out," I say.

"Iritka," my dad says, taking a deep breath. "Your mom loves you very much, but she doesn't know how to show it. Don't get upset with her. She doesn't mean it. It's from her past. Just ignore it."

I sigh. I have heard those three words my whole life. *Okay, Irit,* I tell myself. *Be open to it. Maybe he is right.*

"Yeah," I say, "OK. I'll try." I get out of the car, and we walk upstairs.

"Hi, Mom," I say.

"Hi," she says. "How was your flight?"

"Good. Glad to be here. I'm starving."

"Do you want chicken *paprikash*? I made it today."

"That sounds great," I say, keeping things light.

I open the fridge and see all that my mom has prepared. My favorite, carp with jelly, is in the fridge. She buys the carp at her favorite fish market because she trusts the carp will be good. The storeowners kibitz with her and are good to her. They never steer her wrong with the fish they choose for her. Her preparation for this dish takes over an hour. I eat this first before moving on to the paprikash, and then, of course, I can't resist the walnut and prune *rugelach* that I know also took my mother hours to prepare.

We spend the night watching television together. As I sit in the brown rocker, I look over at my dad and mom sitting on the couch. We're watching *Magnum P.I.*, one of their favorite shows, and my dad has his arm around my mother's shoulders. They seem happy, sitting there next to each other. I don't remember seeing demonstrations of affection like this when I was growing up, but I probably just wasn't paying attention. Somehow, now, it feels different. It feels nice.

I wish I could ask Edna if she remembers my parents being like this when we were younger, but she isn't here. My sister was going to come visit, but she had to cancel at the last minute because one of her boys got sick. She lives a 6-hour drive away from here, in Clarks Summit, Pennsylvania. My nephews Ryan, Marc, and Mike are now 12, 9 and 6 years old. I miss seeing them. They always make me laugh.

I look back at my parents again and smile. I think back to the times we watched TV together when I was growing up. When I was 10 or 11, we all watched the Montréal Canadiens play hockey. I knew the names and numbers of all the players, and whenever they scored, I would get so excited I would kiss the TV, especially if it was Jean Beliveau or Boom Boom Geoffrion who scored. Those were my two favorite players. When the Canadiens fell behind, my dad would get so nervous that he would either leave the room, or worse, shut the TV off. Now I do the same thing. I'm a fickle sports fan. If my team is losing, I get nervous and just turn off the game.

~~~~~~~~~~

I borrow my dad's car the next morning so I can go to my most favorite sanctuary in the world, the mountain that gave Montréal its name. September is my favorite time of the year in Montréal. The foliage is in full bloom. The maple trees blaze with crimson, orange, and yellow. That is what I miss most in California. When I hear people admire the fall foliage there, I know they have never been to the East Coast in the fall.

In 1535, Jacques Cartier, a navigator and explorer from France, climbed to the top of this mountain and called it *"un mont réal,"* a royal mountain. I guess that means we Montréalers are "royal people."

There have been two lion statues standing guard at the base of the mountain since before I can remember. A statue of George Etienne Cartier, the Minister of Defense, stands between them, though as far as I am concerned, the lions are the main attraction.

When I was little, my dad would take my sister and me ice skating at Beaver Lake, and en route, we would pass the lions. I would always wave and imagine that they responded.

When I was teaching, I lived on St. Urbain, which was only about ten minutes from the lion statues. I would always start my morning run at the statues, then run to Beaver Lake and back, about five miles. I always imagined that the lions wished me well before I took off jogging.

I also remember coming here a few weeks before I left for Prague all those years ago. I was wearing bright red shorts that felt like silk and my

Lemoyne School t-shirt, and I just flew. I went eleven miles, and it felt like I didn't even break a sweat. Now, after my accident, running is not an option. I can't remember the last time I ran even a mile.

I look up at the lion statues. That's the feeling I want to recapture. I want to feel the wind in my face as I fly forward effortlessly. Right now, my knees hurt, my back hurts, and my neck hurts; everything hurts, but I take heart that the pain is nowhere near as bad as when I first was injured. One day, I know I will run again. I take a deep breath and start to walk forward, looking at the trees and their solid branches. If the trees could talk, I wonder what words of wisdom they would give me.

This mountain was bought by the city in 1876, and the park was designed by an architect named Frederick Law Olmstead. He was also the architect behind Central Park in New York. The mountain has 250 acres of meadow and forest. Cars are not allowed, only horses and bicycles. Every once in a while, as you hike through the beautiful scenery, you will see a mounted police officer on a horse.

There are two lookouts on the mountain with a spectacular view of the St. Lawrence River and the city. These lookouts are great for romantic dates. I've been to them many times throughout the years. Being at the mountain is like being in the midst of nature and in the heart of the city at the same time.

The mountain has always been my go-to place to clear my head. If I were upset with anyone or if thoughts and worries were going non-stop in my head, I would come to the mountain, and as soon as I started to run, all my thoughts and worries would disappear. I would re-capture that same feeling I had when I was nine years old, looking at the stars from the foyer of my apartment on Dupuis.

Yes, running on the mountain makes me feel alive and unstoppable. I feel like taking off and sprinting, but then I realize that I can't yet. *One day, I will run again*, I think to myself again. After about two hours of peaceful surroundings, I go back to my dad's office, and we head home.

When we get home, my mom is still out visiting her friend, Mrs. Gottlieb, who lives about a 10-minute walk away. Her husband owns a jewelry store, and my dad has bought my mom many pieces of jewelry from him through the years. Mr. Gottlieb is also a client of my dad's. My mom and Mrs. Gottlieb became friends when her son and my sister were in the same high school class. They both speak Hungarian and survived the camps, which created an instant bond.

Dad and I sit in the living room. "Iritka, what will you do with the Chesterfield that Ersie gave you when you move to the bay area at the end of the month?" he asks.

"One of my neighbors is going to buy it."

"Too bad you can't keep it."

"I know. It is so comfortable and cozy. So, is that one just like the Chesterfield you had in Israel?" I ask playfully.

My dad looks at me with his great smile but says nothing.

"Were you telling me the truth about that Chesterfield all these years?" I say. "You were in Bratislava, meeting up with everyone who had the same goal as you, to go to Israel as Israeli immigrants and start a new life after the war. Then, you went up to a pretty woman you hardly knew, and you said … What did you say again?" This story always blows me away so it is fun for me to ask.

My dad takes the bait and says, "I said to her, 'If you have Chesterfield, I marry you.'" My dad taps his fingers on his chair and looks at the huge needlepoint my mom made for him, smiling.

"Did you say that the first day you met her?" I ask, grinning from ear to ear.

"No, maybe the third, but what I didn't tell her was that I always knew she had a Chesterfield."

"Why did it matter so much if she had a Chesterfield?" I ask as I stand up to get myself some water.

"Can you get me club soda?" my dad asks. I rush to get together the drinks and return, sitting on the edge of my seat.

"So, Dad, why Chesterfields?"

"It was so when we got to Israel, we'd have a bed." He smiles, and I see a twinkle in his eye.

"How long before you got married?"

"Maybe four months."

"I guess after the war, people married quickly."

My dad puts his hand on his chin and chuckles. "Well, if you count when I met her the first time, then we knew each other long time. When I was maybe 22, I went to visit my auntie in the hospital, and in the bed next to hers, there was this beautiful girl. She was only sixteen, and she had to go to the hospital because of a skin graft on her hand. She had gotten a horrible burn when she was little.

"After I met her, I made a point to visit my auntie every day and then talk to the girl in the next bed. Her family lived far away from the hospital so she didn't ever have visitors. I felt sorry for her that she was so lonely. Whenever she saw me, she would joke around, and I could tell she liked having someone to talk to. I could tell she didn't like to be alone.

"When my auntie died, I still came to visit her. One day, I tried to kiss her, and she slapped me. I never went back. After your sister was born, your mother told me the story of when she was in the hospital and a boy tried to kiss her so she slapped him. We realized then and there that it was me."

"You probably waited until you got married to even try to kiss her the second time around, right? Things are so different today. You wouldn't understand how dating works. Slapping a guy just for trying to kiss you is just not what happens these days."

My dad pauses, then looks at me and says, "Things were no different then than they are now." He grins. "Do you really think we waited until we got married?"

I stop in my tracks. "Do you mean you and Mom...?"

"Things are no different today. We didn't wait for anything."

I think back to my childhood and how my mom screamed and cursed at me in Hungarian when she caught me kissing my boyfriend Donnie. Growing up, sex was not something ever to be discussed or even thought about. I can't believe that my mom would ever have done anything out of wedlock the way she went on when I was younger. That is too funny.

"Iritka, you okay?"

"I'm just surprised. I'm probably in shock," I start laughing. I wish I would have known this years ago. I never would have gotten so upset at all the things she said to me. My sister had told me time and again, "don't take things so literally and personally with Mom." I guess she was right.

Just then, my mom walks in, and I look at her. I can't bring myself to say anything, or I know I might just crack up.

"Iritka, I have to go back to work," my dad says. "I'll see you later."

I just nod, and try to suppress my huge smile as I strike up a conversation with my mom.

~~~~~~~~~

I take some time to visit my friends while I'm home, but I always make sure to have my meals at home. Otherwise, my mom would be disappointed and upset with me.

There is so much about my parents I don't understand. My mom never speaks about her past, and my father is pretty open about his, but there is a darkness behind both of them that is almost too scary for me to broach. I've probably read all the books ever written about the holocaust. I know that there is much more to the story of my dad's suffering than he's ever shared. I'm nervous about opening those floodgates. The graphic details in the books defy anything that I can relate to. I always thought it was amazing and exciting when I was little, but the more I learn, the more incredible the power of the human spirit to endure and overcome becomes to me.

On my fifth night home, Beth, my cousin, comes over after dinner, and we head off to Old Montréal. In 1642, Paul de Chomedy, Sieur de Maisoneuve, and his 53 men settled in what today is called Old Montréal. With the view of the St. Lawrence River, the spectacular lighting at night, the narrow cobblestone streets, the restaurants and cafes everywhere with outdoor seating, and the many street performers and artisans, it feels like we are in Europe.

We walk around. I love the *joie de vivre* that I feel around me every day in Montréal. It is always the same.

After a couple of hours, we start the 30-minute drive home. I'm glad Beth is driving because at night I love being a passenger and watching everything as it passes by me. I can't help but think how much has changed in my city in the past ten years, and who knows what changes the future will hold.

~~~~~~~~~~

"I need to go to my office and get something. Do you want to come with me?" my dad asks the next morning.

"Sure." I always like spending time with my dad. He is always so calm. In all my years, I have never heard my dad raise his voice. The few times I have seen him angry, he has just abruptly left the house, gone for a drive, and returned calm again. I don't know how he does it. Maybe it's one of his secrets to good blood, something I will hopefully better understand when I get to learn more of his past.

We get in the car and head to the office.

"You know it was very good that I taught your mother to drive," he says as we pull out of the driveway.

"I know. I was amazed that she was able to get her license and pass her test." When we were growing up, the government used to offer English classes to immigrants when English was still an official language, but my mom always refused to go. She didn't want anyone to know she couldn't read or write well, and my dad never had the time to go to school.

I remember I used to say, "Mom, you're not supposed to know how to read and write English when you start. That's why they have the school." She still wouldn't go. Somehow, over the years, she did learn to read newspapers though, and I guess she learned to write well enough to pass her driver's test.

We get to the office, and I get my usual empanada while Dad heads upstairs. He wants to pick up supplies.

Thirty minutes later, we are back home. My dad finds a spot across the street from their duplex, takes the key out of the ignition, and turns to face me.

"Iritka, what do you think will happen to your mother when I die?"

"Dad!" I say, shaken. My mind begins to spin. *Where is this coming from? What is going on? You've never talked like this before. You've never asked me such a serious question.* Dread floods my body. *I don't want to hear this.* Not a word comes out of my mouth.

"Iritka, I'm afraid that when I die, your mother will fall apart. That is why I bought this duplex and sold half of it to Uncle Arnold. That way, she will at least be with family when I am gone."

I feel like someone just punched me in the chest and took my breath away.

"Dad," I say, doing everything in my power to change the subject. "I've got so many health problems, and my body hurts all the time. I'll die before you do."

"Iritka, don't talk like that. The worst fate would be to have my children die before me." My dad pauses, puts his hand on his chin, and starts again. "Iritka, do you think your mom will be okay?"

"Dad, don't talk like this," I say, starting to get angry.

"Your mother depends on me. I do everything for her. I even go shopping with her for her clothes. She doesn't like to do anything without me."

"Dad, you're not going to die, so please don't talk like this."

"I'm not afraid to die."

I look over at him. He looks so calm and confident. "But Dad..."

"Irit, I'm not afraid to die."

I stare at him. My insides feel like they are being ripped apart. I want to put my hands over my ears and pretend this is not happening. Instead, I try to change the subject. It's the only thing I can think to do.

"Dad, all your life you experienced so much hardship, but you still have a twinkle in your eye. I never hear you complaining about your life."

My dad shifts in his seat, and with that ever-present twinkle in his eyes, says, "Iritka, every day that I am free, I am happy."

"But Dad, after the war, you moved to Israel. Weren't you scared in Israel, with the Arabs wanting to kill all of you because you were Israeli settlers and everyone in the *moshav* [cooperative agricultural community] having to take turns standing guard at night in case they tried?"

"Iritka, I was just happy that I had a home and that I had a family. We lived in a community so we were never alone. I was free to get up when I wanted, to drink water when I wanted, and to eat a meal when I wanted."

"But Dad, how come you don't complain about your life? You wanted to be a doctor, but you couldn't go to school because of the war. You wanted to be in textiles in Montréal, but Uncle Frank lied and told everyone you were bad so no one would hire you. You ended up becoming a plumber, who, even when it was a 20 below wind chill factor in the middle of the night, would have to get dressed and go help people with frozen pipes. I never heard you complain, and that is so amazing."

"When I was in the lager, and then in Russia..." He pauses, thinking about his experiences in the Hungarian forced labor camp, and I watch his facial expression change as a dark sadness takes over him, "Every day, every second was spent finding a way to live. Every day there was something new. It was so cold, and we had little food. Every day there was some new punishment. I watched many people during my time there. Many gave up. I knew when they had broken. I could see it in their eyes."

"Why did you go to Israel after the war?" I ask.

"When I got home to Košice, I told everyone that communism was terrible and we had to leave. Israel was the only place that would have us. If we moved to a place other than Israel and weren't sponsored, we would be put in detainment camps. Then, I would have been a prisoner again, waiting to be free. I couldn't stay in Czechoslovakia because I would never be free in a communist country. I felt at home in Kefar Achim, our little town in Israel. The president, David Ben Gurion, came to our *moshav*, and he was friends with all of us."

"He was the president, and he was your friend?"

"We were all the same. We were men and women trying to make our land our home. Israel was our new home, and we knew that as long as we were in Israel, no one could ever do to us Jews what they did in the war. Although there were many problems with the Arabs, because they did not want us to have our land, I was happy and free."

"Are you sorry that you left Israel?"

"When we were in Israel, your mother was lonesome for her family. She wanted to tell everyone, 'Look, I'm married and have two beautiful little children,' So, when your grandmother and Edith offered to sponsor us on our trip to Montréal, I felt we had to come.

"We got to Montréal in the middle of February, and there was a big snowstorm the night we arrived. We were all sleeping in one room in Frank and Edith's house, but that only lasted for about five hours. At 8 p.m., Frank came into the room and woke us, saying, 'Your children are sick, and they have a fever.'"

My dad's face tenses. "You were only three years old."

He closes his fist and takes a breath to relax before continuing, "Frank said, 'I don't want my three children to get sick. There is a room available for rent in someone's home ten blocks away. I will get a cab for you, and I will pay the first week's rent.'"

They stayed there for a month. I look at my dad with sympathy. I had heard that Frank had told everyone not to hire my dad in the textile business because he was not reliable. I also knew he didn't let us stay with him, but I had never realized Frank made us leave the very day we arrived. Somehow, even though I was too little to remember this happening, it seems even crueler that it happened the day we arrived.

"When this happened," my dad puckers his lips, and the muscles in his cheek contract, "it killed something inside of your mother." I can see his whole body tighten as he says this.

"So, why didn't you just stop talking to Frank?"

"Because Edith and your mom were sisters, and your bubby was their mother. We moved to Montréal just to be near them. Your mom so missed her family, and those two were always loving toward us. It was just that Edith married Frank, and he was not a good person. It was his decision to make us leave, not theirs. I couldn't have your mom not talk to her family because of that. It would have killed her."

"What about you?"

He pauses. Once again I notice the tightness in his face. "It was hard for me. Every time I looked at him, I was angry, not for myself, but for how it hurt your mother. I could never understand how he did what he did. Many times, I did consider not speaking to him, but when I imagined what it would be like not to talk to my own sister, Ersie, ever again, I knew I couldn't do that to your mother."

"So," I say, driving my point home, "with all that happened to you, how can you still love life? I know you do. I see it in your eyes."

"Iritka, there is always something good that can come from bad. Positivity is like a plant that we need to keep watering. It starts as a seed, and we have to water it every day. One day, it turns into a flower, and then it just keeps growing. The problem is, people always stop watering and nourishing their plant. They give up too quickly. In everything, there is a positive."

Yes, I think to myself. *Focus on the positive, and don't worry about things you don't have control over.*

"Sometimes it takes people a hundred years to understand."

"What do you mean by that?"

"Iritka, everything is interconnected. What happens now can affect future generations. One day you will understand."

"So, how was the war positive?"

"Every day, I focused on how I could help the other prisoners. I knew as long as I could help others I would be okay. Whenever I could comfort someone or help someone when they were sick, I felt better. I knew I had a purpose, and whenever I was able to, I would give a little of myself to others even if it was just through words of hope.

"I also thought of Ersie and her smile every day. That is what helped me survive. There is always something positive to think of and do in bad circumstances. We just have to look for it. We have to keep looking and never stop. There is much we have no control over, but we can make a difference through how we react to the things around us, the people around us."

I look at my dad and think of the story I always loved hearing growing up. The story of how he played chess with a Russian officer. He won and got a little extra food for his men even though there was too little food for the Russian officers themselves. He made it so his men didn't have to go outside where it was freezing and most of the prisoners would not have made it. *That is my dad in a nutshell,* I think to myself, *always thinking of others, always wanting to help others, always finding a way, and never giving up.*

"What will happen to your mother when I die?" my dad says again.

I can't handle this anymore. I cross my legs and fight the urge to put both hands over my ears. My dad leans towards me, and I can feel tears running down my face.

"I don't know," I finally respond in a shaky voice. "What will happen to me?"

"Oh, you'll be fine," he says calmly, "but what will happen to your mother?"

I want to scream at the top of my lungs, *PLEASE STOP THIS.* My body aches from head to toe now. "Dad," I say, "you'll outlive all of us. I don't want to hear this." I don't know what brought this on. I don't want to. I can't handle this. I can't ask. I want this feeling to go away. *Please tell me this is a bad dream.*

Intuitively, I know where this is going. I also know that I cannot handle it. Dad is not going to let me walk away from death any more than he would let himself walk away from life.

Tears are running down my face, and my dad just looks at me for a long time with one of the most loving, accepting, and calm looks I have seen on the face of this larger-than-life father of mine as if he is trying to will me to his level of comprehension, love, and acceptance. Once again, he says:

"Iritka, I'm not afraid to die."

9

1984

As we express our gratitude, we must never forget that the highest appreciation is not to utter words, but to live by them.
- John F. Kennedy

I arrive at the dormitory at the hospital. It is a one-story, long, thin, beige building. I was told before I arrived that there would be 18 physical therapists from all over the world in the dorm for the next three months, six of whom had already been here for three months. I walk in, and the second door to my right is my room, number 3. I put all my belongings in the drawers and closet, and there is a knock on the door.

"Hi, I'm Petra. I'm in the room next to you."

"Great. I'm Irit."

"Where are you from?" Petra asks.

"Originally, Israel, then Montréal, and now California. What about you?"

"I'm from Germany. I've been here for three months. I'll be here another three months, too. It's been a lot of fun so far."

"You have an accent, but it doesn't seem like you're from Germany. Where did you learn English?"

"We studied English in school, but I lived in Ireland for two years so I confuse people with my different accent. No one can figure out exactly where I'm from."

"It's cool that you speak two languages fluently. That's common in Montréal but not in California. So, what do I need to know about the dorms?"

"If you would like, I can give you a tour of the place," Petra says.

"Sure."

"I'll start by showing you the kitchen," Petra says.

We walk through the double doors; the kitchen is huge. There are three fridges, two rectangular tables, and one round table.

"You will have half a shelf in the fridge and a shelf in the pantry. We have communal stuff. Here is the kitty, the box we put money into for communal food each week. As you can see, there is plenty of prep space for cooking. We eat all our meals here."

We walk out of the kitchen and pass the pay phone. To our right is a huge living room with a television.

"Let's go outside," Petra says. "I'll show you the grounds."

As we take a walking tour of the grounds, Petra tells me a little about the program.

"For starters, Claire is the director. She is the one in charge of the program. We all try to be on her good side. She is a little taller than you and always wears blue. She has short, grey, curly hair, and she wears maybe a size twelve."

"Yeah," I say. "We were told that Claire is the liaison between the school and the students. She is the one I have to call if I can't come to class or if there are any problems."

"You'll meet her tomorrow when you start class. She is well organized and runs the program well. We're all grateful for that, but with her, you never know where you stand. One day she's friendly, and the next day she's the exact opposite."

"So, the less contact the better," I venture.

"Exactly," Petra says.

The next day, 12 of us from all parts of the globe start our 3-month rotation. We begin every weekday in the classroom, learning proprioceptor neuromuscular facilitation techniques. The popular name for that is PNF. We also spend time every day seeing patients. The patients we see are neurologically impaired, recovering from strokes or other neurological problems. They live in the hospital for three months for rehabilitation and receive treatment daily. It is nice to see that the techniques we learn and use can really help patients with their gait, balance, flexibility, strength, and movement. The patients I have been given aren't too heavy, and I'm grateful because the work is physically demanding.

~~~~~~~~~~~~~

When the first weekend arrives, we head off to the Bay Area to explore, with Fisherman's wharf and its famous clam chowder in bread bowls a "must" first stop. We take a cable car just for the experience, and as we ride, we stand, hanging out of the car and watching as other cars and people go by. I keep wondering what would happen if I accidently were to fall out of the cable car, so I grip the rail tightly.

The next weekend at 4 a.m., Petra, Maya, Joy, and I leave the dorms and head to Mount Tam to watch the sun rise. We park and begin our trek. After 45 minutes, we find a spot and wait for the sun to peak its head up and say hello. Petra and Maya have taken a class on how to get what you want in your life, so as we wait, we create wish lists. Most of the items on our lists are probably the same: meeting our soul mates, health, happiness and enough money to do whatever we want. I sigh happily as I finish writing mine. Something about being close to nature makes me feel like anything I ask for will be received. I can tell everyone else feels the same.

~~~~~~~~~~~~~

Two months pass by with weekend treks to different regions in the Bay area. Some weekends we just hang out, reading, listening to music, and connecting with the different therapists. I will have to go back to USC in a couple of weeks to present my oral thesis with Debbie, and then, after I finish this PNF rotation, I will graduate.

"Hi, Dad. How are you doing?" I ask. I always love calling my dad. We speak 2-3 times a week, and many times it's just for a few minutes, just to touch base.

"Iritka! I'm so glad you called. I was just thinking I wanted to call you. It's cold here in Montréal. It's minus five today."

"It's 70 degrees here. You should come visit," I suggest.

"Iritka, I saw this bracelet in Mr. Gottlieb's jewelry store today. It has three types of gold: white, yellow and rose. It changes colors depending on what kind of light it is in, so it looks different during the day than it does at night. I knew when I saw it that it would be perfect for you. I want to send it to you. It's for your birthday."

"That's great, but it's not even December yet. My birthday is in July. I can wait."

"I know, but I want to send it to you now. What's your address?"

"I'll be finished in a little over a month, and I'm coming straight home. So, I'll get it then," I say, confused by his persistence.

"But I want to send it to you. It is beautiful, and I want you to wear it soon."

"Dad, it's November 29th. It doesn't make sense to send it. I'll be home in about a month."

"But I want you to have it now."

I guess he is like me. When he gets really excited about something he wants to share it pronto, but my dad is usually much more patient than I am.

"Dad, I'll wait till I see you. Anyway, I have to go. We're having Indian food for dinner tonight at the dorm. One of the physical therapists is from Bombay, and she said she would introduce us to real Indian cuisine. Next week is my turn to cook. I'm cooking Hungarian."

"I'll send you the bracelet."

"Dad, I can wait. Thanks for the bracelet. I'll call you this weekend."

"Iritka, I love you," he says.

"I love you, too; 'bye, Dad." I hang up the phone. Something feels odd about that conversation, but I let it go. I decide to touch base with him over the weekend when I have more time to talk.

~~~~~~~~~~~~~

I love the program I'm in, but it is challenging on my body. Even when we are in the classroom, we have to practice, so it's hard work physically. Many of the techniques require us to provide resistance for the patients, and some of these patients are heavy.

I'm always happy for the weekends because I get a break from the hard physical work. Hiking seems to help me, but I don't even carry a knapsack anymore because they're too heavy. Instead, I just take a small water bottle. One of my new friends in the program calls me a "wuss," an American term I'd never heard before. For some reason I find it funny, maybe because I know it is so far from the truth.

My eyes open. It's 6:35 am on Sunday, December 2, a day off for me. *Yes, another day off from work,* I think happily.

I get dressed and walk about 200 feet down the corridor through the double doors to the kitchen. Shaila is sitting there, eating her breakfast. Shaila is our Bombay representative, as she often proudly proclaims. She is slim, maybe 5'8", and all legs, with short, almost black hair. She always wears huge, gold-rimmed glasses that she is blind without. California is the first place she's ever traveled outside her country. In fact, she had never been on a plane before coming to California.

"Hi, Shaila. You're up early." I grab some coffee and sit next to her. "What are you up to today?"

"I'm getting my second bicycle lesson from Maya and Petra. I can't wait to tell my friends back home."

"How did you get the bike?"

"One of the staff physical therapists at the hospital got a new bicycle last week, and when I told her I had never ridden a bicycle, she gave me her old one. I feel so lucky," she says with an enthusiasm that is contagious.

I flash back to when I was ten. My dad came home at 7:30 one evening and told me to come out to the foyer. There was a surprise waiting for me: the coolest blue bicycle ever. The bike was as old as I, but I didn't care because, to me, it was new. It had been a gift from one of my dad's customers.

The next morning, I went out early and practiced in the parking lot of two apartment buildings that stretched approximately a block. I didn't want any help, so I practiced by myself. In the afternoon, I went out again to practice. That evening, when my dad came home, I summoned my family and showed off to everyone. The day before had been the first time I was ever on a bike, and now I was riding by myself. I felt on top of the world. This was the best present ever.

"How did you like my Indian dinner?" Shaila asks, breaking me out of my reverie.

"I loved it. Besides the delicious food, I loved how you taught me, through food, about the Indian culture. I especially loved eating with my hands. Permission—finally!—to eat with my hands and be praised for it. I loved taking the food with my right hand, and it was the first time I had Dahl. Oh, and I loved the Indian bread, the rotie. Good thing I'm not a lefty. Do people do things reversed if they are left-hand dominant?"

"No, you eat only with your right hand. The left hand is not the clean one, so if you're left-handed, you learn to use your right hand," Shaila says. "It is your turn this coming Thursday, right? Are you going to make an Israeli dish?"

"No, I'll go Hungarian and make chicken paprikash and nockerly, which are basically dumplings. It's so easy to prepare, and it's delicious. For dessert, I'm going to make my famous chocolate flourless nut roll cake with walnuts."

All of this talk about food makes me hungry, so I go to the fridge, take out some strawberries, blueberries, and yogurt, and mix them together at the table. "Would you like some?" I offer.

"No, thanks. So, tell me more about the cake," she says.

"Oh, it's actually my mom's recipe from Czechoslovakia. This chocolate cake is so good, the students I used to teach actually called it 'chocolate decadence.'"

I leaf through the Sunday times until I reach the sports section. It is my favorite part of the newspaper because the worst news you can hear in it is that a team lost.

"Do you like to bake?" Shaila asks.

"Not really. I developed a reputation as a phenom baker with my students, but I never told them that was the only cake I knew how to make."

Petra walks into the kitchen. She has become a good friend. "We have the Jewish-German connection," I would say to my dad, and he would laugh—Petra, with her ingrained guilt for being German because of what her people did before she was born, and me, with the unexplainable need to forgive those who were not even a part of it.

To me, people fall into three categories: those who help others, those who stand by, and those who do harm. Is Petra the person who, during the war, would have risked her life to save the Jews? Or maybe she would have been too afraid to risk her life to help? Even if she was too afraid, I am sure she would not have turned in Jews who were in hiding. She, for sure, would not have been one of those vicious ones, the ones who would kill for pleasure.

"Petra, after my dinner next week, can you do your mime performance? You told all of us you used to perform when you were in Ireland, so it would be great to do the same for us."

"Sure. I have created a new piece called, 'The Fly', where I do PNF techniques on a fly. It would be the perfect thing to perform for you guys."

The phone rings.

"I'll get it," Petra says, walking into the hall right outside the kitchen to answer the pay phone.

"Irit, it's for you. It's your Uncle Jusie."

I can't hide my shock at that announcement. It's only 7:30 in the morning. Why is he calling? He never calls. It is always my Aunt Ersie who calls. All I can think as I walk into the hall is, *That's weird. Why is he calling so early?*

"Hello?" I say.

"Irit, I'm so sorry to be calling. I'm so sorry to be the one to tell you, but your father … your father … he had a massive heart attack. He's gone. I'm so sorry. The funeral is on Tuesday so everyone can get to Montréal. Your aunt is flying out of Los Angeles. I can make your arrangements, too."

"No."

I hang up the phone.

I can't breathe. I can't talk. *This can't be. This must be a bad dream. I'm having a nightmare. I've had this dream before. Irit, pinch yourself. Wake up, Irit. Wake up. Please, wake up.* My whole being shuts down. I'm paralyzed. My legs are wobbly, my heart is exploding, and knives and daggers are going into every part of me. *This can't be. Please, God, let this be a bad dream. Please, wake me up. You can't take away my father. He was my ally. Why did you take my dad? Please, Irit, wake up.*

I walk into the kitchen as if possessed, tears streaming down my face.

"What's wrong? You look like you've seen a ghost," Petra says, panicking.

"My dad," I say in between sobs, "this can't be. My dad, he died this morning. I have to call my sister. This can't be true."

I somehow get back to the phone. *Please, please, answer the phone.*

"Hello?" I hear my sister's voice on the other line.

"Edna. Is it true?

She pauses, then says quietly, "It's true. He was at a customer's house and said, 'I don't feel well. Can I have some water?' Then he collapsed. The paramedics got there 20 minutes later, but it was too late. Al, the kids, and I are going to drive to Montréal in about two hours. We're making all the arrangements, so we may not be able to pick you up whenever your flight gets in. Just take a cab."

I hang up and think of the conversation I had with my dad just one year ago. I was on his bed, and I said, "Dad, you work so hard. When it is your turn to go, you'll probably say, 'God, not yet, I have one more customer.'" I remember he had laughed at that.

Now he has died at a customer's house. I guess I wasn't too far off. *Please, wake me up from this bad dream.*

Maya, a physical therapist in our dorm, sees me, and says, "I'm so sorry your dad died. How old was he?" I can't think. It is like someone else is answering.

"Seventy."

"Well, you're lucky that he at least lived a long, good life and you had a good relationship with him. My dad died at fifty."

You're crazy! I want to scream. *Lucky? My whole world just collapsed with what seems like a flip of a switch—and you want me to feel lucky?* I just look at her, stunned.

One person after another offers condolences. I am amazed by how many say, *"Well, at least he lived a long life, and you were close."* I am speechless.

Petra comes to my side as I sit in my room. "You have to call Claire," she says. "Here's her number."

I take a moment to collect myself and then head to the payphone and dial. "Hello, Claire? This is Irit. I just found out–" Once again, tears run down my face. I pause to recover my voice. "My dad, he died this morning. I have to fly home … I'll be back in nine days."

There is static and then her voice.

"If you're gone for nine days, don't come back."

I freeze. "Claire, in the Jewish faith, after the funeral of someone in the family, the immediate family sits Shiva for seven days. It is a period of mourning and prayer."

"The most I'll allow you to take is five days."

F----you! I want to scream at the top of my lungs. *No wonder everyone says you have no heart. No wonder everyone hates you! I could get away with it,* I tell myself. *Say f--- you, say f--- you!* Instead, I say, "Then I won't be back. Goodbye."

Petra is at the phone beside me.

"I can't believe she did that." Petra looks as shocked and outraged as I feel. "Don't worry, I'll pack your bags and take care of all your belongings. Do you want me to book your flight?"

"No. Thanks, Petra."

I get on the phone again. I have no clue how, but I make arrangements. My flight departs first thing in the morning. It's just easier to go to Montréal on a direct flight, so I decide not to go with my aunt.

"Do you want me to do anything?" Petra asks.

"Thanks, but I don't even know what I want or need," I say as the numbness of grief takes over my body.

~~~~~~~~~~~~~~

Rich, the staff physical therapist, comes over when he hears the news. "Come to my house for dinner," he says after listening to my plans. "You can stay the night, and I'll drive you to the airport. You can keep your Mazda in my driveway until you get back. Just leave me the keys."

"Yeah, that would be good. Thanks," I say. I am scared to be alone right now, so I am grateful for this offer.

When I arrive at his place shortly after five, he has a big meal of chili, garlic bread, and salad prepared.

I look at all the food he so generously prepared for me, but I can't bring myself to eat it.

"You've got to eat something," he says.

"It's hard to do anything right now, let alone eat." I look up at Rich. "You know, my dad … he ate so fast all the time. It drove me absolutely crazy. I used to tell him he would win a gold medal for being the fastest eater if they had such an event. It wasn't until I read a book about survivors of the war who had experienced extreme hunger that I realized my dad's fast eating was actually common."

"I'm sorry for what you're going through."

I nod in response but continue on, "Last year, I remember it well, I was studying something in neuro anatomy that, of course, I have forgotten since. The phone rang, and it was my dad.

"'Iritka,' he had said. (He always had a warm and loving tone when he said my name.) 'Guess what? I'm finally eating slowly.'

"I was in shock, and he said, 'They pulled my top teeth, and I can't chew anything, so I can't eat quickly.' We both laughed at that.

"I just can't believe it."

Rich is a tall, good-looking man. I notice his broad shoulders for the first time as he pulls me into his arms. He looks so loving and appealing to me in this moment of despair. I begin to cry as he holds me. I don't want to let go. I want to stay here in his arms forever. For a few seconds, I forget the emptiness I feel, the pit in my stomach. I forget the pounding in my head, and I forget the loneliness and sadness that envelops my soul, my being.

The hours pass. Rich stays up with me.

Finally, I'm on the plane. Somehow, with Rich, everything had seemed a little easier to deal with. Now that I'm alone, the uncontrollable sobbing starts up again. *God, how could you do this to me? Why did you leave, Dad? You told me that as long as you were alive, I'd be safe. You'd help me if I needed it. You knew. It's not fair. You tried to tell me when I was in Montréal. I remember. You parked, turned off the ignition, turned toward me, and said, "I'm not afraid to die."*

The guy sitting in the seat next to mine leans over and says, "Excuse me, but it must be bad. Boyfriend stuff, I bet. Well, there are plenty of fish in the sea. Another guy will come your way. It's not worth all the tears."

I look at him incredulously. "You've got it all wrong. It's my dad. He just … collapsed. He died yesterday … wasn't sick … just collapsed and died."

"Oh, I'm sorry," he says. I seem to have scared him off because I don't hear another word from him through the rest of the 6-hour flight. Six hours of tears pass, and yet, I feel no better.

I arrive at Dorval airport in Montréal. *Bienvenue,* the sign at the airport welcomes me, the sign that was always so comforting.

Welcome to Montréal? They clearly don't know what happened.

I hail a cab and notice the phrase written on all the Québec license plates. I get swept up in memories. *Je me souviens. I will remember.*

I will remember the diversity I love, the *joie de vivre* of the people, and the beauty and elegance of the city that freezes up in the winter. I will remember my dad taking me to Beaver Lake on weekends to skate.

I will remember the government trying to change my city as I knew it. The French were so intent on retaining French heritage via the French language. French became the official language, so all bilingual signs on the city streets were removed and replaced with French-only signs. Millions of dollars were spent on that endeavor, and now tourists, and for that matter, people like my mom and dad who did not speak French, would have no idea what the signs meant. Yet, of course, the government was simultaneously trying to encourage tourism.

The French were making laws so that the French would prevail. The French believed that unless these rules were implemented, the French language would eventually disappear and the French culture would be compromised. This did not make sense to me because in my eyes the rules were making it harder for both the French and English living in Québec. Doctors were told that to practice in Québec, they would have to be paid only two thirds of the salary of their English counter parts in other provinces. Businesses had to pay a lot to stay in the province, resulting in a big exodus. Even small business signs like my dad's had to be in French. *Schaffer Plumbing* was illegal. It had to be *Plomberie Schaffer* first, and then, if he wanted the English, a *Schaffer Plumbing* sign could go underneath. He had to follow these rules; otherwise, he would lose his business. The craziest law that affected my dad was the law that all plumbers had to take a new plumbing test to stay in business, and, of course, the test was in French.

"Dad, what are you going to do?" I remember asking anxiously. "You don't speak, let alone read, French."

"Iritka," he said with a laugh, "the test will be multiple choice, and if Louis Chartier passes, so will I." Louis Chartier was his longtime friend and employee.

"What do you mean?" I asked.

"I'll sit next to him."

True to prediction, he and Louis passed, and, of course, with the exact same score. I wonder what went through my parents' heads with all the insane laws developing in Montréal. They were seeing so many friends and businesses leave Montréal and more and more English rights taken away in the name of the ultimate dream of a separate Québec. Would English-speaking people be safe? The government wants us to remember and to know, but can my parents ever forget? *Je me souviens.* I remember the phone call that shattered my world ... tears well up in my eyes. *Can't I escape? Isn't there a place I could go so I don't feel all this? So I don't remember?*

The cab driver stops and says, "1984 Ward Street; you're here." I give him 12 Canadian dollars and head to the front door.

I ring the bell and walk up the 15 steps to the apartment. It was just three months ago that I walked up these stairs, so happy to be visiting. Now, as I walk up the stairs, all I feel is horrible emptiness.

My mom greets me. I can't bring myself to give her a hug. She never hugs me. It's like we have an invisible wall between us and neither of us can break through it. *Ok, stay strong. Don't cry.* My three nephews, Ryan, Marc, and Mike, run to me. "Eareat!" they say, and I get swarmed by hugs and kisses. For the first time since I heard the news, I smile.

~~~~~~~~~~~~~

"Irit, do you want orange juice?" Marc, who will be nine in two weeks, asks me.

He, in his 4'2" frame, is so innocent and confident. "I'm making it fresh from the juicer. I'm really good at it."

"That's great. Did you know that you are my favorite middle nephew in the whole universe?"

"But Eear," he smiles, playing into our usual routine. "I'm your only middle nephew."

"That's ok, you're still my favorite middle nephew."

"Do you want to play chess?" Ryan, my oldest nephew, asks me. He brings the chess board and pieces to the table and sets it up. "You choose the color," he says, "and you can start."

My heart aches as we begin. Chess, the game my dad was a master at, the game that saved his life when he was a prisoner of war in Russia. Chess, the game I learned how to play before I could even read, the game my nephews learned from my dad as well. My dad explained the roles of each of the pieces to me year in and year out, telling me, "Before you make a move, make sure your piece is protected. If you make a move and your piece is not protected, you will be caught off guard and then, checkmate." I was always too tired to stay focused on protecting the pieces, though, and when I got distracted, Bam! I would make a mistake and, like he said, checkmate. My dad was always focused, always on guard. He was the master of chess; no one could beat him.

The doorbell rings. It's Aunt Ersie. She took a direct flight from Los Angeles. The hugs go easy with her. Aunt Ersie is my dad's sister. In a weird way, I feel like this proves it ... this time he really is dead. No more false alarms. Forty years ago, she got a letter from the Red Cross that said my dad was "shot and killed while trying to escape to the Russian front." She had grieved, but then he came back. He wouldn't be coming back this time. If only someone could tell me this is a big mistake, too, and he is coming back.

My eyes start to tear up as I remember my plan to interview my dad. *Dad, I told you I would write down your story,* I think. I look at Aunt Ersie and decide to ask her for help. *Maybe she would have some clues about what Dad always meant about good blood. She knew him better than anyone. Maybe Barna will have clues.*

My thoughts trail off as pain takes over. Someday I will somehow get these answers, but I can't even think about it right now.

~~~~~~~~~~~~~~

My brother-in-law, Alan, and my mom have a special bond. He has a special way with her that I always appreciated and liked to watch. Whenever I saw the soft side of my mom, I felt more connected to her. It always showed me that maybe we could be closer one day. A few years after Al married my sister, his mother had gotten sick. Ryan, their son, was only two at the time, so my mom traveled to Clarks Summit to help out. Al's mother passed away, and within two years, his dad died of a heart attack. Al was always grateful to my mom for all her help. She has become an important parental figure for him, and Al is the perfect son-in-law for her. In her eyes, he can do no wrong.

Edna and Al have taken on the task of making funeral arrangements. Today they are in the kitchen trying to choose a coffin. My dad never wanted anything gaudy and extravagant, just simple and elegant, so they choose pinewood.

There are so many people. Everything is a blur. Suddenly, we are arriving at the funeral service, and my mom faints as we walk in. Growing up, my mom would faint at will whenever she heard something she didn't want to hear from me. Actually, she fainted whenever she heard anything from anyone that she didn't want to hear. I just didn't realize it wasn't all about me back then. My sister always knew she would come to, but I was always afraid that she wouldn't.

What I didn't know then was that she just had a low threshold for stress, probably from holding in all her secrets from the war. She would just get so overwhelmed and upset that the only way her body could cope was to faint. For me, when she fainted, it felt like the end of the world. Today is no exception. Her fainting is too much for me to handle. People rush to her side, and when she comes to, Al takes her arm and guides her to her seat. I just stand on the side, trying to hold it together.

Edna, Al, my Aunt Ersie, my mom and I sit in front. My mom won't stop sobbing. *Please God*, I pray, *please don't let her faint again. I can't handle it.* I just want to scream.

One by one, people fill the room. So many people, about 300, are here to pay tribute. How did they all know? In the Jewish tradition, burials are supposed to occur within 24 hours, but because so many of us were coming from long distances, the rabbi said Tuesday would be fine. That made it 48 hours.

Mr. Bass, one of my father's biggest customers, comes over to offer his condolences. "Your dad was such a kind and generous man. No matter what time of day or night, if there was a plumbing problem, he would take care of it," Mr. Bass says.

I remember hearing about Mr. Bass from my father. I did the bills for my dad when I lived here, so I knew his name well. He owned so many apartment buildings and gave my dad so much work that if Mr. Bass did not call him for a few weeks, my dad would worry that he had found another plumber. Dad depended on Mr. Bass' business.

Next, Mr. Rothberg comes to where we are all seated. "It was an honor to know your dad and husband; he was one of the gentlest and kindest men I knew," he says to all of us.

Mr. Rothberg was the one who had wanted my dad to give up his business and become partners with him in his 200-apartment complex. My dad was to be in charge of all the maintenance and help with rentals. The apartments were half empty then. My dad wanted to do it, but my sister and I were still little so my mom was afraid that if he invested all their money and it didn't work out, we would be left with nothing. He would have been a millionaire a few times over. *You would not have had to work so hard,* I think, sadly. *There is a waiting list to get into those apartments now. Your life didn't have to be so hard.*

Mr. Specton comes over and introduces himself, "Mr. Schaffer was like family to me. I'll miss him," he says.

I knew of him, as well. He was the eccentrically gay attorney from my dad's stories. *Gay* was not a word we ever discussed, and yet my dad was so accepting. He always smiled when talking about him. Yes. My dad helped Mr. Specton a lot.

My dad bought the duplex five years ago, and it came with an in-law apartment. My uncle, Arnold, my mom's brother, bought the other half of the duplex from my dad. He lived in the downstairs unit. It was bigger than my dad's unit because it had a stairway that led to a big family room, which the upstairs unit did not have. They agreed that, since Uncle Arnold had the bigger apartment, my dad would get the in-law apartment and use it to store plumbing supplies.

When my uncle first bought half the property, he was happy with the arrangement. After four years, however, my uncle suddenly decided that my dad's portion was more valuable because of the in law apartment. My dad found this out for the first time via a lawyer's letter. The letter stated that my uncle felt my dad should reimburse him for the inequity in property. Mr. Specton was so outraged by what my uncle was trying to do that he helped out. He wrote a letter stating that my dad would switch properties and move downstairs to my uncle's home and my uncle could move to the upstairs unit and also have the in-law apartment. He stated that my dad would consider that equal in value.

After the issue was resolved, Mr. Specton would not accept payment for his help. He said that after all that my dad did for him, it was the least he could do. My uncle later apologized and said it was a misunderstanding, but for my father, it took a while to get past the hurt. "How could family do that?" he would ask.

One by one, people are still filing into the auditorium, and then, the dreaded question can be heard, "Do you want to see the deceased before we close the coffin?" In the Jewish tradition, there is no public viewing, but if someone wants to say good-bye, they can have a private viewing.

"No, I can't. I'm afraid I'll be haunted by the picture of him," I say when it is my turn to answer.

"I want to see him," Aunt Ersie says. She gets up and slowly walks through the door, clutching her black purse. She returns within ten minutes saying, "he looked so peaceful, almost smiling."

It is zero degrees, cold, crisp and windy, but sunny as we walk through the cemetery. Nature appears to be opening up its skies to my dad.

My mom keeps sobbing, murmuring, "yoi eeshtanam," (*Oh, my God* in Hungarian). Thank goodness for Alan. He is so gentle and comforting with her. He is the only one who can calm her. Alan is the best son-in-law, and brother-in-law for that matter, that you could ask for. I'm relieved as he walks on one side of my mom, with my sister on the other. I don't know if I could handle watching after my mom today. I can barely watch after myself.

Irit, be strong, I keep saying to myself. I don't want to cry in front of everyone. I'm afraid if I start, I will never be able to stop. I will completely lose it.

The coffin is put into the ground. I take the shovel, pick up some earth, and throw it over the coffin. In the Jewish tradition, everyone takes some earth and puts it over the coffin. The patter of the earth hitting the coffin forces everyone to accept the finality, the end, of the passing. *Dad,* I think, *with this earth, I am burying your unconditional love, your heroic acts, and your healing abilities, which shaped my perspectives.* I feel a piece of my heart rip apart, and I say to myself, *Stay strong, don't break down now, not in front of all these people.* It's too much for everyone to handle with my mom also breaking down.

~~~~~~~~~~~~~~

We sit Shiva, which means *seven* in Hebrew, named for the seven days of mourning. The deceased's mom, dad, grandparents, sisters, brothers, sons, and daughters stay in the house for one week and sit on stools to mourn and pray for their beloved. My mom, my sister, Aunt Ersie, and I, sit on the special stools provided. Each one of us has a rip that we make on a piece of clothing opposite our hearts, representing our grief. All of our mirrors are covered with sheets so that we remember not to look at ourselves. That is another rule for sitting Shiva.

Prayer services are conducted three times a day for my dad, and there must be a *minyan,* meaning a quorum of ten Jewish male adults, present to pray at each service. If ten men cannot be gathered, the synagogue typically helps out, but for my dad, that is not a problem. There are always enough men.

So many people come with food for us, and they pay respects. We receive stuffed cabbage, chopped liver, chicken and matzo ball soup, dumplings, *cholent*, bagels, lox and cream cheese, chocolate, cake, strudel and so much more. So many people help comfort us. Then the seven days pass, and everyone leaves.

Since the program director told me I didn't need to bother coming back to finish my rotation, I had decided to stay an extra couple of weeks in Montréal with my mom. While there, Kate, my instructor from USC calls me to offer condolences on behalf of all the teachers. She tells me she was appalled when she heard about Claire's reaction and apologizes for it.

I am relieved as she tells me that the head of the department decided that, since I had completed two months of the rotation and that was the full length for some of the other rotations, I would not have to repeat it to gain credit. The only thing remaining in my education is my master's dissertation, which I will present at the beginning of January. I hang up the phone and take a deep breath. I guess it is time to get back to work.

~~~~~~~~~~~~~~

Three weeks have passed, and now it is my turn to leave. I was going to come home in January for two months to record my dad's story and study for my state boards, but now everything has changed. I will study in California and work as a physical therapist in training until I get licensed. I will apply for my green card, and then I will see what happens.

On my last day home, I go into my dad's study and look at the unopened jewelry box on his desk for the hundredth time. I know my bracelet is in it. I have looked at the box every day since I arrived, but I still do not have the strength to open it.

Dad, how could you abandon me like this? I think. *I wasn't prepared. Now who am I going to talk to? You have been my buffer and my protector.* I look at the gold and silver box and take a deep breath. With tears welling up in my eyes, I open the box. The bracelet has three types of gold with different link formations, giving it a dainty and elegant look. I hear my dad's words, "Iritka," he had said, accentuating my name. "It is perfect for you." I remember I could feel him smile as he said those words.

I start sobbing uncontrollably. Just then, my taxi arrives, honking its horn. My mom comes downstairs and helps me with my luggage.

I look at my mom one last time before I leave. She looks so helpless and sad. I feel a gut wrenching pain in my abdomen as I hear my dad's voice echo through my mind. *What will happen to your mother when I die? Is this her pain I feel now or mine?*

I lean over, give her a kiss on the cheek, and say good-bye. I already know I'll call her the second I get to California. I get into the cab and look up at my mom, my uncle Arnold and my aunt Rose. I remember my dad's conversation with me in September in that silver Malibu. *I sold half the duplex to Uncle Arnold so that when I die, your mom will not be alone. She will be taken care of. Iritka. I'm not afraid to die.*

~~~~~~~~~~~~~~

"Where are you going?" the immigration officer asks at the airport.

"San Francisco," I say.

"Do you have anything to declare?"

I look at my bracelet, gracefully and loosely nestled on my left wrist, and my throat clamps up. I look at the officer, and I say, "No."

"Have a good trip."

"Thanks," I respond and head toward gate 54.

~~~~~~~~~~~~~~

Irit Schaffer

10

1988, June/July

Courage is resistance to fear, mastery of fear, not absence of fear
Mark Twain

Whoa! I look up at three 50-foot poles. They look like telephone poles, swinging back and forth, going right and left. *Oh my God,* I think, *are we supposed to go up these poles and jump onto the trapeze eight feet away?*

I am in Austin, Texas at a two-week seminar about communication skills, the tools I need to better understand the world, or maybe to better understand myself. Today, there is a rope course staring me right in the face. This was the one thing I determined I was not going to do when I signed up because, of course, I was afraid of injuring myself again. Now, somehow, here I am with so many others, waiting for my turn to climb.

As I stare at the swaying poles with the sun shining in my face, fear takes over. I start having doubts, but that little voice inside of me keeps asking, *How will you feel if you leave and miss out on this experience without even trying?* I stay in line for my turn.

More than three years have passed since that phone call on December 2nd. I am visiting Austin for this seminar; I now live in San Francisco. I am starting a new job when I get back. I will start off working mostly with outpatients, and once in a while, I will also work with the inpatients. I secretly hate working with inpatients because I'm always afraid that a patient will faint, or worse, die when I get them out of bed the first few times after surgery.

"Is the pole going to come out of the ground?" I hear myself asking, but I'm really just talking to myself.

"No! It's rooted into the ground," Ed responds loudly to the whole group. He looks over at me. "The rope course," Ed says, "is a physical metaphor, and it should be about more than just climbing to the top and jumping."

"I went skydiving from 8,000 feet once. Why do I still feel afraid of heights?" one participant asks. I'm glad I'm not the only person feeling fearful.

"That's a good question." Ed smiles. "When you're at 8,000 feet, it is too much of a distance for your brain to relate to; 50 feet is much easier for the brain to comprehend. It's important that you use this experience to help you in your everyday life. Otherwise, it will just be a momentary high, and that's it. We are a group of PhD psychologists who are trying to help people transform their lives. That's why we do these rope courses. If there is something you can learn from this, what would it be?"

I have not really gone back to fun, adventurous activity since my car accident in Physical Therapy School. The doctor I saw in PT school told me that I had the neck of a 70-year-old and that it was something I would "have to live with." That is the catch phrase for doctors when they have no clue what to do. My neck tightens up even more at this thought, or maybe it is from my fear.

I hear Ed's instructions once again, "Think of something you would like to overcome. Think of finding another way to see the world, or think of letting go of fear, and then embark on your climb. You'll be harnessed, and there are rungs to help you climb the first 48 feet. At that point, you will have to figure out a way to get yourself up the last two feet to the top of the pole. Once you reach the top, jump onto the trapeze eight feet away." I can see the pole swaying slightly, and my fear of getting hurt creeps into every cell of my body. Just like that night when the cops pulled me over, I can see the next day's headlines: *Canadian woman, in an attempt to work on a physical metaphor, plunges to her death.*

"Partner up," Ed says, "with the person standing next to you. That way, when you go up the pole, you will have a partner to help you if you get stuck. We all get stuck at certain points in our lives. You should ask each other what you would like to hear in those moments. What do you want your partner to say when you feel that you cannot move another inch. Remember, it's not just about climbing. Make it personal. What do you want it to mean for you?"

John and I are paired up. He is tall and a bit of a stud, with six-pack abs, not an ounce of fat on him, and short, curly blond hair. He doesn't look like he could be afraid of anything.

"You can learn a lot about yourself through these courses," Ed continues after we pair up. "Some people are internally driven; others are externally driven. Internally driven people are self-motivators; externally driven people may need assurance from others on a regular basis. Neither is good or bad; they just are."

"Have you done stuff like this before?" John asks.

"I've done scary stuff," I say, "but I'm still petrified."

I look at the pole, and I think, *Why is it always so hard for me? What is it that I have to remember or what is it that I have to forget?*

"Are you ok?" Ed asks, breaking me from my thoughts.

"Yeah! I was just, well, I'm just trying to figure out what this climb will mean to me."

"What do you want it to represent?"

"I guess … letting go? I love doing things that are physical, but I seem to hold onto the fear of getting hurt, so I don't do anything, and then…"

"Any step you take is a step toward success. Embrace the challenge, and set yourself up so that you succeed."

"I've heard that before. Easier said than done," I say with a nervous laugh.

Ed looks at me understandingly. "It's normal to be scared. Just remember what it represents to you."

Ok, I think, focusing. *I want this to represent me letting go of my fear of getting hurt. I want to have fun again.*

"Who is going first?"

"John is," I say quickly, before John can say a word.

"Make sure you know what type of support John needs," Ed says.

"When I go up," John says, "I want to be told that a chariot of four white horses will pull me up if I get stuck. It has to be white horses."

I look at him, wanting to laugh, but he looks so serious that I do everything in my power to contain myself.

"Ok," I say, in the most serious tone I can muster. I look at him in his muscular 6'2" frame and say, "Go for it. I'll help. Good luck!"

Three quarters of the way up, John stops. He can't go further. I wait for what seems like forever. He hasn't moved.

As stupid as I think it is, I say, "John, the chariots of four white horses are there ready to pull you up. Tell them when you're ready."

"Ready!" he yells.

"They're pulling you up."

He climbs the rest of the way up effortlessly, makes it to the top, stands on the pole, jumps toward the trapeze, misses, and is hoisted down via his harness.

Go figure, I think. I don't know whether to laugh or just be impressed by what transpired. I never would have imagined using a phrase like that to help anyone. I guess that is what the phrase 'different strokes for different folks' is all about.

John comes down, and he's beaming. "Thanks for your words of encouragement. They helped me get to the top," he says.

"It's your turn," Ed says encouragingly.

"What do you need me to do?" John asks.

"Actually, I want silence so I can coach myself, or maybe you can just say, 'you can do it' once, but then I want silence."

"Got it," John says.

I put my feet and arms through the harness with the rope over my left shoulder. Ed and the gang will use that rope to maneuver me down if I stumble. Only three of the participants so far have managed to hold onto the trapeze, so there is obviously a good chance I won't be able to. Wearing my yellowish green shorts and pink t-shirt, I head to the base of the pole. I take off my sunglasses, give them to John, and say, "I'm ready."

Ed does one last check to make sure I'm secure, then I lift my tennis shoe-clad feet and start the climb. The pole feels maybe 10 - 12 inches in diameter. My legs shake as I go from one rung to another. I can't stop. It's as if my legs are doing their own jittery dance and I have no control. I stop for a moment to pull myself together. *Dad, how did you do it?* I ask. *I mean you lived in danger for so many years, and you were never able to stop and regroup. You had no harness.* I look down. That is a big mistake. *Yikes,* my stomach feels like someone has squeezed it as hard as they could. *Look up,* a voice inside of me says. *Keep going.*

With each rung I climb, I stop and say, *Good job, keep going.* About three fourths of the way up, I freeze. *Ok, don't look down.* I hear John say, "Irit, you can do it," over and over again. I look down and once again, fear gushes into me, but I manage to move my finger to my mouth and say, "shush."

I need silence. I don't want to look down again. Somehow, I keep moving up one rung after another until there are no more. Now I have to reach approximately two feet higher to get to the top of the pole.

Irit, many others have done it; you can, too. Something within takes over, and my right foot is propelled to the top, then the left one. It feels effortless, weightless. It brings back a memory.

~~~~~~~~~~~~~

I was seven. My cousin Emily, Frank's daughter, was six. We were walking in the country where we stayed during the summers. I was on the inside. Emily was on the outside. There were no sidewalks. A car came quickly and was about to hit my cousin. I grabbed her hand and hoisted her over myself. She landed in the ditch. It was effortless. It was as if she didn't weigh anything. I had tried to repeat that feat on many an occasion in the ensuing years, but I could never get beyond yanking her arm. Her feet remained planted on the ground.

I find myself standing on the pole as it moves left and right and keeping my balance. I look at the sun. Its rays hit my face and cloak me in warmth. Then, I look at the trapeze.

You did it. You climbed to the top, I say in awe. *Wow!* I just stand there taking in what I have just done, not ready to take the next step. The trapeze is maybe eight feet away, yet it feels so close. *Ok, jump toward the trapeze,* I think. *This is a new beginning. On the count of three...* I take a deep breath and count, *1 ... 2 ... 3.* I soar through the sky with that same effortlessness with which I had reached the top, and somehow, both my hands reach the trapeze.

My hands grip the bar as my body sways through the air. *Now let go,* I think, but I continue to hold on. I can't let go. Fatigue has taken over, and I close my eyes. After what feels like an eternity, I let go.

As promised, the rope guides me back to the ground. I land and my legs feel like spaghetti. I grin from ear to ear and look up at the top of the pole. *Yes! I did it. Yes, a new beginning.* I make a fist and raise it to the sky.

I can see Ed approach me with his beaming smile. I give him a big hug.

"Thank you, thank you so much," I say.

"This is what I love about my job. Now you might want to get out of your harness."

"Oops!" I say. I had totally forgotten that I was still attached.

I head to the table where our souvenir t-shirts are waiting to be picked up and notice a brochure, *Swimming with dolphins of the wild in the Florida Keys.* It is another event run by Ed's company. There are 16 people in each tour, and it includes two days of swimming with wild dolphins in the ocean and two days of swimming with dolphins at a sea park.

I run to Ed.

"I have loved dolphins ever since I saw *Flipper* on TV. I want to sign up. Does it fill up quickly?"

"It shouldn't fill up today, but it will fill up within the next couple of months, so you should make the commitment by mid-September."

"I'll sign up today," I say, with an excitement I had forgotten existed since my accident. "This is truly a great day!"

"Wasn't the rope course awesome?" Barb, another San Francisco participant asks. "I've always wanted to go skydiving, and after today, I decided I'm going to do it. Do you want to go? Wouldn't that be another great way to push yourself? There is a skydiving place back in San Francisco near where you live in Byron."

"Yeah, why not?" I say. "At this point, I'm ready for anything. How about if we go on my birthday in three weeks? Does anyone else want to go?"

"You're not going to back out?"

"You have my commitment." We shake on it.

I'm still dancing inside with the excitement from my climb. Exhilaration and electricity fill every cell of my body.

The next two weeks fly by, and I finally return home. After the excitement wore off, I couldn't believe I had committed to skydiving, but there was no turning back now. I was glad that I had convinced six other people to come with me because the more people who agreed to go, the easier it would be for me to follow through.

But what will it mean to you? I can hear Ed's voice say.

~~~~~~~~~~~~~~

When I was ten, I was going to my piano lesson with Mrs. Ferenz and was about to ring the bell so she could let me in when a stranger came and blocked my path. He asked if I wanted candy. I did, but he scared me, so I said no. He still wouldn't let me get to the bell. I started to cry. He pulled out a knife, put it to my throat, and said, "If you cry, I'll kill you." The tears kept rolling down my face. I couldn't move. I couldn't speak. He pulled me away from the door and pushed me against a railing five feet away. It seemed like

I was there forever. I remember he put his hands on the skin on my abdomen and the tears just kept rolling down my face.

Suddenly, we heard a noise, and he pushed me aside, said I was the wrong girl, and ran away. I rang the bell, ran up the three flights of stairs, and told Mrs. Ferenz, the piano teacher from Budapest, what had happened in a hysterical voice. She, in her heavy Hungarian accent, said, "Don't make up stuff just because you're late."

In that instant, a belief system got implanted in my mind: if you tell the truth, you won't be believed.

I went home and started having nightmares every night. I would dream that I was being chased and couldn't move. I refused to tell anyone what had happened, but my dad was concerned because I had said I didn't want to play piano anymore. My mom and dad had noticed that the changes started after my last piano class, so my dad called the teacher. Mrs. Ferenz told him what I had told her. They were mad at me for not telling them. After that, the nightmares only happened once in a while, but I still flash back to that sense of helplessness when I am frightened.

~~~~~~~~~~~~~~

When I get scared, I hold my breath and feel paralyzed. I start thinking there is no way out. *I want to be able to function when things are scary,* I think, *that is what skydiving will be for me.*

The phone rings.

"Hello."

"It's Chad. How was your seminar? How are you doing?"

"Great. I am so jazzed about everything that has happened. There are so many stories I have to tell you. A bunch of us are going skydiving on my birthday. You want to go?"

"Sure. That would be great. You want to go to lunch? I'd love to hear about your trip."

"I'd love to share."

"How about if I pick you up in an hour?"

"Great. See you soon. 'Bye." I hang up the phone.

Chad is a doctor I met about a month ago at my last job. He was fascinated when I first told him about the seminar I was attending and wanted to hear about my experiences when I returned. He is 5'10, with blond hair, blue eyes, and broad shoulders. I've always loved broad shoulders. Maybe it is because I like the way they feel when I'm being held, or maybe it is just because my knight in shining armor has always looked like that in my mind. Regardless of the logic behind my adoration of broad shoulders, it definitely produced a bit of a crush on Chad.

Chad has many interests, and he's smart. Smart is important to me. I figure it means that I, too, am smart. I'm enamored by what he does. He is a surgeon, and a brain surgeon at that.

I start to get ready, and an hour later, Chad picks me up in his black Mercedes. We head to the Cliff house, a restaurant overlooking the ocean.

We get seated. For a Saturday at lunch, it's surprisingly slow.

I'm chatting away, and Chad just listens. He seems so calm and attentive.

"You're not going to believe it, but after skydiving, I'm going to go swimming with dolphins. The tour is five days, and it's led by the same people who ran the ropes course."

"Are they dolphins of the wild?" he asks.

"Yep. Isn't that totally cool?"

"I'd love to sign up. Maybe I can take Nick." Nick is Chad's 12-year-old son. "He's going to a boarding school on the East Coast, and his mom, who lives on the West Coast, has to agree to take him out of school for any trips. I hope he can do it."

"Why is he out east?" I ask.

I can tell the question makes Chad a little uneasy. He combs his fingers through his hair and presses his lips together before saying, "It's a long story." He looks away, deep in thought, and sighs. "Nick has a learning disability and a behavioral problem, but like I said, it is a long story. But maybe his mom will let me take him, and you can meet him."

"Why wouldn't she let him go?"

"You don't know her." I can see the masseter muscles in his cheeks jutting out as he clenches his teeth. "We are not on the best of terms, to put it mildly, but that's for another time. You think he would want to go?"

"What 12-year-old would not like to be in the water with dolphins?" I ask with excitement. "If you want to go, you should let Ed know and secure a spot."

"I'll find out tomorrow. We'll see about his mom."

"I'm famished. Let's order," I say.

~~~~~~~~~~~~~~

On my birthday, July 31st, ten people show up for the sky diving extravaganza. My new boss, Carol, is one of the ten. I met Carol at work, and we instantly became friends. I have become a confidante for her, and she always bounces ideas off me.

We head in and start learning about the process. Chad asks many questions along the way, mostly about what to do if something goes wrong. I would never even think of those crazy questions, but Chad is an expert at seeing the danger in everything. After four hours of listening to the instructor explain all that could go wrong, we sign waivers releasing the company of any liability. I'm not sure the forms would hold up in court.

We all suit up. I'm nervous, but I'm as ready as I'll ever be. *What did I get myself into?* I think. *I hope I live to tell this story.*

We are all ready, but the winds are strong, so we're waiting for the green light to take off. After thirty anxious minutes, our instructor returns and gives us the news, "The winds are too strong. The jump is cancelled."

I breathe a sigh of relief.

"Sorry, guys, but we will have to wait for another week," the instructor says. Chad automatically signs us up for a jump two weeks later. The other eight guests gracefully decline a future jump. I think they chickened out, and I don't blame them after all of that build-up. The problem is, I told all my patients that I would go skydiving, so I knew I had to follow through. When I first floated the idea, I had been sure that the only reason Chad wanted to jump was his interest in me, but I was wrong. He seems more eager to do it than I am now.

~~~~~~~~~~~~~~

"You want to go to Ocean Beach?" Chad asks when we get back to San Francisco. It's still early afternoon.

"Great idea," I say, happy to spend the rest of my birthday in one of my favorite settings, the beach.

We get there, and after a few minutes of walking, I get a sudden urge, an urge I haven't felt for a very long time. I take off running for the first time since that accident in Physical Therapy School almost four years ago. Every time I got close to feeling good enough to run again, something got in the way. Worst of all, I'd actually sustained another injury since the car accident in Physical Therapy School, which set me back in my recovery big time.

I build up speed. I can hear the roar of the ocean and feel the salt in the air. The wind is blowing in my face, and I keep going, faster and faster. I feel light. Everything is effortless.

After maybe five minutes, I stop. I pump both fists into the sky as the sun shines on my face. "Yes!" I scream out in exhilaration. *Dad, guess what?* I think. *Today, I'm not just better. I'm great.*

I feel so energized and unstoppable. I start running again. In this moment, I am so thankful to my dad for teaching me about two of the important ingredients of good blood: *to believe in the possibility of healing and to focus on what I can do, not on what I can't do.* Once again, I pump both my fists in the air as the sun shines in my face.

That week, I start playing tennis again. I join Chad's tennis club, and we decide to take lessons together. We're at about the same skill level, but he always somehow finds a way to pull ahead when it's match point. I'm still rusty from not having played for so long, but the truth is, I also just don't have the killer instinct to beat him. My competitive nature has not kicked back in yet, but it will. For now, it just feels really good to be able to serve effortlessly and to volley back and forth.

~~~~~~~~~~~~~~

Chad calls me every day after my birthday. I know he wants to meet up, but I keep postponing. He just split up with someone a few weeks ago and it just doesn't feel right yet.

The day of our rescheduled jump arrives, and since we already had the training, we are given the jumpsuits and are in a small plane heading up 10,000 feet within 20 minutes. I am doing a tandem jump, meaning I will be harnessed to the front of my instructor, Bob. I close my eyes and try not to see the headlines: *Canadian girl killed when chute malfunctioned.*

"There's not much for you to do except plant your feet when we land, so have fun," my instructor says.

We go up, and in no time I hear the key word, "*Doooor!*" This is my cue that it's time to exit.

"Are you ready?" my instructor asks.

"My life is in your hands," I say.

I'm becoming more petrified with each passing second. I sit by the edge of the open door, with the wind howling in my face, causing my cheeks to puff out. The look on my face shows my increasing levels of terror. He motions to me, and it's time.

We jump … It's surreal. I see other skydivers, and I'm mesmerized. We have been told to take in a picturesque glimpse of the Sierra Mountains, but I can only notice the skydivers. I feel like I am watching a movie. Everyone seems so graceful in their movements. I'm mesmerized, and I completely forget where I am.

We keep falling, and then the chute opens. We're jerked up at top speed. I feel like I have been shot out of a cannon. Then, everything is slow and calm. I'm in good hands. Everything is smooth sailing, and we finally land.

Chad comes over. Both of us are grinning from ear to ear.

"Do you want to go again? It could be my birthday present to you; as many jumps as you want."

Ed's voice comes back to me. *What would you like it to mean to you?* I want to let go of my fear of paralysis in the face of danger.

"It would be great to get to where I can jump out of a plane by myself and land in the bulls eye pit," I say. "Let's go for it."

"Perfect. We'll sign up."

We hang around and lie down in an empty field nearby. Everything is so still. The sun is shining, and it's maybe 90 degrees. We're lying there peacefully when Chad reaches over and puts his hand on my abdomen. That's the moment everything changes. I am not sure why, but a little voice inside of me seems to be warning me about something. It's a gut feeling that I can't explain, but I ignore it. He's really nice, so I try to just let it go.

~~~~~~~~~~~~~~

I am spending more and more time with Chad. I love that he is so calm. He never raises his voice. He always wants to be with me. He is attentive and affectionate. I feel accepted and heard when I am with him. He gives me flowers and writes me poems. It feels nice to be so wanted and to feel that I can do no wrong, but I can't shake the feeling that something is off. Maybe it's because my previous relationships never ended well for me. *But this time it is different.* I tell myself. *He is so considerate and kind.*

Chad and I spend a lot of time together playing tennis, cycling, and running. He is always attentive and caring. He calls a few times a day just to say "Hi," and he always says something nice. It is so different from what I am used to. In my past relationships, conflict and criticism reigned. Now, everything is flowing and effortless. It is healing for me to feel that kindness and love.

~~~~~~~~~~~~~~

About four months after our first skydiving experience, Chad decides to attend a spine conference in Phoenix. He invites me, saying it would be fun to have me join him, and the hotel has a spa, a large swimming pool, and tennis courts. It is going to be a 3-day trip. I figure, *why not*?

However, while in Phoenix, we are also going to go visit Chad's dad. Chad thinks it will be easier on him if I go along, but I'm not really keen on that idea, especially since I know he and his dad don't have the greatest relationship.

We arrive at the hotel in Phoenix, and it's got all the bells and whistles. It is a four star hotel. We don't get much time to settle in before its time to meet up with Chad's dad. Chad hasn't seen his dad in over a year, and they don't talk much on the phone. Chad says the less time they spend together the better. He still resents his father for divorcing his mom when he was seven and for rarely being there in his formative years. Even now, when they talk, it feels strained.

"Are you sure you want me to come with you to your dad's?" I ask. "I'd be perfectly happy to stay here." The hotel seems so lavish. I secretly wish I could just hang out here.

"Baby doll, it would be great to have you with me."

We unload our luggage into the hotel and then head out in our rented Chrysler Lebaron convertible.

"So, tell me something about your dad," I say as we cruise along.

"He got a PhD in Political Science. He served in the marines, and then he worked as a civilian for the CIA before becoming a Dean at a college."

"You're kidding? That's pretty impressive."

"I guess, but he never talked about it. In fact, there is a lot about my dad that I don't know. We never had much of a relationship."

Before long, we arrive. The house is on the corner. It's one level, and there is a garden out front.

"Chad, I'm nervous," I say. "If you can't stand being around him, why would I want to meet him?"

"Don't worry. It'll be fine. Besides, we won't stay too long."

Chad's dad opens the door. He's in his seventies, about two inches shorter than Chad, and he has a full head of grayish white hair.

"Hi, Chad," he says formally before turning to me, "Nice to meet you."

"Hi," I say.

"My name is Richard. Come on in." We enter the foyer, and I look around at the décor. It seems inviting. *Ok*, I think, *I can handle this*. "Chad told me your name, but can you repeat it?" Richard continues.

"Irit, pronounced ear-eat," I say.

"Where's that from?"

"I was born in Israel."

"Oh, that's nice. My wife had to go out, but she should be back soon. Let's go in the den in the meantime. It's cooler there."

I walk in and see two walls of books and a bar cabinet made of oak. The cabinet has two tall glass doors, where wine glasses and tumblers are stored, and below are two pullout drawers for beverages.

"Would you like something to drink?"

"Calistoga, no ice," I say.

"What about you, Chad?"

"Same, but with ice."

He gets to work on our drinks, reaching for the bucket of ice on top of his cabinet.

"I had surgery two weeks ago, and I'm doing great."

Surgery? I think to myself. *Why didn't Chad say anything?*

"The surgery was so good you can't even tell there was surgery done," Richard says.

Chad takes a sip of his drink and says, "That's good."

"Are you a nurse?" Richard asks, turning his attention to me.

"No, I'm a physical therapist."

"Same thing," he says. "You're in the medical field."

I look over at Chad at this comment and raise my eyebrows. *Those are most certainly not the same thing,* I think.

"I would highly recommend this surgery," Richard continues. "I feel great now. You can't even tell that I had a penile implant. You want to see?"

I almost drop my drink. Chad and I say, "No!" in unison, but it is in vain.

I can't seem to control the bubbles of laughter that want to explode from my belly as Chad's father, this man I just met, drops his pants to show us the surgery he is oh so proud of. *Ok,* I tell myself, *think of something serious.* I can't. *Think of something sad.* I can't. *Stay professional. Please!* I look at Chad, and that's a mistake. My lips stretch into a smile, and I almost lose it again. I bite my lip, hard, to try and create pain. I know if I start laughing, I won't be able to stop. I'm afraid to speak, so I just keep quiet.

Somehow, the time passes, and we're back in the car.

"I'm so sorry." Chad says, turning to me before pulling away from the curb.

I look at Chad, and I can't hold it in any longer. I burst out laughing.

"Baby doll," he says again, "I'm so sorry."

~~~~~~~~~~~~~~

Three weeks pass, and we're heading to Byron to go skydiving again. It will be my eighth and Chad's twelfth jump. As we drive, we pass field after field of grass with cows grazing. The journey mostly crosses flat land. Windmills come into view. Once we are close enough to see the blades turning, I know we will be near.

"It will probably be another five minutes before we get there. I'm going to jump twice today, what about you?" Chad asks.

"No, one adrenaline rush a day is enough for me."

"It gets easier when you do two," Chad says. "You aren't as anxious the second time, so you can just enjoy it."

"No thanks! Once is plenty for me."

I look at Chad's hands on the steering wheel. He looks so calm and confident. Meanwhile, my stomach is doing major somersaults. I always start panicking as soon as I see the windmills. They are the reminder of what is ahead. *How did I get myself into all this?* I think. It is hard for me to remember that it was my idea originally.

"Baby doll, we're here. What's wrong? Are you nervous about the jump?"

"No, not really."

"Well, I'll meet you inside. I'm going to pay for us."

As I get ready, I'm way more nervous than excited. It's supposed to get easier with experience, but it doesn't.

When my jumpsuit is on and the parachute is safely secured, I head to the plane.

"You're jumping for your eighth time today," our instructor Ron says. "You don't need headphones anymore."

Fear grips at me. "No way! I don't think you understand. I wasn't born with navigational skills. I can't maneuver myself when both my feet are planted on the ground. I even get lost in places I'm familiar with. I need headphones."

"You'll be fine," Ron says.

"No way! When I'm in the air, I want you guys to direct me. Trust me, without the headphones, I'll end up far from here, and you'll have to drive and get me." *Besides, I don't want to end up in wires and get electrocuted,* I think, but I keep that reasoning to myself.

"I've gone without headphones for the last six jumps. It's not so hard," Chad says. "You can do it."

Even after seven jumps, four of them solo, my fear that I will land in wires somehow stays strong. I can see the headlines: *Canadian girl electrocuted 6000 feet above ground because she didn't know which way was north.*

"I want my headphones," I say with conviction.

"You don't need them. You'll do fine," the guys protest.

Yeah, right. I think. I see another headline: *Canadian girl killed because she missed her mark. She landed in water and drowned.*

"I want my headphones," I say with nervous certainty.

"You'll feel great when you realize you can do it yourself without our help," Ron says.

She didn't live to tell her story ... "I need my headphones."

"Alright, here are the headphones," Ron says. "Let's go."

We board our little plane. The propellers are already moving. Ron goes in first, then Chad, and finally, me.

Chad will jump first. He is about 195 pounds, maybe 15-20 pounds over my liking and 75 pounds more than I weigh. The heavier people go first to avoid any air collisions, so he moves toward the door. Ron decides that he is staying in the plane instead of jumping out after I do. That is the "prize" for it being my eighth jump. *Well, at least I have my headphones.* I think. Our ascent continues, but I try not to start worrying. I know I still have time since Chad has to go first.

"Dooooor," Ron screams, the signal that the door is about to open, and the signal for Chad to exit.

"I'll see you down there," Chad yells over the sound of the propellers.

"Have a good jump," Ron says, and Chad is gone.

The door shuts, and our ascent begins again, this time for me. I thought I was nervous before, but my stomach is getting worse by the second. I can't believe I'm doing this. Before every jump, I go into this panic mode, but each time I land I forget about the fear, and in my excitement, commit to another jump. Now my fear is in full force. *What was I thinking? My mom is right; I am out of my mind. Good thing my dad is not alive. He'd agree with her on this one. Even I agree.*

I look down at my brown jumpsuit. My parachute is strapped on. Everything is a go. *Breathe,* I think, and then I hear the word that I dread.

"Dooooooor!" Ron shouts.

A gust of wind hits my face. The fury of the wind beckons me to get up and go through the door. I stand on the platform, 10,000 feet from the ground. On my own count, I will exit the plane and fall into the abyss.

"Are you ready?" Ron yells. With everything deep down inside of me resisting, I yell, "Yes!" Somehow, the louder I say, "Yes," the more convincing I usually am to myself.

Ok, on the count of three, I say to myself. The wind is howling so loudly I can hardly hear myself think. *1 ... 2 ... 3, and off I'll go.* Everything is a blur, but I am still standing on the ledge. *Just do it. There is no turning back, no quitting.*

I hear Ron scream, "Have a good jump!"

1 ... 2 ... 3! I say. Somehow that makes it easier. I plunge into the sky. I do one somersault after another, but it's not intentional. *Extend your arms,* the little voice inside of me keeps saying. I do so, and after a few more somersaults, my body finally balances. The odometer, which had started at 10,000 ft., now reads 7,000 ft. I did 3,000 ft. of somersaults. *Keep focusing,* I think, *6,000 ... 5,000 ... don't forget, at 3,000 pull the ripcord.* My arms are extended like wings. *4,000 ... 3,600 ... 3,200. Get ready ... 3,000.* I pull and am jerked up as my chute opens. Suddenly there is nothing but silence, stillness, nothingness. My body is in a state of relaxation, and I feel the exhilaration of pure peace.

This is the point where the headphones usually tell me which way to pull the cord, right or left. Yet no sound is coming from them. The headphones aren't working. *What did they say about where to pull? Into the wind? Away from the wind? Which way? Where is the wind?*

I stay calm. My survival mode kicks in, and it knows I need to be calm. I start to coach myself, *Just do it the way you did it seven times before. It was always the same. You see the landing pit. Keep maneuvering toward it. You're on your own, but you'll be fine.*

There is still no fear in my mind. I have no thoughts, except on my goal. I see the landing pit. I'm right on course as I get lower and lower. Everything feels as if it is going in slow motion. I descend lower and lower, and finally, I see the crew from below. I'm headed for the bull's eye. *Wow!* I'm going to be hitting the bull's eye, and I didn't even get help through the headphones. I see the team on the ground frantically motioning with their hands. *What is it? Oh, turn. They want me to head in the opposite direction. Ok.* I start turning into the wind.

Is that what they wanted? I guess so, because they stopped motioning. I'm going faster than usual, and the little voice inside of me commands, *Get ready for a parachute-landing fall.* I hit the ground and do the log roll they taught us to absorb the shock.

Bull's Eye!

I land in the pit. This is amazing. I did a perfect jump right into the middle of the landing pit.

Ron comes over, and his voice quivers as he asks, "Are you ok? You were heading away from the wind. We taught you to go into the wind! Thank goodness, you did a parachute-landing fall. I was sure that we were going to have to call an ambulance." He seems to be very tense, which seems bizarre to me because I feel so happy.

"I didn't realize I was in danger. My headphones weren't working. Besides, the hard part was jumping out of the plane. I'm always scared I am going to get tangled in wiring somewhere up above and get electrocuted."

"No one here gets tangled in wires. There aren't any around here. The real disaster is if a chute doesn't open, and after that, most injuries occur with the landings. You have to pay more attention," he says disapprovingly and walks away.

All of a sudden the exhilaration I had been experiencing from having jumped and landed right onto the target by myself vanishes. I'm left with the empty feeling of somehow having done something wrong.

You should have done it differently, I can hear my Mom saying.

What about the congratulations? I think, I had gone skydiving to face my fear of paralysis in the face of danger, my fear of fear. I am proud of myself for that.

Chad comes over to me with his suit still on.

"My jump went great. I heard you had a close call. It's important to pay attention to the wind. Are you ok? Did you hurt yourself?"

"I'm fine," I say.

"It will be easier next time," he says and gives me a hug.

"No, I'm done jumping."

"Are you sure? I know you'll be fine."

"I have nothing more to prove to myself. I jumped by myself, didn't use the radio, and landed in the bull's eye, which was an amazing feat in itself for me, so yes, I'm done."

~~~~~~~~~~~~~~

Irit Schaffer

11

1988, December

Letting go of expectation of how it should be allows for possibilities beyond what we could ever expect

anonymous

"So, are you ready for the experience of a lifetime?" I ask Nick as he walks into our room. Chad and I had reserved two rooms in a beach-front hotel for this trip, one for us and one for Nick, Chad's 13-year-old son. Chad had been worried that Nick's mom wouldn't let him come on the trip, but, surprisingly, she thought it was a great idea and was supportive of this experience for him.

Nick smiles and nods. "I love the water. It will be fun to be in the ocean with the dolphins."

Chad had told me Nick has some learning and discipline issues, but all I see is a kind, considerate and enthusiastic 13-year-old ready for an exciting adventure.

It is a dream come true for me finally to be here to swim with the dolphins. It has been over six months since I did the rope course that sparked my adventurous spree. I went skydiving eight times and decided that the only "doooor!" I ever want to experience again is the kind I can walk through. Chad jumped 20 times and then finally decided to call it quits, too. Skydiving was about letting go of fear for me, and now, I'm hoping the dolphins will help me bring more light, joy, and love into my life.

This tropical paradise, with exotic trees and plants, is home to famous coral reefs and water life. The blue waters are quite enticing. I can hardly wait to dive into the ocean and play with the dolphins. I also can't wait to see Ed again. His ropes course had been so much fun. I know these next few days will be awesome.

"It's almost 7 p.m., so we better get going," I say with excitement. We head out, making a few wrong turns, and finally find the meeting room. I have butterflies in my stomach. This is where we will begin the orientation for our adventure with the dolphins.

Ed is standing outside the door, and I rush up to him. He is about 6'0" and has silvery grey hair. His belly makes him look like a huggable teddy bear to me.

"Hi, Ed," I say and give him a big hug.

"It's so nice to see you," Ed says.

We walk into the room, and there are 12 other participants waiting. We do some group activities to break the ice, and then Ed pairs us up into groups of four. We will be in the same groups when we go into the water.

"Chad, Nick, Irit, and Brian, you will be in one group."

"Hi, you guys. I'm Brian, and I'm ten," a short, chubby-faced boy says. I notice a scar on his left cheek and jaw as his smile lights up the room. He is wearing blue jeans and a t-shirt with two dolphins on the front. His parents are standing beside him, wearing t-shirts with the Make-A-Wish logo on them.

"I'm here because of the Make-A-Wish Foundation," Brian says excitedly. "I had a rare cancer in my jaw, and the doctors thought it was terminal. I had surgery, and then I used crystals to heal. You want to know more about crystals? I have a whole bunch here."

"Ok, Brian," I say, completely drawn in by this little boy. "I'm all ears. I don't know much about crystals except they look nice."

"I see your name tag, but how do you pronounce your name?"

"Ear-eat."

"Irit, this crystal is tourmaline." He holds up a dark black, opaque yet shiny gemstone. "It's used for protection. It helps you stay grounded, which is important in healing. This one is malachite," he says, holding up a bright green spherical gem that has a silky luster to it. "Its history dates back to ancient Egypt, and it helps with tissue regeneration. This is a quartz crystal, and it helps cleanse the environment. It is used for protection and cleansing."

"What is that deep purple stone you have on the gold chain around your neck?" I ask.

"Oh, it is an amethyst pendulum. It is used for protection and helps smooth out negative energy. It also opens up the seventh chakra."

"The seventh chakra? I'm not too familiar with the chakras," I say, impressed. "Brian, you have the wisdom of an elder. Are you sure you're only ten?"

Brian smiles. "That's what people tell me. They can't believe I know so much."

"We'll be in the water at the same time. Are you excited?"

"What fun!" Brian says, but I can tell he is still too focused on his crystals to change the subject. "If you want to know more about crystals and how to use them, even to protect your home, I'll share it with you." He has such a knowingness about him that he exudes a confidence beyond his years.

"Maybe I should take you home with me because I need all the help I can get," I smile down at him. I can see his parents behind him bubbling with pride.

"You're not going to swim with the dolphins, too?" I ask them.

"No, only Brian will. The Make-A-Wish Foundation only paid for him, but it will still be great to share in his experience."

At this point, Ed calls everyone's attention back to him.

"I'm so happy to have all of you here," Ed says.

"Will we swim with the dolphins tomorrow?" Brian asks excitedly.

"No. Tomorrow you will go into the pool at the hotel and learn to use your snorkels and fins. You will learn how to move and make sounds like the dolphins. It's not a given that they will show up or that they will play with you if they do on dive days, so we will teach you how to better communicate with them. This will give you a better chance at having a great experience in the water. We will take you to swim with the dolphins the day after tomorrow."

That will be December 2, I think. *It has been four years since that phone call, the call that changed my life forever.*

"Do you think they'll play with me?" Nick asks.

"I bet they will. You've told me what a good swimmer you are, how you love the water, and how you like to dive deep. How can it not be great?" I say. Nick beams.

Sometimes I forget how young he is because he is so tall, almost the same height as his dad. Nick reminds me of the students I used to teach, the ones with spunk and a rebellious streak. They were always my favorites for some reason.

~~~~~~~~~~~~~~

"You better get ready, or we'll be late," I say to Chad the next morning.

"Don't worry. We still have about 45 minutes. I'm going downstairs for some breakfast. I'll meet you at the pool. I don't want to be late."

I drink freshly squeezed orange juice and have eggs sunny side up with toast. It's always so yummy. I get to the pool, and I'm one of the first people there besides Ed.

"How are you today?" he asks.

"Great. It took me a while to fall asleep last night because I was so excited. I'm so jazzed."

"Well, tomorrow will be the big day. Today you'll learn the ways of the dolphins in the water. I want you to meet Kyle. He will be our instructor. He is going to take you all in the pool today to teach you."

Kyle is tall and has golden blond hair and a bronze tan, probably from working outdoors. He is muscular, not an ounce of fat on him.

"Do you need equipment?" he asks.

"Yeah, I need snorkels, fins, and a mask."

"We have some time, but I'll start setting you up."

Finally, everyone arrives, and Ed starts.

"Let me formally introduce all of you to Kyle. He'll be our guide for the next few days. He is an expert on dolphins," Ed says.

"Hi," Kyle starts, "and welcome to the Florida Keys. I'm a scuba instructor, and I've also worked with dolphins for over four years. It is always fun to educate people about my favorite mammals. Dolphins are friendly, but they may or may not play with you. In fact, they may or may not show up. They're fed when they do, but some days, even when they visit, they decide not to stay and play. They love kids most, probably because of their innocence and playfulness. Any questions?"

Chad raises his hand. "Have people ever been upset with their experiences?"

Why would Chad ask that? I wonder. Chad was the one who asked all the 'What could go wrong?' questions about skydiving, too. My guess is that it is a result of his education. As a surgeon, you always have to be thinking of what could go wrong so you are prepared for anything and can act accordingly. I guess that mindset is so ingrained in him that it transfers over to all areas of his life. It never even occurred to me that this experience could be anything but great.

"That's actually a good segue to the story I'd like to share," Kyle says. "We once had the CEO of a large company on the trip. He really wanted to swim with the dolphins. I won't say his real name, but for purposes of this story, I'll call him Evan.

"Everyone went into the water in groups of four, like you all will, and the dolphins did come around and play, but they avoided Evan. On the second day, Evan didn't want to share his time with anyone because he didn't want any competition for the attention of the dolphins. When he went into the lagoon, he paid for four people so that he could be alone. He was sure he had it all worked out. Only problem was, even though the dolphins showed up, they still refused to go near him. He did this for one more day, but the dolphins wouldn't budge."

"So, what happened?" I ask.

"He was so angry that he actually broke down after the third day and cried. He even admitted it was the first time in his life he didn't get what he wanted."

"So, why didn't they play with him?" Brian asks.

"Dolphins are very playful, and they operate with their sensors. They can feel your energy, and they gravitate toward nice and playful energy. Evan was trying to force his will on them. I told him that unless he changed his attitude, the dolphins would stay away. They could sense his negative energy, and they didn't want to spend time with him."

It's the same thing with healing, I think to myself, *the more we try to force it, the more resistance we encounter and the harder it is to heal, not just physically, but emotionally as well.*

"So, did he finally lighten up?" I ask.

"No, after three days of rejection, he stormed out and went to Sea World, where he knew he would be guaranteed attention from the dolphins and a picture to show whomever back home. The dolphins were trying to teach him something, but he didn't realize it."

"So, how do we get them to realize we're nice?" I ask.

"That's what we'll be doing today. We'll teach you to become more like the dolphins. We all like people who like us and are similar to us. The same rule applies with dolphins, so we will teach you how to become more like them.

"Dolphins swim by moving their fins up and down. Their tail is so powerful that it can push them straight out of the water. They undulate in the water, meaning that they bend their bodies in an S shaped wave. This wave begins at the head and moves down the body toward the tail, pushing them forward.

"We will teach you to undulate so that you can move your hips and upper bodies, making waves and propelling yourself forward with your fins. First, you will bring your hands together in front of you and put your feet together. After that, you will make the same undulating motion as the dolphins. It's a wavelike form. Dolphins also make sounds. One of the easier sounds to mimic is the clicking, so we will practice that today, too."

"But we'll have snorkels, and we will be underwater," I say. "How will that work?"

"Dolphins talk in the water, and so will you. Don't worry. It's easier than you think. Anyway, enough talking, all of you should get familiar with your snorkels and fins, and you'll have all day today to practice undulating and making sounds like dolphins. We will be here for an hour this morning and then for another hour between three and four. Remember, dolphins are probably one of the most playful mammals, so if you want them to play with you, be playful. Tomorrow we leave for the ocean at 7:30 a.m.. Have fun."

~~~~~~~~~~~~~

I wake up the next morning to a flood of emotion. Today's the day, December 2, the day that changed my life forever. My dad's heart stopped, and a piece of me was ripped from its fabric. I always want to pick up the phone and call him, like before, just for a few minutes to say I love you and hang up. But there is no phone, no phone number, to call.

My dad, my rock of Gibraltar, is gone. He survived so much.

It is December 2. It is still painful for me to think of my dad, but today I'll be in the water with dolphins. Dolphins have brains 40% larger than ours, and I have been told they can send out healing energy. They have supposedly helped many people because they can sense problems. Maybe the dolphins will know what I need. I want to see this day in a different light. I need to learn how to remember my dad without feeling all this pain. Maybe the dolphins will give me light. Maybe they will spark my hope that perhaps life should and could be celebrated on this day.

"You better get out of bed. We have to be ready to leave in 30 minutes," Chad says.

"I'm awake," I say, quietly. "I'm just thinking of the dolphins. I wonder if they'll play with me like Flipper did on the TV show, especially since today is December 2."

"Don't get your hopes up. Remember what Ed said: they may or may not play with you, and they gravitate to kids. They'll probably play with Nick and Brian. In a way, we aren't so lucky that the kids are in our group because it will lessen our chances," Chad says.

I shake my head at this. *They will help me heal,* I think. *They will sense it. I just know it.*

I get out of bed and grab all my gear. I'm ready.

~~~~~~~~~~~~~~

We arrive at the center, and a person I have never met greets us. His tag reads "Ken." I look around and see that Kyle is also there.

"Welcome. Today is an exceptionally warm day at 85 degrees, so you all lucked out," Ken says, and a murmur of excitement goes through the group. "Before you all have the privilege of going into the water, there are a few things you must know, certain rules you must follow. These dolphins are wild and have not been trained. You are a guest in their world. Do not approach them; let them make the first move.

"You cannot touch the dolphins unless they invite you to, and no matter what kind of experience you are having, you *cannot* hang on to their dorsal fins. Any questions?"

"I have a question," Chad says. I chuckle to myself, wondering what worst case-scenario question is on its way now. "Has a dolphin ever hurt anyone?"

Of course not, I think. *That answer is obvious.* My thoughts are interrupted when I hear the instructor answer, "Yes." I stop in my tracks, thinking I must have heard wrong, but then the instructor continues.

"Once, a dolphin kept banging into the chest of a 30 year old woman. In fact, she got bruised up on her left side. She was the first person that ever had to go to the Emergency Room from this program. She thought the dolphin had broken one of her ribs. We were baffled and shocked. There was no explanation. We didn't understand what would have provoked the dolphin to do that.

"The woman had tests, and while she was wrong about the broken rib, the physician did notice a lump on her breast. They ran more tests, and it turned out that she had breast cancer. The cancer was on the left side, where the dolphin had kept nudging. That woman was convinced that the dolphin was trying to warn her by nudging her so often. She is sure that the dolphin saved her life."

I beam at this story. Dolphins are so playful, so in the moment and so loving. Maybe the high vibration and frequency they exude allows them to tap into a higher power that shows them what humans need. I am often frustrated by the limitations of the medical world. Maybe we could learn from dolphins. How could a dolphin just automatically sense something like a tumor?

I hear Ken continue, "Dolphins are known to be healers, and many times people have said that being in the water with dolphins has changed them forever even if they only experienced it once.

"You will have 45 minutes today. Though, of course, you can get out any time before that."

I turn to Chad, "So, if the dolphins don't play with us, does that mean we're not nice people, like Evan, that CEO?"

"Irit, don't be ridiculous." He laughs.

"Irit, Chad, Nick, and Brian," Kyle announces. "It's your turn in five minutes. Get ready."

I wet my fins and put them on. Then I put the mouthpiece of the snorkel in. I brace myself. Getting into the water is the hardest part. The water seems really cold, so, just like with skydiving, I decide I need to count down to prepare myself, *1 … 2 … 3.* I plunge into the deep. The cold pierces my skin for a minute before my body finally acclimates.

OK, use the snorkels. Use your fins. Undulate, I say to myself. *Mimic the dolphins.* Then, three feet away, I see one and then another and another. My heart starts to pound, and fear takes over.

Oh, my God, I think for the first few seconds. They are humungous, about 12 feet long, and moving gracefully and quickly through the water. *Yikes, they could pummel me in one fell swoop, and then I'm history.* Before I can be overcome by fear, I think of *Flipper* and all the things I have heard about dolphins helping humans, and I instantly relax. My heartbeat slows.

I see one dolphin that is dark grey on the top near its dorsal fin and almost white on its underside, and there are two others. They're moving fast. Suddenly, one dolphin leaps out of the water. *What fun!* I watch them swim by, but they're completely ignoring me.

Ok, I say to myself, *undulate.* I move my hips and upper body, just like I was taught. *Come on, dolphins, come over and play with me. I so desperately want this day to be special. Come on, dolphins. I'd love to play with you.* Everything falls on deaf ears.

The three dolphins keep swimming, totally ignoring me. I see them get close to Nick and Chad. Brian is no longer in the water. I don't know why, but the thought leaves me pretty quickly with the dolphins swirling around in the water. *Come on you guys, at least one of you can come and play with me, right? I don't understand.*

Ok, I tell myself. *Keep trying. Make clicking sounds like they taught us. Undulate. Try again. Keep trying.* I am trying so hard, and yet the dolphins are taking no notice.

After what seems like an eternity but was probably just 10-15 minutes, I get so exhausted from trying that I give up.

I start to swim around in the water, noticing little fish and plankton. The water is so clear I can see all around me through my mask. I begin singing through the snorkels, maybe more humming than anything. It feels so peaceful I forget where I am and what I had wanted. I get caught up in my own little world under the sea. I forget there is anyone else in the water. I am mesmerized. It feels like the water is nurturing me.

All of a sudden, I feel something on the back of my knee. I turn around, startled. *What is that?* I think. *Where am I?* Then, one foot away from me, there he is.

A dolphin is staring right at me. We look at each other, our faces almost touching. His eyes are so big and kind. They penetrate my heart, my soul. The dolphin knows me. The dolphin understands me. It seems as if he knows everything about me. In this instant, I feel one with the universe, and it is pure love and light.

He prods me in the stomach, and I turn. I roll to the right, and he rolls to the right. I dive underneath him, and he dives underneath me. We keep copying each other's movements and mirroring each other. We are completely connected.

I touch his smooth skin and he turns. He jumps into the air, makes a squealing sound, and lands about 18 inches from me. I laugh through every cell of my body. He turns me over time and time again. Now I notice the other dolphins coming around. They all want to play with me.

My dolphin, apparently feeling protective of his territory, intervenes. Only he is allowed to play with me. The others just watch from the periphery. He and I are immersed as one in a world that I never dreamt possible. The world of the sea has opened up to me. I have no thoughts outside of this moment and the next and the next. Thoughts of my father, my injuries, and the people watching completely evaporate. It is as if nothing exists except my friend and me.

Too soon, it is time for him to leave. I can sense it as my dolphin friend says goodbye, so I get out of the water.

"Irit," Ed says, "That was amazing. You were playing with that dolphin for over 30 minutes. The dolphins are never that playful with just one person."

I smile. I feel an incredible sense of inner calm and peace. The dolphin knew that I needed to open up my heart and to remember to celebrate and embrace life. The dolphin was helping me heal.

"Irit," Nick said, "I can't believe it. The dolphins were close to me and Dad, and then something changed. They just surrounded you and wouldn't leave. You were like a magnet. What did you do that made them come to you?"

Once again, I smile. There are no words to explain the magic that had just happened. It was beyond my mind's understanding. I had made a dolphin friend for life. I see his black eyes, so soothing and comforting, filled with knowledge and wisdom and love.

"I can't believe it," I say when Chad comes over to me.

"That was great. They came near me for two seconds and then took off," Chad says teasingly.

"Maybe tomorrow … What happened to Brian?" I ask, looking around.

Ed answers, "He got scared, so I will go alone with him tomorrow."

"Oh, well, I'm glad he will get to come back with you tomorrow. I know the dolphins will look out for him."

~~~~~~~~~~~~~

The next day, we're back, but it's in the sixties and cloudy.

After ten minutes, there is still no sign of dolphins. The energy in the air feels different today. The magic of yesterday is gone. Today is just another day.

Chad and Nick are in the water with me, but it feels lonely and cold without the dolphins, so I get out. I sit on a dock, and I start doubting my experience from yesterday. It seems so bizarre that when a magical experience occurs that is so poignant and real, self-sabotage emerges, filling our minds with doubt, not wanting us to take the next step forward because it would mean letting go of what was.

I throw a ball in the water and suddenly see the silhouette of a dolphin.

"Hey Irit, do you want to play?" I imagine him saying through his soothing squeals. He throws the ball back to me.

For about ten minutes, we throw the ball back and forth. My new dolphin friend keeps making squealing sounds, leaping up into the air, and diving deep below the surface before finally saying goodbye.

Yesterday, when our eyes connected, the dolphin showed me a new world, a world of the sea and all that lives there. Through its gentle and wise eyes, the dolphin showed me that we are all visitors on this planet and that it is important to respect all that is. Through its eyes, the dolphin showed me that the universe is more expansive than anything I could ever have imagined and that we are all one. We are all interconnected. I remember my dad told me that once. He always understood. He always said, "Everything around us is a part of our world. It is all interconnected."

"But Dad," I would protest, "what does it matter if something is happening far away from me?"

"Iritka, it does. One day, you will see."

I understand now.

Dolphins naturally help others in need. They saved that woman's life when they kept hitting her ribs. My dolphin saw the darkness in my heart and used the light of joy and love to dissolve the heaviness and pain so I could heal. Today, the dolphin stamped it in even deeper, reminding me again what pure love and pure joy feel like.

The dolphins are our role models. Their positivity, joy, gentleness, love, and desire to help others are amazing. Those are qualities that we should learn to access, qualities my dad accessed— the qualities that allow us access to our own good blood and our own qualities that will allow us to heal.

At dinner, Chad says, "Irit, the dolphins came close to us today, but they didn't want to hang out like they did with you. I thought maybe they would stay longer since you and Brian weren't around.

"Yeah, you have to tell us what your secret is," Nick adds.

I smile and raise my glass. "I want to make a toast," I say. "It is a toast I have known since I was a little kid. It is one word, and it is always said at times of celebration.

The boys lift their glasses to mine.

"Lechaim," I say. "*To life.*"

~~~~~~~~~~~~~

Irit Schaffer

12

1940-1991

When I despair, I remember that all through history the ways of truth and love have always won. There have been tyrants and murderers, and for a time they can be invincible, but in the end they always fail. Think of it—always.

Mahatma Gandhi

Mr. Rosen, my sixth grade Hebrew teacher in Talmud Torah Elementary School, says that on the Jewish New Year, *Rosh Hashanah*, the *Book of Judgment* for the coming year is opened up. Every person's signature lies in this book of life, and when the great trumpet, the *shofar*, is blown in the synagogue, it marks the beginning of the New Year. Each person's fate for the upcoming year is set in motion.

Rosh Hashanah is my favorite holiday because my mom makes all the desserts I love from scratch: flourless chocolate nut roll cake, chocolate éclairs with homemade custard, and strudel, not to mention the bowl of chocolate for the nut roll cake that she spends at least 30 minutes whipping on the stove and that we get to wipe with our fingers and lick when she is done. I shake my head, trying to rid it of chocolate daydreams and focus on Mr. Rosen's lesson.

"About a week after *Rosh Hashanah*," Mr. Rosen continues, "is *Yom Kippur*, the Day of Atonement. It is the holiest day of the year. It is the Day of Judgment. At the end of this day, God decides who will live and who will die."

"You are all too young to fast the entire day, but adults fast for 25 hours, from a half hour before sundown to nightfall the next day. They pray for forgiveness, and they pray that God will pass over their names and their children's names and let you have a happy new year. If you pray enough, maybe God will pass over your name even when you have done badly. On this day, according to the *Talmud*, one cannot eat, drink any liquid, work, drive, wear cosmetics or leather sole shoes, or have conjugal relations."

Johnnie raises his hand. "What does conjugal relations mean, Mr. Rosen?" Mr. Rosen blushes and quickly tries to find the right words, but before he can, Johnnie, the class rebel, blurts out, "You mean no sex?" and everyone laughs, except, of course, Mr. Rosen.

The kids fast until 12 p.m. on *Yom Kippur*, and then we feast on all our mom's desserts. Of course, by 10:00 *Yom Kippur* morning, my stomach starts growling, and I think of my Dad. He told me that during the war he was always hungry. I try to think what that would feel like. I can't even go without food for a full day, let alone many days and months. *How does the body adjust? How can one last?* I wonder, and then, like with all things I don't understand, I decide to stop worrying about it. I figure that one day I will understand. One day I will make a point of figuring it out.

~~~~~~~~~~~~~

We get dressed up to go to evening services. My dad is in his grey suit and tie. *Yom Kippur* and *Rosh Hashanah* are the only two days a year he gets dressed up. My mother is dressed in a dark suit. She looks very much in control, as she always is. We are all ready to light the memorial candles.

Yom Kippur always reminds me of the family members I never knew. There are memorial candles for all immediate family members of my parents' families who have perished. The purpose of these candles is to help us remember our relatives' existence and to pray for their well-being. There are four candles for my family.

First, there is a candle lit for my grandfather, my mom's dad, who died a few hours after his liberation from the death camp of Bergen Belsen because his heart gave out.

The next candle is for my uncle Deju, my mom's brother, whom my sister looks exactly like, or so they say. He had volunteered to go to Auschwitz because, at the time, it meant that his parents would be spared. We are told his fate was sealed in the ovens.

The next candle is for my grandfather, my Dad's father, who my dad does not even remember because he died at the young age of 26 from complications with pneumonia following an emergency appendectomy.

The last candle, my favorite, is for my dad's mom, my grandma, whose fate was also sealed at Auschwitz. I love hearing about her. My grandma had a heart of gold. I am told she always showered her love on my dad and my aunt Ersie. Dad told me she was kind and gentle and had a calmness about her that rubbed off on others. I look at my mom and can't help but wish she was like that.

The candles that are lit are a constant reminder to me of the war that was. In our household, the "H" word is forbidden around my mom, as well as asking anything about the war. We weren't supposed to talk about anything she did not want to hear. Sometimes, when we broke these rules, her legs would buckle under her, and she would fall to the ground. She would always recover quickly, and then my dad would take us aside and say, "It was the war that made her upset. You must be quiet about it." I never understood why he would say that. It's funny, my Mom is silent as a stone, but my Dad is always talking about the forced labor camp and Russian POW camp he was in. Why can he handle it, but she can't? I look at her. I can't help but wonder why she is so stern so much of the time. She often looks like every day is her *Yom Kippur*.

I don't know much about my mom's war experience, but I do know she could have escaped. She had papers, but she chose to stay with her parents. I also know that her most important possession is the gold chain she always wears around her neck. It reaches all the way to her chest. Her father gave it to her and told her to put in the lining of her shoe for safekeeping.

"What are you doing?" my mom yells, breaking me out of my pensive trance. "Get your jacket on. We have to go now, or we'll be late." Whenever I ask my mom why she is yelling, she yells back that she is not. It's just her voice. She can't help herself.

We arrive at the synagogue, and the greetings begin. Mrs. This and Mr. That come up to us, all saying the same things.

"My, I can't believe how much you've grown. You're still so skinny. You need to eat more," They greet my sister, too, but they never say to her, "You're too fat. You need to eat less."

I just say, "*Shannah Tova*," *Happy New Year*, over and over again.

Finally, after ten minutes of greetings, everyone finds their place. The men sit on one side of the synagoge, the women on the other. The men put on their *teffilin* prayer shawls, and the married women cover their heads. Before the *Kol Nnidre*, the services for *Yom Kippur*, the rabbi begins by thanking the contributors to the synagogue. First, he lists the people that gave $500, then $1000, and then more. Around me, I hear people telling each other, "that was so generous of you," "what a mitzvah (*good deed*) you do with your donations," and, "you will be blessed."

The Rabbi gives his sermon. He talks about forgiveness, and he talks about how it is important to be good, to give to others, to pray for those less fortunate than us, and to do *mitzvot* for others. As he speaks, I think of Uncle Frank. He gives generously to the synagogue and is always praised for that *mitzvah*, so I guess he is blessed, but he is only nice on Saturdays and holidays! Shouldn't he be good every day? So he prays … so he gives money … it doesn't change the fact that he is mean. Does anyone know what he did to us when we came to Montréal? It definitely was not a *mitzvah*.

The service ends, and I hold onto my Dad's hand on the way home. When we get inside, I ask, "The rabbi talked about forgiveness, and I was wondering something. You talk to Uncle Frank, and you go over to his house. Does that mean you have forgiven him?"

My dad pauses, then says, "It's hard for me to forgive, and it's hard for me to forget. One day you will understand. Now, go to bed."

~~~~~~~~~~~~~~

That *Yom Kippur* was over, and then the next came and went and then the next and then the 20 next. As I look out the airplane window, Chad brings me back to the present.

"You seemed lost in thought."

I turn away from the window of the plane that is taking us to Prague. "I was thinking of the Jewish holidays and how I grew up."

"The guide book says that Prague is a city made up of 600-year-old architecture that has been virtually untouched by natural disasters and wars. That will be amazing to see. One of the other attractions is the Jewish Quarter. It says here that there are six synagogues, a town hall and a cemetery. It didn't get demolished because the Nazis wanted to make a museum for the 'extinct race', so artifacts from all over Europe were stored here," Chad says.

"I grew up immersed in the Jewish culture. We kept kosher at home, and it was cool to celebrate all the holidays. The Hebrew school I went to emphasized the holidays, and it was always fun. It helped us feel connected to our heritage and ancestry. It will be cool to check out the Jewish quarter."

Chad turns to me and asks, "Why do Jews keep kosher?"

"Because the *Torah* says to do so, plus my mom's family has been doing it for generations. It is tradition."

"What does keeping kosher mean exactly?"

"Kosher means fit, proper, or correct. Keeping kosher means that we can and cannot eat certain foods, and there are certain ways these foods have to be prepared. The *Torah* forbids consumption of blood. It is the only dietary law that has a reason specified in the *Torah*. We don't eat blood because the life of the animal is contained within the blood. This only applies to the blood of birds and mammals though, not to fish. Thus, all blood from the flesh of kosher animals is removed. The other big thing is that we have to have separate dishes for certain foods. Growing up we had separate plates for dairy, meat, and a third category, called *pareve*, or neutral, which was food that could be eaten on any plate. On Passover, it is forbidden to eat leavened foods, which are also called *chametz*. Any utensil that is used throughout the year is not allowed during this holiday because it contains *chametz*. It is always a massive cleaning job when we prepare for Passover. Completely separate dishes and utensils are used during it."

"So what happened if you went out?"

"We never went out on Passover, but when we went out any other day of the year, the laws didn't apply. My favorite was always when we got Chinese takeout. Imagine eating Chinese pork, the forbidden, non-kosher food, as takeout at home."

"You mean you ate non-kosher at home? How did your Mom explain that one?"

"It was on plastic," I laugh. "There are a lot of contradictions that can't be explained, but on Passover, everything is by the book. My mom is emphatic about Jewish traditions. It's the way she is. I guess the traditions are her connection to her heritage, but I also think they are important to her because they are comforting and connect her to her childhood memories. I actually loved being immersed in all the cultural traditions growing up. I'm grateful to my mom for it."

"Look at this picture of the Prague castle. It's the oldest castle in Europe. I'm so excited to see all of this stuff. I've never been to this part of the world," Chad says.

"I'm just glad you are coming with me and are going to meet my family. I can't wait to finally go to Kosice and meet all the people who meant so much to my dad. There is no appendix to stop me like last time."

"If your mom thinks following the Jewish traditions is so important, does she have issues with you living with me since I'm not Jewish?"

"Actually, the word she would use for that is *Goy*. That's the word for a non-Jew," I begin, pensively. "You're a doctor, so she thinks our relationship is good overall. Plus, you're a neurosurgeon, so that's even better. But all the bragging rights I would get from those things are out the window since you're not Jewish," I say laughingly.

"Actually, being Jewish no longer holds the weight it once did. When my cousin married a non-Jew, after the intial hoopla, everyone ended up embracing him, including my mom, and it changed our family's entire mindset."

"Would your Dad have cared when you were growing up?"

"When I was 18, I met this absolutely knock out-guy on the squash courts named Robin. I was in my first year at McGill University in Montréal, but unfortunately, I was still living at home. On our fourth date, he picked me up from home under the scrutiny of my mother, the inquisitor. She made him come inside and asked him question after question, trying to find out if he was Jewish. I felt like I was dying a slow death from embarrassment. I just wanted to get out of there, fast. Fast would not be fast enough, but he held his own and was very elusive. I was impressed.

"When we finally got out of the house, he said, 'Would your parents care that you are dating someone who isn't Jewish?'"

"I laughed and said, 'Well, if my mom knew, she would probably faint and have a stroke, a heart attack, and/\or a nervous breakdown. I'm not sure in which order. My dad wouldn't care, but he would probably have a heart attack from worrying about my mom.'"

"What happened?" Chad asks.

"He did a great job with the interrogation, but for some strange reason, he said he didn't want to go through that again," I laugh. "That, of course, made sense to me, so that was the last time we went out. I was mad when it first happened, but now I just find it funny.

"What is really amazing is that he ended up getting a Rhodes scholarship. Education was extremely important to my parents, but at that point, I guess even a Rhodes Scholar would not have held any weight. He would have to be Jewish.

"My sister had it worse, though. My sister dated this guy Bobby for three years. He actually was Jewish, but my parents still did not like him. He was from a part of the Middle East where, culturally, women were not considered equals, at least in the era when my parents grew up.

"My mom would scream at Edna and threaten her, saying her usual 'You are going to give me a heart attack and stroke' line, but it wasn't a good strategy with my sister, since she never took those threats seriously. She would just ignore it. Even my dad, who was usually accepting of everyone, was on her about it, saying, 'He comes from a background where men don't treat women right.' It was one of the few times my parents were in total agreement."

"So what happened?"

"Thanks to their alliance, Edna spent two and a half more years with him than she probably would have otherwise. I really don't think they would have lasted that long if my parents hadn't fought so hard against it.

"My mom and dad are like night and day. My whole life I felt like the guy in *Fiddler on the Roof.* I'd look at my mom and say, 'on the one hand,' and then I would look at my dad and say, 'on the other hand.' It was always that pull and push, but they had a special bond and connection that was beyond what I could understand."

The flight attendant comes by, "Would you like a drink and mixed nuts?"

We both pull our trays down. Suddenly, the airplane starts to rock and the fasten seat belt signs light up. Even our trays are shaking from the turbulence. We're sitting in the exit row, and I'm beside the window. As I look out the window, I smile. Even with all this turbulence, this flight experience sure beats hearing, "*doooor!*"

"I'm so glad we're going to Prague," Chad says.

"I'm glad you will meet Barna and Jofie. I feel like I have known them forever. One of the things that I will always cherish is the day I got out of the hospital after my emergency appendectomy. Peter, Katy, Barna, and Jofie had a celebration feast waiting for me. We hung out in Barna's living room, sipping wine, tasting different cheeses with crackers, and eating cold cuts and Jofie's brownies. What made it so special was that I know the food cost a week's wages for them. To add to it, Petr had to wait in line for over two hours and use a connection to even get the meats. The outpouring of love that I received is something I will always hold in my heart. I can't wait to see them again."

"It's pretty amazing what we take for granted. How did he and your dad know each other again?"

"Barna and my dad were childhood friends. Then, Barna's sister, Elli, married into my dad's family; so, they were not only friends but also family. They also were in the Hungarian forced labor camp together until my dad escaped."

"Do they speak English?"

"No, I'm thankful that I can speak Hungarian well enough to communicate. I'll translate for you. You will at least be able to speak with Barna's son and daughter, Petr and Katy. They speak English. I hope you'll be ok with not being able to understand the conversations a good part of the time. I know it can be stressful."

"I lived in Japan for two years after medical school, and I studied Russian, German, Spanish and Chinese, not that I remember any of those languages well. I'll be fine."

"I didn't realize you had studied all those languages," I say, surprised and impressed. "My dad spoke eight. I was always so amazed by that, but he never studied any of them. He learned on the fly."

"I would have loved to meet him," Chad says.

The seat belt signs are turned off. Over the intercom, the pilot proclaims that it should be smooth for the rest of the trip.

"Both Petr and Katy are doctors. Petr is a cardiovascular surgeon, and his wife, Melada, is a pediatrician. Yet, under communism, being a physician holds little status. It is not a revered profession like in America. In fact, they are so low on the status list that when Petr got married, they had to jump through hoops just to get housing. They lived separately with their respective families for two years after their marriage before they could get their own home."

"That seems absurd compared to how things are in the States. So, what was the process for them to get housing?"

"Under the communist regime, there were only two ways to get a flat. First was through the state, which would take 10-20 years. Second was through a cooperative, which would take 2-7 years. With the cooperative, you first had to become a member, which cost 15 months' salary. Even then, one had to get the flat through partial help or self-help. Self-help meant putting 2,000 hours of work into the building of the complex.

Petr chose the partial, which meant he and his family had to put 500 hours into the building of the flat. Once the building was complete, the cooperative administration decided by lottery which flat they would be in. On top of that, Petr will have to pay an annuity for the next twenty years.

Only then will the flat be his. Their son was already one year old by the time they moved in.

"Well, communism fell two years ago, so does he still have to pay the annuity?" Chad asks.

"Yep, it still has to be paid up."

About an hour later, the plane lands, and I feel excitement swirling inside of me.

"Welcome to Prague," I say as we walk through the gateway.

Everything is quick, not like when I was here under the communist regime. Going through customs is easy, and I'm not forced to buy currency. I feel like I am being met with much less suspicion.

"Let's take a cab. It will be much easier than public transportation," I say.

"I think it's a great idea to be staying with a relative. It will give this trip a much more personal feel. Who are we staying with again?"

"Ruja. Ruja's husband was Frank's brother, so we always knew her as our aunt. She speaks English, so it will be easy for you. She used to live in Montréal but moved back here to be with her sister after several family struggles. It's good this way. Barna won't be upset that we aren't staying with him since we are still staying with family. A hotel would be out of the question. They would be eternally insulted if we tried to do that, but their space is a little small for the two of us. We're invited for lunch tomorrow, though, and I think I'm ready to just spend tonight in. I'm so exhausted from the flight."

~~~~~~~~~~~~~

The next morning, we leave early with directions in hand to do some sightseeing around the city of Prague. It is still a little cool. So, we wear jackets.

We decide to walk most of the way in order to see as much as possible. We walk across the famous Charles Bridge, which was one of my favorite places to visit the last time I was here. The bridge connects the various parts of the city and is the main footbridge for locals and tourists. I still have the sketch Petr gave me on this bridge all those years ago. It always reminds me of the beautiful view of Prague and the history of all the statues.

"Look at all the artisans," I say in awe. "It was bare when I was here last. It wasn't part of the communist edict." It is still early, but the place is filled with tourists and maybe some locals. It feels much more alive and vibrant than it did under the communist regime. I love the cobblestone pavement we're on. It almost feels new to me—maybe because the vibe is so different from the last time I was here.

"I read that there are three bridge towers and that the one on the old town side is considered one of the most astonishing gothic buildings in the world. I can already see why," Chad says, gesturing to the building in the distance.

I lean on the 3-foot high stone railing and look out at the water. The sun is shining on the Vlatava River, and the water is calm. I breathe in the beauty.

"Look at all the saints lined up on the bridge protecting us," I say. "There are 30 statues of saints along the bridge, but this one, the 16th, is the special one. It is of St. John of Nepomuk."

"Why is this the special one?" Chad asks.

"Because, if you touch the plaque beside the statue saint, you will have good luck, and you are guaranteed to return." I touch the plaque with both hands, hoping that will give me even more luck.

"Do you want me to take a picture of you next to one of the saints?" I ask.

"Sure, but get the river and the city in the background. Everything is so breathtaking." He looks around and picks one of the statues to stand next to.

"OK. Smile," I say. I snap a few pictures, and we head off to the front of the Prague Castle.

I feel like I am in a fairyland. The palace is immense. It includes cathedrals, a monastery, gardens, and three courtyards. It is solid, massive, powerful, expansive, and just incredibly breathtaking. The two guards here—who are not allowed to move as I remember from my last trip—are guarding the first courtyard, known as the Courtyard of Honor.

I lean against the wall, maybe one foot from the guard, and I smile as he maintains his stiff, motionless posture. I scan his blue uniform, grey pants, white gloves, black shoes, and military cap. His rifle is by his right side, standing up as if also at attention. This is a job I will never understand. It reminds me of all the people who had to stand at attention and not move for far too long during the war for the amusement of their captors. I always wonder how it is even possible to stand for hours on end, especially when forced to. I bet the brain has some sort of turnoff mechanism. *Maybe the brain goes into a survival mode allowing people to do the impossible. Kind of like how I lifted my cousin up when that car was about to hit her when I was seven. I still don't know how I did that. Or maybe it is a higher divine presence that gets accessed, or maybe...* Chad takes my hand, bringing me back to the present.

We walk inside and are surrounded by the immensity of the building. This is the largest ancient castle in the world. It is 570 meters long, about 128 meters wide, with an area of 7.28 hectares. It was originally built in the 9th century, but it has gone through many reconstructions over the centuries, which brought in the baroque, the gothic, and the Rocco influences. The architecture in here is mind-blowing. It is like walking into a space captured in time.

"It's magnificent," Chad says.

"This is the official residence of the president of Prague," I say. "Gustav Husak, who was the president of the communist party, lived here until 1989. Vaclav Havel became president in 1989, but supposedly he unofficially resides somewhere else because the living quarters in here are surprisingly small and not that comfortable."

We continue our tour of the castle. The beauty and detail in the construction is breathtaking. "Imagine the history written and hidden in these walls. We think we're so evolved, but look at what preceded us. This is from over 700 years ago. American architecture pales in comparison to this," I say.

We walk along, and Chad takes pictures. Finally, we get to the third courtyard of the Prague Castle in front of the Vitus Cathedral. "This is the largest cathedral in the country. Look at the intricacies, the art, and the stained glass. The bell tower is 97 meters high. It has the influence of Gothic and Baroque architecture," Chad says excitedly, quoting all of the travel books he had been reading in preparation for this trip.

We walk inside, and I have to stop. The ceiling goes so high! The stained glass, the art, the massiveness of the structure—it all freezes me in my steps.

"They buried the kings here, and there are 14 statues of Czech saints. I'm surprised that the communist regime left this all intact, considering they didn't believe in religion."

We continue our walking tour and get to the old city. We are near the famous astronomical clock, called the *orloj*, which is mounted on the southern wall of the Old Town City Hall in the Old Town Square. There are three components to the *orloj*. There is the astronomical dial, representing the sun and moon, the walk of the apostles, and the sun-dial, with medallions representing the months.

There is a crowd gathering at the base of the clock as the time clicks on, nearing 12:00. "Watch for the apostles, Chad." I say, excitedly, "I remember this from the last time I was here."

We wait a few minutes, and then the clock strikes twelve. Twelve wooden apostles start to parade by the window above the dial, and some of the sculptures start to move. Death holds its hourglass and beckons the sculpture of a Turkish Man, who is shaking his head in response. There is a statue representing vanity, portrayed by a man with a mirror. Miserliness is shown through the statue of a man with a moneybag shaking a stick. Not all the sculptures move, but all of them have been crafted beautifully. There are sculptures for an astronomer, a chronicler, a philosopher, and an angel. There are also twelve medallions, each representing one of the zodiac signs. When the apostles finish their journey across the windows, the golden cockerel on top of the clock crows, quivering its wings. The bell rings, the clock chimes, and we all disperse.

~~~~~~~~~~~~~~

We take a cab and arrive at our destination.

"I bet this motorcycle is Barna's," I say gesturing to one in the lot. "He had a bike in this exact same spot over ten years ago when I was here."

We climb three flights of stairs, and the door opens. It is as if I had left only yesterday.

"Iritka, it is so nice to see you," they greet me. Then they turn to Chad and say, "Please make yourself at home." I translate for him. Barna is wearing a short sleeve, checkered brown shirt with brown suspenders for his dark green pants, and big brown glasses. His smile is mischievous and playful, just like I remembered. Jofie has short, dark hair and big tinted glasses. I love her short sleeve, round neck pullover. It is hot pink and vibrant green with many different patterns. I love the colors.

"Petr and Katy and their families are on holiday in the country, so they won't be here today," Jofie says.

We catch up for a few minutes. Then I help Barna set the table while Jofie is in the kitchen. Jofie comes out with the food, the smile on her face letting us know how happy she is to feed us. I look at the food: Hungarian goulash, potatoes, and cucumber salad. My mouth starts watering.

"Chad, the more you eat, the better you will look in their eyes."

"It smells delicious. What a treat!" Chad says.

The food is delicious, and before long, lunch is over and the dishes are cleared. Barna and Chad sit on the couch, and I sit opposite them.

"Barna, can you tell me about the war? I want to get information for a book." I had told him when I was planning the trip that I wanted to get some information about my dad. So, I know he is prepared. At least, I sure hope so, but I am still nervous about asking.

Barna looks around the room, then takes his glasses off, cleans them with a napkin and puts them back on as I wait in anticipation.

"I have never talked about the war to anyone. After the war, I wanted to forget, so when Petr and Katy were growing up, I never mentioned it. If they asked me questions, I said, 'No! I will not talk.' But now, for Zoli..." He looks at me, pauses as if fighting an internal struggle, and then says, "I must help you. I must do this for Zoli even though I had promised myself I would never talk about it again." I watch as every muscle in his face tightens.

I know that if I had not said I was writing a book Barna never would have had the courage to open up. It had to have a meaning beyond him, a bigger purpose. To hold this kind of secret for so long must be so hard on the body. I think of my dad and close my eyes. I take a deep breath, knowing the emotions Barna's story will probably bring up. I am ready.

Barna begins, "Well, you know that in 1944 I escaped the Hungarian labor camp. I was a prisoner in Russia for two months, and then I joined the Czech army.

"Maybe you can start with when you were first forced to leave home," I say.

"In 1938, the first Vienna Arbitration assigned Kosice to the Hungarian kingdom. In October of 1940, Hungary joined Germany, Italy, and Japan in the Axis alliance, and in 1941, Hungary decided to join Germany in the war against the Soviet Union. Finally, in December 1941, Hungary, along with the other Axis powers, declared war against the United States.

"At first, it was not so bad. The first alliance in 1940 just meant we had to sign up for the Army, though I wasn't a good soldier."

"What are you talking about?"

"I have some pictures. I'll show you." Barna goes into his bedroom and comes back out with pictures. "I have kept it in a box for all these years. I never showed it to anyone," he says, a hint of excitement in his voice. He hands one to me, and I smile as I take in the photo.

"I can tell that's you on the left and my dad on the right, but I don't recognize the middle guy."

"He was our friend, Danny."

They are all wearing uniforms and holding on to their own respective bicycles and rifles. I pause, surprised, "You had rifles? I had no clue you were given rifles."

"Yes, they gave rifles to us, but they did not have bullets. That was not allowed."

"So, how come you are the only one smiling in the picture?"

"I was smiling because we had just found my rifle. I was such a good soldier that I lost my rifle."

"You lost your rifle?" I say with a laugh.

"Yes. When I lost it, we were all worried because I would go to jail if we didn't find it."

"So, what happened?"

"I remember saying, 'Zoli, what are we going to do?' He said, 'We will find it. We just have to keep looking.' We combed every inch of the field, back and forth, back and forth, until Zoli found it."

"How did you lose your gun?"

"We had sat down in the field for a little break. They weren't as strict with us at that point. Then, I forgot about the gun when we got back up. I told you, I wasn't a very good soldier."

"My dad is so serious in this picture." "Zoli was serious most of the time. He used to tell me, 'You'll see, it will get much worse.'" Barna looks at the picture again, and this time it's as if he has gone back in time. I can see flickers of youthful joy and anguish cross his face as he travels back.

"So, how long were you in the army?" I ask, breaking him from his reverie.

"Not for long, maybe a few months, and then we were allowed to go back home."

"How was that?"

"It was hard because of all the new laws. In 1939 alone, there were 350 edicts made against Jews. By 1941, every Jew had to wear a yellow ribbon in public. Next, there were laws that if we went on trains, we were only permitted in the third class. We were forbidden in many public places. We could not swim or play organized sports, either. The worst thing about all of these edicts was that it made it hard for Jews to find work. The laws practically forbid people to hire us."

"How did you manage?"

"We stayesd at home a lot. I was in love with a girl named Julie, so I spent a lot of time with her in her home." Barna takes off his glasses and takes a sip of his soda water.

Barna, Danny, & Zoli

Zoli, second from the left

Barna

"Zoli was a great swimmer, and he had an excellent physique. I kept telling him that if he dated it would take his mind off the situation. There were so many girls interested in him.

"But Zoli would say, 'I cannot get serious now. I will not be able to make any promises to anyone that I can keep. I will not be able to take care of anyone; it will just be one more person to worry about. Now I must focus on how to get more food for all of us.'"

"So what did you do for food if you couldn't work?"

Barna takes another sip of his drink. "We had very little food. Every day I asked, 'Zoli, what are we going to do?'

"Zoli would just say, 'We'll find a way.'"

"That sounds like him. So, what did you do?"

"Well, Zoli realized that one way to get food was through farmers. He would say, 'The farmers have the food. What can we do for them in order to get food in return?'

"He came up with a plan. Most farmers did not have pictures of their families. The technology was really new back then, but our friend Danny, from the photo I showed you, was able to take photos and develop them in his own darkroom. Zoli said, 'We will go to the farmers, take pictures, and develop them in Danny's dark room. When we return, we can ask them if they want to trade food for the pictures.'"

"So, what happened?"

"Zoli went to families and took a lot of pictures. When he returned with the finished products, they loved them so much, they not only gave us food but also money."

Barna laughs at the memory. "For six months, we were living better than ever. We went to many farms. The farmers were always happy to see us. They gave us a lot. Our friends and family started coming to my house or Zoli's house to eat. We had plenty of food, and all our friends and family had plenty because of us."

"No wonder he loved taking pictures so much," I say. I can still hear my Dad's voice inside my head, saying, *'Remember, pictures are important. You will be happy later that I am taking all these pictures. Now smile,'* and click and click and click the camera would go. He always took so many pictures.

"After those six months, a new law came into effect. We had to enlist again, and this time we did not have uniforms or rifles. We were being sent to the forced labor camp, or *Lager* as we called it." Barna takes his glasses off, rubs his eyes, and then puts them back on.

As time goes on, Barna tells me more stories. I translate them to Chad.

"My dad said that for a while he would get sent home on leave without any notice, and each time he went home, his mother, my grandmother, would have food ready for him. She always knew when he was coming even when no one told her.

"We had no phones then, and your grandmother, Pepe, she just knew things. I don't know how. She was special."

"Barna," Jofie calls from the kitchen. Barna excuses himself and heads in to see what Jofie needs.

"Irit," Chad says, "the kindness that I feel from Jofie and Barna is amazing. It's different in my family. My mom is very kind, but she is much more reserved and not as openly affectionate. My dad never shows that kind of warmth."

Barna comes back into the room. "Jofie needs something from the store," he says. "I'm going to take my motorcycle. I'll be back in maybe 20 minutes. Do you want to come with me?"

"No, thanks," I say, and I smile.

I look around the room. There is a sense of warmth and comfort in here, which I felt the moment I walked into this apartment for the first time. I can easily tell what Chad means. Everything is so orderly and neat. There is not much room, but the high ceilings create the illusion of more space. Two connecting glass doors separate the living room from the bedroom. When Katy and Petr were growing up, the bedroom was further divided between them. Katy had the space to the left as her bedroom. I look at the single bed in the opposite corner. It was my bed when I was here last time and Petr's bed growing up.

"I'm so amazed at all the stories. What did Barna mean by your grandmother knowing things?"

"My grandmother, Pepe, whose real name was Josephine, was an amazing person. She died before I was born, but through all the stories I feel like I knew her. The story that sticks in my mind is the last time Dad ever saw her. He came home and was going to surprise her, or so he thought. Instead, he walked into the flat and saw that his mom had set the table with her best china and tablecloth. His favorite meal was prepared, and she had even made dessert.

"'How did you know I was coming home?' my dad asked her. She just smiled. '

'How did you get the food?' he asked. They were struggling for money and food more than ever since the laws were making it so hard to work.

'I found a way,' she said.

"When he left to go back to his brigade, she gave him a letter and said, 'Do not open it until you leave here. You have to promise me.'

"'OK,' he promised. They hugged, she held on tight and told him how much she loved him, and then he left.

"She had known that would be the last time she would see him. That's what the letter had said. Every night he would read the letter to his brigade, and every night, many of the men would have tears in their eyes. 'It was like their own mother was writing to them,' he said."

"What happened to the letter?" Chad asks.

"When he was shot, it got bloodied, so it was destroyed. I always loved hearing that story about my grandmother and the letter. Even though I never knew what was in it, I wanted to cry each time my dad told the story. I would make him tell it to me over and over again when I was growing up. It's like each time I would hear about her, I would somehow feel closer and closer to her."

"I hope you will eat dessert with us," Barna says as he walks through the door. Chad and I smile and follow Barna into the kitchen. He hands Jofie the milk and cream he had picked up so she can make the whipped cream for our coffee. I watch Jofie in action and ask if she needs any help. Of course, I know the answer to that before I even ask, but I figure I should try.

Before we eat, Chad takes a picture of Jofie with the food. Jofie smiles, and I can see in her face that she is proud of her ability to feed us. My mom is the same way. They show their love through food.

We are served homemade apple strudel and coffee.

"The strudel is delicious," Chad says. "I can't believe the whipped cream is homemade. Tell them thank you for me."

I quickly translate and then reply, "This is what I grew up with. My mom would make a little coffee and a lot of homemade whipped cream. She would whip it by hand until it was ready."

After dessert, we head back to the living room.

"Where were we?" Barna asks.

"Let me ask you a new question. You mentioned before that my dad was afraid to get serious but you were in love with Julie. What happened to your girlfriend?"

"We got married during one of my leaves in 1942. It was tough to start a new marriage at this time, but we did it. At first, the Hungarians were not so bad, but they slowly took more and more away from us. Each day we would say, 'at least it can't get worse than this,' and each day it would get worse. We started moving toward the Russian front, so we were not given leave anymore.

"As time went on, we got less food, and we had to work harder and harder. The officers who ruled over us became known as the 'Hungarian Nazis,' and we were called the Jewish Brigade, the Jewish Legion, and the Jewish Suicide Squad."

"What happened to your wife?"

"My wife was killed in Auschwitz in 1944."

As he says those words, I think of my grandmother. In her letter to my dad, she had said she somehow knew her fate was sealed. I think of Uncle Deju, whom my sister looks exactly like. He also knew that he needed to sacrifice himself for his parents, and he died in Auschwitz. I think of my grandfather who, on the day of liberation, allowed others he had perceived to be sicker than he to go before him. He died of a heart attack, waiting for the next convoy. I think of my mom who had endured the unthinkable but could never utter a word about it. As the reality of all of those stories hits me, it is hard for me to comprehend. I want to stop and take a breather because it is so hard for me to hear, but I know I can't because Barna is open to continuing. I take a deep breath.

"Aunt Ersie gave me a letter that my dad sent to her in Aruba. It was written in 1942. Can you read it? I can't read Hungarian." I get my purse and take out the envelope.

I give Barna the letter, and he reads it to himself before responding.

"You know the letter is cryptic," Barna says. "Zoli intentionally wrote it very poorly; otherwise, it never would have been sent. Everything was censored at that point. It's amazing this even went through. I'll read the letter to you and then tell you what it really means."

~~~~~~~~~~~~~~

All families together. Work for Horthy for 20 cents a day. I had to take the job. Can you imagine, Ersie, to be a plain soldier with no rank? Especially for me, when I was thinking of the Army, I got the worst job, and with bad luck, I became a soldier. I hope for not so long if nothing comes in the way.

I send you some pictures. I'm in the Army only for four weeks. I hope you recognize me since I lost a few kilos.

I have to finish my letter because I have to go to the barracks. I am the maid in the room. I have to sweep the floors. But not a lot to sweep, because the room is not large, but there are forty people in the room. The most important thing is everyone is Jewish.

The sergeant calls us the Jewish Legion. I wish you and Jusie the best, and I hope you will be a very happy couple. Many times I kiss you. Zoli

~~~~~~~~~~~~~~

"And now here is what Zoli was really saying in the letter:

Horthy is in power. We are forced labor. We are separated from the non-Jews, and we have no rights.

We're not being given much food, and we're basically starving.

We just hope we will be allowed to return home again, like in the past.

It's overcrowded, and I'm forced to do menial work. The Jews are prisoners. We have been separated from non-Jews, and we are treated harshly. We are called the Jewish Legion.

~~~~~~~~~~~~~~

"Who was Horthy?" I ask.

"He was admiral and regent of Hungary. He made an alliance with Nazi Germany in exchange for the land we lost in World War I. That's how Kosice became part of Hungary again."

I translate to Chad, but I am watching Barna as I do so. He is getting fidgety, and I know he is uncomfortable.

"Let us take another little break," Barna says. He gets up, takes a spray bottle, and starts spritzing the green plant in the corner of the room. The plant almost reaches the ceiling. I watch as he works, and then, out of the blue, he turns and aims at me. He gets me, and I smile. I can see that sly smile I love so much radiating across his face, revealing his *joie de vivre,* a love of life that hasn't left him. After the tension that had built up in me during the storytelling, his sense of humor breaks through my spirits and lifts the pressure from my shoulders. Suddenly, a sweet memory comes back to me, and I can hear my high school students squeal as I squirt them with a water gun, their playful protests egging me on.

~~~~~~~~~~~~~~

I get up, laughing, and take this opportunity to go to the bathroom. I pull the cord that flushes the toilet, and as I head back to the other room to wash my hands, I flashback to the day I had my appendix out. I had been in the bathroom for what seemed like forever. It was so long ago, yet it seems to me like yesterday. Barna is inviting me into his memories, and it seems as if it is unlocking some of mine.

I return, and Jofie leads me into the kitchen. "I want to show you some pictures from before the war," she says. We sit at the table, and I take in the view from the window before turning to the pictures. Jofie is stunning. In one picture, she's wearing a royal blue and white fitted suit that looks like it came from Saks Fifth Avenue.

"I made all my clothes back then," she says when I comment on her suit. "I also made my father's suit in this picture. There were so many children in my family that there was no way we could all afford to buy clothes. There were ten of us: five girls, five boys.

"My father worked hard, and he was always serious. He did not show much attention to me separate from my siblings. One of the nicest moments I had with my father was when I gave him that suit. He was so happy. He stroked my right cheek with his two fingers just like this." I watch Jofie put her index and middle fingers to her right cheek. "I can still feel his touch on my face. I can see the look on his face, how proud he was. That was the most special moment for me. That was the first time I remember him showing me such attention." She smiles. "This is the first time I have ever shared that story. I've never told anyone that before, not Katy, nor Petr."

Jofie and I smile at each other like we just shared some great secret, which, I guess, we really did. I watch her face and eyes light up, warming the room. We go back into the living room to find Barna showing Chad a book about Prague. Barna smiles at me.

"You want more cake?" Barna asks with approval. I know that me wanting seconds makes them happy. Actually, thirds and fourths would make them happy as well, but that was beyond my capacity.

Chad gets more cake and coffee as well, filling his cup mostly with the homemade whipped cream.

As we eat, I look at Barna and ask, "Can we continue?"

Barna takes a deep breath and says, "Yes, let's continue."

"What happened the day my Dad escaped?"

"There was a Hungarian officer who watched out for your father. You could just see it. There were many bad officers, but there were some, though not many, who tried to help as much as they could. One of the nicer officers got your dad into the kitchen, and it saved him. The officer warned Zoli to stay away from the sergeant because he wouldn't live to see the next day if he went near him."

"My dad told me that, too. He said that was why he knew he had to escape that day."

"He asked me to go with him. I couldn't. I just knew that if I went, I would die. We hugged, and then he ran off. I heard he was shot and killed.

"In 1944, I escaped to the Russian front, and then I got into the Czech army. That's how I survived."

"What was it like when you saw Dad again after the war?"

"I didn't see your dad again. That was the last time we said goodbye."

I stop in my tracks. I can't believe it. They were like brothers. They never had a chance to reunite? Somehow, with the way my dad spoke of him, it had never occurred to me that their communications were never in person.

"I met Jofie after the war, and we moved to Prague," Barna continues. "Zoli came back to Kosice, but it was not easy to travel then, so we didn't visit each other. I spoke to him once on the phone, and we sent letters. He tried to convince me to go with him to Israel. He warned me about the dangers of communism, but I didn't want to leave. 'Nothing could be as bad as what came before,' I said to him. He always answered, 'You don't understand.'

"I am sorry we never saw each other again in person," Barna says, and I can see the regret in his eyes.

I am stunned. I can't believe that I never knew until today that they never saw each other again. 'Barna was like a brother,' my dad would say to me, and every year he would send Barna packages. The more money he made, the more he would send. 'The more I have, the more I can give,' he would say to me.

"Zoli worked so hard when he went to Israel and then Canada. It was only in the last ten years that he started to have it easy. My life here has not been so hard. There were many things we could not do, but it was not so hard to deal with. Zoli refused to come back to a communist country, though, and nothing could change his mind."

I hear my dad's voice from when I took my first trip out here. 'They will lock me in jail and throw away the key, and then it will be too late for anyone to help.'

"There were many times in my life where, if it weren't for Zoli, I would not have survived."

Barna gets up to get club soda, and I stand up and stare out of the bay window in the living room. I look at the tree and the leaves rustling in the wind. It is so peaceful.

"Would you like something to drink?" he asks me and gestures to Chad.

"No," we both say after I translate.

We all sit down again, and I let out a sigh. Barna lets out a sigh, too. We all sit in silence for a moment until Barna says, "I'm ready to continue."

I take a deep breath and start again, "Barna, my dad told me and Edna that a horrible thing happened on *Yom Kippur*, but he never told us what it was. Do you know that story?"

"Of course, I was with him. As usual, he saved my life. *Yom Kippur*, that's right," he says, as if he had forgotten and wasn't too eager to remember. "In many ways, every day became our *Yom Kippur* in the camp. Hunger and starvation was our way of life. There was always a gnawing feeling inside our bellies. Our stomachs were always growling, begging and praying for the minimum sustenance it would receive. Every day was made up of the same nightmares. Yet, we could never wake up. The nightmares were in the air, in everything we did, in everything we saw. *The Jewish Brigade.* What a name! It was a special unit of the Army that gave Hungarian rulers the opportunity to dish out cruelty daily. It was a unit that was privy to senseless beatings. If you didn't stand at attention properly, you were beaten for it. If they didn't like the way your hair looked, you were beaten for it. If they didn't like the color of your eyes, you were beaten for it. If you appeared to have a smirk on your face, you were beaten for it. You could be beaten with a stick, a hand, the butt of a rifle, or you could be pummeled with a boot on any part of the body. Anything could happen at the whim of the Hungarian guards, all for their sporting pleasure.

"The Jewish Work Unit was another name used for us because we were always working. I remember we would have to load five trucks full of hay, never knowing why we did it, never daring to ask, not that it mattered. The trucks were loaded and then sent off to some unknown destination. Many times we loaded the hay only to unload it in the same place. The hay would be put back in the barns with the ultimatum that if you didn't finish the job properly, you would miss dinner.

"'Properly,' no such standard existed. It just depended on how cruel the Hungarians wanted to be that day. Imagine, a piece of stale bread with murky soup and maybe part of a potato, or maybe some cabbage, that would be the fuel for a full day, a full day of labor in the cold, in the rain at that. The 50 of us liked sleeping in the barn, at least, because the hay would give us a semblance of warmth, though it was never really warm enough to ease our chilled bodies."

"How did you endure all that?"

"I don't know, but I remember two of our brigade, Chaim and Joseph, who were Chasidic Jews, the ones who wear the black kaftans and black top hats. They had beards that were straggly and went all the way down to their chests. They also had twirly ear locks from never shaving their side-burns, and they always had their prayer books by their sides. They were always studying, always praying, and yet, now, they were like us, lacking any semblance of their past life."

"Yeah, Chasidic Jews actually scared me a little when I was growing up in Montréal," I say laughingly.

"Irit, they would make me laugh and give me hope."

"How was that?"

"They would, on Fridays or holidays or whenever, take imaginary wine and say the blessings. They would light imaginary candles and say the blessings. They would hide a morsel of bread in their pockets and later pull it out and say the blessings. That is, when they felt they were not within earshot of the guards."

"Why is that something you remember so clearly?"

"Because, no matter what the circumstances, no matter how bad things got, they would keep their faith and go through the motions of being Jewish. It seemed so absurd to me that it made me laugh, and even more important, it helped me believe when holding onto belief in anything was getting more and more difficult. They still prayed on *Erev Yom Kippur* (the eve of *Yom Kippur*), even though, at that point, the rest of us thought it was ridiculous to pray and ask for forgiveness and atonement.

"The morning of *Yom Kippur*, at around five or six, the Hungarian officers, with rifles in hand, came storming into the barn, ordering us to get to attention. Then, came the surprise.

"The soldier said, 'Today is your *Yom Kippur*, and this is your lucky day. Today we will give you a chance to renounce your religion. If you convert today, you will be set free and return home.'"

"So, what happened?" I ask.

"I thought to myself, *What are words anyway? I'll say whatever they want me to if that enables me to leave this hell-hole. If God is awake, he will understand.*

"As I was about to put my right foot forward, I looked over at your dad. Zoli stood there, at 6'2", with little semblance of his athletic physique left from his years of playing soccer and swimming. I saw his eyes piercing into my soul, not enabling me to move. I could hear him yell, *This is a trick. Do not move.* Yet, not a word came out of his mouth. I saw him do the subtlest shake of his head possible so he wouldn't get caught, and I kept my feet planted, rooted into the ground. I was paralyzed in my place by his look. I noticed Zoli also gesture to Ben, George, and Jon. Ben and George stepped forward anyway. All in all, twelve stepped forward.

"The officer said, 'Who else wants to be free, to become Christian, and to be forgiven for your sin of being a Jew and scum of the earth?'

"There was a silence that seemed to last an eternity. I kept wanting to step forward. I so desperately wanted to believe that they were telling the truth. I kept looking at Zoli so I would have the courage to stay put.

"The officer finally opened the barn door, and the twelve men marched behind him, with the other guards at their sides. We kept standing there, afraid to speak, afraid to move since the door remained ajar.

"Then the order was given, 'Stand at attention in one line.' I heard the cruelest laugh and the order, 'Shoot.' All twelve men fell to the ground, bullets through their bodies. No more breath would ever come into their lungs."

"Did you cry?" I ask.

"I couldn't. I just stood there, frozen. The guard came back in and let out that same evil laugh. I wanted to kill him with my bare hands, but I looked at Zoli and stayed put. He told me with his eyes, once again, that now was not the time. Then, the next order came: 'Dig.'

"That night, Chaim and Joseph prayed and said, '*Yiskadal v'yiskadash*,' the Jewish prayer for the dead. Someone blurted out what many of us were saying to ourselves every day, 'How can you still believe in God?' They answered, in unison, as if they had practiced this for a lifetime:

'How can there not be a God? We are still alive.'"

~~~~~~~~~~~~~~

Zoli, second from the right.

Men in the Hungarian Forced Labor Camp

Zoli in the front middle, with white turban

13

1991

Hatred does not cease by hatred, but only by love;
this is the eternal rule.

Buddha

Once again, I fasten my seatbelt, and Chad fastens his. This plane will take us to Kosice, the city my dad grew up in.

"Finally, I will be able to bring all the stories my dad told me about his childhood to life," I comment to Chad.

"What is the language of the people there?" Chad asks.

"Slovak, but when my dad was growing up, everyone spoke Hungarian. It was part of Hungary until 1918 and then again during the war. It's only 20 kilometers from the Hungarian border."

"Was your dad born there?"

"No, he was born in Hernandesce, Hungary. When he was about three, his dad died of pneumonia. His mom tried to maintain the farm for a couple of years, but she couldn't manage it without his dad. So, they all moved in with the family of her mom and stepdad, the Weinbergers. The sad part was that there was no work for my grandmother in town. She worked almost two hours away taking care of another family and their two children, so my dad and Aunt Ersie just lived with their grandparents most of the time.

"Aunt Ersie told me that when they were five and seven, they would only see their mom on Wednesday nights and weekends. Whenever she left, Aunt Ersie and Dad would get into one bed, hold each other, and cry themselves to sleep. It's like they set a pact that they would be there for each other.

"My dad always said that during the war, it was his memories of Ersie that helped him remember the good in life. It was her love that kept him going."

"I'm glad I met your aunt. Even at her age, she is so regal."

The plane starts moving, and within a minute we're up in the air. I look down at the beautiful land of Prague, wishing to return some day.

"There were two women that my Dad always talked about for as long as I can remember, Ellinani and Margitnani. In Hungarian, '*nani*' means *aunt*. I'm so excited that I'm going to meet these great women," I say.

"So, they are your aunts? Do you know how they are related to you?"

"Ellinani became my dad's aunt through marriage. She is actually Barna's sister. When he was about ten, she moved into my dad's house. Margit was my dad's step-grandfather's daughter, so it's a distant relation, but she was always protective of him.

"Whenever he told his stories, it was as if they were larger than life to him, so, of course, now they are to me, too. I was supposed to meet them the last time I was here, but then I had the appendix surgery, and well, you know that story."

"If they're anything like Barna and Jofie, I'll be happy. I can't get over their hospitality. I mean, they didn't even know me, and yet I never felt left out. It was like I was part of the family."

"Well, Chad, you are through me." I look at Chad as he shrugs. *Doesn't that make sense?* I think. *We have been together a long time ...* but I say nothing.

"How long are we going to be in Kosice?" Chad asks.

"About four days; then we head off to the Tatra Mountains."

"I am amazed by how Prague seemed to have escaped most of the bombing in World War II," Chad says. "Everything is so old and beautiful. It is breathtaking."

I nod. "I wish my Dad hadn't been so afraid to return. I wish he could have seen the people he loved so much again. Before the war, he had believed in the socialist way of the world. He felt that communism was the way the world should be. Everyone would be treated equally. After what he lived through, however, he vowed never to return to communist soil. 'They say one thing in the books, Iritka,' he would say, 'but it is not at all like the books.' There was nothing anyone could say to change his mind.

"You know, you're like him in some ways," I say. "You're soft spoken and generous. You never yell, and you care about people around you."

I halt in my comparison at that point and reflect. My dad's eyes were dark brown and kind. He always had that twinkle, that sparkle, in them. I look into Chad's eyes. *But you don't have that sparkle*, I think, *and it bothers me*. As quickly as I think it, I erase the thought from my mind. I don't know why, but Chad's eyes have always troubled me. It is a strange fixation of mine.

The flight is short and sweet. After only an hour, I hear the flight attendant say, "Fasten your seatbelts. We will land in Kosice in ten minutes."

"Chad, I'm so nervous. I have no idea how we will recognize them."

"They'll find you."

"I hope so."

"It will be fine," he says reassuringly.

My stomach is tangled up in knots, and yet, at the same time, I am bubbling with excitement. I am finally going to meet my family.

One by one, the plane empties. We claim our luggage and wait outside. It's sunny, about 85 degrees. I know we are in a different country, yet all the people look just like they do at home. It's not until I hear the language buzzing around me that I fully realize where I am. I look around, the sun shining on my face, and then, from maybe 60 feet away, I hear my name and see five people waving at me. We head toward each other.

"Iritka, it is so nice to meet you," I hear a chorus of voices saying in Hungarian.

Chad and I get hugs from everyone, and we each get a bouquet of flowers with an assortment of tulips, roses, and irises.

"Iritka," Marika, my dad's cousin says, "you look just like Zoli."

Just my luck, I think to myself. I have always been well aware that I inherited my dad's face, big nose and all, rather than my mom's beautifully proportioned one.

"This is Latzi, my husband," I hear her say.

Latzi gives me a hug and a kiss. Latzi is 65, and Marika is 63. I got their ages from Aunt Ersie in preparation for my trip.

Next I meet Ellinani, who stands at about 5'1", with short white hair and big brown glasses. She looks at me and immediately pulls me into a hug; my great Aunt Ellinani, the woman that my father spoke of with such love, the woman I always wanted to know, the woman I felt I always had known. Her eyes are so kind, her smile so radiant. My heart melts.

"I am so happy to finally meet you in person," she says in Hungarian, and I get another hug and kiss on the cheek. I look at her and think, *You're 88 years old, and your posture is better than mine!*

"You look just like your father. Too bad he never came back to visit," she says.

Elllinani's daughter, Eva, and her husband, Sandor, introduce themselves to me. Eva is 65, and Sandor is 70. Once again, I am smothered with kindness.

"We are so happy to finally meet you," I hear over and over again in Hungarian. "We are so sorry that Zoli never came back to visit."

I introduce everyone to Chad and start translating for him. Ellinani, Eva, and Sandor live in a two-bedroom apartment. It was determined before we arrived that Chad and I would stay with them. A hotel was, of course, out of the question.

I look at this group of five that make up my family and my heritage. Three of them are wearing short sleeves, and I suddenly notice the number 17260A on Marika's arm. My eyes scan the rest of the group, and I notice other numbers on some of their left forearms. It feels like someone is squeezing my heart as hard as possible. *That must be their constant reminder of the war, the war I am going to ask them to talk about. I hope they want to talk. I hope I'm not bringing them distress by asking.*

"You must be hungry," I hear the Hungarian chorus again. "We have food prepared."

"We will all go to our house," Ellinani says.

I translate for Chad. I'm glad Chad is with me because he is always willing to eat, which bodes well for his relationship with everyone in my family. The more you eat, the more you care in their eyes. That must be in our Jewish blood because as the years have gone by, I, too, have started to feel that way when people come over. Yikes!

We drive in two cars, and 20 minutes later, we arrive. I look at the apartment complex. It reminds me of tenement housing, almost like barracks with brown cement. The apartments are square and efficient. The building is three stories. They live on the third floor, and, of course, there is no elevator. We walk through the door, and I watch my great Ellinani as she walks up the stairs. She moves quickly, never stopping to catch her breath. She is the first one up. I look at her, and it is like she is surrounded by white light. She has such a pure smile. No wonder she meant the world to my Dad.

I walk into the apartment. A transformation has occurred. Outside, the building looks plain and dreary. Inside, the home looks inviting and warm. There is a big kitchen with a little cot in the corner just like at Barna's. I notice a long dining table with embroidery on it. There are even embroidered coasters under the crystal vases that are famous in this part of the world.

"The embroidery is so beautiful," I say in Hungarian.

"Ellinani made it," Sandor answers.

I look at my great aunt, and she smiles that beautiful smile.

"You know," Ellinani tells me, "your Dad has written to us about you since you were born. I wish he would have come to visit us while he was still alive. We told him it would be okay and that things had changed, but he said no."

"I know, Ellinani. My dad always talked about you, too."

"Iritka, I am so happy that you finally came to Kosice. We were so disappointed when you had your appendix out in Prague and never made it out here. Now I am happy. I can finally be with you."

I think of all the years I had hated speaking Hungarian. Now I feel so lucky that Ellinani and I have a language in common. I stare at the intricacies of a needlepoint on the wall. It features a regal woman and man with trees and flowers in the background.

The aroma in the kitchen is so inviting my mouth starts to water.

"You must be hungry. I made the food before we picked you up. Eva is heating it up now."

Within a few minutes, Eva beckons all of us to come and eat. Eva and Ellinani are about the same height. Eva is maybe fifteen pounds heavier than her mom. They both have short hair that is perfectly in place though Eva's hair is brown and Elli's is white.

I feel much warmth from them as they serve vegetable soup with dumplings, beef stew, cucumber salad, and green beans.

"It will be so nice to show you Kosice. We will be your tour guides. Is there anything special you want to see?" Sandor asks. He has dark brown hair with grey mixed in and a receding hairline. He has a round face with a serious look about him, as if he were trying to protect everyone. He is wearing a short sleeve shirt with khaki pants and a brown belt.

"I'd like to see where my dad grew up and where my grandmother had to live because of her work when my dad and Ersie were young. I'd like to see the school they went to and the synagogue they went to. I'd also just like to see what Kosice is like."

"Not all the buildings are still there," Latzi says.

"Then just show me where they were. That will be good enough for me."

"We will take you. There is also a part of Kosice that we will show you that is just like it was when we were young," Latzi says.

"That will be great."

"How is the food? You hardly have any on your plate," Eva says with concern.

"That's because I've eaten most of it," I say reassuringly.

As usual in my family, I take and eat a second helping and the question arises again, "Do you want more?"

"No, thank you. I'm full. I already had two helpings."

"Chad, do you want more?" I translate.

"Sure, I'll have another little bit." I smile. He may not speak their language, but he is fitting in with my family just fine.

"Marika and I will clean up, and then we will all have dessert," Eva says.

I look around the room and explore a little more while they clean up. The wall unit has two shelves full of books, one shelf with crystal wine glasses and goblets, and another shelf filled with Bohemian crystals and Czech plates. I love their tall ceilings, and the beautiful windows covered with lace curtains that Eva made herself. I am interrupted in my explorations when Ellinani takes my hand and says, "I want to show you something." We head into her bedroom. I follow her eagerly, excited to see what she has to show me.

"Iritka, two months before your dad died, he sent me a letter, and I still have it. Would you like it?"

"I'd love it," I say earnestly, "but I can't read Hungarian. Can you read it to me?"

I look at my aunt who, like me, is skinny. Elli has on a white, lacey long sleeve pullover and a black skirt that I know my Aunt Ersie had sent her. Her gentle voice begins:

~~~~~~~~~~~~~~

Thirty-seven years passed like it was yesterday. I will always cherish the time I spent with you when I lived at your house after the war. Every night I made the fire. I remember it always. Of the whole family, you are the closest to me.

Ersie said that she wants to bring you to California. I thought I would finally see you after 37 years. I don't want to believe that all this time has gone by.

The best time in my life was when I was with you, Elli, the two months before I went to Israel. I would love to talk to you in person at least once.

Barna and I speak on the phone and in letters. I would love to send a package, and I want to know what size everyone is. Send me the measurements. I would love a picture of Eva and Marika.

Vera [Elli's other daughter, who now lives in Israel] goes sometimes to Boston. I will look her up. When he was here in Montréal, Petr said that he "loved Elli." What's not to love?

Edna still looks great, like she is still twenty. Irit meets with Ersie a lot since she is still in LA. Ersie has had lots of disappointments. Jusie is a good man, but he is very nervous. His daughters also run away from him.

Tell me if you want anything. With an open heart, I'll send it.

With much love and kisses,

Zoli.

~~~~~~~~~~~~~~

"Iritka, I'm so happy you are here," Ellinani says once more as she finishes the letter. "We will spend a lot of time together. I wish I could have seen Zoli again, but I am blessed to have you here."

I try in vain to hold back my tears.

"Let's have dessert," Ellinani says softly. We head back to the table, which is now covered with cheese strudel, apple strudel, and poppy-seed cake, more homemade delicacies from my great aunt.

"I only want the apple strudel," I say, "because that is all I have room for." My statement falls on deaf ears. "I'm full," has no weight in these circumstances. All of the desserts are piled onto my plate.

"You need to at least try them all," Marika says.

I look in her eyes. Everyone seems so happy to be able to give something to us that I succumb. I eat the apple strudel and the poppy-seed cake, but I try to leave the cheese strudel.

"I'm allergic to cheese," I say.

"Iritka, a little of this won't kill you," they urge.

I look at Chad, take a deep breath and finish everything on my plate. I just can't say no, regardless of what my stomach may have to say afterwards.

"Have seconds."

This time I'm really too full to cave. "I can't."

They look at Chad expectantly.

"Have seconds," they say again, and I translate.

"I'll have a little bit more of all three. It is absolutely delicious." Everyone beams at him. I look at Chad as he eats and laugh in disbelief. Thank goodness he was never one to say no to desserts.

"Would you like cognac?" Sandor asks. "It makes the food digest better."

"Ok. Just a little bit," I say. "Chad," I remind him as he eats, "you know we will be eating again with Marika's daughter and the rest of her family in three hours, right?"

"Good thing the food is so great," he says good-naturedly.

We finish eating, and the table is cleared.

"Come," Marika says, "let's sit on the couch and talk. Barna says you are researching for a book and would like information."

I am relieved that I am not the one who brought it up. Marika, Eva, and Ellinani sit on the brown couch. I look at Elli and, as always, she radiates gentleness and inner peace. I see great kindness in Eva, but there is also an inexplicable deep sadness in her eyes. Her posture, like her mom's, is erect, sending a message of strength and wisdom.

Chad and I sit in chairs facing my relatives. Marika sits next to Eva. She, too, wears glasses. She has short brown hair, with "not even one white hair," as she so proudly states. Every hair is perfectly in place, and she is wearing a brown-and-white top with a brown skirt. She has a mischievous, playful look in her eyes, almost like innocence, yet at the same time, she seems rooted to the ground with incredible strength.

Sandor takes a seat on the brown chair, and Latzi is the last to sit down. Latzi is maybe 6'2", and he is like a teddy bear. He wears big glasses with black rims and has a receding hairline with black hair mixed with a little grey. He has dimples, and when he smiles, I feel him exude gentleness. As with Sandor, I get the sense that he is always protecting his family from the cruelty of the world.

I'm about to begin when I notice the numbers again, always a reminder. I take a breath and say, "I know it is hard for you to talk about the war, but I would love to know more," and add, looking at Chad, "Chad, I'll translate so you can take notes. At least, that way you will be involved."

"Iritka," Latzi says with caution, "I have never talked about the war before."

"Nor I," another of the relatives says.

"Nor I." A chorus of voices rise.

I look at them nervously. I know this will be hard for them. I'm not sure what to say.

Finally, Ellinani breaks the silence, "We will help you because it is for Zoli." She looks at Eva, Sandor, Marika, and Latzi as if saying this is a must, and then she smiles at Chad.

"Chad," I explain in English, "no one has ever talked about it."

"Irit, are you sure this is a good idea?" he asks, expressing my own concern.

"Chad," I say, trying to reassure myself just as much as him, "it is important that they share their history not just so the world will know but also so they can heal. When you let go of secrets and people bear witness to it, it can help. Thankfully, they are willing to because it is for a bigger purpose. It just might be hard."

I take another deep breath and start in with my fractured Hungarian. It is much easier to understand it than to speak it.

"You were all in Auschwitz." I get affirmative nods from everyone. "When did you go?"

"In 1944, when the Germans took over and new laws swept the country along with renewed orders to get rid of the Jews," Eva answers.

"Eva, were you married before the war?"

"No, I was only 18."

"I was only 17," Marika pipes in, and Elli adds, "Vera, my other daughter who now lives in Israel, was only 13."

"So, maybe you can start from the beginning. Who would like to start?"

They all look at each other, and then Eva begins, "We were all shipped out in cattle cars. There was nowhere to sit. There were no toilets, and there were about 70 people per car, maybe more. I remember watching my father on the ride. Within 24 hours of us getting in the cattle car, his whole head of hair had turned white. In 24 hours, he became an old man. We got there, and we were sorted alphabetically, so Marika and I were separated.

When Vera got off the cattle car, the officer there asked her how old she was, and when she said she was 13, he quietly said, 'Tell them that you are 18. Don't forget. You are 18.' The officer knew that if you were a child, they put you in the lines where you would not return."

It is hard for me to listen to this. It's as if I am there watching it all as it unfolds. I'm taking in the cruelty and injustice. As I witness them being crammed into a cattle car, I feel like someone has punched me in the stomach. I pause and tell myself to breathe.

Eva continues in a very matter–fact-way. She seems detached. That is probably the only coping mechanism she can use when speaking about this dark part of her life.

"We stood in line, waiting for our destiny, and we got separated from Vera," Ellinani picks up where Eva left off. "When it was my turn, they asked, 'How old are you?'

'42,' I replied. I was put in a line to the left with many of the older women and the children. Eva followed me.

I saw Vera waiting in another line, and I knew I had to get to her.

"'Eva,' I said, 'we will run to the line where Vera is waiting.'

We took off.

A German officer yelled after us, *'Was ist los?'* (What is going on?) But just at that moment, another cattle car full of people arrived, and there was a big commotion. We were lucky because they forgot about what we did.

Now me and my two girls, Eva and Vera, were in one line, together. As we waited in this new line, the German officers asked each person, 'How old are you?' and, 'What work do you do?' *Why are they asking these questions?* I asked myself. I looked around and tried to figure out a plan. If they were putting us to work, the factory would be best I decided. That way we would not be as cold. I figured that in the factory, they would want people who worked with their hands. I told the girls, 'Vera, Eva, tell them you can do anything with your hands.'

Then it was my turn in the line.

'How old are you?' The German officer asked.

'28.' I lied this time.

They motioned me to go in a different line than the one Eva and I had been in before we ran, the line that led everyone to the showers. We had been saved.

It was Vera's turn.

'How old are you?' he asked.

She said, '18,' heeding that man's words of advice.

'What do you do?'

'I can sew, cook, and fix things.'

She joined me in the line. Now it was Eva's turn."

"Yes," Eva says, picking up the story once again. It is hard to believe that they have never spoken of this time before. Their narrative flows so smoothly from one person to the next it feels effortless. "I said the same thing, and then I was in the same line as them. We were shipped off to work in the factory."

I am on the edge of my seat, "So, what happened?"

"We were in the factory, and every once in a while, I would be able to steal extra food and share it," Ellinani says.

"Weren't you afraid they would catch you?"

"It didn't matter." I look at Ellinani in awe when she says this. She risked everything for the sake of her girls. She always cared about more than just herself. She could see the bigger purpose. I think of my mom. I know that she gave up her Christian papers and went into hiding with her parents because she knew that is what she needed to do. She, too, understood the bigger purpose. Maybe that is part of why they all survived. They weren't focusing just on themselves. They were focusing on others, on the big picture.

"Another two weeks of the war," Ellinani continues, "and I would not have made it."

"Why is that?" I ask.

Eva bursts out at this point as if she is still perturbed by her mother's selflessness, "Because she was giving Vera and me most of her food portions, which was nothing to begin with."

"You needed it more," Ellinani says calmly.

Eva just gives her mom a look of exasperation that no words could express. She then crosses one leg over the other and places her hands on her thighs. "My father," Eva says, "he was not one of the lucky ones."

Latzi combs his hands through his hair and chimes in for the first time, "Sandor and I were strong and young. We had played many sports before the war. When we were put into the work lines, we were used for hard work. Our strength helped us survive."

"Did you know Marika before you were sent to Auschwitz?"

"No, Marika and I met after the war," Latzi says.

"What about you, Sandor?"

"I was in Auschwitz, too, but I didn't meet Eva until maybe ten years later."

"Marika, were you in the same factory as Eva?" I ask, turning to her.

Marika closes her eyes for a minute, and I wait, hoping she isn't upset.

"No," she finally says, "we were separated alphabetically. My group was shipped out to a camp in Krakow, and then eventually we came back to Auschwitz."

"What was it like there, Marika?" I ask.

"When we were shipped to Krakow, they said it was too crowded. That was never what you wanted to hear.

'All of you in this line,' the German officer ordered. 'You will all be in line for the showers.'

"We knew what was going to happen. Many of us were reciting the Shema prayer as we were all loaded into the shower. But no water came out. There wasn't even any gas. We heard someone outside complaining, 'The gas is not working.' We were let out, and after that, we were put into the work line."

I take a breath and wait for Marika to continue.

"I was strong so I survived. I remember I had a dream that I was eating one of my mother's favorite cakes. It was poppy-seed cake, like we had tonight. I could smell and taste it. I was so upset when I woke up," Marika says.

"Many people had dreams of food," Eva says.

"What is something that stands out in your memory, Marika?" I ask, wanting to know more. Everything she has told me so far has completely blown me away, and I want to know more. Her strong resolve and inner peace, despite what happened, or perhaps because of what happened, is something I wish I could get a better grasp on.

"When we got off the cattle train for the first time, a German officer gave me a barrette. He put it in my hair. It was pointless, though. I would have no need for a barrette. My hair would be shaved that same day, but still, I remember it was like he was trying to do something nice. That gesture somehow gave me comfort and strength, reminding me that kindness still existed in humanity. It was a constant reminder that I held onto while there was so much evil surrounding me."

I watch everyone as the stories are being told, and I can see Sandor and Latzi clenching their teeth.

"What was the worst thing for you?"

Marika pauses, then leans forward as if she is about to bare her soul. "We were all saying, 'if we die, we die,'" she says, "but then, one time, I had to work outside and move stones from one place to another and dig the earth. It felt like we were digging graves even though we weren't. A German officer pushed the butt of his rifle into my back, and he laughed a horrible laugh. I looked up at him, and it was the most afraid I have ever felt. I will always remember the face of that man, that face of a killer, that face of evil. It will probably be the last image I see as I take my last breath. He scared me more than anything else in the war."

"He knew the power he had over you," Eva says with a voice of understanding. "He could feel that you were terrified so he was fueled by your fear. That's why he could affect you that way." I wonder if she is speaking from her own experiences with such terror, but I refrain from asking. I know I need to let Marika finish telling her story.

"How did you survive him?" I ask.

"There was another German officer. He saw me, and I don't know why, but he probably saved me. He told the other officer, 'I want her to help me.' He then came to me and said, 'Can you wash my socks and clothes?'

I answered him with confidence, 'I will be glad to. Surely I can do a great job for you.' He must have known how it was for me because he made sure I was never near that other officer again. That is what saved me. I could feel it."

I flash back to the cop who stopped me in LA that night I took the wrong exit. He knew I was afraid. I was almost paralyzed by fear, and somehow that seemed to fuel him to harass me. It was as if knowing I was afraid energized him. It made him want to use his power over me. Like the German officer who saved Eva, the kind cop who shielded me from his partner made sure I would be safe. Even with all the bad my family and many others endured in the camps, which was beyond imaginable, there always seemed to be a few kind people who, out of the blue, gave them hope, and those are the stories that stick the most: the soldier who gave Marika the barrette and the one who had her wash his clothes, the soldier who warned my dad to stay away from the officer who had it in for him, and the soldier who warned Vera to say she was 18. They reminded my family not to give up, to believe in the good of mankind.

"Did you cry in the camps?" I ask.

"No," everyone answers in a chorus. I had meant the question just for Marika, but it seems to be an important point for the whole family. I had touched on something.

"I have not cried once since they took us to the camps," Eva says. "If I started, I probably would never stop."

Those words shake me, and I feel a vice grip my heart.

"*Freedom through work*," Marika says. That is what the sign at the front gates in all the camps read. That sign constantly mocked us."

Marika pauses, and I can tell she is done for the day. "So, you want to write this down in a book?"

"Yes," I manage to say. I am having a hard time fighting off tears. "Thank you for sharing your story."

"When will you finish your book?" Marika asks.

I look around the room at the shelves filled with books.

"I don't know."

"But what if someone reads it, and they don't believe it is true?" Marika asks. "Everything is true and worse than what I have said. Everything is true. There was even worse, more than anyone could ever imagine."

Her words pierce my heart. I look at her left forearm and the numbers branded on it. "The world knows," I say. "The world knows it is true, Marika." It breaks my heart that she even has to question that.

Marika leans back on the couch. "Do you know, Iritka, that I still have no grey hair? It is all natural," she says.

I smile as I look at her thick brown hair. It is truly amazing. After all that she went through, how is that possible? A lot of women would want to know her secret.

"After just one day on the cattle car, my dad's hair turned all white. Marika is a marvel," Eva pipes up.

At this point, Ellinani cuts us off, "Let us stop for now. We can talk more tomorrow."

"It is time to go to my house," Marika says. "My daughter, Eva, her husband, Thomas, and their little 4-year-old, Peter, will come visit us there for dinner."

Boy, I think to myself, *there are a lot of Evas and Peters in this family.*

~~~~~~~~~~~~~~

We head to Marika's house, and the family routine continues: food and more food. We have big meals at each family stop.

My Dad, who was the fastest eater on the planet, taught me well. I know I should eat slowly and chew my food more because it helps with digestion, but that is easier said than done, especially with my training. Actually, it just may be part of our Jewish lineage. Still, once again, I try to eat slowly because as soon as my plate is empty, there is more food on it.

"You're too skinny. This is good for you," is the mantra of my family, and I take it as a sign of love.

"Chad, when we go to the Tatra Mountains, I think I'll go on a fast," I say that night over dessert.

"Irit, it's a resort known for its food."

"That's ok. The way I feel now, my stomach will need a break."

"Would you like some cognac? It is good after a meal," Eva, Marika's daughter, says in Hungarian.

"Ok … just a little," I smile.

That night, we head back to Eva and Ellinani's home, where Chad and I are given the master bedroom with two single beds put together. We were not allowed to sleep on their roll-out couch. It was an argument we could not win.

"Irit, your family is amazing," Chad says as we drift off.

~~~~~~~~~~~~~~

The next morning, I awaken early, and as I walk into the living room, I am greeted by Ellinani's warm smile.

"Did you sleep well?" she asks.

"Yes, it was great."

"Iritka, I am so happy that I finally know you. You are so much like your father. Let's go in the kitchen. We will eat together," she says.

We sit at the table, with the window to our right overlooking the many apartment complexes in the area.

"Ellinani, what was it like when you saw my Dad for the first time after the war?" I say, always trying to get more insight and wanting to know as much as I can about my family.

"We had heard that Zoli got shot and died so when he came home in 1948, it was like seeing a ghost. I couldn't believe it. I thought maybe I was dreaming. He was so skinny, but yes, it was our Zoli. He stayed with me after the war, and I will always remember the dream he told me he had after he got shot."

"The dream? He never told me about a dream," I say, my ears perking up.

"I think that's because when he told a few people about it, they just thought, 'poor Zoli, he is saying crazy things because of the war.' They didn't believe him, so he stopped talking about it. But I knew. I believed him. He told Ersie, too, so she knows. You should ask her about it when you go back to California."

"Can you tell me about the dream, Ellinani?"

"Of course," she says. "Zoli told me that when he got shot, he was on the ground in a pool of blood. He couldn't feel his hands, and he was cold all over. He passed out and then woke up in a field full of the most beautiful flowers. The weather was beautiful; the sun was shining; and the meadow went on forever, farther than the eye could see. He experienced the most peaceful feeling he ever had in his life. He stood up and just kept walking in this meadow of beautiful flowers and birds. He said that every color had a magnificent brightness, like nothing he had ever witnessed before. He said even the birds had a brightness and glow that was beyond beautiful, and then, from behind him, he heard his sister, Ersie. 'Zoli, please come back. I need you,' she said. It was that voice, full of love, which made him come back. The next thing he knew he was awake. He was in so much pain, and he was angry that he was not in that field anymore. Then he heard a Russian officer say, 'He is alive. Kill him.'"

Ellinani ends the story there, but I know the rest. The bullets would be removed, and a doctor would save his life.

I think back to the hundreds of times he told me that story. I can't believe I never picked up on that. So many times, I now realize, he had said, *"I had a dream, and then I woke up,"* but I had never thought twice about it.

He was probably right not to tell too many people. No one in those days had heard of near-death experiences, or at least no one believed they were legitimate. Maybe it was this dream that gave my dad his deep understanding about life. He had told me that day in Montréal in the silver Malibu, *I'm not afraid to die.* Maybe he was ready to return to his beautiful meadow.

"Iritka, what are you thinking?" Ellinani asks

"I'm just glad to be with you."

Ellinani smiles at me. She has a beautiful smile that reaches to her eyes and creates that sparkle that my dad always had.

"Ellinani, when your husband died in Auschwitz, how did you deal with it?"

"I knew I had to go on, so I just thought of Vera and Eva, my children. They were only 13 and 18 when we went into the camps. After the war, it was hard for all of us. So much of what we had before the war was destroyed, and so many family members and friends were gone forever. We were on food stamps, and there was still not much to eat. There was a big famine in 1946 and 1947. It was even worse in Russia, where your father was."

"Ellinani, I look at you and you are so peaceful and happy. How do you do it?"

"I am happy to see you," she says, smiling.

"But Ellinani, you don't seem bitter at all, yet you saw things in your life that no one should have to."

"I was one of the lucky ones. I was in the factory."

"But it was still horrible, Ellinani," I say. *Lucky?* I think. *She is just like my dad.* Once again, I flash back to the silver Malibu and hear my dad say, *"there is a positive in everything, you just have to keep looking for it."* I desperately wish I could understand how he and Ellinani have such inner peace.

"Yes, it was horrible," Ellinani replies calmly. Then, as if she has already changed the subject in her mind, she smiles at me again with that smile that tells it all. She is happy.

"Ellinani," I ask as a question comes to me, "if you were to give advice to a teenager, maybe 15 or 16, what two things would you say to them?"

Ellinani looks out the window and then looks at me. She smiles. "The first and most important thing is that the greatest gift of life is the gift of love. That is what makes me want to get up every day: people like you, my family, and my friends. Iritka, the Nazis, they didn't understand anything. Their hearts ... they could not feel, or they wouldn't have done what they did. Love? They had no idea. No one who did what they did could, and so they knew nothing about life."

"But how do you—"

"Iritka," Ellinani cuts me off, "I forgave the Nazis because I knew they knew nothing about love, about life, about what is important."

I look at Ellinani, and I want to give her a big hug.

"The second thing I would tell them is you have to exercise your mind and body every day. I exercise every day. I also read and do crossword puzzles to keep my mind sharp. My heart is not so good, so I can't go up and down the stairs all the time. I make sure that I do my exercise in the house every day for about thirty minutes. I always tell Eva that she doesn't exercise enough." I can't keep from laughing at that. My 89-year-old aunt is telling her 65-year-old daughter to exercise.

"Iritka, it is so nice to finally be with you. I'm so sorry that I have not known you all my life, but," she reflects, "but I am lucky, because at least I get to know you now."

I look at Ellinani, and my heart feels warm and tingly. She seems so close to being made of pure love.

~~~~~~~~~~~~~~

That afternoon, the questions begin again. Everyone tells their stories, and I am amazed that each of them survived. At times, it is hard for me to hold back tears, yet not one of them seems to bat an eyelash. It's like they are glad to finally open the floodgates of their secret memories, which have been locked up for so long.

"What was it like after the war?" I ask.

Eva seems uncomfortable and shifts positions a few times. "In 1946, '47 and '48, we were on food stamps. We didn't have much. When your dad came back in 1948, he wanted all of us to come to Israel. 'Communism will be terrible,' he warned us. He was the only one who decided to leave, but, in the interim, he found work in a store, and he could sell anything to anybody. He had been good at that ever since I can remember."

I laugh, thinking of how much my Dad loved buying stuff for all of us in the factories. He always liked to give.

"With his first paycheck from the store, he surprised me and bought me a bike so I could get to work more easily. I remember he said, 'Evaka, I am going to Israel, and this is for you. It takes you too long to get to work. This will help you.' He would not take no for an answer. I had that bike for 30 years." Eva falls into a reflective silence and then says, "Let us stop for now."

"Tonight we will take everyone out for dinner as we promised," I say.

"Iritka," Eva says, "Margitnani does not feel well so she will not come tonight. We will take you to her place tomorrow before you head off to the mountains."

Eva gets up, and everyone else follows suit.

"Ok, at least I will spend some time with her," I say though I am a little disappointed that I haven't gotten to meet her yet. I wonder what she is like, this other woman whom my father always talked about.

~~~~~~~~~~~~~~

We head off to a restaurant called Paprikash. The men there are in suits and ties, and the women are dressed in nice skirts and matching jackets. Three tables are put together for our big group, with a total of 11 place settings. We order beer for the adults, along with different types of soup, like borsht, cabbage, and matzo ball, cucumber salad, and five entrees for all of us to choose from. We then have dessert and coffee and end the evening with some brandy. They say brandy puts the right edge on the meal.

When the waiter hands us the bill, the total cost is equal to $33.00.

"Irit, this has to be a mistake," Chad says, flabbergasted.

I translate, but Marika's daughter says, "No, this is how much it is. For us, this is more than a week's salary. Communism fell two years ago in our country, but our economy is bad and many people do not know how to run a business under capitalism. There are too many choices now, and people are not used to handling choices. Remember, we were always told what to do and where to live. Under communism, people got paid whether they worked hard or not so there was no work ethic in place. If you were lazy, it didn't matter. Now it does matter, but people don't understand so they are still acting like they did before. They do not know how to adapt. There have been many problems because no one is teaching us how to live under this different system. There will be more problems; you will see."

Wow, I think, *you've lived under communism your whole life. You were never exposed to anything but the communist mentality. How do you know that the foundation for how people interact in business and in life has to be different now when so many others don't?*

"Funny," I respond, "maybe four months ago I read in the newspaper that many of the people who win big in the lottery lose it all pretty quickly because they don't have the mindset it takes to be wealthy. They are not comfortable having money so they lose it all or spend it all and go back to their comfort zone. They end up self-sabotaging."

At this point, Sandor interrupts, saying, "Now we will take you for the best ice cream in Kosice. It is maybe a 10- minute walk from here. It will be our treat."

"No," I insist, "this is our evening. Let us have the pleasure of treating."

This is the first battle that I have won since arriving here three days ago. We reach the ice cream shop, and everyone gets two scoops, one vanilla and one chocolate. I decide to only get one scoop. I was going to pass altogether, but all of their looks said, *if you don't eat, we will feel bad.* At this point, I decide my lactose intolerance will, once again, have to take a back seat.

"Let me take a picture of all the family together," Chad says, and we all assemble and pose until we hear the click, click, of the camera.

As we take pictures, I look around at my family. Ellinani is in the middle, standing proud in her blue and white suit. Latzi is looking like a giant next to Elli, and he is busy eating his vanilla scoop of ice cream. Sandor is at the very end, with ice cream in his mouth, looking at the camera. I am next to Elli, and Marika is beside me, standing confidently and smiling. Eva is beside Marika, and she, too, is looking proud. This is my family, and I feel right at home even though I have only known them a few days.

We take a bus back, and after 20 minutes, we get to Ellinani's apartment. Once again, Ellinani is the first one up the stairs, no huffing or puffing.

I chat with Ellinani and Eva while Chad and Sandor attempt to speak to each other with the little German that Chad remembers. Sandor gives

Chad a book on Czechoslovakia, which includes Kosice as part of the Czech Republic.

"This is for both of you, a memento from us," he says.

"I can't accept this," I say. I know it must be valuable.

"This is for your memory of your visit. We will be hurt if you don't accept this gift. Your dad was so good to us, there is nothing we could ever give you that would be enough."

I chuckle as I think of all the times my dad sent packages, not knowing how much the relatives would receive and how much the government would take.

"Dad," I would say when I was about 12, "if you don't think they will get most of the packages, why are you still sending them?"

"Well, hopefully they will get some of it. That will be better than nothing," he would answer.

I smile thinking of the last time I came to Prague, with my suitcase nearly full of nothing but presents from my dad and Aunt Ersie. I had to solicit a stranger to lift it into my car.

Chad and I say goodnight to everyone and go into our bedroom.

"Irit, your family is amazing. What stories, what courage!" he says.

"Chad," I say, finally voicing the question that I had been wanting to ask forever. "You're a doctor. According to your training, how could any of these people have survived? I mean, they endured human conditions that were beyond cruel. They were degraded and constantly told they did not deserve to live."

"Science tells us that stress affects our body and will break it down. Yet this is way beyond any stress that we can comprehend. Couple that with starvation, harsh winter conditions, little clothing, little food, if you can even call what they ate food, hard and meaningless work, gun wounds, infections, and forced labor. After all that, their bodies healed, and their spirits were not broken. There is a lot that we don't understand in the medical field. You can't really explain your family's stories in scientific terms. That is for sure."

"I know the life changing moments where the showers didn't work or they switched lines and the officers got distracted could be called fate, destiny, divine intervention or even coincidence. But, look at what all these people endured on the physical level. People would be forced to go half naked and stand at attention in the freezing cold day in and day out, and some of these people didn't even get sick! How did they do all that heavy menial work for hours and hours with little food and water? Their bodies kept going," I continued. "When I'm physically exhausted and hungry, I can't think clearly. Yet, my dad, who was so depleted physically, was clear enough in his mind to win one chess game after another with the Russian officer.

"You raise great questions, Irit, but I don't really have answers I can give you. The body heals in ways that are beyond our understanding. I wish people would understand that, so they wouldn't be so quick to tell people it is false hope to believe in the possibility of healing.

Your family is amazing. They defy anything I could make sense of in scientific terms. The fact that they survived is a miracle in itself, and the fact that they can be so kind and not jaded toward humanity impresses me even more. There is a lot in medicine that we don't know. It is all a matter of more research to be done and more to understand. We just haven't reached that level of knowledge yet."

"Maybe we're not headed in the right direction to explain this. Take the placebo effect, for example. Someone takes a pill, and they believe it will help them heal. This strong belief allows the brain and body to take over and do what it needs to do to heal. Maybe that is an area we should focus more on. When someone believes something will heal them, how does that alone allow healing to occur?"

"Yes, science can be flawed, but there is more and more research being done and maybe one day we will have a better understanding. A lot of times people believe things like that are genetic or just unexplainable so they stop probing. It is hard to measure things like that."

"But what triggers the genetics in one person and not the other?" I ask. "That's what I would love to learn."

"I would have loved to meet your dad. His story of survival defies anything I could ever have been able to explain from my medical training."

I fall into silence. There is so much about the human will and human power that is greater than what we understand, and I know that is an important part of the equation. That is probably what allows "miracles" to occur, but how *can* science measure that?

"Baby doll," Chad says, breaking through my thoughts, "why don't you come into my bed?"

"We're guests here, and the walls are thin," I say laughingly.

"We'll be quiet."

"No way. Stay on your side."

"Baby doll," Chad pleads.

"No way. Good night, and sleep tight," I say with a smile. I close my eyes, and I can see my Ellinani's smile.

~~~~~~~~~~~~~

Irit Schaffer

14

1991

You must not lose faith in humanity. Humanity is an ocean; if a few drops of the ocean are dirty, the ocean does not become dirty.

Mahatma Gandhi

4:30 a.m. That is what the nightstand clock says. It is quiet. Chad is asleep, and everything is still. It seems as if the whole city is asleep, the whole world for that matter. I imagine that this is the moment of the night when calmness and all other forces of nature try to balance out all the chaos of the world.

I think of my Ellinani. Today is the last day we will spend together, and that puts a pit in my stomach. I have to remind myself that this is not *good-bye*; this is just *until next time*. Today is a new beginning. This trip is now becoming just another chapter in my past, but it isn't over yet.

Today I will finally meet Margitnani. Margit is the daughter of my step-great-grandfather. She is the one who always shielded Ersie and my dad from their step-grandfather, her father. My dad told me that story many times in my youth. Margit's father did not believe Zoli should get more food than the others even though he was a growing boy and loved participating in sports so Margit and Elli would always hide food for him. When he was hungry late at night, my dad would go to his secret place and eat.

Chad wakes up and slides over to my side of the bed to put his arms around me. I hear sounds in the next room. I think it is my Ellinani so I squirm out of Chad's grasp.

"Chad, I'm getting up," I whisper.

"Baby doll, stay in bed a little longer," he says sleepily, but I get up anyway.

I walk into the living room and see Ellinani walking out of the kitchen.

"Good morning. Did you sleep well?" she says.

I look at my great aunt, with that endearing smile and that glow on her face that I have come to know so well, and my heart melts.

"Yeah! I slept great. What about you?"

"I slept well, too. Come. Let's have breakfast together. What would you like to eat?"

"Just some orange juice and toast. I'm not very hungry. I can make it myself though."

"No," she insists. "You are our guest."

"Ellinani, will you be coming with me to see Margitnani?"

"No, I don't feel well, and I don't want to climb all those stairs."

My Ellinani has a bad heart, but the doctors here are not the same as in Montréal. Here they refuse to do surgery on her. They say she is too old so surgery is not an option for her. It's amazing how Elli knows how to listen to her body and adapt. If she is tired, she stays home. If she feels the stairs are too much, she won't go out, and she'll rest. She knows her body is talking to her, and she never complains about it. She just listens. My mom and dad were the same way. If Dad had a headache, he would say, "I need to lie down so it goes away." If he was tired, he took care of himself and cancelled what he was going to do. I think this trip has helped me better understand the importance of listening to your body. Doctors can only know so much about your body. You are the one living in it. No one is more of an expert on what you need and how you feel than you are. You just have to listen.

A few hours pass, and it is time for the goodbyes before we head off to meet Margitnani. This is hard for me. I will miss these people. I feel so connected to all of them. It will be hard to leave them behind.

Ellinani looks at me and says, "I am sorry I have not known you longer," and then, in the same breath, she switches gears, saying, "No, I am grateful that I have had this time with you. I am glad I have finally spent time with Zoli's daughter." I bet that is how she stays so peaceful. She always tries to look at the world through a lens of light and positivity.

I want to cry, but I do everything in my power to hold back. Somehow I know that I need to. I am in a room full of people who have amazing resilience, strength, and wisdom. I think of Eva who hasn't cried once since the war. I just know I need to stay strong.

~~~~~~~~~~~~~~

Chad and I climb into the back seat of the Skoda and are soon en route to Margit. Sandor is driving, and Eva is in the passenger seat.

"Irit, was Margit in the war, too?" Chad asks.

"No. It is kind of ironic because her dad was ultra-religious. He did not want her to marry anyone but a Jewish man. She married Tibi before the war despite her dad's protests. Tibi is Christian, and because of him, she got false papers. She was able to pass as a non-Jew. So, in essence, he saved her, and they have been married over 50 years."

Before long, the car stops. My heartbeat quickens.

I count as we climb 58 stairs and the door opens. Sandor and Eva enter with ease and make themselves at home. I am nervous and excited at the same time.

"Iritka, finally. It is so nice to meet you," Margitnani says, and she gives me a big hug. "You look so much like your father."

I stand back and look at her. Margit is 91 and maybe 5'5". She is wearing a brown-and-beige dress with a v-neck, showing all the wear and tear of life on her skin. Her eyes are deep, wise, calm, and gentle.

Tibi comes up next. He is 93, maybe 5'6" in frame, and wearing a white shirt and brown pants with suspenders. He has big glasses with brown frames. He pulls me in for a hug, and once again I make the introductions for Chad.

They go back to their chairs, pushing the crossword puzzles they had been doing aside. Both of them seem as sharp as can be. We sit down and start getting to know each other.

"Iritka, I heard that you all had a great dinner yesterday. We are sorry that we could not go with you. I just didn't feel well, but I'm fine today. I am always careful not to overdo it."

"We missed you, but I am so happy to be here today, and I'm so glad you feel well."

"Did you know that three years ago I had an emergency abdominal surgery? The doctors were surprised I made such a speedy recovery."

"I remember hearing about that," I say. I remember how my Aunt Ersie had told me the doctors didn't think she would make it at all. I remember that because I had felt so sad that I would never get to meet her. Now here we are, three years later, sitting around her flat. They have lived in this same flat for over 40 years. I look around and happily settle into my seat as I listen to Margit talk.

Food, of course, is prepared, and the aroma makes me excited for the yummy food even though I'm not very hungry.

We are served weinersnitchel, mashed potatoes with onions, matzo ball soup, cucumber salad and chocolate brownies. As we eat, Chad speaks some German to Tibi and Sandor, basic stuff that I know Chad will translate for me later.

My translating has gotten better as the trip has gone on because I'm trying to include Chad as much as I can.

"Margitnani, do you have any pictures of my grandmother?" I ask.

"No, but I have one picture of my mother, your great-grandmother."

I remember that my great-grandmother's first husband had died after my grandmother was born. She then married Hermann Weinberger, Margitnani's father, who was 20 years older. My dad didn't like him, but he loved his grandmother. Margit's father was religious and strict. He always made my father pray first thing in the morning. It was always traditional Jewish prayers, and at first my dad would pretend to pray. Then, after his grandfather realized this, he made my dad pray out loud, would hit him if he didn't pray right.

"In this picture, my father is 80 and my mom is 60," Margit says.

I translate to Chad and show him the picture.

I look at the picture. My step-great-grandfather is sitting in his chair, rigid as can be. He has a white beard and what seems to be a permanent frown plastered on his face. I can't believe my grandmother is only 60 in the photo. She looks much older. You can see the rigors of life had gotten to her. There is a sadness and resignation about her, but she still exudes a softness. She had my grandmother, Pepi, from her first marriage, and then she had six more with Margit's father. One of their children, also named Sandor, married Ellinani. That's how she ended up moving into the house. All my childhood stories are coming to life. It is so wonderful to hear the stories from a new perspective and to be in the presence of these people as they share their history.

"Margitnani, my dad told me you used to hide food for him."

"Zoli was a growing boy, and he played many sports. My father would not give him extra food even though he needed it, so I would hide food in the pantry. My dad was especially tough with Zoli. From the time he was

Grandmother Jeanette Havas

Grandmother Jeanette Havas and Step Grandfather
Hermann Weinberger

five, Zoli would have to go outside and help on the farm. His hands would always be chapped from milking the cows and helping with other chores outside, even in the winter."

I look around the room, which is decorated with bohemian vases, crystals, paintings, needle-point and bookshelves.

My eyes meet Aunt Margit's, and I see her warm smile.

"It was hard for Ersie and Zoli. They missed their mother so much and only saw her on Wednesdays and weekends. I was ten years older than Ersie and Zoli. I had to look out for them."

"Aunt Ersie told me you were also one of the matchmakers who brought her and Jusie together."

Margitnani smiles. "That was many years ago, but I remember it like it was yesterday. Ersie was in love with a boy named Michael. She was so sure that they would be married, but his family had a lot of money. One day, Michael came to Ersie and broke her heart. We were so worried for her. We all told her she would meet someone better, but she was so sad. She didn't want to be with anyone else."

I remember that story well. I flash back to Aunt Ersie's kitchen, with her purple place mats, her favorite color. We had just finished lunch, and I asked, "How did you meet Jusie?"

She laughed, and said, "Irit, when I was 24, I was with this boy, Michael. He was the person I thought I was going to marry and be with forever. We were together two years."

"Really? What happened to him?"

"He came to me one day, and I could tell something was wrong. 'What is it?' I asked. 'Did someone die?'

'No, Ersikem,' he said. 'Something worse. My parents do not want me to marry you. You come from a family with no money, and they said they would disinherit me if I marry you.'

I thought that this could not be and that that maybe somehow we could convince them otherwise, but I was wrong.

'Ersikem, I am so sorry,' Michael said.

Margit, Elli, and Zoli all said, 'You will find someone better,' but for two years, I did not want to be with anyone else. I wanted to be with Michael, and that was not possible.

One day, Margit invited me for lunch and said, 'Wear one of the outfits you made. They are always so beautiful on you.'

I agreed, but I was a little confused. When I showed up, there were place settings out for four people.

'Margit, what is this?' I asked. 'Who else is coming?'

It was Judy, her good friend, and Judy's nephew, who had recently moved from a nearby town to Aruba. She didn't tell me this, of course, but he was looking for a wife. He had a job with Esso Oil, and his name was Jusie. Before I could say a word in protest at the set-up, there was a knock at the door, and in came Jusie."

"So, was it love at first sight?" I asked.

"Irit, I hardly said a word the whole afternoon. I wasn't interested." Ersie started laughing.

"What is so funny?"

"A few days later, Margit came to my house and said that Judy, her friend, had told her that Jusie cold not stop talking about me. He couldn't believe you had made such a beautiful outfit, she said, and he said that you were were even more beautiful than the dress and wants to ask you out."

"Were you flattered?"

"I was surprised because I had hardly said anything to him. What I didn't know was that Judy was telling her nephew that I had said he looked like a movie star with his tan from Aruba, he was the best looking person I had ever met, I thought he was so interesting, and I wanted to go out with him."

"Did you say that?"

"No, I didn't say that."

"For four weeks we went out on dates, and each time we came back, Margit or Elli would tell me through Judy that they had found out that he said the most flattering things about me and that he was falling in love with me. Unbeknownst to me, Jusie was hearing the same things about me.

"After four weeks, he asked me to marry him. I had to give my answer within two days because he was going back to Aruba. Esso Oil had to get the exit papers for me if I said yes." Ersie laughed again.

"I never said anything about Jusie to Margit or Elli, and Jusie never said anything about me to his aunt. They made it all up so that we would want to get together. We only found out after we were married. The matchmakers had made everything up. They were good."

"Irit?" I hear my name and come back to the present in Margit's living room. "Would you like some soda water to drink?"

"No, thanks," I say. "Tell me more of the story."

"Our matchmaking worked," Margit picks up the thread of the story. "Jusie asked Ersie to marry him. He went back to Aruba in 1938, and he sent for her in 1939. Even in 1938, the situation was bad. When Jusie went to Aruba, he had to stop in Germany. Jusie was with some other people on the trip who were denied food because they were Jewish. One of the guys got hurt and was bleeding, but the pharmacy would not serve Jews so he had to clean the wound himself. Ersie left for Aruba in March of 1939. We were so happy. We had been afraid she would stay behind for Michael."

I nod and I can hear my aunt Ersie's voice again as she continues to share the story with me in her kitchen.

"March 3, 1939, I remember that day well. Zoli had had a feeling that I might change my mind so he kept telling me, 'Jusie is a good man. He will provide for you. The situation here will get worse. You will not be strong enough. You must leave.'

My mother had worked hard all her life. She never complained though. She told us it was all worth it because she had me and Zoli, the greatest joys in her life. She, too, told me I must leave. 'You will be safe that way,' she said. 'You will have a family one day, and you will tell them about me.'

Zoli and my mother took me to the train station. Laws were splayed about, forbidding Jews to be in public places, like parks and universities. My mother said, 'You see, it is good you are getting away now.'

We got to the train station and Michael was there, waiting for me.

My heart felt like it was going to jump out of my body. It was pumping so fast. If, at that moment, Michael had said, 'Marry me,' I would have stayed. Instead, he said, 'Ersikem, I am so sorry that I wasn't strong enough to stand up to my parents. I will always remember you, and I am glad you will be going to a place that is safe.'

'But Michael –' I had said, but he stopped me.

'If anything ever happened to you, I would never forgive myself. You must go.'

We hugged, and then I went back to Zoli and my mother.

'Ersikem,' Zoli said to me, 'You will see. One day, you will realize that you are the lucky one.'

I heard the train whistle blowing, and it was time to leave. We all hugged. My mother would not cry. She didn't want me to cry. I felt my feet go up the few stairs to the train compartment. It was as if they were moving without my assistance.

I sat down and tried to glimpse Zoli and my mom through the window. There was a Dutch man next to me who gave me his seat so I could look out more easily. Zoli was standing beside my mother. His arm was wrapped around her shoulders, and they just stood there. Our eyes fixed on each other. Then, the train began to move, and their faces disappeared from sight. The way they looked in that moment is still imprinted in my brain.

Would I ever see them again? What would happen to Michael? What if this is a big mistake? All these thoughts were swirling in my brain. I had not seen Jusie in six months. The man next to me asked me where I was going. I told him, 'Rotterdam,' which was also his exit. I told him that, after Rotterdam, I was going by boat to Aruba, where I was getting married. I had received papers through Esso Oil.

One hour passed, and we were in Germany. The train stopped, and a German officer came toward us.

In his gruff German voice, he said, 'Passport.'

I gave him my papers and birth certificate as requested. He looked at me, put my birth certificate in his pocket, and said, 'Jew, get off the train.'

'But,' I said, not sure what to do, 'I have papers.'

He refused to give me back my birth certificate. The gentleman next to me, the Dutch man, said, in fluent German, 'She has the proper papers to leave. She is going to get married and live in Aruba.'

The German officer would not budge. Once again, he gave his order, 'Get off the train,' but the Dutch man persisted.

All I could catch at that point were the looks on their faces because they were speaking too quickly for me to translate. The Dutchman stayed calm, and, at one point, I thought the officer would force both of us off the train so he, too, would lose the right to leave. Finally, after what seemed like an hour, the German officer gave me back my papers and moved on.

The Dutchman and I spoke very little for the rest of the trip. We got off the train at Rotterdam, and I never saw him again."

"When you arrived in Holland," I asked, "what did you do?"

"I went to a hotel. I had no money and I was afraid to go out. Jusie had told me to wait at that hotel until I heard from him and got money. After almost two days, a friend of Jusie's arrived at the hotel with a bouquet of violets, my favorite. Jusie had told him to get the flowers. That was the first time since getting on the train that I felt myself relaxing. He had paid for my boat, and I was finally headed to Aruba."

"What happened to Michael?" I asked, and I could see Ersie freeze, as if it was still hard for her to acknowledge it.

"He was beaten to death by the Nazis about six months after I last saw him."

~~~~~~~~~~~~~

"Irit," I hear my name and look up to see Margitnani smiling at me. I shake my head to clear it. *Focus,* I tell myself, *you only have so much time with her.*

"I miss your father," Margitnani says to me. "I wish he had come back to visit, but I am glad that I finally met you." Each time they say it, and it seems almost like a mantra at this point, I am reminded of the deep love my family had for each other.

"I know. He always said he wished he could see all of you again." I can still hear my dad's loving voice.

"After the war, it was not easy for us. There was famine everywhere. My parents died, along with many of my other relatives and friends. I was just happy that Ersie was in Aruba so at least she was safe. The Red Cross sent Ersie a letter saying Zoli had died, and Ersie told us. I still remember the day we found out Zoli was still alive," Margit says.

I remember the beaming look on Aunt Ersie's face as she told me the story in her kitchen. "I got a letter from Zoli in 1948. I was sure I was dreaming. It was too good to be true," she had said. Even all these years later, there was a sense of excitement in her voice, as if she were discovering he was alive all over again.

"What was it like when you saw my dad for the first time?" I ask Margitnani.

"I couldn't believe it. It was like seeing a ghost. Before the war, Zoli had a physique like an Olympic swimmer. When he came back, his upper back was curved, and his hair, which used to be thick, was now thin and wiry. He said it was from typhus."

"He was only home for a few months before he left," she continues, a sense of sadness coming over her. "He wanted us all to go to Israel with him, but only he went. None of us could bring ourselves to leave."

I translate for Chad again. It must have been so hard for all of them. They finally got Zoli back but then had to say goodbye for good soon after. I know that after he moved to Israel he never saw any of them again.

"The food will get cold. Let's eat now." I hear the magic words that get my attention.

"Would you like some wine with the meal?" Margit asks.

Chad and I both decline.

"The war was over in 1945, why didn't your dad return until 1948?" Chad asks me.

"He was in the Russian Prisoner of War camp. One year, the Russians let all of the Hungarians out of the prison, but the Hungarians said my dad was now Czech because he had come from Kosice. In 1945, Kosice had become a part of Czechoslovakia again. The next year, they let out the Czechs, and the Czechs said he was Hungarian because he was born in Hungary. Finally, he somehow managed to get his name on the transport. I'm not sure how, but my dad told me that's how he eventually escaped."

After lunch, Tibi went back to his crossword puzzle.

"We do puzzles every day. It keeps our minds sharp," Tibi says, excusing himself. "We read books, too, and we go for walks. It is important to stay active."

I smile. They sound just like Ellinani, so healthy and alive for their ages. It is inspirational.

Too soon, it is time to say goodbye.

Margitnani hands me a brown bag. "Here is food for your 6-hour train ride to the mountains. The food on the train is not good."

I take the bag and give her and Tibi a big hug and kiss.

"Thanks," I say, "thank you for everything."

"It was nothing."

"No, this has meant a lot to me. I have known you since I was a baby, through my father's stories. He was right about everything. You are amazing."

Margit smiles.

I walk down the 58 stairs, and before I get into the car, I look back. Margit and Tibi are standing on the balcony, side by side, arms over the railing, with joy pouring out of their smiles. They wave to me, and my heart stops.

I know this will be the last time I ever see them. My stomach knots up. My chest feels as if there is a hundred pound weight on it, suffocating me. I get into the back seat, Sandor gets in the driver's side, and I turn around one last time. They are still there, Margit and Tibi, looking so peaceful and loving. The car starts, and I just keep looking at them until they are no longer in view.

Knowing that I will never see them again and knowing many of their stories will go with them makes it feel like that chapter of my family's history is closing forever. I have met the wonderful people who shaped my dad's life on this trip, and now it is in the past. I wish I could just hold on. Tears come streaming down my face. I am glad Eva and Sandor can't see me. Chad is sitting beside me. He looks at me and takes my hand, comforting me.

We get to the train station and are guided to track number 16.

"This is the train that will take you to the Tatras," Eva says.

"Thank you so much," I say, trying to hide my puffy eyes and choked voice.

"It was with great pleasure. We are so glad we could meet you. We are so happy you could stay with us and that we finally have met Zoli's daughter."

Eva and Sandor say goodbye, and we all hug.

"Until the next time," I say. We all hug again, and then I watch them walk away.

As I am standing at the station, I close my eyes. After this week full of stories and emotions, it is like I am transported back in time on these tracks in Kosice. I can hear the German officers. I can see the people milling about. I can see the fear on the faces of those with arm-bands. It is as if I am there. I can see a black cloud sweeping over the sky, portending the doom that would be.

My grandmother, Pepi, stood here on March 3, 1939. I have never even seen a picture of her. The few pictures my dad's family had before the war were never found, but I knew her through my family. I experienced her warmth, kindness, and devotion. I witnessed her work ethic and never complaining attitude. I wish I'd met my grandmother, Pepi. She had the qualities I always craved.

What was it like for her to see Ersie leave? My grandmother, she knew things. She knew them before they happened, like when she gave my dad the letter the last time they saw each other, the one he read to the men in his labor camp, or as they were also called, the Jewish brigade, the letter that got soaked with blood and was forever lost when he got shot.

I can feel the sadness. I can feel my family. How can all of those things have happened? The whistle blows, the same whistle that had beckoned Aunt Ersie onto the train.

"Irit," Chad says, "let's board."

Then I see the cattle cars, the same ones that left these tracks all those years ago, the ones that carried maybe one hundred people in a single 8x10 car. There was no place to sit, and no place to pee. Everyone was holding onto the few belongings they were allowed to carry. I imagine Eva's father, with all his hair turning white overnight, and my grandmother Pepi, who knew her fate when she headed to Auschwitz. I imagine the rest of my family, who all left from these tracks.

My mom and her mom, Josephine, were in the next city over, also on other tracks. The cattle cars only had tiny holes for air. The tiny holes were where they could see the outside world, the world that they were leaving for the gates of hell, where the sign at the front gate read, "freedom through work." The eyes were all one could see from the outside, eyes with many different colors and temperaments. There were eyes filled with despair. There were eyes filled with condemnation. There were eyes filled with disbelief. There were eyes filled with horror. There were eyes that were simply numb. All eyes going right to the soul. How could this have happened?

"Come on," Chad says patiently, "it's time to board. We're in first class."

First class is only about $10.00 more, which is nothing to us but a fortune to the locals.

"Baby doll," Chad says, wrapping his arms around me as we settle into our seats. We are the only ones in this compartment. "Thanks for making me feel so comfortable with all your family. Your translating made a huge difference. Your family's hospitality, their courage ... and to see the numbers on their forearms! It is something I will always remember. I cannot imagine how they survived or how they are so kind and warm after all they endured."

"Yeah, they don't teach that in medical school."

"No."

"I guess that is just another case for the power of hope," I say.

"Irit, look at the book Sandor gave me."

"The book he gave us," I remind him.

"Of course. Look at the castles and the countryside. After we leave the resort in the Tatras, let's check them out."

"That would be nice."

"I booked us into this posh resort. We will get a queen-size bed, and we can sleep in as long as we want, with no one we know in the next room," he says flirtatiously.

"Yeah," I answer as I look out the window, still too wrapped up in my own thoughts to focus on him.

"Hey," Chad says, trying to cheer me up, "I know how to make you smile."

"What?"

He takes out the brown paper bag Margitnani gave me and lays it on the table beside us.

"Let's eat."

~~~~~~~~~~~~~

Irit Schaffer

15

1992-1995

When one door of happiness closes, another opens; but often we look so long at the closed door that we do not see the one which has been opened for us.

Helen Keller

It seems like everywhere I turn at the hospital, someone is saying hello to me. This hospital is small and filled with employees who truly care about their patients.

When I got accepted into the physical therapy program at the University of Southern California, I decided that I would do my best to be on the leading edge and be among the best in my field one day. I also vowed that I would always work in a facility that would allow me the freedom to grow to the best of my abilities.

Here we are encouraged and paid to take professional development classes, which is a big plus for me. I teach most of the back and body mechanics classes to patients and staff at the hospital.

"Good morning, Irit. It's so nice to see you," Lisa says to me as I walk in through the doors. Lisa is our receptionist, and she is always welcoming to the patients and staff. "Your new patient is early. She is sitting in the corner on the right. Here is her chart."

Olga is 74 and had to have surgery on her left shoulder because of a rotator cuff tear. After the surgery, she developed a frozen shoulder, so now she is here to see me. I go into the waiting area and see her. Maybe 5'1", she sports short and curly white hair. She has a European feel to her, maybe Sicilian.

"Hi. I'm Irit," I introduce myself. "Nice to meet you."

"I'm Olga. Nice to meet you, too," she says.

"Follow me," I say, and we head into the treatment room. "How are you?" I ask as she settles into her seat.

"I'm a little nervous. I went to physical therapy sessions a few years ago, and they really hurt. The doctors said, 'no pain, no gain,' but I hurt a lot after treatments. I couldn't stand it. Is it going to be the same?"

"Well, let me evaluate you, and we'll see what we can do to make it more comfortable for you." One of the things that I remember most from my classes at USC is how important it is for patients to feel safe and trust their therapist. Trust is something that has to be earned, and the more comfortable the patient feels, the easier it will be for the therapist to help. This always resonated with me, especially as a teacher and coach.

"I can't raise my arm past my shoulder," Olga says as I begin my evaluation.

"Ok, so that's only about 90 degrees."

"I also can't move my hand behind me past my waist, so I can't fasten my bra."

"Do you feel any pain in your shoulder?"

"Yes. There is pain where the small incisions are, and at night, my whole shoulder aches. Is the therapy going to hurt a lot?" she asks again with trepidation. I can tell she is scared of what is in store for her.

"I'm going to do things a little differently for you," I say. "You shouldn't feel much pain today."

She breathes a sigh of relief. I smile. I know what it is like to be in pain, and I also know how to make treatment less painful so I am excited to help her.

Very gently, I do some hands-on mobilizations with her shoulder and then say, "We will start with some exercises to increase your range."

When I say, "exercises," I hear Olga's sharp intake of breath.

"That is what hurt so much," she says.

"We'll do it differently," I promise. "First, I am going to have you crawl your hand up the wall. Stop when it hurts. When you bring your arm down, you can use your other hand for support. We'll mark the spot so you can see your progress."

She raises her hand, and I mark the spot.

"How are you doing?"

"Fine so far."

"Athletes use visualization all the time in their training, so I am going to have you do the same. Visualize raising your arm up the wall with its full range of motion five times before you actually try it. Breathe out as you raise your hand. If you need to stop to breathe in, do so, and as you raise your arm, exhale. Ready?"

Olga closes her eyes, and I watch her as she visualizes. Then she brings her arm up the wall.

"Wow. I went three inches further than the first time, and it didn't hurt to do it."

"The trick is to breathe, which helps you relax." I teach her a few more exercises that she can practice at home, and the session ends.

"This was great. When is our next appointment?"

"Check with the front desk. The end of this week would be great. Remember, practice visualizing, and breathe as you exercise."

Next, Dorothy, an African American lady in her 60s comes into my office. She is a new patient, too. She is maybe 40 pounds overweight and recovering from a fractured ankle.

I do the evaluation. This one is easy. We just need to improve her range of motion and strengthen her ankle. After that, she'll be fine. After we practice the exercises, we use a balance board to help her with proprioception, strength, mobility and balance in a fun way, and then I do some hands-on work.

"It feels much better than when I came in. Thank you," she says.

"You're welcome," I smile.

Dorothy leaves, and I head to my office. With the exception of Carol, my boss, all of the physical therapists in our department share an office. I go to my desk and do my least favorite part of the job: note taking. I know it is important to take notes on the conditions of our patients and the progress they are making, but I also know that most doctors just want to know if the patient is better. They don't really care about the why or how in physical therapy.

Carol walks into the room with two new referrals and hands them to me.

"These are earmarked for you by the orthopedist and the neurologist," she says to me. "What do you do, ask the doctors to refer you? No one else gets special referrals."

I get a knot in my stomach as I look at her and say, "No."

I am not sure why, but it seems like ever since Carol became more confident—or maybe less confident—in her role as leader, she has started to hold some sort of grudge against me. When she first started here, she and I were pretty close. She would often call me into her office and ask for advice on choices she was making for the department, but now it seems as if she thinks I am preventing her from being the shining light of the department. She doesn't seem to realize that the more we all excel in our jobs, the better she will look because she is the head of our department.

Lisa comes into the staff room with her great smile, and it immediately makes me feel more at ease.

"Your next patient just called and cancelled."

Great, I think to myself. *I needed a breather, anyway.*

I walk out of the office and immediately bump into one of my former patients.

"I just saw my doctor and didn't want to leave without saying hi to you," he says.

"How are you? You look great," I say, surprised to see him.

Chris was one of my first patients here. He had fallen off his roof and messed up his back and had to have surgery on his right wrist and left elbow.

"My arm is great. I have been working for almost three years now since that fall. You were amazing. It's thanks to you that I was able to get back to work. I just wanted to stop by and catch up."

I was amazing? I think. *I just believed it was possible and didn't get in your way. It was all you.* Chris was easily one of the most inspiring patients I have ever had.

I remember the first day I met him. I read his chart and felt overwhelmed by all that was wrong with him. I had no clue how I would be able to help. I didn't think I was skilled enough yet. I braced myself and went to the waiting area to introduce myself.

"How are you?" I asked politely.

"Great," he had said, with a big smile on his face.

I looked at him in utter amazement. *You have a cast on your left hand, a brace on your right hand, and you're walking with a cane. How can you be great*? I wanted to say. Instead, I went with, "Great? How come?"

"Look, I can move my wrist a millimeter."

I still remember that moment like it was yesterday; the look in his eyes, the determination that said, *I won't be stopped.* I knew at that moment that he was going to heal beyond what people thought possible. I also knew that

I would be the best person to treat him because I was probably the only one in the department who would believe it was totally possible for him to make a full recovery. He guided himself through the treatment plan, and I just followed the basic steps for increasing range of motion and strength.

Chris had worked as a mechanic at an airline before the accident and was determined to get back to work. However, in order to return, he had to be able to lift over 40 pounds and pass other physical tests. The orthopedic surgeon who had operated on his elbow and wrist didn't think he would ever be able to do it, but Chris wouldn't take no for an answer. After only four months, he took the test to go back to work.

"Chris, how did the test go?" I asked him when he came to his next session.

"I failed," he said, "but I'll get it next time."

Two months later he retook the test, and I asked again, "How was it?"

"I failed, but I did better than last time," he said, always the optimist. "You watch, third time will be the charm."

His physician told me privately that he hoped Chris wouldn't be depressed when he failed again, but I had said, "Don't count him out." My family had overcome impossible conditions, and it was obvious that Chris possessed the same qualities of good blood that my dad had always displayed. He believed he could do it and didn't let negativity get him down.

On the third try, he passed.

I smile. Now here he is in front of me, three years later and healthier than ever. I look at him and see that familiar glow in his eyes, that sense of knowing.

"Thanks again for all you did for me," he says. "I couldn't have done it without you."

"You're welcome, but you did it all. You were my teacher, and I am the one who should say thank you."

"How did I teach you?" he asks.

"You just did," I say, but in my mind I keep going. *You reminded me never to forget about the power we have inside of us to heal.*

"I'm glad that you worked with me."

"Me, too. It was great seeing you."

I head back to my office, treat a few more patients, and then take a phone call. It is Dr. Alan Jones, one of the orthopedic doctors at the hospital.

"I have a proposition for you," he says. "If you're free in about 30 minutes, can you come to my office?"

"Sure, I'm off to lunch now. I'll drop by right after."

"Glad you could come by," Dr. Jones says, opening his office door. "I'm in charge of scheduling in-service classes for the doctors. Doris, the head of nursing, went to your communication seminar last week, and she said it was valuable in helping her with her staff."

Chad and I lead communication seminars for health care practitioners and educators about once every other month. We have even gotten some of the staff members here to participate. The communication tools that we teach help us better understand our colleagues, patients, and ourselves for that matter.

"She also said that you gave a talk at the American Back Society about motivating the unmotivated patient. She recommended you to give an in-service on communication to our doctors. Would you like to? It is a paying opportunity."

"I'd be honored." I beam.

"How about January 15 at 9am?"

"I usually have a partner come to the seminars with me. Would that be ok?"

"It would be great!"

"Thank you so much. I can't wait."

I head back to the clinic, giddy with excitement. The date for the in-service has been secured. On the way into the physical therapists' office, I bump into Carol, and I eagerly tell her the news.

"I can't afford to let you take that time off," she says in a stern voice, and my heart sinks. "We're too busy. Chad will have to do that himself." I stand there in disbelief as she adds, "You're very good at doing PR for yourself, but everyone else in this department is just as good as you are. I've decided that next month everyone will start teaching so that you don't do it all. Everyone should get recognition."

She heads into her office, and I walk numbly into mine. No one takes notice of me as I sit down, bewildered.

A few minutes later, Carol comes in to announce her decision to have everyone teach, and she walks out amid stunned silence.

Bill is the first to speak, "I hate teaching."

"So do I," says John.

"What is that all about?" Belinda asks.

I'm fuming, and my brain starts churning, trying to figure out a way to make the in-service happen. *I know,* I think. *I'll ask for a vacation day and not tell her why. Then she cannot stop me.*

I feel as if handcuffs are being put on me, restricting me from doing the best job I can do. Suddenly, a little voice starts creeping into my mind, reminding me of the pact I made with myself when I became a physical therapist, but I push the voice aside and focus on the work ahead of me.

~~~~~~~~~~~~~~

"How are you all doing?" I ask my class that afternoon.

"I wanted to talk to you," Linda says. "It's been four months since I started the class, but I'm still no better."

"How is that?" I ask. "You're stronger, and you have more flexibility. I can see it in what you are able to do. Last week you told me you went on a 5-mile hike and had no pain! Plus, your gait is so much more fluid."

She stretches against the wall, then looks at me and says, stubbornly, "I don't feel better."

"How much of the time are you in pain?" I ask.

"Ten percent of the time, but the other 90% of the time I am worrying that the pain will come back."

Unfortunately, this is a ritual I go through with many of the patients who have a hard time recovering. They focus on their pain, and when they have no pain, they focus on their fear that the pain will return. It is my job to help them key into a positive outlook, like Chris intuitively had. No one who focuses only on the negative can heal properly. There are many studies to prove it.

Everyone begins stretching while Linda and I talk.

"Is there a pattern for when the pain comes on?" I ask.

"Yes, it's in the morning, especially when I take a shower. I wash my hair every morning, and I have to stand in an awkward position because the showerhead is so low."

"Are you in pain for the rest of the day after you take a shower?"

"No, but I keep waiting for that sharp pain to hit."

"OK, but how was the pain four months ago?"

Linda sighs. She knows where I am going with this. "I was in pain most of the time."

"It seems like the shower is your biggest problem right now. Why don't you get a handheld nozzle and see what happens?"

"That's a good idea. I'll try that," she says, and she reluctantly joins the group to start class.

We start off doing exercises on the green ball for core strengthening, stretching and balancing, and to finish, we do 15 minutes of relaxation.

Once this class ends, I head upstairs to teach another class, this one for participants in the chronic pain program. This is our first class together.

I look around and see 12 people sitting and waiting for class to begin. I introduce myself.

"Hey, guys, I'm Irit, and I'd like you to start off by introducing yourself. Tell me a little bit about yourself, but do not talk about your pain. We will spend plenty of time talking about that later."

"Hi. I'm Jim," the first man stands up, "and I've been in pain for almost two years. I have problems sleeping, and I am in pain almost all the time." Even as he says this, I can see him unconsciously put his hands on his lower back and start massaging it.

"Great, nice to meet you," I say and then turn to look at the woman to Jim's right. "Now let's learn about you," I say. "Let us know, do you work? Are you married? What are your interests?"

"I'm Danielle, and I'm married and have two kids." She says, then, just like Jim, she can't refrain, "I haven't been able to work for almost four months because of the pain in my back."

One person after another stands up, and even though I remind them not to speak about their pain, it seems like they can't help it. It has become a part of their identity. I know that feeling only too well.

Their body language is telling it all. The room feels very heavy. I'm being sucked into their negative energy. I look out the window of the classroom and watch the trees swaying in the wind. Then an idea hits me out of my desperation to lift the heaviness I feel in the space.

"Ok, you guys," I say with excitement. "We're going to try something new. I need a volunteer."

Jim comes to the center of the room.

"Ok, close your eyes," I instruct him. "Think of a time when you were in horrible pain. What does that feel like? Intensify that. What does it look like? Intensify that. Do you hear anything? If so, intensify that. Now keep this feeling, open your eyes, and walk twelve feet."

Jim has taken on such a severe limp as he walks that it blows me away. Calmly, I say, "Stop. Now come back to the place you started and shake that feeling away."

"That's funny," Jim says. "That's how I had walked when I was at my worst. I forgot about that."

"Now close your eyes and think of something totally fun and exciting. If you can't think of that, think of what would happen if you had one wish and it came true. Intensify that. What does it look like? Intensify that. Do you hear anything? If so, intensify that. Now keep this feeling, open your eyes, and walk twelve feet."

Jim walks forward again, and this time his head is up, he has a smile on his face, his gait is quick, and his posture is much more erect.

"Ok, shake that feeling off. Now I want you to think of that first episode one more time, but this time I will walk beside you and make sure you maintain the posture you had the second time around. Ready?"

I put my hand on Jim's back to guide him. I raise his head and remind him to smile because that is what he did the second time, and he walks forward without a limp.

"How was that for you?" I ask.

"I couldn't think of the pain," Jim says.

We divide into groups, and I walk around helping out.

"When I hold my head high, I literally can't think of the time I was in pain," a student says, and the rest agree.

~~~~~~~~~~~~~~

"That seems ridiculous. She should be glad that physical therapy is getting so much recognition," Chad says after I relay the conversation I had with Carol to him.

"I don't know."

"You should think of starting your own practice. You're good enough."

"Nah, I don't think I'm good enough yet, I'm still learning a lot here. Besides, it's still fun," I say.

"Ok, but you should think about it. You'd be really good. I could refer people to you as well."

"I'm going for a run," I say. This conversation is making me tense. I just want to feel the wind in my face as I pass all the redwoods and leave my stress about Carol behind. "You want to join me?"

"I'm tired. I'll stay put."

~~~~~~~~~~~~~~

Every day at work I see a new success story. Every day I learn something new. Yet, every day, the tension between Carol and me grows. The days pass, and soon, holiday festivities are in the air. I head into the office and smile as I see the Christmas decorations hung around our department. Tomorrow is the start of the one-week break I had requested months prior.

The first patient I am seeing today is Olga. Her shoulder is almost back to normal, and she no longer has any pain so it will be a pretty simple session.

As she comes into my office, I see a present in her hand.

"This is for you," she says excitedly. "Open it and try it on." I open it and am surprised to see a handmade blue-and-white ski sweater.

"It fits perfectly," I say, stunned by how much work she had to have put into it. "This is unbelievable. I've never gotten a present like this before. I'm speechless."

"Just wanted to say thanks for all that you have done for me. Merry Christmas!"

"Wow," is all I can say.

My next patient is Dorothy. I laugh as she also enters with a present in her hands. I am starting to feel spoiled. I open the box to find a pair of red booties.

"I knit these for you," she says. "Hope they fit."

"I can't believe this. Did you talk to my last patient?" I ask.

"Actually, yes. I just wanted to thank you. Merry Christmas! I hope you like it."

"Like it? I love it. Thank you so much."

My next patient comes in and gives me a red-and-white hand-knit scarf. My eyes start to tear up at the generosity of these women. I never expected anything like this. During every other Christmas season I have had here I only received candy from some of the patients, which I didn't even eat. This year, I don't get candy from anyone, just all of these unbelievable gifts made especially for me.

As the day goes on, I get more and more gifts, and that afternoon, when Carol walks into the physical therapists' office to talk to me, I tell her, in an excited and incredulous tone, "Look at these beautiful gifts. Isn't this amazing?"

Carol scans my pile of gifts and then gives me a stern look. "This isn't right. Did you tell them to get you presents?"

I look at her blankly. I feel like I am about to say something that I know I will regret. So, I hold back the worst thoughts that are coming to mind, but I can't help bursting out in sarcasm, "No, but that's a great idea. Imagine how much more I could have gotten had I asked."

Carol walks out without another word.

~~~~~~~~~~~~~~

Two more weeks pass, and it is the day before my in-service class with the doctors. As I am walking down the hall, Carol stops me, and I feel my stomach knot up in a now all too familiar way. *What now?*

"I heard you are giving a talk tomorrow. I thought I told you I can't spare you for the talk," she says.

"I know. That's why I took it as a vacation day. You approved it." *Ha! Ha!* I think to myself while trying to keep an innocent look on my face.

Carol pauses, then says sharply, "The day after tomorrow, I want to do your evaluation. I will get the secretary to reschedule your patients from 9-10 am."

I get home, and once again, after I relay the story, Chad says, "You should think of getting into your own practice."

"No. I'm not good enough yet. I'll be fine. I'm too well liked."

~~~~~~~~~~~~~~

Friday morning I go into Carol's office with my nerves on edge, and she begins the evaluation.

"You have time management issues," she begins. "You spend too much time with some patients and end up making others wait up to 5 or 10 minutes sometimes. That is not fair to the patients who have to wait. Also, your paperwork is not acceptable."

Carol goes on and on, listing every single fault she can find with me until, finally, we get to the communication portion of the evaluation.

At least, the worst is over, I think foolishly. *I know I'll do well in this one.*

Carol looks at me coldly and says, "You have difficulty getting along with staff. That will have to improve."

"What?" I blurt out, "You must be kidding?"

"No. I've heard complaints about you."

"Who is complaining?"

"I can't divulge that. It's confidential." My eyes bore into her. *What did I ever do to you?* I want to scream, but I hold it in.

Finally, she strikes me with the final blow. "And the last thing is you have too much fun. You are not here to have fun. You are here to do a job."

"But … if you have fun, it makes a better work environment," I say.

Carol smirks at me as if I am some naïve little girl and says, "You have a lot to work on."

I know there is no arguing with her. She has finished talking.

~~~~~~~~~~~~~~

Six weeks later, the director of the hospital comes by my office to say good bye.

"The hospital will not be the same without you," he says. "Wish we could change your mind."

I smile and say, "That means a lot to me. Thank you."

~~~~~~~~~~~~~~

16

1992-1995

We could never learn to be brave and patient if there were only joy in the world.

Helen Keller

I pull over at 2044 C Street in my rented car. I park and check my hair in the mirror. My lipstick is on, and my jeans have been pressed. Aunt Ersie says I should always look my best, so if I don't, she thinks it is somehow a reflection on her. I walk through her garden of lilac bushes and reach the glass door to the kitchen.

Aunt Ersie opens the door, and the aroma spilling out of the kitchen automatically makes me hungry. I reach out for a hug but then pause.

"You have a walker. What happened?" I ask.

"The doctors say it is poliomyelitis. They don't know what causes it, but they gave me prednisone. I had it before Jusie died, but it got better. Now it's bad again."

It has been almost a year since my uncle died, but the memory of the phone call is still vivid in my mind.

"Irit," Ersie had said, "I'm so sorry, but your Uncle Jusie died in his sleep last week."

"When? How? When is the funeral?" I asked in disbelief.

"We already had the funeral. I didn't want to call because it was better that you didn't come."

"Didn't come? What about sitting Shiva?"

"I decided not to have a Shiva."

"But that doesn't make sense."

"Irit, it is just too difficult for me. I don't feel well, and I didn't want to have everyone go out of their way."

"But everyone would have wanted to pay tribute," I said.

"I don't feel well," she repeated and hung up.

A part of me understood, but I was disappointed that I couldn't say goodbye to Jusie. My aunt doesn't want anyone to see her unless she is strong. I guess that could be said of all my family members. We all tend to do that very well.

Since paying tribute during Shiva wasn't an option, I decided to go to the beach as I often do when I am sad and say goodbye to my uncle in my own way.

"I am so glad you are here. How was your flight?" Aunt Ersie asks while gesturing for me to sit.

"The trip was easy. There were no delays at either end. So, what are the doctors doing for you?" I ask.

"They're giving me steroids."

"Be careful. Steroids help at first, but if you're on them too long they can become a problem."

"Don't worry. The doctors know. I went to physical therapy, and they gave me some exercises. Maybe you can help me with them later."

"Absolutely. I'd love to. We can do that now if you would like."

"Later would be good. I'm so happy you could come visit. You look so good. Zoli would have been so happy to see you like this."

I smile at the warmth that oozes out of her. My aunt's home is very inviting. Her dining room is filled with Chinese teak furniture and has a sliding glass door that overlooks the garden and the gate that leads to her pool. I go into her bathroom, which is in the entryway for her bedroom. It has a light purple sunken bathtub and a huge glass window that takes up a whole wall; on the other side of the bathroom is an atrium filled with green plants and trees. It makes me feel like I am in a lush forest as I look around. I have never taken a bath in here, but I wish I could. I'm sure it is very peaceful.

When I return, we sit down in the kitchen. My aunt serves an apple crisp made with corn flakes. She gave me the recipe a few years ago, but hers always comes out better than mine.

"How is work?" Aunt Ersie asks as I take a bite, savoring the sweet apple flavor.

"I'm taking a little break from having a full time job. For now I just want to work for the physical therapy registry so I can pick and choose the days I want to work. Plus it will give me a chance to see what options are out there. "

"Have you started your book? I found some letters and pictures. Remind me to give them to you."

"I haven't yet, but that's awesome about the photos and letters. I definitely want to see them."

Aunt Ersie fidgets in her seat for a minute and taps her fingers on the table before finally saying, "I miss your dad." I smile at her sympathetically. I know the feeling.

"I still can't believe my dad never told me about the dream he had when he was shot," I say. "I mean, it was the most incredible dream. Why didn't he share it with everyone? I mean, it's like he was in the beyond, in this amazing place of beauty and peace, but he was called back to life by your voice. That isn't something that should be kept quiet. That is amazing!"

"He was afraid people wouldn't understand. When he first came back from the war, he did tell people, but they all thought he was crazy. Ellinani was the only one who understood, but after that, he kept quiet. It was his own little spiritual secret."

I sit in silence, wondering again if I really would have understood the implications of his dream growing up.

"You know, he told me once that he wasn't afraid to die. I was so scared when he said that that I never asked him why. I wish I had. I wonder ... maybe it was because of the dream. Maybe he wasn't scared because he knew he would just return to that beautiful place of bright lights that were more beautiful and magnified than anything else he had ever experienced."

"He always said to me, 'Ersikem, I don't ever want to be so sick that people have to take care of me,'" Ersie says pensively. "He didn't want to become a burden. He would rather just pass on peacefully, independent to the end."

"He said the same to me."

"I'm the same way. I can't stand this walker. I don't want anyone to see me like this. I'm going to wait until I don't need the walker before I visit friends again."

I look at Aunt Ersie. She looks so serious and sad. I try to reassure her, "Aunt Ersie, you still look great. You're probably the most beautiful 82-year-old person I know." I wait a beat and then smile mischievously, "You're also my favorite aunt in California."

"I'm your only aunt in California," Ersie says sweetly.

"But you're still my favorite," I say earnestly, and we both laugh. I have said this to my aunt since I can remember. It is our own little special way of communicating, which I have since transferred to my nephews, carrying on the tradition. "Well, if that's how you feel about it, then let me help you with your exercises, so you can get strong enough to walk without a walker," I say, getting back to the matter at hand. My aunt brings out her instruction sheet and starts doing the leg exercises with the yellow theraband the doctor gave her.

"Did they teach you about breathing?"

"No."

"I'll show you. Usually when you exert yourself, you exhale. The breathing is the most important part. We didn't focus on breath work in school, but through my experience with yoga and chi kung, I have gotten a better understanding of the importance of it.

Ersie tries the first exercise again, this time taking very calculated breaths. "Am I doing this right?"

"That's perfect." We do each exercise on the sheet, and I show her how to breathe properly with each one.

"It would be horrible if I had to have someone take care of me," Ersie says, but before she can continue, she is cut off by Suzie, her daughter, knocking on the glass door.

"Irit, my cousin, how are you? I'm so glad you are here."

Suzie is my artistic cousin. She even owned an art gallery for a while. She also loves shopping. She buys all the designer clothes and gets tired of them quickly, which is a plus for me. When I was in Physical Therapy School, I would come over to her house in West LA and get hand me down clothes from the most expensive boutiques in town. The clothes never looked worn. Probably because most of them weren't. I always felt like I had just won a shopping spree in Beverly Hills. Suzie now makes furniture of stainless steel, marble, and glass. Her furniture has been shown in *Interior Design* magazine, *The New York Times*, and *Architecture Design*, to name just a few. Yet she, like me, suffers from the it's-never-good-enough syndrome.

"Suzie, your friend Jack called me to check in, and he told me something about you that made me laugh," Ersie says.

"What did he say?" she asks with a good-natured grin that shows she knows some sort of punch line at her expense is on its way.

"He said, 'Suzie can make any man a millionaire,'" Ersie pauses, smiling, "'that is, if he starts as a billionaire.'"

Suzie laughs. *Yes,* I think, chuckling. *I don't know this guy, but he is right on. That is my cousin.*

~~~~~~~~~~~~~~

I return home, and I go running almost every day. Chad and I play tennis about once a week, and we bicycle together about twice a week.

After a two-week break, I start at an employment agency that finds me work in facilities that need temporary help. This is perfect for me right now because it gives me the freedom to work whenever I want and I get to go to different facilities on a regular basis. I decide to take it easy for a little while and prepare for Chad and my next holiday this coming summer: a trip to Paris, Rome and Florence.

Chad and I have been together for almost five years now. He and I are still teaching communication seminars, but it's starting to take a toll on me. The teaching part of the seminars is fun, but I always have to figure out ways to get more participants, and I hate making those phone calls. If I made phone calls for others, it would be fun and easy, but because it is for me it feels like I'm bragging about myself and that doesn't sit well with me.

When I complain, Chad reminds me that he is doing all the slides and handouts and that it is my job to get participants. I have to just keep at it every day, but I feel so much pressure from him. It just doesn't seem worth it anymore. I feel like teaching together has become too draining on us and on our relationship.

~~~~~~~~~~~~~~

I stand in the corner of the room, and I can see that Chad is preoccupied with a slim, tall woman with long blond hair almost to her waist. I keep trying to get his attention, but he is ignoring me. After each attempt, I feel a deeper and deeper wedge come between us.

Suddenly, the scene changes. We are standing outside, and I watch them as they drive away together, leaving me behind.

As I awaken, my heart beats fast. I turn to Chad and wake him up.

"Chad," I say, visibly upset.

He groans as he wakes up and mumbles, "What's wrong? Why did you wake me up?"

"You cheated on me. How could you?" I say on the verge of hysterics.

"What are you talking about? Irit, you were dreaming. Go back to sleep."

"You cheated on me."

"Irit, it is called a dream. It's not real." Chad says irritatedly, and he turns his back to me.

I sigh and look up at the ceiling, trying to calm myself down. I have felt like things between me and Chad have been tense lately, but whenever I try to talk to him about it he tells me it is all in my mind. *I know it was just a dream,* I think as I start to fall back to sleep, *but it felt so real.*

~~~~~~~~~~~~~~

"Irit, I am not happy," Chad says abruptly, halfway through his meal of broiled scampi. I take a bite of my wild salmon, savoring the taste, before responding.

"Maybe we should do more fun things," I say pensively. "We've been too serious. I feel it, too. I'm the queen of fun, though. So, that should be easy enough to manage."

Chad sits quietly and takes a few more bites of his meal before continuing, "Irit, I'm not happy, and it's you. I'm thinking, maybe you should move out."

I feel like I have been punched right in my solar plexus. I can't breathe. The world switches into slow motion. I am so confused. Just that day we had gone on a two-hour bike trip, hung out at the house, and now here we are, halfway through dinner at a nice restaurant. Suddenly he is unhappy?

"I need space."

"Space," I say. "But you always wanted to spend more time together." I pause, trying to hold it in, but the question still slips out, "Is there someone else? Like in the dream I had two weeks ago where you were with another woman."

"No. I told you, that was just a dream."

"Are you sure there's no other woman?"

"Yes, but I am not happy."

"Chad, we can work it out," I say. "Let's go to counseling."

"No, I think it's you."

"Chad," I say. I am completely caught off guard. "You never said anything before. You don't even want to try to work it out?"

"I just started feeling this way recently."

I lose my appetite and push my plate away.

"I need space. I'm not happy," I hear again. I try to hold back, but I can't.

"Chad, are you sure there isn't someone else?"

"No," he says, a note of aggravation in his voice, "but I want you to move out as soon as possible. Maybe when we are apart I will have a better perspective."

~~~~~~~~~~~~~~

That night in bed, I toss and turn. I want to talk. I keep beginning, but Chad always cuts me off.

"I need my sleep," he says.

"But Chad, we need to talk," I say.

"I have to do surgeries tomorrow. You will give me a heart attack if you don't let me sleep."

Those words take my breath away. He sounds like my mother. He doesn't have heart issues. He doesn't need sleep. He is just shutting down on me, and there is nothing I can do. I can't believe it. I can't speak, and I definitely can't sleep.

~~~~~~~~~~~~~~

When the morning finally arrives and Chad wakes up, he is cold as stone. There is no emotion, no caring, and no friendship remaining inside of him. It is as if I never knew him. My heart has been ripped apart.

I move out, and six weeks later someone else moves in.

I keep thinking, *If only ... If only I had done things differently, if only I had been different, if only, if only, if only ...* The record plays over and over in my head, causing me deep sadness, emptiness, and regret.

I had red flags nagging at me from the get go, and yet I still went down that road. His eyes, I always wondered about his eyes. They never had had the warmth that I so loved and craved. My dad had great eyes. All I can do now is question myself. *What is it that always makes me go down the wrong path?* Whenever other options, other paths come to me, I find reasons not to take them. Somehow, I am always drawn toward the Chad type, the ones who, in spite of their broad shoulders, will never be there for me.

~~~~~~~~~~~~~~

Eventually I get back to my routine, but it's still hard for me to concentrate. I just don't feel like working, and I'm having a hard time being alone. After a couple months of this, a friend shows me a brochure for a 3-month intensive class that she thinks might be good for me. The class taps into the inner child through the mediums of art, dance, and writing. Better yet, the first month is at Sea Ranch, a community dedicated to preserving its natural beauty. The next day, I sign up, and before long, 14 other participants and I are headed up to this new community.

I arrive at Sea Ranch, and the surrounding beauty awes me. The homes we are staying in are nestled into the landscape, and most have a view of the Pacific Ocean. The smell of the salt from the ocean spray creates gentle breaths of clean ocean air.

I am placed with five others in the home closest to the ocean, The next day, our class begins. Each day, there is a theme and a project on self-discovery. Most days we go into the water and then do drawings and write about our experiences. Later in the day, we head to the dance studio where we have movement exploration.

It's nice to be immersed with so many creative individuals. Life is beginning to flow back into me. Yet, every morning, like clockwork, I wake up at 2 a.m., and the negative 'it's my fault' tapes play on full blast. I lie in bed as my brain works overtime, dwelling on thoughts that I know do not serve me. If any of my patients were to tell me that they didn't believe they could ever be better or that they only focused on the negative, I would have told them that, until their mindsets shifted, they would have a hard time healing. I know I need to incorporate the same mindset to heal my heart as I do to heal my physical body, but I feel so stuck. As hard as I try to talk myself out of this feeling, I can't. It is definitely easier said than done.

One morning, we head to the redwood forest, where we are blindfolded. Our task for the hour is to walk in the forest and hug as many trees as possible. My mind goes completely quiet. I have to be so focused that I have no choice but to be present. As I hug a redwood tree and walk in what feels like cool moss, I feel at peace for the first time.

Too soon, it is our last evening at Sea Ranch, and I am hanging out with the occupants of one of the other homes. They turn the music on and start doing free flowing creative dance. Two of the girls from this house are classically trained dancers, and one of the guys is a professional modern dancer. So, everything they are doing looks beautiful. I sit and watch, but when Enya starts playing, they ask me to join them. I'm wary at first because they are all such great dancers, but as we start to dance together, something magical happens. It feels as if we are all one, moving about in our uniqueness, and each of us is somehow an extension of the other. Bubbles of joy start streaming inside of me. I am having fun again, without a thought or care in the world. Once again, I'm shown what is possible in life, and I breathe it into every cell of my body.

~~~~~~~~~~~~~~

I think someone is looking out for me, because as soon as I complete my 3-month program, a friend calls me to tell me about a private practice physical therapy position that would be perfect for me. I begin my new job three days later and am working four days a week, which is ideal for me.

The job is pretty easy because at the moment, Tim, my boss, doesn't want me to do any hands-on work, which is the hardest part of the job. I only have to guide the patients through exercises. Tim is a fitness buff, and he emphasizes the importance of regular exercise. He is a colonel in the army reserves, so he is disciplined, and some say he runs his exercise program like a boot camp.

Tim wants the program to be the same for everyone, so those with back problems have to go through the same prescribed exercises and those with knee problems have their regimen and so on. There are some female patients who ask him to oversee their exercise programs because they like to flirt with him. His wedding ring, reminding them he is married with two teenage girls, doesn't stop them. Others are intimidated by him and ask me to oversee their exercises instead.

There are two massage therapists on staff to do body work and modalities on the patients. The facility has a gym with workout equipment that men and women share, and there is a small room designated for women only. It is used especially by those who are shy about working out with the opposite sex. There is a co-ed swimming pool and a steam room for men only. Tim often lends out t-shirts and shorts for the male clients to work out in. The shorts look like the oversized white underwear that someone's great grandfather would wear. They are good because they can be worn in the steam room, and the good news for Tim is that no one would ever want to steal them and take a pair home.

I'm satisfied just working in the gym for now because I don't want to expend much energy. I work out in the gym with Tim and others three days a week. I run every other day. I think I could run a marathon and still not be tired at this point. I bike on the days I don't run.

I still feel sad and wish I could have changed so much about what happened with Chad and me. I'm still putting him on a pedestal and putting much of the blame on myself, but it is not with the same strong intensity. I'm not fixated on Chad every second like I had been for so long.

~~~~~~~~~~~~~~

"Muscle energy is a direct approach for increasing range of motion and normalizing dysfunction," our instructor explains. "It involves the voluntary contraction of a patient's muscle in a controlled direction at varying levels of intensity against a counterforce applied by the practitioner. The tissue is moved toward a barrier, and the direction of motion is toward the restriction."

I am in Tucson for a three-day seminar on muscle energy for the spine. The teacher demonstrates the technique on one of the students. Before the demonstration begins, the student can't move his head to the right. After this technique is applied, he has his full range of motion. Another student, who can't bring his hands past his knees, volunteers next. After the technique, he can almost touch his toes with no pain.

The seminar is fun, but there is a lot of information to take in. I am exhausted, so I go to bed early.

The next morning, I wake up with a horrible headache. It feels like a vice grip around my temples, and my neck is tight. I decide to ask one of the assistant teachers to work on me, and after about forty-five minutes, my headache is gone.

"I can't believe that. No one has ever been able to alleviate my headaches like that before," I say. "What techniques did you use?"

"I was doing cranial work. Those techniques aren't offered in this class, but you should look into them."

~~~~~~~~~~~~~~

Not even two weeks after the seminar, I'm in a car accident, and my car is totaled. I made a U-turn where I wasn't allowed to, and a car in oncoming traffic was speeding. So, I was broadsided.

When the ambulance arrives, I am bleeding from a cut on my head, but I keep telling them I'm fine, except, of course, for the bleeding. Unfortunately, the paramedic tells me they have to take me in no matter what I say. Sometimes people think they are fine, and then they drop dead from unknown complications.

As we wait for the all clear to head to the hospital, the paramedic asks me if I want to be covered up so the people in the cars crawling by can really have something to wonder about. I laugh, but I say no. I am too superstitious for that. I don't really want to tempt fate.

Within a week, I'm running again. I won't let this get me down. During this past year, I have changed jobs and have lost my boyfriend. I am not about to let a little accident and a totaled car stop me now.

~~~~~~~~~~~~~

A few mornings later, I head to work in my rental car. I am waiting at a red light when I hear the crashing sound of metal on metal and my car is shoved to the side. A car that had been turning left and was going in the opposite direction of me lost control and found me. There were two hits in just a few seconds. First, the car broadsided me, and then my car broadsided a parked car. Everything happened so fast1 I am shaken. My neck and upper back automatically start to feel tight.

How can this be happening? I ask myself in disbelief. *I was waiting for the red light to change. I wasn't even moving!*

I call the office first thing to tell them I am going to be late and then wait for the police to arrive.

~~~~~~~~~~~~~

I can't complain much about my body to the people at work because I don't trust that I will keep my job if I complain. As it turns out, this job is perfect because I am not using my body much, so I can heal.

Unfortunately, traditional physical therapy and the exercise program that Tim put me on after the second accident are making me worse. I'm getting headaches every day, not anything like in physical therapy school, but still bad. Tylenol helps sometimes, but sometimes I just have to suffer through it.

~~~~~~~~~~~~~

If anything, the second accident encouraged me to take more classes. I am always looking for new ways to heal.

Ever since the woman at that course in Tucson did cranial techniques on me, it has been on my radar of courses to take. Now, I am finally going to meet one of the most important mentors on my healing journey in a course at Esalen in Big Sur, California, a region on the central coast of California where the Santa Lucia Mountains rise sharply above the Pacific ocean.

Esalen is a retreat center and residential community offering courses in the humanities and science. It was founded in 1962 by Michael Murphy and Dick Price with a vision of exploring and better understanding the world of human potential. I am going for five days to take my third craniosacral class. The craniosacral system, as I learned from my previous class, is a functioning physiological system that possesses its own physiological rhythm. The craniosacral system influences and is influenced by the nervous system, the musculoskeletal system, the vascular system, the lymphatic system, and the respiratory system. This system shows us that what happens in one part of the body can affect the whole body.

There are different hypotheses for how the craniosacral system works, but the agreement among doctors is that when there are imbalances or restrictions in this system, they can manifest as problems elsewhere in the body. I have been practicing these techniques on my patients ever since taking my first class, and I am shocked at the improvements. It still amazes me how such a light touch therapy can be so powerful.

The grounds of Esalen are made up of 120 acres of land divided between mountain and ocean. A feeling of peace and calm envelops me here, making me forget all of my worries back home. Esalen is famous for its mineral hot springs and baths facing the seaside cliffs, a must see while I'm here.

Today in class I am finally going to meet Dr. John Upledger. He is the osteopathic physician, who developed and simplified craniosacral techniques. Much to the chagrin of fellow osteopaths, he offered these classes to non-osteopathic health care practitioners and lay people who had an interest in learning these techniques. He is a pioneer and visionary in the field. I have heard about him through many colleagues. When I heard this class would be at Esalen, I signed up immediately. Another perk of signing up for the class is that I can ask Dr. John, which is the name he prefers, for advice. I have been having horrible headaches since my last car accident. I have an osteopathic physician working on me in San Francisco, but it isn't helping much.

The class begins, and I hear Dr. John start off by explaining his philosophy. "The body has an inherent wisdom, and it has an innate ability to heal. When something goes wrong, our bodies try to tell us, but many times we just don't know how to listen.

"The body never lies," he says, "so the more you develop your skills to listen with your hands, the better you will be at creating balance in the body and enabling it to heal itself."

Yes! I want to shout. That has always been my philosophy, too.

The first day of class flies by, and I now understand why I have heard so much about Dr. John. I'm excited about the class, but by dinnertime my head is splitting, a regular occurrence since my last accident. I can't focus on anything else. I head over to the drink station to get some green tea hoping that will help, and Dr. John is right behind me. I decide to take this opportunity to talk to him.

"Hi, Dr. John. I loved your class today," I say, and we exchange pleasantries. "I was wondering ... sometime during the week can you evaluate me and give me some advice? I have been getting these horrible headaches ever since I was in an accident, and the osteopath in town hasn't been able to help."

"How about now?" he asks.

"No. I don't want to bother you now," I say politely and then automatically scold myself. *Are you out of your mind? If he offers, say yes.*

"Don't be silly, this is a good time. Let's go now. Your face actually looks kind of green," Dr. John says.

"That's how I feel, too," I say. Now it makes more sense why he is so willing to help me out right away. I probably look terrible.

We go to the classroom, and I lie on the table. Dr. John and Lee, one of his assistants, start working on me. My head is throbbing, but as they put their hands on me, I begin to feel like I'm floating. Lee is working on my lower back region, and Dr. John is at my head. After about five minutes, I hear and feel a gust of wind being pulled out of my sacrum, the triangular bone at the base of the spine. It is the same gust of wind I had experienced when Dr. Goode took away those unbearable headaches in physical therapy school. I drift in and out of awareness as I am being worked on. I feel like I'm floating, and then, suddenly, I start reliving the car accident I was in when I was in physical therapy school.

"Treatment is like peeling an onion," Dr. John says. "Old injuries will come forth during the process."

"I'm reliving an old accident," I say, surprised. It is like he read my mind.

"I know."

After an hour, they finish, and I get up and head to my room. No sooner do I get to my room than I rush to the bathroom to throw up. When I lie down again, the accident from physical therapy school begins playing over and over in my head. I'm reliving it in my mind and in my body. I can picture it all and feel the jolt as pain starts shooting through my body. How is this possible? I know the body has a memory, but the accident was ten years ago.

I wake up to the sound of the ocean. My head feels good, and I get up. It is 7 a.m., so I head for the baths. As I walk outside, I look up at the sky. This is the first time I have looked up without using my other hand for support in a long time. It had been too painful before today because of the cervical limitations. I continue on my way. I am still getting sharp shooting pains once in a while, but I feel so much better. I sit in a mineral bath on the cliff and gaze into the beauty of the Pacific Ocean.

"How are you?" Dr. John asks when he sees me at breakfast later that morning.

"I feel better today than I have since before the car accident, but when I got back to my room last night I threw up. I kept reliving a car accident I was in ten years ago."

"It will take at least another month before you feel a lot better, but this was a start."

The course ends, and I leave feeling bewildered and amazed. The body has a wisdom that is beyond our mental awareness. I am excited to share what I have learned with Tim in his private practice.

~~~~~~~~~~~~~~

I call Aunt Ersie on a regular basis. She stopped using the walker and seemed to be alright until about a month ago when she developed shingles on her head and face. The nerve pain is probably similar to what I had in PT school. The doctors have given her strong pain meds. Every day she seems to be getting weaker, and the doctors keep upping the pain meds. The more drugs she is on, the worse she is feeling and the more symptoms she is experiencing.

She is using a walker all the time now because she is so weak. She is having difficulty moving around within the house. She has even become bladder incontinent at times, and the doctors don't know why. I wonder if it could be a side effect of the many meds. I know this is totally devastating to her. She has always been a private and independent person. Now she has a Hungarian attendant staying with her and watching over her at all times.

"She does not make good chicken *paprikash*," my aunt says in frustration every time I call. Everything the attendant does reminds Ersie of what she can't do anymore and it is taking its toll.

"How are you?" I ask Ersie over the phone as I sit on my couch Monday night.

"The doctors say it takes time, but I am in so much pain," Aunt Ersie says.

"Maybe I should come visit. Some of the work I do helps pain. In fact, I worked on someone with shingles, and it significantly lessened the pain. "

"The doctors say nothing will help. Only time," Ersie says.

"It doesn't hurt to try."

"Irit, I can't take care of myself properly. It feels like it is just getting worse, and the pain is too much. Every day it is worse, and every day I need more and more help. I don't think I can take it much longer."

My body tightens, and I go numb. "Please don't talk like that," I urge her. I can drive down tomorrow and work on you. Maybe it will help with the pain."

"I miss your father. I wish I could talk with him."

"I know. I miss him, too."

"I want to get off the phone. I'm tired and I want to go to sleep. Irit, I love you."

"I love you, too." I hang up the phone and immediately call Suzie. My heart pounds as I fill her in on all Ersie had said.

"The attendant is there," Suzie responds. "I'm going to her place tomorrow morning, so I'll call you and let you know how she is."

The next day she calls and says, "Everything seems fine, but my mom says to wait to come visit. She's better."

The following day I go to work. It is April 6th, the day of Uncle Jusie's death, so I know it will be a tough day for Ersie. When I arrive home, I notice there is a message blinking.

I press the play button.

"Irit, my cousin," I hear Suzie say, and in between her sobs I hear, "the police were here. The attendant went shopping for my mom. When she came back to the house, the attendant saw the walker standing close to the deep end of the pool. She found my mom in the deep end."

The message cuts off, and there I am, standing in my kitchen, trying to breathe.

~~~~~~~~~~~~~~

Alison, Aunt Ersie's granddaughter and Suzie's daughter, speaks at the funeral. Alison could do no wrong in her grandparents' eyes. It is identical to how my mom is with her grandchildren.

"My grandmother Ersie," she says, "represented love and creativity. Everything she did was out of love and kindness. She gave, gave, gave and always from her heart.

"Her favorite question was, 'What do you want to eat?' Everything she made became my comfort food. Everything she sewed became my favorite thing to wear. Her pleasure in life came from giving, and I always felt it.

"She was the epitome of creativity. Yes, she was an amazing seamstress. Yes, she was an amazing cook. But it went beyond that. Everything she did was so detailed because she cared that much. She always cared deeply, and it showed in everything she cooked, everything she sewed, everything she said, everything, everything, everything."

I feel so much emotion welling up inside of me. Aunt Ersie was a proud woman, and she lost everything that was important to her. I'm still very angry at her for leaving us, maybe not at her so much as at our medical system and maybe not even angry at the medical system, just very disappointed.

The side effects of the many drugs Ersie took contributed to her downward spiral, yet she never questioned any of the decisions the doctors made. She trusted that they knew what was best for her. She also believed that if she questioned any of her doctors' choices, they would be unhappy with her.

Yes, they tried to help her, and yes, they cared. Yet, their focus was to alleviate the pain at all costs. Did anyone take into consideration what was important to her? Did anyone share the side effects the drugs would have on her physical and emotional independence? Ultimately, it would affect what was of utmost importance to her.

Maybe nothing would have helped Aunt Ersie. Maybe it was her fate to go now, but other options were not given to her.

~~~~~~~~~~~~~~~

17

1997-1998

Everyone has a doctor in him or her; we just have to help it in its work. The natural healing force within each one of us is the greatest force in getting well.

Hippocrates

Two years have passed since the phone call from Suzie, and I'm exercising in my living room when the phone rings.

"Eear!" I hear on the other end, and I light up.

"Hey Marc, how are you? How is my favorite middle nephew in the whole wide world?"

"I'm your only middle nephew." I hear him chuckle that same chuckle I have heard since he was a small boy.

"Well, you're still my favorite middle nephew." I smile and feel warmth wash over me as I remember teasing Aunt Ersie in the same way.

"You're not going to believe it. You know how I lost the election for student body president at Pitt by three votes this past school year?"

"Yeah! I'm sorry. I can't believe, with the amount of students enrolled at the University of Pittsburgh, just three votes would determine who was president. I guess every vote does count."

"Well, when I lost the vote, I decided to graduate. Had I won, I would have just taken fewer courses per semester and graduated the following December when my student body term would have been completed. So, since I graduated in the spring, I applied for a job in New York and guess what?"

I can hear the excitement in his voice, "You got the job?"

"Yep. My title will be *client relations and marketing assistant.*"

"That's great. So, what does that mean?" I say.

"I take care of office duties for the person I work for."

"Congratulations!"

"That's not all. They want me to work in their satellite office," Marc says.

"That's good," I say, not really sure what that means.

"The satellite office is in San Francisco."

"You're kidding!" I say so loud that I'm sure all my neighbors hear it. My whole body is about to explode with excitement. I can hardly contain myself. "Are you serious?"

"My flight is in ten days, Saturday, June 28th."

"I can't believe this. That is so awesome."

"So, I was hoping I could stay with you for a few months and then get my own place."

"You can stay as long as you want. Yay!" I say, giddy with excitement. "What about your car?"

"The company is paying for my car to be shipped. Well, I have to go, but I'll call you back to let you know the exact time of my flight arrival, okay?"

"See you soon. I can hardly wait."

"Me, too."

I hang up the phone. I can't believe it. He is 21, and it's his first full-time job since graduating from the University of Pittsburgh. Yay! 1997 is a good year.

I sit down in my living room, smiling. When Marc turned 13 and had his bar mitzvah party, I was the only adult allowed in. "She's my aunt from California. She's a skydiver, and she does ropes courses and other cool things," he would tell all his friends.

I can't wait to actually have him in my life for more than a week at a time.

~~~~~~~~~~~~~~

Before I know it, I am at the baggage claim in the San Francisco Airport, and I see Marc coming down the escalator. He is tall, muscular, and confident in his blue jeans and brown leather jacket. I give him a hug.

"I like your jacket," I say.

"Thanks, it was a birthday present."

"How was your flight?"

"Good. I can't believe I'm here."

"Me, neither." As I look him up and down, I notice his eyes are identical to mine. Some days they are green, some days brown, and they have that twinkle that I always saw and loved in my dad.

Marc gets his luggage, and we head to my car, a silver 900S Saab. I had shopped around a while before settling on that car. It is supposed to be one of the safest out there, or so they say.

"When does your car arrive?" I ask.

"Monday between 4 and 6 p.m.."

"What kind of car is it?"

"It's a Mitsubishi 3000GT. It's a sports car. Dad bought it for me as a graduation present."

"That's nice. What color is it?"

"Dad got this great deal for me. We bought it sight unseen. Dad spoke to the dealer on the phone."

"What color is it?"

"Well, when he bought it, Dad told me it was silver with a tinge of purple in it ... Dad's color blind."

"Uh oh." I laugh.

"It's very purple, with no silver."

"A sports car, though; that's cool."

"Oh, look!" Marc says excitedly, "We're going onto the Golden Gate Bridge. I remember it from when I was here last. I was 15, and we drove from San Francisco to Squaw Valley to go skiing."

"Yeah, I remember, too," I laugh. "You were 5'8", but every day you told the ticket person you were under 13 so convincingly that you got away with getting a child's ski ticket. I couldn't believe it."

"Eear. You should know better. Of course, they would believe me. You know I can talk my way into and out of anything."

"How tall are you now?" I ask.

"I'm 5'10". You think I could get away with it again when we go skiing this year?"

"I'll disown you if you try."

We arrive in Mill Valley, my town, and I open the door to my one-bedroom apartment.

"The living room will be your bedroom at night. The closet in the dining area is huge, so you can use that for all of your stuff."

"Wow! The view from the living room is spectacular. Can I open the sliding glass door for a better view?" Marc asks.

"Sure. The view is of Richardson's Bay, and beyond that are the mountains. At night it has an even more magical feel. You'll see. To the left is the pool and Jacuzzi. You can use them any time. It's part of the amenities of the complex."

"Great, thanks!" Marc says, still unable to take his eyes off of the view.

I look straight ahead to the island of Redwood trees. It is marsh land and Miwok Indian territory now. It's also a state bird sanctuary, but there has been a push to develop there. So, one of these days, sadly, they're going to tear down the trees. Every time I look at the trees, I feel them asking me to help them not get torn down. Yet, there was nothing I felt I could do.

Drawing Marc's attention back to my place, I say, "I got you a futon that folds out, but you will have to put everything away in the mornings. Sometimes I use this room to see patients. See, here is the folded massage table that I use."

"When did you go into private practice?" Marc asks. This is news to him.

"About six months ago."

"Was it hard to leave your old job?"

"That job was fun. It was exactly what I needed at the time. It had a pool and a gym, and I was learning a lot. My boss, Tim, even paid for my first craniosacral class."

"So, why did you leave?"

"I took more classes, and my boss was impressed with the results that I was getting."

"That's good …" A confused expression crosses Marc's face.

"Well, he took a class, but he wasn't getting the results I was getting. He wasn't getting any results."

"So, did he take more classes?"

"He took two classes, but he told me it wasn't the route he wanted to pursue. I also think he got frustrated because he would work on patients and then they would request I work on them the next time."

"So, what happened?"

"Tim called me into his office one afternoon as I was finishing my paperwork."

"And what happened?" Marc curiously asks again.

"He told me that he wanted me to be in the gym, overseeing exercise; it was not cost effective for me to do hands-on work. Finally, he just said that craniosacral work was not the direction he wanted his clinic to go in."

I can remember that moment so clearly. "But I am helping people in ways that will benefit your clinic," I had said.

"Regardless, I'm going to start being the only one doing hands-on work. If that isn't what you want for your career, then maybe it's time for you to think about opening your own clinic. That way you can follow your passion and help people in the way you see fit," he had said. I flashed back to all those times Chad said the same thing when I was having issues with Carol."

"Is that when you left?" Marc asks, bringing me back to the present.

"No, as you know, I'm stubborn about letting things go. I decided to cut back my hours to three days a week, and I took another position two days a week at a center that helped clients afflicted with HIV and AIDS. I was still resistant to opening up my own place, finding every reason not to."

"Ok, but you still didn't tell me why you left."

"One day, I watched someone leave in a lot of pain. She had pain in her arm and wrist that was keeping her up at night. She was not improving, and I could tell that she was in even more pain after Tim's treatment than she had been when she arrived. I thought I would just try to help the best I could, so I told Tim that what the patient needed was work in the neck and thoracic region because her pain was probably being referred to the wrist from those regions.

"He wouldn't listen. He said that the doctor had only prescribed work on the wrist, so that's what he was going to do. I told him to call the doctor and ask to try working on those areas. Tim refused and reminded me that it was *more economical* for him to have me work only in the gym.

"When he said that, I realized that he just didn't buy into what I believed was important in helping people. I also realized then and there that Tim was right when he told me to consider opening up my own practice. If I was to make a difference and be the best I could be like I had promised myself at the beginning of my career, I couldn't do it here. If I wanted to make a difference in people's lives and give them more options to healing, like I'd wished Aunt Ersie had had, the only way I could do it was to open my own practice. It finally became crystal clear that this was something I had to do. All my resistance disappeared. I knew this was the new door I needed to go through. I wrote my letter that afternoon, giving two weeks' notice."

"So, now you have the best boss ever?" Marc smiles.

"Yep!" I laugh.

I smile to myself thinking of all my bosses throughout the years. Dr. Cole's actions probably affected me the most. He got promoted to the school board right after I went back to school. Within four months, I received a card in the mail from him. Before I opened it, I thought to myself, *Oh no, I've left teaching. Please don't say anything negative now!* I started feeling queasy. I opened the card and read what he wrote. I couldn't believe it. I was in shock. It was beyond anything I would ever have imagined.

"First, I'd like to apologize for not being at the banquet," the letter had said. "I heard it was an amazing event. Congratulations! I'd also like to thank you for all that you did for the school, both as a teacher and as a coach. I'm sorry that I never supported you in all your efforts."

It was like my brain couldn't figure out what I had just read. I had all these belief systems in place about me not being good enough. They were all based on my assumption that my issues with Dr. Cole had somehow been my fault, but that was not true. I will probably never know why Dr. Cole acted the way he did with me, but after the letter, I finally realized that it was his stuff and his issues that were the problem. It was something I should not have bought into.

"Can you work on me sometime?" Marc asks.

"Sure." I say excitedly. He had had a bad injury several years back, and I had actually been hoping to try out some of my techniques on him.

I serve him chicken *paprikash*, which I prepared in advance yesterday. It's my can't-miss-easy-to-make meal. We eat, and then Marc spends the rest of the evening unpacking and settling in.

"Tomorrow, I'm going to the city at around 6:30 to do Qigong. If you'd like, you can come with me, and then we can go out for breakfast with the group. I have some things to do in the city after that, but you could explore by yourself for a few hours."

"What's Qigong?"

"It's a healing martial art with a lot of breath work. We do it in the park. Try it. That's the best way for you to understand what it is."

"Interesting."

"It gives me more energy throughout the day. I actually didn't do it to help with my work, but it ended up giving me a better understanding of what I'm doing and how the body's energy works."

"In college, I did Chung Moo Doh," Marc says. "It's also martial arts. I did it for over a year. It helped me get strong again after the accident, and it helped me get back to doing all kinds of sports."

"That's good. You can decide in the morning if you want to join me."

The next morning, Marc is up before me. We head to the city and as we drive, the fog makes it hard to see anything. The clouds look like they are touching the ocean. Only the top of the Golden Gate Bridge can be seen. It looks like the top of a drawbridge, beckoning us to enter a castle in a faraway land.

"I can't see anything, but it feels so magical," Marc says.

"I know. The fog means it's officially summer. Every day here there is a new breathtaking scene to behold. You'll see."

We get to Huntington Park, and after Qigong class, we join everyone for a Dim Sum breakfast. My Qigong teacher is Chinese. We call him Sifu, the term used for master in the Chinese culture. As usual, he orders for us. He always orders more than we could ever eat. It reminds me of my family in Europe.

We finish, and the group of us head to my Qigong teacher's clinic to meditate. I go to the clinic 3-4 times a week, but meditation is hard for me. I'm told that with practice I'll get better, but thoughts that I didn't even know I had come to life when I sit still.

"Marc, I'll finish my meditation, and then I'll see you back here at 2:00 p.m.. That will give you three hours. Is that OK?"

"Perfect."

When I finish meditating, or rather, attempting to, I run a few errands. I get to Huntington Park a few minutes early.

"Eear, you're never going to believe my day," Marc says when he spots me. A big smile is spread across his face.

"Why are you laughing?"

"Well, I checked out my office. It's in the financial district. Then, I headed to Market Street. There were these three guys with chessboards, so I stopped. The first guy was a skinny Chinese man. He had black jeans and a black leather jacket. His hair seemed to be slicked back with the help of a whole bottle of gel. Next to him was a rabbi. He had on the black kaftan, black top hat, big grey beard, ear locks and everything. Next to him was an African American guy, dressed in a blue suit and tie. The protocol was to pay for each match because they were playing on a bet. I wanted to play, so I paid five dollars and played with the Chinese guy.

"It was so bizarre. As we were playing, a Walter Matthau look alike came by to watch wearing a white-and-red sundress, and in the background, a gay pride parade started to pass by."

"That's right. I forgot. It's on the last Sunday of June," I say, trying to keep from laughing. "San Francisco is a little different from Pittsburgh, huh?"

"Just a little," Marc smiles.

"So, did you win?"

"Eear..." Marc says, giving me a playfully scolding look. "I'm the best. Should you even ask? Grandpa taught me well."

"How many games did you play?"

"Only one."

"Why?" I ask, shocked at his restraint.

"Because ... well, the guy tried to hustle me."

I stifle a laugh. "Welcome to San Francisco! It is a unique and diverse place. That's what I love about living here."

"This view is unreal," Marc says as we cross the Golden Gate Bridge once again. "You can see the Pacific Ocean, the sailboats on the water, Alcatraz, and the mountains."

"It's especially beautiful when the sun is rising and setting. I love driving to and from the city every day."

We get to my apartment, and Marc asks, "Can you work on me later this afternoon?"

"I'd love to. Actually, I'll work on you now."

"Great."

When he was a senior in high school, Marc had been shot in a hunting accident and was in the hospital for two weeks. The bullet shattered his pelvis, severed his urethra, and fragmented his bladder. The doctors were not sure that he would make it through the night, but after four months in a wheelchair, five months with a cane, and five surgeries in nine months, Mark managed to play rugby in his sophomore year of college. I think he joined the team just to prove he could.

"I've heard the story of how you got shot from your mom and dad, but never from you. Are you okay telling me how you got shot? I just want to get a more complete perspective and maybe some more clues about your healing abilities."

Marc takes a deep breath, closes his eyes, and reconnects to that painful memory. "Pops, that's the nickname for the 83-year-old in our hunting party, and I were waiting for Dad and the others in the hunting party to arrive. He was behind me, and we heard a rustling sound. Pops was startled and lost his balance. His rifle went off accidently, and the bullet went through my butt. I fell, and I'll never forget the smell of my burning skin. My body turned cold, ice cold, but the pain was like a burning hot iron searing through my flesh."

"I remember you said afterward that you had been afraid they would try to take the bullet out without putting you to sleep first. Why was that?"

"When the paramedics arrived, I just kept thinking, *please put me to sleep when you take out the bullet.* I don't know why.

"En route to the hospital, the ambulance was in a car accident, and the IV came out. I could feel the saline burning into my wound. It was horrible. When we finally got to the hospital, someone actually asked me if I would be an organ donor."

"What did you say?"

"I was appalled. I remember thinking, *What? Does your sister need a liver transplant or something? Why would you ask me that?*"

"I guess people don't realize that saying something like that can have serious consequences for someone's ability to heal. Did that comment make you afraid that you weren't going to make it?"

"No." Marc pauses. "Never. I thought what was said was totally out of line. It wasn't a way to help people. I didn't know until a few days later that the doctors were not sure I would make it through the first night.

"Before the surgery, the nurses kept trying to make sure I was awake. So, whenever they came by, I would pretend to pass out, and then I would open my eyes and wink. They kept panicking. It was funny."

"Why did you do that?"

"They were cute." Marc smirks at the memory before continuing, "Everything seemed so heavy. Even the air was heavy. I remember thinking I had to make it lighter. I don't know why. I just had to change the heaviness."

"It's pretty amazing. The bullet shattered your pelvis, severed your urethra, fragmented your bladder, you had five surgeries, and look at you now."

"Eear, why would you think it would be any other way? I'm just the best at everything. You should know that by now," he breaks into a laugh. "I knew I would get better. I just didn't know how long it would take."

Marc has always focused on the positive. When he was 13, he was the shortest kid in the class. His mom always told him to eat more because she was worried he wouldn't grow. I always loved his answer because it was so him. "Mom," he would say, "I'm only 13. Wait until I'm 21, and if I haven't grown by then, then worry. Now, it's a waste of energy. In fact, if I'm short, I'll be short. Why worry about something that we have no control over?"

My dad was the same way. Both of them were never concerned about not healing. *They put their trust in the unknown, not letting fear be part of the equation.* All their energy went into healing, with nothing left over to focus on the fear that they couldn't or wouldn't heal. They both could effortlessly tap into their good blood.

"I bet the hospital staff was surprised because first my classmates had a minister and priest come to the hospital, and then my dad had the rabbi come. I know there were many prayers said for me in several different churches and synagogues because of my friends and family. I had a lot of support to help me heal."

"Do you think all the prayers helped?" I smile. I am in awe of the outpouring of love he had experienced.

"I don't know, but I was glad I had the support. The doctors were surprised at my quick recovery. I went home after two weeks, on the day before my 17th birthday, and the doctors had thought I would be in the hospital for at least 4-6 weeks."

As we continue talking, I start to set up the massage table. It only takes about 30 seconds, and we are ready to go.

"OK, get on the table," I say.

My apartment is really not a bad place to do treatment, with the view of Richardson Bay as a backdrop. I start at Marc's feet and scan his body. I feel the restrictions in his pelvis. I feel around, allowing the tissues to guide me, and then I gently, with intention, start the treatment.

"I feel a surge of electricity going down both legs, and your hands are so hot," Marc says after a few minutes.

"That's good. That's the energy moving around."

"My stomach is gurgling."

"That's common. It means your body is relaxing."

"I'm really tired all of a sudden, Is that part of what you're doing?"

"Just go with it," I say soothingly.

Marc closes his eyes, and after about 40 minutes, I end the session.

"That was so relaxing. I felt like I was floating. Sometimes, when you were working on my head, I could feel it in my pelvis. Why is that?"

"Our bodies are made up of fascia. They are the tissues that connect every muscle, tendon, organ, and blood vessel in the body. The fascia give the body its shape. If you took all the bone structures out of your body, it would still retain its shape because of the fascia. There are a lot of reasons why you would feel it in other areas of the body, but the fascia is one possible reason. Injuries in one area of the body can create a pull and affect other areas."

"That felt different from any of the physical therapy I have had."

"That's because they don't teach these techniques in most physical therapy schools. When I was in a car accident five years ago, traditional physical therapy was making me worse. Not long after, I took a muscle energy class and was impressed by the instructor, so I went to her clinic in Connecticut for five days of extensive treatment. Most of what the physical therapists were doing on me was craniosacral, myofascial, strain counter strain, and visceral work. After that experience, I knew I had to learn the hands-on approach. Osteopathy was developed by Dr. Andrew Taylor Still in the late 19th century, but for the longest time, classes were not offered to physical therapists, so it wasn't even on my radar in school."

Marc sits up and stretches, "What do you like best about this form of treatment?"

"The philosophy behind these techniques resonates with my belief system, which is that the body heals itself and one part can affect the whole. These techniques teach you to listen with your hands in a subtle and precise way. It helps you to find areas of dysfunction and then to facilitate a release. We're always striving for normal motion, and when energy gets stuck, it creates dysfunction and, in many instances, pain. The body is our ally. It tries to guide us, but many times we don't know how to listen. I am always taking more classes to help me understand the body's language better."

"Well, this was cool. Thanks."

~~~~~~~~~~~~~~

Later that afternoon I show Marc my running trail along the water. It's about three miles. After we get back, I start to prepare dinner while Marc looks through the books on my shelf.

"Here's an interesting book," he says. "*How to Win Friends and Influence People*. Dale Carnegie must have used me for inspiration because I already do that so brilliantly."

"It was written before you were born," I laugh.

"No matter. We should write a spoof book," Marc says.

"Yeah, *How to Lose Friends...*" I say.

"*And Alienate People*," Marc adds.

"That would be a great title."

"Now all we need to do is actually write the book," Marc says.

The time flies, and before I know it, it's 10:30 p.m.. I help him set up his bed and head in to my bedroom. After hitting the pillow, the next thing I hear is the alarm.

~~~~~~~~~~~~~

At 6:30, Marc and I head into the city.

"I can't get over the view. Today it's still foggy, but it has a different feel from yesterday. It's like we're totally immersed in the clouds today," Marc says.

I drop Marc off at the bus stop, and after participating in my daily Qigong class in Huntington Park, from 7:00 to 8:15am, I head to my office ten minutes away.

My first client today is Tommy. He was walking with his toddler in a store one day when a carpet dropped from above and hit him on the head. He suffered a concussion, along with headaches and upper and lower back pain. The headaches and the back pain are getting better with treatment; that part was easy to help him with. The problem is that he is still struggling to comprehend things. Ever since the accident, he hasn't been able to understand anything he reads or remember simple things. The brain tests show his IQ has been affected by the accident. Today, when he comes in, I am finally going to try a new technique on him to hopefully help with his head and neck issues.

During the fourth craniosacral class I took, I had volunteered to be the demo for mouth work. The instructor kept telling the class that it is a great treatment for people with herniated discs, neck injuries and head injuries, and I thought of Tommy immediately. However, after being the demo, I didn't feel as comfortable with the idea of performing the work on Tommy because the experience had been painful. I gagged a lot, and it was the most painful craniosacral treatment I've ever had. The teacher ended up saying I was the perfect demo because he was able to show the class what can happen in the clinic when someone has jaw issues. (My jaw problems dated back to my accident in physical therapy school.) I know the treatment helped me a lot, but I am still afraid to try it on a patient because I don't want to inflict that kind of pain. Plus, I'm not confident that I will do the techniques correctly since I have never tried. I'm afraid I may do more harm than good.

Two weeks ago, however, I had a dream, and when I woke up, all I could remember was being told to work in Tommy's mouth. *Today is the day*, I tell myself as he gets on the table. I put on the latex free gloves and gently begin to work. After all my anxiety, it doesn't even hurt him. He actually loves it.

At the end of the session, he sits up and says, "I'm feeling clearer. I don't know how else to explain it, but I feel clearer."

Go figure, I think to myself. Another example of how I waste my time being afraid of something for no reason.

"This is so hard to explain, but I feel clear again. I feel clear," Tommy repeats. "This is the first time … the first time I have felt like my old self in a long time. Thank you."

Wow. I'm amazed, but I keep that to myself. I feel so lucky because my patients are my teachers. I always look forward to what I can learn each day from them.

My next patient for the day is Liane. She and I actually met when we were both teaching in the chronic pain program at the facility we worked at. She gave birth a couple of months ago and called me because she was having a lot of foot pain. She asked me if I knew someone who might help. I offered to myself, so here she is.

"Hi, Liane. It's so good to see you again. How are you doing?"

"I'm okay. It's good to see you, too. I really hope you can help me."

"I'll try. First, I need to get your history."

"During the birth eight weeks ago, I had two epidurals and then eventually ended up having a C-section. In the middle of the night after the surgery, I freaked out because I couldn't feel my right foot. My whole right leg felt numb, like a block of ice. At the same time, I started having problems breathing. The doctors said it was from my low blood pressure. After a few days, I was taken off oxygen because I no longer had problems breathing, but then I got really depressed. I started getting constant, dull, achy, throbby pain in my leg and foot, along with intermittent electrical-shock pains that took my breath away. It felt like waiting for an earthquake. I never knew when it would happen again, but I knew it would. Now, I keep thinking, 'What if I'm never able to hike, dance, or walk without pain again?'"

I take a deep breath and look at my tabletop fountain with its soothing sounds. I've dealt with those feelings before. It sounds like nerve pain. Fortunately, that is something that I may be able to help with.

"What are the doctors saying?"

"The tests didn't show anything. The physical therapists said they couldn't help me. The neurologist said it takes time to heal from this type of leg and foot pain and sometimes the pain never goes away. So, basically, I'm breastfeeding, I'm popping vicodin, and I still feel the pain constantly."

"Is the vicodin alright to take when breastfeeding?"

"The doctors said it wasn't going to affect my baby, but if I felt I had a choice I would rather not have to take it."

I get to work, "Ok, Liane, get on the table, and let's see what we can do."

I place my hands on her feet and move my way up her body, doing the diagnostic evaluation I was taught in my craniosacral and myofascial classes. I go back to her right ankle and follow the principles of the three planar fascial release techniques. I use these techniques as a guide at the beginning of all of my treatments, and then I let the body take over and guide me on how to continue. After about 20 minutes on the foot, I feel a release in my hand. It's like putty that just gave way.

"I just felt a big release of tension. How are you doing?" I ask.

I see tears in her eyes.

"You ok?"

"When you said there was a release, I could feel it. The pain had gone away for the first time since I gave birth." There is a pause as her tears start flowing again. "For the first time, I feel hope."

I continue to work on different parts of the body, and then the session is over.

"I feel so much better. It's as if a weight has been lifted from my shoulders. See you at our appointment in a week, and once again, thanks!"

~~~~~~~~~~~~~~

I take a break and walk on Van Ness Street, passing by all the hustle and bustle of traffic and the fast pace of people's lives. I'm mesmerized by my own thoughts. The body is so amazing. It talks to us loud and clear if we just try to listen. Every day I'm learning new tools to help me become better at listening to that inherent wisdom. I am so lucky to have all these people lie on my table and teach me so much.

I reflect back to the conversation I had with Tim in his office. Tim's vision focused mostly on using exercise to help people heal, and that is very different from mine. I wanted him to accept and buy into what I think is important, but the truth is, and it was hard for me to accept back then, we are both right in our different perspectives and we both have different strengths as physical therapists. I take another deep breath and head back to my office.

~~~~~~~~~~~~~~

My next patient is Theresa. She is 63 and started seeing me because she had debilitating knee problems and sciatica. She had an epidural and went to physical therapy through her health plan. The pain in her back was gone, but she still couldn't move four toes on her right foot. She was told by her doctor and physical therapist that she might have to live with it because there was nothing they could do.

On top of that, whenever she eats and does other fine motor activities, she has tremors. Right now, she is on high blood pressure medication. I remember that in physical therapy school, Dave, one of our instructors, had told us about the side effects of high blood pressure meds. He gave the lesson a personal twist since he was on them and experienced side effects; tremors, and impotence being the two main ones. He banged it into our heads that we should *always* ask about the side effects of medications because the side effects of meds can end up being the source of their problem. I looked up the side effects of her drugs and the word *tremors* jumps out at me. She was going to her doctor that same day, so I told her to ask her doctor if that may actually be the source of her tremors.

This afternoon she arrives, as usual, with a great big smile on her face. She's one of those people who find pleasure in the little things in life, and it's contagious.

"So, how are you feeling?" I ask.

"Great."

"And how is your body?"

"Better. This is only our fifth session, and I can move my toes now without a problem. I do the exercises you taught me in my Jacuzzi, which is so nice, and I love the marble exercises. It takes the monotony out of the exercises. My knee still hurts, but it's better."

"Did you ask your doctor about the tremors?"

"Yes. She said that it couldn't be from the medicine."

"What did she think the cause was then?"

"She had no idea why I keep having tremors, but she said it definitely couldn't be side effects of the drug."

"So, what do you think?"

"I'm not sure. It can't be from the drug, or my doctor would know it."

I sigh. The doctor says it can't be from the drug even though it is a common side effect, but if the doctor does not know what the cause is, how can she say with certainty that it is not from the drug? I just wonder why some patients are not more proactive in their own care. They accept the answers given to them as truth, even when the answers don't make sense.

"I love what you do on my head. I don't understand it, but each time you do that stuff, I get into such a relaxed state."

"It's in that relaxed state that powerful healing occurs, and it allows your body to do what it needs to do. Sometimes the body gets stuck and can't do the necessary corrections on its own. My job is just to bring balance back into your body so that your body can take over and heal itself. I facilitate the healing process. Your body does the healing."

"Well, whatever you do, it feels great. I'm feeling better than I have in a very long time. Thank you."

The session ends, and Theresa gives me her big smile once again.

~~~~~~~~~~~~~~

Next on my list is Gary. He is a 25-year-old who hurt his back. "How are you today?"

"I'm ok."

Gary gets on the table and, as usual, I feel around to check what's going on with his body.

"Gary, what's up with your neck?" I ask, feeling a tense point.

Gary laughs. "I didn't want to tell you what was wrong. I was testing you, as you know I do each time I come here. Once again, you passed with flying colors. I was feeling really good, so I went back to Tai Kwan Do, and I'm not sure what I did to my neck but it hurts."

His problem is an easy one to fix, and after treatment, he has no pain.

~~~~~~~~~~~~~~

When I'm done for the day, I do some shopping and head home.

"How was your day?" I ask as I walk in to find Marc in the living room.

"Great. I met my boss, and she's cool. How about you?"

"Sometimes, I think I should pay my patients for all that I learn from them, but of course, I don't tell them that."

"You want to play tennis?" Marc asks.

"I haven't played since I was in the car accident," I say hesitantly, "but yeah … why not? I still have my old tennis racket."

"Are there courts around here?"

"The recreation center is five minutes away. There are outdoor courts there. We can see if one is available."

"My car actually came about a half hour ago. You want to drive to the tennis courts in it?"

"Great idea!" We get outside, and his car is easy to spot. It stands out with its very purple color. I smile.

We get to the tennis courts, and Randy, the tennis pro, is there. He introduces himself to us and says, "You have to be a member to play. It's about $50 a year, less for the second person."

"That's no problem," I say, as excitement and anticipation take over. "Can we play now?"

"Sure. There's no one here. Head on in, and here's my card if you want lessons."

Marc and I start to volley for about fifteen minutes, and I start to get back the feel of it.

"Do you want to play a match?" Marc asks.

"Sure, but let me practice my serve first. That used to be my strength."

After about ten practice serves, the match begins.

My serve is inconsistent. I ace one and then miss the next six. I can't help but smile though. I have always loved tennis, but with all of my accidents it has been too long since I have played. We volley back and forth. Before I know it, I am serving, and it's match point in Marc's favor.

My first serve is a bullet, but it just misses the line. Before I can try again, Marc sits down in the server's box.

"What are you doing?" I yell out.

"Well, I'm just so sure that you're going to miss that I figure I can sit here and watch you instead of running around for no reason."

Between laughs, I say, "This isn't fair. You're making me laugh."

I aim at Marc once again, and I miss. I hate losing. Marc starts running around the periphery of the two tennis courts, his tennis racket above his head, singing, *I am the champion of the world,* though not nearly as well as Queen. While he's running, I start throwing tennis balls at him from mid-court, hitting the target only twice.

We head home and after dinner, Marc asks me to work on him again.

"Every time I exercise I have a throbbing, sometimes dull, sometimes sharp pain at the incisions and in my upper leg that lasts about a day."

We get the table out, and Marc goes into his deep healing place almost immediately. It's like he's asleep, but he can hear everything. He definitely inherited my dad's healing abilities. After about 30 minutes, I stop.

"The pain's gone." Marc says, stunned. "That's a first. Thanks."

~~~~~~~~~~~~~~

The next day, I finish work early and, unbeknown to Marc, call the tennis pro. Carrying out my plan to get even with Marc for beating me at tennis. I sign up for a lesson that afternoon and the following day.

A few days later, I am ready. Marc gets home, and I make the challenge.

"I'll beat you six games to one," I say confidently, "I don't want you to feel too badly, so I'll give you a game."

"You dreaming?" Marc smirks, "Remember what happened last time?"

We get to the courts and rally, Then, I start the serve. I smile as I see Marc working up a sweat. I have him running everywhere on the court. The match ends, and now it is my turn to sing and dance around.

"How did you do that?" Marc asks suspiciously, "You got so much better in just a few days!"

I burst out laughing and decide to confess, "Marc, I took two lessons this week."

"That's not fair," he says, breaking into a grin.

"Oh, well," I say with my mischievous smile.

"I'm taking a lesson," he declares competitively.

"We can take a lesson together," I say good-naturedly.

"You know, I just realized that the throbbing pain I have had every time I've played a sport since my accident isn't here. This is the first time in five years. It's amazing."

"Maybe we took care of it. Time will tell."

We get home, and the phone rings. It's Tommy, my patient who had a concussion.

"I had to call and tell you," he says excitedly. "I got home from treatment, and I was so exhausted I slept right away. When I woke up this morning, I took a shower, and it was the first time since the accident that I automatically knew where the soap and my razor were in the bathroom. I know it seems like nothing, but that is not what it has been like for me. Everything has been a struggle. Especially with the simple things, I just had no clue where anything ever was. I'm back. I know it. I'm back, and I had to call to tell you."

"That's great," I say, and I can feel my heart swelling up. "Remember, your brain is still pretty fragile, so take it easy."

Once again, I'm blown away. I'm gaining more confidence in the skills I am learning every day. I am amazed by the wisdom and the power our bodies have to heal daily. I was taught that craniosacral work could help concussions. I wasn't convinced because I wasn't sure I was good enough to help him, but I figured I had nothing to lose by trying.

All of Tommy's neurological tests had shown he had brain damage, and the doctors had no solution for him. I'm blown away by the amazing powers of the body to heal itself when we remove blockages through hands-on work.

I do the same things every day since I opened my clinic, but it always feels different. I start with Qigong at the park, and then, during the week, I work either in the city or out of my home. Every day, one patient after another teaches me something new. It took me a long time to get here, but I am so glad I now have my own clinic that I can run my own way.

~~~~~~~~~~~~~~

Two months pass. Marc is now on a local soccer team, and we're both in a tennis league. Whenever something goes wrong in practice or in a game, he asks me to work on him, and I am more than happy to.

My routine continues as normal. I am at my office today, and Liane is my next patient. It's been a month since I last saw her. I go to the waiting area to greet her.

"Hi, Liane. How are you doing? How is your son?" I say.

"He is great! I can't believe how much better I feel. I've been dancing and hiking with no pain. I just started feeling pain again a couple of days ago, so I'm glad you could see me. It's not that bad right now, but I'm freaked out that it will get worse. I saw my neurologist last week. I told him about my treatments with you and how I could feel the pain go away as you worked on me."

"Was he impressed?"

She shakes her head and says knowingly, "He looked at me and said, 'Improvement with treatment was just a coincidence. It was just time that helped.'"

We get to work and midway through the session her foot pain is gone.

"Thank you so much for introducing me to this type of treatment. I wish doctors would know more about it," she says. "It just seems like they aren't even willing to give it a try because it's not what they know."

"I know. There are so many people who could benefit, but some doctors just don't know what they don't know. They give advice but they don't know about all the options available. Usually they just dispense drugs and say the side effects of those are better to deal with than the pain, but sometimes the side effects are greater than the original problem."

"It is hard to explain what you do. It's so subtle."

I smile. "The best way to understand it is to have a problem. When it goes away with treatment, you get it."

"Thanks for all your help," Liane says.

"You're very welcome."

~~~~~~~~~~~~~~

I've begun to jog around the 4-block radius surrounding Huntington Park in the mornings. I jog for about 30 minutes before my Qigong class, and whenever the class is dismissed, I get stopped by strangers who ask me what we were doing. I explain that Qigong is about healing and breathing and ask them to join us next time, but they always look at me skeptically and respectfully decline.

~~~~~~~~~~~~~~

The months pass quickly, with seeing a lot of patients and referrals that keep coming, and before I know it, it's Thanksgiving. Marc was supposed to move out after three months and get his own place, but he decided to stay with me longer because he wasn't sure if he might go back to school to get his MBA and didn't want to commit to a rental agreement. That works out well for me because I love having him around.

My family didn't celebrate Canadian Thanksgiving so I didn't celebrate Thanksgiving until I was in the States and had friends invite me over, but Marc grew up in Pennsylvania so Thanksgiving has more significance for him than for me. This year is Marc's first Thanksgiving away from home, and it's my first one doing the cooking. I am excited but nervous. I don't want to ruin Thanksgiving for Marc.

The day arrives, and when it is ready, I take the bird out of the oven. I am totally impressed with myself. It is a beautiful golden color, and it smells amazing. Marc takes pictures while I brag, and then the carving begins. However, after a couple of minutes carving, something falls out of the Turkey and flops onto my countertop. My boastful bubble is burst as I reach for the bag full of giblets.

"Oh no," I say, shocked. "The cavity was frozen when I checked, so couldn't find them. I thought the giblets were already out. I've poisoned us."

For the rest of the meal I'm worried about it, but Marc just thinks it's funny. To my mortification, that story is the first thing out of his mouth when his parents call. He laughs, but I'm horrified. I am freaked out because I think I might have somehow poisoned us by cooking the turkey with the bag inside. After some research, though, I realize I haven't done any health damage. It just took a little while to figure out. Another example of how I waste my time worrying over nothing.

Despite my panic attack over the turkey, dinner is delicious. When we are done, we put the dishes away, clean up the kitchen, and then settle down to a game of chess. After about an hour, the game ends, and I win.

"Let's play again," Marc says.

"Not today, but how about we set up a challenge? Whoever wins ten chess games first gets treated to a fancy dinner by the loser, and, of course, the loser has to acknowledge the feat of the other."

"I'm hungry already," Marc jokes. "Where are you going to take me?"

"You mean where are *you* going to take *me*?"

Later that night, Marc goes out with friends, and I stay home and watch *The Shawshank Redemption* on TV. I've seen it three times before, but I still love watching it. At one point, I decide to turn down the volume and watch the body language of the actors. Body language is such an important part of communication. Studies have shown that between 50% and 65% of communication is portrayed via body language. Words are only about 7%, and the rest is tone. Doctors, for example, are considered authority figures. They are meant to be experts in everything they tell their patients. If a doctor doesn't believe a patient will improve, that belief will come through in the doctor's body language. The patient will feel it, and that can affect the patient's own ability to heal.

The months continue to pass. I'm doing fun things at work, and I feel blessed that I am getting such good results and such interesting cases. Marc's pain near his incisions and leg hasn't come back. Liane's pain went away for good, and Tommy even went back to work.

"Marc, it's for you. It's Robyn," I say, holding the phone to my chest as I call to him. He gets up and takes the phone eagerly. Every time they're on the phone together, he laughs a lot. I smile as I watch him grin from ear to ear.

"Marc, you should go out with Robyn," I say when he gets off the phone. "You seem to have such a good time with her."

He brushes my comment aside, saying, "We have been great friends since the moment we met the first week of college, but that's all. Even her parents love me. They didn't like the last guy she went out with, so they actually told her to dump him and have me move in instead."

"That's a different response from most parents."

"I told you, it's because they love me. Then again, what's not to love?" he smirks.

"I love the fact that you are so humble," I say sarcastically. "Is she still going out with him?"

"No. Are you ready for our match?" he says, changing the subject.

We have kept up our chess competitions over the past several months. Right now, he is beating me 9 to 7. Today will be my come back. The game begins, and there is no joking or witty banter. There is too much at stake for both of us; our pride hangs in the balance. The game goes on for almost an hour. We are even, and then I make a move. I take my finger off my knight and, after a split second, put it back, realizing my queen is in jeopardy.

"Eear," Marc gasps, and a grin spreads across his face as he notices my mistake, "you took your finger off the piece. It's final."

"But it was only for a split second!" I say in anguish.

"You know the rules."

"But if I do that, you'll get a big advantage. Don't you want to win by outplaying me and not just as a result of me making a split second mistake?"

"A rule is a rule."

I acquiesce angrily. I then watch as I lose my queen and my composure. Marc wins.

"Who is the best?" Marc keeps boasting. "You know, I'm getting hungrier and hungrier by the second. Which French restaurant are you taking me to? Remember … I am the champion, champion of the world. Grandpa's influence was obviously greater on me than you."

"Ha, ha, ha," I say sarcastically. If it weren't happening to me, I would think it was funny, but now I have to hear him saying exactly what I would have said had I won. It would have been more fun for me to be the one rubbing it in.

~~~~~~~~~~~~~

Almost a year to the day that he got here, Marc leaves. His first stop is Las Vegas. After two weeks he gets to Pittsburgh, his new home, and I get a phone call.

"Guess what? I took your advice," he says happily.

"What was that?" I ask, confused.

"I asked Robyn out, and now she and I are dating."

~~~~~~~~~~~~~

Two years quickly pass, and before I know it, Marc calls once again, "Guess what?" he says with excitement. "Robyn and I are engaged. We set the date, and we're getting married next summer."

~~~~~~~~~~~~~~

Irit Schaffer

18

2002-2004

Courage is... the knowledge of how to fear what ought to be feared and how not to fear what ought not to be feared.

- David Ben Gurion

Life continues for me as usual. Qigong is helping me stay calm, centered, and balanced. It is also helping me in sports because I am now able to stay relaxed and focused at the same time. I have been playing in a mixed singles tennis tournament and actually made it to the finals. So far, I am undefeated. I'm surprising myself.

It's pouring outside as I drive to the office in my new car. My old Saab died on me in the middle of an intersection about a year and a half ago. Fortunately, four guys immediately came to my rescue and helped me move the car to safety before anything bad could happen, but I took it as a sign that it was time to say goodbye to my Saab. After a lot of research, I decided on a BMW 325 I series.

I've had my car for a little over a year and am happy with it because it's so safe. As usual, safety was a major prerequisite for me when choosing a car. Even with the rain outside, I feel safe when I fasten my seat belt.

I cross the Golden Gate Bridge on my way to work, pay the toll, and then, a few hundred yards later, traffic stops. As I come to a stop, I can hear the screeching sounds of tires that are out of control. I look in my rear view mirror and don't see anything, so I relax, but then, *bam*. I hear the sound of metal crunching as my car jolts forward, and I can feel my seatbelt squeezing my chest. I stay in my car, dazed and bewildered. There are no cars behind me yet, but I am afraid to get out of the car because I don't want to get hit again by the oncoming traffic. I look around and see a green pickup truck facing sideways. I watch as he corrects his car and, as traffic starts to move, drives off.

There is no shoulder for me to pull off on, and I panic as the traffic starts to pass by me, thinking I'll get hit again. I drive my car to the nearest parking spot and take a deep, shaky breath before getting out to assess the damage.

The car wasn't as badly bent up as I had thought. It's a good thing I bought a sturdy car. I wait for the person in the green pickup truck to find me, but I know that is wishful thinking. Typical! My neck and upper back feel tight. I have my appointment book with me, so I call to cancel with a few patients before dialing the insurance agent. The agent tells me that I have to go to the police station to report the accident so I head over. I find the station, and when I get inside, I start seeing double. My hands won't stop shaking.

I know I'm hypoglycemic because this has happened to me before after skydiving. It used to happen to me all the time after physical activity when I was 12 and 13. I would always drink orange juice and feel much better. I call a friend, and she meets me at the police station with some orange juice she bought me in the nearby convenience store.

Somehow I fill out the report and go home. I park my car and go inside. The adrenalin, which has been in overdrive since I got hit, is released as soon as I get home. I totally crash.

~~~~~~~~~~~~~~

The next morning, I call to make an appointment with the osteopathic and internal medicine doctor next door to my office. I have never met her, but fortunately, she has an opening the next day.

A friend gives me a ride into the city, and I use my right foot to push down an imaginary brake the whole way. She drops me off at my office, and I go next door, where the appointment will be. I walk up the ten stairs and wait for the doctor.

"Hi. I'm Dr. Rita B," I hear her say, and I look up.

She was born in India and is about the same height as my mom, 5'2". She has long dark hair and looks fit.

"Hi. I'm Irit," I say. "I have an appointment. It's nice to meet you. I'm actually your next-door neighbor. I work in the building right next to this. I'm a Physical Therapist."

"Great to know there is a PT next door." Rita smiles, and that makes me feel more at ease. I notice her eyes and am drawn to the intensity, the razor sharp focus they exude. It makes me believe she works hard at honing her skills.

"Irit ..." She repeats my name as she looks over her records. "I see you were in a car accident."

"Yeah," I say and describe the details. "My neck and upper back are sore, and honestly, I'm petrified to get back into my car. I got a ride here, and I was sure we were going to be in at least five accidents during the 20-minute drive."

"Was this your first accident?" Rita asks.

I laugh, "I've been in so many I think I should start wearing a helmet in my car."

Rita cringes comically and then smiles, "Well, let's get you on the table, and, hopefully, make you feel better."

Rita puts her hands on me, and my body starts to relax. My body seems to trust her hands, and I can feel myself unconsciously loosening up.

"You're body is in shock, so let's try and calm it down," she says softly.

"Shock?" I ask, surprised.

"Not from the medical standpoint, of course, but from the osteopathic perspective. The fluid mechanics, the visceral mechanics, and the range of motion of the tissues are frozen in time. Even your primary respiration is muted." I am encouraged to hear her say that. She seems to understand what is happening with my body in a way that I *know* the average doctor wouldn't. Many doctors would just say, "Give it time, and your body will be back to normal."

"Yeah, it's like my sympathetic system is in overdrive, and I'm in a constant fight-or-flight mode. It feels like I'm just holding my breath most of the time."

"Exactly. You are," Rita says.

The session ends, and I make another appointment for next week. As I head home, my body feels like it's breathing more freely than it was this morning. I decide to take two weeks off from driving. I will also take a week off from seeing patients, and I will get a ride when I need to see Rita. I'm not ready to get behind the wheel again, not yet, anyway. It is hard for me to cancel on my patients, but I know I need to give my body more time to heal.

The next time I see her, Rita once again works on calming my system down. "Every time you get in a car, your system goes into that panic mode," she says when I tell her about my fear of getting back behind the wheel.

"I would actually call it fear or terror, not panic," I tell her. "I get paralyzed by it. I'm set up to see an EMDR (eye movement desensitization and reprocessing) therapist soon. They are supposed to help people deal with trauma."

"Good, that should help. I'll see you in a week. Let me know how that appointment goes."

I start to see the EMDR therapist, and after about three sessions, I start driving again, but I still won't drive in rain. Whenever I stop at a light, I'm sure the car behind me won't. If a car is tailgating me, I know I'll get hit, but with my EMDR therapy, I am starting to freak out less often.

~~~~~~~~~~~~~~

Eight months pass, and I'm still having body and car issues. After eight sessions, I had decided to stop going to the EMDR because I felt like I had plateaued, but I know I need to find a new way to let go of this crazy fear.

"Irit, how are you doing?" I hear the usual question from Rita.

"I think I have some bigger car purpose or something, and that's why I keep getting in accidents. It's like fate. It's like there is something I have to learn about fear, pain, people yelling at me, people leaving the scene. That happened to me in the car accident in PT school and now again with this accident. It was even the same kind of car both times, a green pick-up truck. I feel like I'm in my own version of the movie *Groundhog Day*, having car accidents again and again until I learn to change my thoughts and attitudes, until I do it right and can let it go. Ever since my last accident, I have been having car dreams with similar themes at least three or four times a week. In one, I lose my car, which is probably telling me to not drive. In another, I am driving, and my brakes fail. Then, of course, there are the dreams where I am in the car accident. I know that it's harder for me to heal when I relive the experience and the fear that goes with it too often, but it just creeps into my dreams. I really don't know how I would be handling things if I weren't doing Qigong every day and seeing you for treatment once a week."

"The problem is, every time you freak out, you go back to your old patterns of injury. Your thoughts affect your physical body. So, every time you go into your state of fear from the accident, your body replays the accident and goes back to the same pain patterns. There is a lot of scientific research to support the theory that our thoughts affect our physical body. Now, why don't you lie on the table?"

~~~~~~~~~~~~~~

"You're not going to believe what happened yesterday." I say the following Monday when I go back to see Rita. "I was waiting at a stop light, and a car behind me hit me."

"You were in another car accident? I'm so sorry!" Rita says.

"The guy was apologetic." *At least now I'm getting apologies and not hit and runs. That's an improvement,* I think to myself. *I must be doing something differently.*

"He said his mother was sick, and he was in a rush to get her to a doctor. He just put his foot on the gas and wasn't paying attention."

I lie on the table. Once again, as the tissues unwind and the blood starts flowing easily, my body starts to breathe, and I feel better. I'm not sure if the latest accident actually set me back, or if it was just the fear that my body would tighten up again that set me back.

I always relax at work. It is the one place where I somehow let go of all thoughts and all judgments. I tap into the wisdom of what the body needs. I call it my 'god space' because I always seem to tap into a magical and mystical experience. I tap into one of the important ingredients of good blood; *trusting in the unknown and knowing it will somehow work out,* which is something my dad and Marc have always done intuitively, and something that I need to do more of outside of work.

~~~~~~~~~~~~~~

Six months later, I am with all of my family in Worchester, Massachusetts for a wedding. It's raining, which is still a big trigger for fear in me, but I'm trying to keep myself calm. Suddenly, the driver in front of us puts on the brakes. My sister slams hers, but there is not enough room.

Bam!

I don't feel any pain in my body. It really wasn't a bad accident, and I consciously know that. Suddenly, though, I get hysterical. I scream at my sister for not stopping in time. I scream at the rain. I scream at everyone and everything. My family tries to quiet me down, but when I get to my hotel room, I start crying and can't stop. When my sister enters my room to check on me, I become hysterical again.

"Do you know what it is like to live in pain 24/7?" I ask between sobs. "Do you have any idea what it's like when everyone tells you either it's your fault, it's no big deal, or you should have done this and you should have done that? People always yell at me when it's their fault, and I'm the one who ends up taking the fall by being in constant pain!" I say at the top of my lungs. "Do you have any idea?"

I am totally out of control. I know it, but I don't care. I'm not screaming at my sister. I'm screaming at all of the car accidents that I have been in and all of the pain that I've experienced.

My mom, sister, brother-in-law, and nephews are the witnesses of my breakdown. I know they've never seen me like this. Neither have I, for that matter. So, they just let me yell. I think they're afraid I'll explode at them if they try to intervene.

~~~~~~~~~~~~~

The next day, I'm feeling better than I had before the accident. My body feels lighter, and I'm feeling an inner calmness. It is as if my breakdown released a huge amount of tension. Surprisingly, there is no pain in my body, as if I have released some blockage that had been in my body since the car accident in Physical Therapy school, when the driver got out of his car, yelled at me, and took off.

~~~~~~~~~~~~~

I return to the Bay area and to work. Barbara is my next patient. I've worked with her for three years. She reminds me of my aunt Ersie in her regal ways and her determination to always be perfectly dressed and perfectly mannered. Barbara is the descendant of many generations of native San Franciscans. Her family was the 'who's who' of the historical community.

"There are very few of us left," she once told me. "I was born here, and so was my father. Whenever we went outside back then, my father would always wear a suit, and my mother and I would wear a dress, a hat, and gloves. My mother would have been horrified to see me wear jeans. It was just not acceptable. It was different from today." I remember noticing the pair of blue jeans she was wearing at the time. There were flowers embroidered on the sides of her pant legs, giving even her blue jeans an air of elegance.

"Hi, Barbara. Come on in," I say when she arrives at my office, "How are you today?"

"Well, everyone tells me how great I look," she pauses. "I just wish I felt the way I look. I'm 86 years old, and it feels like it."

Her cell phone rings. "Oh, I forgot to turn it off. Let me get it before we start," she says apologetically.

"Hello? Oh, Mary, I can't talk. I'm at my healer's for some energy work."

I smile as she finishes up the call. I like hearing how I am perceived. I am her "healer." I do "energy work." That is perfect, yet it always surprises me to hear others say it that way.

Barbara hangs up and then turns to me, "My right shoulder is sore today, and so is the right side of my neck."

As usual, I use my hands to find where the body is telling me to go, but halfway through, Barbara says, "This session is terrible." If that comment came from anyone else, I would think, *oh no*, but with her, I don't skip a beat. "Why is that?" I ask.

"Because I am not seeing purple."

I laugh. "Seeing colors is not a prerequisite for a good session."

"I never saw colors before I started seeing you. My acupuncturist doctor was impressed because he said when you see colors you are tapping into a very high level of healing. Besides that, it's just so wonderful. It starts off with light pastel colors, and then, from the edges, it turns to purple, and then the whole field becomes vibrant purple. It is so lovely."

Barbara closes her eyes, and I start to do craniosacral work on her head. Finally, I can tell that Barbara is in that deep relaxed state where she thinks she is sleeping. I know she isn't sleeping, though, because if she were sleeping she wouldn't be able to hear me when I speak. In this deep healing state, she hears everything I say. It is the state that people who meditate for hours strive to reach.

All of a sudden, coming out of her deep reverie, Barbara says, "I see purple."

"Thank goodness," I answer laughingly.

The session ends, and Barbara walks out of the room into the waiting area where she runs into her friend, and my patient, Marg.

"Marg, I didn't know you were seeing Irit today," Barbara says.

Marg smiles, "You know that at our age there is always something ailing us."

I can't help but wonder if that isn't the truth at all ages. I have been working as a therapist for almost 20 years now and have had patients from all age groups and all walks of life, all with one thing in common: the need to heal.

"Are we still going to get together for a walk this afternoon?" Barbara asks.

They continue to talk as I set up the room for Marg's session. Marg referred Barbara to me. She is 85 years old, and her mind is very sharp. She is about 5'8", and she dresses impeccably, eats healthily, and is up on all the latest health alternatives.

She is an inspiration to me. Marg had pain in her left hip for over six months before seeing me. She had what doctors call, "deterioration of the hip." The cartilage surface of the hip joint had worn away. The doctor told her it was like 'bone on bone'. She hadn't wanted to go the surgery route, but then she fell twice in one week, making her hip feel even worse. Her doctor suggested Physical Therapy to strengthen her body before surgery, and one of her friends recommended me. I remember it was such a struggle for her to maneuver the 15 steps to my office when she first started.

"The first time I fell," she had told me, "I was at Cala Market, and I fell into the cheese bin. I was so embarrassed. No one seemed to notice, though, so I had to get out of that predicament by myself. The second time, I was at the Cathedral Plaza, and I fell again. Once again, no one was there to help, so I had to get myself, and my pride, back up."

She never ended up getting that surgery. It's been over three years since I first saw her, and she has not fallen once since then. She can also now sleep on her left side, and she walks up and down the stairs without pain.

After I work on Marg, my next patient, Marilyn, is waiting for me. She is the definition of a teacher disguised as a patient for me. She is 5'7" and a perfect example of the power of the mind, body and spirit.

When Marilyn was 30, she had horrible headaches. Her doctors kept telling her it was because of stress and she should try losing weight. She was popping 10-12 Tylenols a day to try to ease her pain, and a year into this, her friend urged her to see a neurologist and get a brain scan.

She had the scan, and doctors found a cyst. Soon after, they operated and injected her with a steroid, Decadron. The swelling reappeared a day later, and she had a second emergency surgery to drain the cyst, followed by a second steroid injection of Decadron.

Almost two years later, she started feeling a pain in her hips, so she started to research the side effects of Decadron. She read that no one really understands the mechanism, but it can affect blood flow to the hip and may cause osteonecrosis. She was eventually diagnosed with avascular necrosis, meaning her bone tissue was starting to die due to a lack of blood supply. She believed it was because of the steroids, but the doctors were not sure because necrosis due to steroid use was rare. As she read more about the effects of the steroid, she found that it actually wasn't uncommon for necrosis to occur 23 months after surgery, and it had been exactly 23 months after her surgery that she developed her symptoms.

She ended up having hip replacements for both of her hips, Eventually she had to have her right hip replaced again. She was told that she should anticipate shoulder replacements and possibly knee replacements, too, because she was diagnosed with necrosis in those joints as well. After her hip surgery, she was taking a lot of Motrin, but she did not feel that was a viable long-term solution. She did some research and found a holistic internal medicine doctor. The doctor recommended an acupuncturist for pain relief and a Feldenkrais practitioner for exercise. Feldenkrais is aimed at reducing pain, expanding patients' movement repertoire, and expanding their awareness of how their body works. The doctor also told Marilyn that long-term use of NSAIDs like Motrin, could lead to serious adverse side effects, such as gastrointestinal bleeding. She followed the doctor's advice. The acupuncture helped alleviate her pain, and the Feldenkrais method helped her get into shape without having flare-ups of pain and inflammation.

However, Marilyn had started experiencing a disabling vertigo, and the doctors had no idea what was causing it. They suggested more medication, but a friend of hers suggested me instead. That was over a year ago.

Now, Marilyn works out in the gym daily. She does one hour of cardio a day and a weight program designed by her Feldenkrais practitioner. She swims twice a week, does the Reiki process on herself daily, and meditates. She has also changed her eating habits.

She sees me and her Feldenkrais practitioner every other week, and she sees her acupuncturist once every three weeks. Her shoulder pain is gone, and its range of motion keeps improving. She had knee pain when she started with me, but it is no longer problematic. Her hip's range of motion has improved. She no longer has vertigo, and she no longer needs her blood pressure meds because her blood pressure is back to normal.

"Come on in, Marilyn. How are you feeling today?"

"Good. I had the weirdest experience, though. A psychotherapist who also works out at my gym asked me, 'How do you stay motivated? Is health your motivation? How do you get out of bed? How do you get yourself to go the gym every day?'"

I look at Marilyn, and I smile, waiting to hear her response.

"It's just strange because I don't really have to actively stay motivated. It makes me feel good to exercise, I told her. It's part of my day. I miss it when I don't do it. I feel like my brain is in a fog when I don't work out. Then she asked me what I enjoy doing to improve my health."

"What was your answer?" I ask.

"That I always look forward to acupuncture, Feldenkrais, and sessions with you. It's like I'm gradually feeling better and better as I get older instead of worse. It makes my life better."

"Were you ever afraid you wouldn't get better?" I ask.

"Nooo. Why should I be afraid? In fact, when I had my first hip replacement, the pain meds made me sick, so I didn't want them. My doctor said I healed so quickly because I wasn't afraid. He also said I must have a high tolerance for pain because I didn't want the meds."

I look at her and feel blessed to know her. She is a reminder of what is possible in the healing world. She has good blood. It never even occurs to her to focus on what she has no control over. She doesn't spend any time focusing on fear, fear that she will not heal, fear of 'what if I don't', 'what if I will never be able to', or 'what if this will limit me'. She just accepts what is. She trusts in the process and in the unknown. She spends all her energy focusing on what she needs to do to get better, and her body responds by allowing itself to heal.

She also exhibits two other keys to healing, to good blood: being gentle with herself and listening to her body, like Ellinani and Margitnani always did. When she works out, she is always paying attention to the signs her body sends her. If a part of her body is hurting, she doesn't push through it, she redirects what she is doing so it is always safe. If she is tired, she doesn't work out as hard; she will just do gentle work. She, like my dad and Marc, exhibits all the qualities that make up good blood. They all do it intuitively, and they are role models, teaching us what is possible.

Marilyn lies on the table, and her body guides me to where I should start. She goes into a relaxed state, and so do I.

~~~~~~~~~~~~~

My patients teach me new things every day. I see firsthand what fear or any kind of resistance does to the body. I can also feel with my hands what happens when we let go of that fear and resistance.

I know that I have to conquer my own crazy fear of driving. Just like with my patients, I can feel how it is affecting my body. This crazy fear has made me more understanding and compassionate for those who have a hard time letting go, but I also know that facing my fears will help me be a better therapist. So, although I am petrified, today I am flying to Greer, South Carolina, home of the two-day BMW high performance driving course. It's finally time to face my fears. The course here is half the cost of a similar course at home, and even adding in the plane fare and hotel, it is still worth it to be here. The bonus is that after the class ends, I will drive to Charlotte and spend a few days with my youngest nephew, Mike.

I park the SUV I rented outside of the training building. The rental place upgraded me because they were out of the cheaper cars, and I'm glad because this car seems safer. I look at the ultramodern building in front of me. It looks almost like it is made of glass because of all of its windows. Just above the entrance is the sign, BMW Performance Center. I take a deep breath, and I walk in, find the classroom, and take a seat. There are eleven of us, but I sit in the back by myself.

A man enters and goes to the front of the room. He is wearing beige slacks and a white polo shirt with the BMW logo on it, the attire all the instructors wear.

"Hi! I'm Bob. I want to welcome you. I am a racecar driver, and I'll be one of your instructors. It is always fun to teach people not only about high performance driving, but also about how to be better drivers in general."

Better drivers, I think. *Now I know I'm in the right class.*

"Why don't you all introduce yourselves and say why you're here," Bob says.

The introductions start with row one.

"Hi! I'm Howard, and my wife gave me this as a birthday present."

"Hi! I'm Steve, and my wife gave me this as a birthday present."

"Do you guys know each other?" Bob asks, smiling.

"No, we met about ten minutes ago," they laugh.

"Hi! I'm Elizabeth, and my boyfriend gave this to me as a present because I've had three speeding tickets in the last two months."

"We better watch out for you," Bob says.

"Hi! I'm Ben. I'm interested in racing. I'm actually interested in the racecar driving course, but I was told I had to complete this class first."

I hear similar responses from the others, and finally, it's my turn.

"Hi! I'm Irit, and I'm here," I sigh and begin again, "and, well, I'm afraid of driving because I was in a few accidents where I was stopped and I got pummeled."

I hear a sigh from the class, a collective, *oh no.*

"Maybe those who hit you should take the class," Bob says.

"If I could track them all down and make them, I would. That's not a bad idea, but I'm always afraid I'll be hit, so I've become the driver I fear most on the road. I'm afraid of becoming one of those people that end up causing an accident because they are so timid. I need to get my confidence back and have fun driving again."

I hear another sigh from the class. I can just imagine what they are thinking, *What the heck is she doing here? She'll be holding us back.*

"The cars you will be driving are the 330 BMW series. There will be two people per car, and we have an uneven number, so one of you will have to go solo."

Passenger? Are they out of their minds? I'm even more afraid of accidents when I'm a passenger. *I have to go solo,* I decide.

"Who here gets seasick?" Bob asks.

I know where this is leading, so I blurt out, "I was in a sailboat last week, and I got seasick," before anyone else has a chance to respond.

"Irit, you'll go solo."

Thank you, Rick, my neighbor and friend, for taking me sailing last week. I think, thankful I won't have to be a passenger. I know my imaginary brake would be on non-stop when they were driving and worry that this fear might get in the way of my healing.

"We'll start by familiarizing you with the car. You'll alternate between driver and passenger. Irit, you'll go twice for each activity. We'll teach you the principles of the techniques, and then you'll go out and practice. You'll have walkie-talkies in the car so we can instruct you if you need it. Any questions?"

No one says anything.

"We'll start with the positioning of our hands on the steering wheel, and then we'll proceed to the concept of cornering, a very important part of racing as well as basic driving," Bob says. "It's the cornering techniques that can make or break a race.

"Now, when you turn, the important thing is to look where you're going before you start the turn. You brake, then start the turn, and then accelerate out of the turn. We'll have instructors positioned where you should be looking when you go in and out of turns. Let's go out and practice. Have fun."

Fun, right. My hands are trembling, and I haven't even started. I walk outside with everyone else. The track is huge. It looks about the size of two football fields.

"To the far right," Bob says, "is the skid pad, which is maybe one quarter of a mile with a grass patch in the middle. We have sprinklers to make it a wet course, and close to the skid pad is another course where we will have timed races with two people on the track at the same time."

"Awesome," I hear someone say.

"Let me show you to your cars, and you can head to the middle where we have the cornering course set up."

I get in my car, a black 330 BMW. It still has that new car smell of leather. I wait for my turn. I see the course, with about eight pylons in an S shape. I hear my name, and I start. My hands are trembling. My heart is beating quickly. I am about to make the turn, and I hear my name, "Look ahead to where you want to turn," the voice says. "See where I'm waving? That's where you have to look."

I hear my name over and over again, telling me the same thing: look ahead, always keep your focus ahead. And I see the waves and the smiles encouraging me. I think I'm probably setting a record for how many times a participant's name has to be called. It is my reminder to focus on becoming a better driver.

Now they have us switch partners, and I go again.

After we finish the first course, we go back to the classroom and review some principles of driving. Next we will practice how to avoid an accident by changing lanes. We head out to the track and start off practicing at 35 miles per hour, and then we repeat the exercise at increased speeds until we finally each practice accelerating to 55 mph.

I get behind the wheel and start accelerating. My nervousness is growing, and I end up turning before I'm supposed to.

"The cone is where you're supposed to turn," I hear the instructor repeating through the walkie-talkie. *I know that*, I think, *but it's easier said than done.* I tell myself to breathe because, of course, I am constantly holding my breath. I wait for my turn again. I hear my name and practice again. Finally, it is my forth attempt, and I have to increase the speed to 55. My hands and feet are trembling.

"Relax and have fun," I hear the instructor coach me.

"Right," I mumble under my breath.

I start and pick up speed until I see 55 mph on the gauge. I reach the cone, and this time I turn right on time, avoiding the anticipated accident.

"Great!" I hear the instructor tell me for the first time. I feel elated, and I'm ready to pack it in for the day with that success under my belt. Then I hear, "Change drivers. Irit, go again," and I sigh. Every time they say, "change drivers," it just means I have to go again since I'm on my own. My hands are clammy, and my heart is probably beating at a rate faster than I've been driving. *Here we go again.*

~~~~~~~~~~~~~

The next morning we're back in the class, but now we have a new instructor, Jim. My whole body aches from being so tense the day before, and I can feel the 4-letter word that has been my constant companion that past year kicking in again: fear.

"Today there will be two of you on the track, and you will be at opposite ends. You will each be timed. This is a good way to practice turns. Any questions?"

"What if I'm going too slowly and get hit?" I ask.

"Don't stop. Isn't that how you always get hit?" the instructor reminds me jokingly.

"Ok."

"You'll be fine."

We get in our cars, and I'm in my normal mode of hands trembling and heart pounding through my chest. I survive the first go round, and the second time around my hands aren't trembling as much.

We get a break, and I sit beside Howard and Steve, the guys whose wives gave them this class as a present. They have been partnered up on the course.

"I told my wife about you last night. I'm glad that you have been able to go twice with all of the courses," Howard says.

"I told my wife the same thing," Steve says. "You're getting better each time you get in the car."

I am a little shocked. I expected both of them to be envious they're not going twice, but instead they are happy for me. Everyone must be seeing, feeling, and hearing the fear inside of me. I am thankful they are supportive, and I tell them so.

We get back to the class, and Jim tells us that our next challenge will be driving on the skid pad. "You'll be learning how to overcome skid conditions and loss of control over front and back wheels. The sprinklers will be on to mimic rainy conditions, and an instructor will be in the car with you to guide you," Jim says.

I don't drive in the rain anymore. I'm too afraid, and I'd rather skydive than drive in ice and sleet. At this point, though, I'm even more afraid of telling the class that so I decide to hold it in. I have knots in my stomach, and I'm queasy. I notice that I'm holding my breath, so I start trying to in-hale slowly. *I've already dealt with so much in this class, and now I have to face this?* I think.

My body starts its fear dance, but the instructor's voice brings me back to the room. "There are two types of skids, rear wheel and front wheel. In the rear wheel skid, the back end of the car starts to slide out in the op-posite direction of where you are trying to turn. So, if you're going around a curve to the left, the rear end slides to the right. To correct this, do not put on the brakes. If you do, it will pull you more into the skid. Instead, turn the car gently in the opposite direction of where you want to go, and then, when the skid stops, turn the wheel back in the direction you were heading.

"The front wheel skid is harder to handle for many people. If you're trying to turn right, the car doesn't turn, but instead it keeps going straight because the front wheels have lost traction on the slippery road. In this case, very gently put your feet on the brakes to throw the car's weight for-ward onto the front wheels and give them more traction. Then, turn the steering wheel back to straighten out the front wheels and get them rolling regularly again."

I go out to the track and get into the car with the instructor, Chuck, who is in the passenger seat. Once again, my hands are uncontrollably trembling.

"Have you ever crashed with someone during this procedure?"

"No. Don't worry. You'll be fine. We haven't lost anyone yet."

"Yeah, right." I say, faking a laugh. *What did I get myself into?* I ask myself. I can see the headlines as I always do when crazy fear overrides my logic. The newspapers in Montréal and San Francisco will carry the story, *Canadian girl, now also an American citizen living in the Bay area, is the first paying customer to die in a southern BMW driving course.*

"You'll be fine," I hear again.

I look at him. He doesn't seem scared, even with me, a trembling wreck, behind the wheel.

"You'll start," Chuck says, "and then just keep turning faster and faster until you go into a rear skid."

I like the fact that this ¼ mile course has grass in the middle. At least, if I lose control and can't gain it back, I will just end up in the grass.

"You ready?" Chuck asks.

"As ready as I'll ever be," I hear myself saying. I remind myself to breathe, and I start. I go around the curves, building up speed, going faster and faster until I lose control and the car slides. I steer into the skid like they said to and then turn the other way, but I do it all too fast so we continue the skid. We land on the grass.

I gain some confidence, now knowing for sure that if I lose control, nothing bad really will happen. After a few tries, I do it right, and I keep doing it correctly after that. I had been so scared of not doing it right, but oddly enough, that is the very thing that allowed me to calm down.

"This is fun," I say.

"You're doing really well. Now, let's practice the front wheel skids. Keep accelerating around the track, and then I'll surprise you by putting the hand brakes on. This will put the car in a front skid. Brake gently, putting the weight on the front wheels, and that will give you more traction. After that, turn the steering wheel back to straighten out and get the front wheels to roll again. Ready?"

I begin driving around the track. I accelerate and accelerate, and then, suddenly, Chuck puts on the hand brake. The car goes into an immediate skid. The car won't turn as I had planned. It is going straight ahead. I do as he instructed, and I quickly regain control. "Wow! This is cool," I say, and for the first time in a very long time, I am feeling confident in my driving skills.

"You're doing great," Chuck says. "This skill is where most people have problems, and so far you have done this the best."

We keep repeating the course, and I'm getting very comfortable with the exercise. The instructor starts mixing it up, and somehow, I intuitively keep making the corrections I need to each time. I feel like I'm in an amusement park and nothing can go wrong.

"We're done. That was really good. Congratulations."

When I get out of the car, my legs feel wobbly, but I'm jazzed. "This is the only time I won't go twice, since we are sitting with an instructor, and now I wish I could," I say.

All the participants and instructors keep encouraging me. The day passes, and finally, we are on our last event for the class: the race. The ½ mile track is set up for us to practice all of the techniques we have learned, and we get to go around it twice while we are timed.

I get in my car, adrenaline pumping once again, and I get the sign to go. I start, and, holding onto my steering wheel tightly, I make the turns as we were taught. My hands relax, and I suddenly find myself accelerating with confidence. I'm completely focused on the course. I get to the finish line, and I brake quickly, like we are supposed to.

After all of the participants go, the results are in, and I come in fifth. I can't believe it. I was dead last in everything on the first day, and now I have managed to beat out some of the other participants, and some of them really love to drive.

I completely let go of all fear as I began the race. I was in the zone, in the moment. I didn't have any thoughts running through my head, just a pure sense of focus on what I intuitively needed to do at any given moment. It felt so liberating to be in this positive place, my body just relaxed. When I finished the race, my body felt great. What a difference it makes on the body when we tighten up as compared to when we relax. Many scientific studies support that, and now I have seen firsthand that even in a sporting event it holds true.

I feel so empowered and confident, and I think back to Ed, from my ropes and dolphins experiences. 'What do you want this experience to mean to you?' I can hear him say. I want to be motivated by excitement in the face of the unknown, rather than be limited and become a prisoner to fear. Fear stops me from being me and stops my body from healing. The feeling I had on the racetrack is what I want more of in my life. I now have a new memory that shows me that when I am scared I have another choice for how to respond. I can make corrections and redirect. Today I showed myself I don't have to live in fear when I drive. The more I experience this way of being, the faster my brain will rewire to make it a much more natural state, and that can transfer over to other areas of my life. This is the best feeling in the world!

We go back to the classroom to wrap things up, and Jim gives out our certificates. I'm the last to get mine.

As he hands me the paper, Jim announces, "The crew here has voted you 'most improved driver in the history of the course,' with the exception of one guy who lived in New York but had seldom driven and didn't own a car," Jim says. Everyone claps and congratulates me.

"Wow," I say with a big smile on my face. "That must mean I really was as bad as I thought when I started."

Everyone laughs, and I head off to Charlotte, driving comfortably in my SUV. I am on my way to visit my youngest nephew, Mike, feeling like a better driver than ever before.

I turn on the radio, and I hear John Denver's song, *I Want to Live*. I start to sing along, feeling connected to the words, '*I want to live. I want to grow. I want to see. I want to know. I want to share what I can give. I want to be. I want to live.*'

~~~~~~~~~~~~~~~

Irit Schaffer

19

2008

May the footprints we leave behind show that we've walked in kindness toward the earth and every living thing.
-Inspired by American Indian philosophy

In the Jewish culture, you always get bragging rights if you have a doctor, a lawyer, or a businessman in the family. In my family, we have all three, split between my three nephews. Ryan is the doctor, Marc is the businessman, and Mike is the lawyer. Though Mike isn't actually working as a lawyer now, he works in the White House, instead, which grants its own bragging rights. All the bases are covered, which makes it seventh heaven for my mom when she gets to talk about her grandsons.

Actually, she's been bragging about them since the day they were born. In her eyes, they have always been perfect. Through all the years, she has never once gotten mad at any of her grandchildren, and she has never criticized anything they do. It's like they have a magical spell over my mom, and it is always fun to watch her interact with them. I get to see her playful, loving side.

This week, I'm headed to Montréal to celebrate yet another Passover with my whole family. I'm excited to see everyone on this trip. There will be four generations in one house. Marc is now married to Robyn, and they have two little ones. Zachary is three and a half, and Jake is 20 months. They will be flying from Pittsburgh. Ryan, my oldest nephew, will also be here with his wife, Michelle, and their little one, Ben, who is also 20 months old. They are driving from Boston, and my sister, Edna, who is Ryan, Marc and Mike's mom, is driving from Clarks Summit, PA. Unfortunately, my youngest nephew, Mike, who lives in Washington, DC can't make it because he agreed to be an usher at a friend's wedding before we all decided to celebrate Passover together in Montréal.

~~~~~~~~~~~~~~

Passover celebrates the beginning of the Jewish people out of exile. At midnight during Passover over three thousand years ago, the Jewish slaves, also called the Israelites, escaped Egypt, becoming free under the first full moon of spring.

On the first two nights of Passover, we have a Seder, which is a Jewish ritual feast marking the beginning of the holiday. We have books called the *Haggadahs* that teach us about the exodus of the Jewish slaves from Egypt. There is plenty of singing, prayer, blessing, wine, and, of course, food. It is the most festive of the Jewish holidays.

It probably takes two weeks of preparation for my mom to get the house clean and rid it of all types of forbidden, leavened foods, called *chametz*. There is a special set of dishes, silverware, pots, pans, and other utensils that are used for Passover only. All the plates, utensils, pots, and pans used during the year are stored away, and for eight days, we use the Passover dishes only. Growing up, Passover, Rosh Hashanah and Yom Kippur were the only holidays where no cheating with foods was allowed.

The first day of Passover has often been a day of crisis for our family. The first time I remember it happening was when I was six. I came home from first grade. We were preparing to go to my Aunt Edith and Uncle Frank's home for Passover, but something went wrong.

"I feel sick, and I have a rash," I said.

My mom called the doctor. He arrived with his black bag, looked me over, and said, "Irit, you have chicken pox."

My dad was happy to stay home, and my mom scrambled to make an acceptable Seder dinner, which was, of course, delicious.

The next year, at about the same time, two hours before we left for Uncle Frank's house, the doctor arrived with his black bag.

"Irit, you have scarlet fever. You will have to stay home for three weeks," he said. My dad was again happy to stay home, and my mom again scrambled to make an acceptable Seder dinner, which was, of course, delicious.

The next year, I came home from school, ready, finally, for a Seder at Uncle Frank's, but the doctor came with his black bag.

"Irit, you have the mumps," he said.

We stayed home. Again my mom scrambled to make a delicious Seder dinner, and again, my dad was happy to stay home.

The next year, two hours before Seder at Uncle Frank's, I said, "I feel achy all over." My mom took my temperature, and it was 103. Once more, the doctor arrived with his black bag. This time, he didn't even know what I had, but still he said,

"Irit, you have to stay home."

My mom scrambled to make a delicious Seder dinner, and my dad was happy to stay home.

I must have finally run out of childhood diseases so we finally got to Frank's the next year. My Aunt Edith is nice, and I always loved spending time with her. I was excited to finally make it to Seder. It was especially fun to be around all our family members during all the singing on Passover because my three cousins have great voices.

My dad was quiet most of the night, but I could see from his face that he didn't really want to be there. No one else noticed, but I knew he could never really forget how Uncle Frank treated us when we arrived in Montréal and how he had made sure no one in the textile business would hire him. My dad was always loving and kind to Aunt Edith and his three nieces, though.

Everything went well that night, and the next year, and the one after that. Then we started having Passover Seder at home, and things ran fairly smoothly until the year I turned 16.

There were seven place settings, and six of us were sitting at the dining room table. Our cousins from my dad's side were visiting from New York. My dad was running late, and we figured he had just gotten a last minute call at work.

After what felt like forever, we finally heard the door open, and he walked in, white as a ghost.

"Dad, what happened to you?" I was the first to speak.

"I was walking to my car. It was at the garage for repair. I crossed the street, and when I was halfway across, a car came. I saw it, but I couldn't get out of the way. I jumped onto the hood while it was moving. The car couldn't stop right away, so I was just on the hood while it moved forward. The people who saw it said it must have been going 35 miles an hour."

The mood in the room immediately changed when he walked in, and now several of us were standing, very alert. I moved forward, trying to make sure he was ok. "Dad, you have to go the hospital," I said. "People can die from shock after something like that. You could have internal bleeding, and you won't know it until it's too late. I learned that in first aid."

"Iritka, I'm fine."

The whole rest of the night I was scared, and after that, I started carrying around the fear that he would die in a car accident or have a heart attack at any given moment. I remember taking a CPR course just in case something happened. At the same time, I kept wondering, how could he jump onto the hood of the car, be with it until it stopped, and have survived?

Once again, Passover and Seder settled down, but last year, my mom's back was bothering her three hours before the Seder. I was visiting from California and offered to work on her. For the first time ever, she said yes. We put pillows on the kitchen table as a substitute for my worktable, and I got started.

After a few minutes, my mom stated, matter-of-factly, "Your hands have turned ice cold."

"Mom, that's the *chi*, the energy and life force that flows through us. Without energy, we're not alive."

"Now your hands are like a hot furnace."

"That's the *chi*, too. That's a good sign," I said.

After a few minutes, my mom's body started shaking from laughter.

"I don't know what's so funny, but I can't stop laughing."

"That's the *chi*," I repeated, chuckling.

"Now, I feel like I'm going to sleep."

"Mom, that's fine. That's what happens for a lot of people," I said excitedly. I knew she was experiencing a powerful treatment. I was removing the blocks, and her body was doing the rest to self-correct.

That was a big moment for me, and that night, when we went to Seder at my mom's best friend's house, my mom had said, "Medi, I don't know what Irit did, but it was better than any medicine for my back."

That was the first compliment I remember hearing from my mother.

~~~~~~~~~~~~~~

"Would you like lunch?" the stewardess asks me.

"No, thank you. I brought my own food."

The plane lands, and as I walk through the corridor en route to customs, I see the familiar sign, *Bienvenue!*, the sign that always made me smile.

"What is the purpose of your visit?" the immigration officer asks.

"I am visiting my mom."

"How long will you be here?"

"One week."

"Do you have anything to declare?"

"No."

"Welcome to Montréal and have a nice stay," the officer says and stamps my passport.

I get my luggage, rent a car, and, once again, am on the freeway, headed to my mom's. I love Montréal. It always feels so welcoming to me even though one has to be on constant alert driving in the city. The drivers here have been ranked as some of the worst in North America. That's probably why we can't make a right turn on a red light here.

I am the first to arrive at my mom's place. I know everyone else won't start arriving until tomorrow at around five in the afternoon.

My mom moved to a big apartment complex a few years ago. She is on the ninth floor and has never been happier. She lives near three of her friends who are like her sisters. It is an extremely secure area, too. Visitors actually have to call the police department for permission to park on the streets at night.

I ring the doorbell, take the elevator up, and knock.

My mom opens the door, and I lean over to give her a kiss, something that has finally, after many years, become natural to me.

"Iritka, you should have parked your car in the driveway," she says in a concerned tone. "The street isn't in a good place." Every time I visit I get the same comment, no matter where I park. I should always have parked in another spot. I smile. I know that is just her way of trying to help, and she is just being her spunky self. She second-guesses herself all the time, too, not just me.

I go into the dining area, and my mom goes in directly after me.

"Do you want food?" she asks. "I made chicken soup, and there is gefilte fish."

I'm hungry. I have been looking forward to eating since landing in Montréal. My mom sits at the table with me as I eat.

"How was your trip?" she asks.

"It was fine. Thank goodness it was direct. Air Canada is usually good."

"My cleaning lady came today so we have to be careful. Don't eat anything in the den."

"No problem," I say.

I finish dinner, and we go into the den to watch *Deal or No Deal*. My taste in shows hasn't changed much from when I was a little girl. I hate any shows with violence. Even if I know what will happen, I still get scared so game shows or shows where the good guys always triumph are more my speed.

When it's time to sleep, I begin to open up the hide-a-bed in the living room and my mom cautions, "Be careful of the plant."

I smile and look at my mom's plant. It sits on a stand that is 12 inches off the ground, and the long, slim, new leaves grow upright as the older ones gently cascade downward. This plant and its stand have been with my mom for over 25 years. It was with her when I was in high school and we lived on Van Horne Street. Then it was with her when my parents moved to Ward Street, and now here it is, in her new place on Honoree de Balzac. The plant and its stand are still intact, but they have always been flimsy, so they are neatly tucked out of harm's way in the corner of the den. When I open up the hide-a-bed, the plant remains safe.

I remember when I first started teaching, my sister and three nephews were visiting for Passover, and Mikey and I were horsing around in the den. Somehow, the plant got knocked over, and the dirt got all over the carpet.

"Edna, I'm in big trouble," I had said in a panic. "Mom will kill me if she walks in here. I can't believe I spilled the plant. That stupid pot has always been so flimsy. Please, try to keep Mom occupied in the kitchen while I clean up."

Before Edna could even reach the kitchen, we heard Mikey, Edna's youngest, scream out, "Bubby! Irit spilled the plant. It's all over the floor," and giggle, as only a 6-year-old would at a time like that.

My mom ran into the room. "*Yoi eeshtanam*," she had exclaimed with a voice of doom and gloom, which meant, *Oh, my god,* in Hungarian. "Look what you did. The rug is ruined."

"Mom, it just needs to be vacuumed. I'll do it myself," I said, trying to calm her down.

"Irit, go away," she said harshly as she pushed me out of the way and went to get the vacuum cleaner. "Get out of the room. You'll give me a heart attack."

My body cringed from my mom's loud voice, and I looked at my nephew and his devilish smile as he said, "Let's go to the park and play."

He looked so sweet and innocent, and I had to laugh at his mischievousness.

I crawl into bed and look at the plant now, still standing strong, and I smile as I turn out the light.

I wake up early and head to my sanctuary at Mount Royal. The lions are gone, and it makes me sad even though I know they will be back. They were taken away to be repaired from the years of harsh Montréal weather conditions, but they will return in a few months. I will just have to spend this trip home without them.

It's spring in Montréal, one of my favorite times here. You can feel everything come alive, and as I walk on the gravel in the midst of the many trees, I notice the colors of the leaves. They are a vibrant green. I touch a leaf that I know is probably only two weeks old. It is soft and silky. The trees are saying hello to a new beginning, a new year of life and growth.

When I get home, my mom is ready to go run our errands for the day. We walk together to the car. My mom is carrying books, and she says, "Let's go first to the library. I will bring the books back and will see my friend Medi; we will trade books and get new ones."

When we reach the library, she gets out of the car quickly. It is so amazing for me to see my mom holding stacks of books. My mom never read a book while I was growing up. She even needed me to write out checks for her. She wouldn't go to school to learn to read or write. She didn't want anyone to know that she couldn't so she wasn't even willing to acknowledge that fact in public. Somehow, after my dad died, she taught herself to read and write English, and she and her friends started to share library books. I never would have believed it. That is what I would call a miracle.

I watch her walk, and I suddenly notice something that I had never paid attention to before. She walks so strongly and with such confidence. She has amazing strength and fortitude, a sheer will that always lets her overcome hardship.

Five or six years back, my mom came to visit me in the Bay area after spending time in Palm Springs with two friends from Montréal. She stayed a week, and I had really hoped I would get her to talk about her past. She never spoke about it, but I used the tool she had used on me all my life: Jewish guilt. She used it well.

"How will your grandkids feel," I asked, "if so many people are willing to help me with the book and you didn't share your story?"

"Iritka, why are you talking such stupidity?" she had said, but I could tell I was getting to her.

"Mom, it is important."

"You want to give me a heart attack? It is in the past. It is not important." She sighs deeply and puckers her lips.

"Mom, tell me, what will we tell your grandkids and great grandkids when they ask why you didn't share?"

"I don't want to talk."

"Okay, but you will have to be the one to tell your grandchildren that you don't want to share and you don't want to help."

My mom sat on the couch and took another deep breath. Her face softened as she paused and finally, said, somewhat sadly, "Ok, I will talk for a little bit."

I ran to get the tape recorder before she changed her mind. I could hardly believe my ears. I had been working on convincing her for so long (that was hardly the first time we had had that exact conversation) that I had started to doubt it would ever happen.

I set up the tape recorder and looked up at my mom. I had asked her so many questions throughout my life with no response. Now here she was, ready to share, and I didn't know where to begin.

"Mom, can you start by telling me what happened when you first had to leave your home?"

"For a long time, we could still stay at home."

"You mean on your farm in Hatalov?"

"Yes, but in 1944, there were new laws. Now we were forced to go work in a tobacco farm in another town in Czechoslovakia. Then we escaped."

"How long were you in hiding in the woods?"

"We were in hiding over three months."

"How many people were with you?"

"First there were many people, maybe 50."

"You had papers to say you were Christian. How come you didn't use them to leave like your other two sisters?"

"Because," she took a deep breath, "I knew I had to be with my mother and father. I just knew they would need my help."

I stop and take a breath. My mom goes from Hungarian to English and back in a heartbeat, but it seems second nature to me because we have always communicated like this.

"Were you in the woods the whole time?"

"After few months of hiding with many others, it was very cold, and my daddy paid someone for us to stay in a farmhouse, in a hole they made for us near the roof of the house. We were safe for one month.

"How did you get food?"

"The Christian husband and wife gave us food.

"How did you get caught?"

My mom's face tightened, and she paused again. After a long silence, she said in a loud voice, "A Jewish informant brought in the Gestapo, and we were captured."

"Why did he do that?" I asked, trying to get more details.

"The informant thought if he told on us he would be freed. His wife was not a Jew so he thought he was safe, but he, too, was rounded up with us. We all were sent to the camps."

I take a deep breath and continue, "So, you were sent to Bergen Belsen?"

"We were moved to a few camps. First, the Germans took us to Sered, a concentration camp in the Slovak state. About a week later, they sent us to Ravensbruck, a concentration camp in Germany, and then, about a month later, we were shipped to the German camp Bergen Belsen, which was a death camp."

My mom crossed her hands and shook her head. I saw all the muscles in her face tighten.

"What happened at Bergen Belsen?" I asked, sitting on the edge of my seat. I had only ever known small tidbits of this story, but now I knew I was about to find out more about my mother. My heart was racing.

My mom let out a sigh and then lifted her head up high and said, "They made us go naked, and then they gave us what to wear. For me," she said raising her voice, "they gave a rotten torn skirt, a torn blouse, one coat with different color sleeves. No stockings, no underwear, but I kept the shoes I had."

My mom put her fingers on the gold necklace that is always around her neck, and a look of triumph spread across her face. My stomach squeezed tight just thinking of how they could be so humiliated, and at the same time, I was in awe of her, amazed at how she could have survived.

"Your Bubby, my mother, and I were put in separate lines, and she ran to mine. After that, we were together."

"You mean she was in the line for the gas?"

"Yes, and they didn't catch her when she ran over, and after that we were together." My mom's hands were on her thigh, and I saw her start tapping her fingers. I could tell she was getting uncomfortable. It was the first and only time she had spoken about the camps in any detail, and she was not giving me any resistance. I was so shocked when I realized I was the one having a hard time hearing the stories and containing my tears. Yet, I knew that I had to continue since she was finally answering questions so freely. It was like she had been holding it in so long that she finally had to let it all out.

I took a breath and asked, "How did your days at the camp start?"

"We stood outside in freezing weather almost naked and we stood at *appel*."

"What's *appel*?" I asked but I knew.

A few years earlier, I had gone to the Dachau concentration camp, and I was mesmerized by the statue of the *Unknown Inmate* erected in 1950 and created by Fritz Koelle, a German Sculptor. In the statue, the prisoner's hands were in his pockets, his foot was pointed sideways, and he was looking up—three things that you could not do when you stood at *appel*; three things that remind me of how much we take freedom for granted.

"You stand and can't move," my mom says. "Then, many times, they shower us with cold water in freezing temperatures, and still we are not allowed to move."

I wanted to stop, but I couldn't. My whole body felt as if it was in a vice. My mom was answering every question and patiently waiting for the next. *I have to be strong*, I told myself.

"What if you had to go to the bathroom?"

"You couldn't move. You just ..."

For the first time that day, my mom cut off before finishing her answer, and I didn't pressure her to continue. I wanted to cry, but I stopped myself.

"What did you do for food?"

"In the morning, we had black coffee and a piece of bread. In evening, we had bad soup with maybe a potato or beet."

"Where did you sleep?"

"On the floor, and I used my shoes as a pillow."

"Did you save Bubby in the camps?"

"Two times I heard the Gestapo say, 'Tomorrow we select people to go to the gas.' When your Bubby said she didn't want to go to work those first few days, I made her go with me. When we got back, there were no older people or sick people left."

"What kind of work did you do?"

"We moved sand from one place to the other."

"Were you scared you were going to die?"

"We didn't care."

My relatives in Kosice said the same thing when I asked them. She, like them, was answering matter-of-factly, waiting for the next question to answer, waiting to finally let it out and be acknowledged and heard.

"What made you go on?" I said, choking back the lump in my throat. I so desperately wanted to take a time out, but all I could do was take a deep breath.

"Every night, your Bubby would say, 'Tomorrow we will be liberated,' and she would hold me. It was what kept me going," she sighed and pressed her lips together before going on, "Every night, your Bubby said the same thing, 'Tomorrow we will be liberated.'"

~~~~~~~~~~~~~~

The car door opens, breaking me off from my memory, and my mom gets back in the car with a book in her hand, this time it is *To Love Again* by Danielle Steele.

"Now let's go get lox and bagels. Do you think two pounds will be enough?"

"I have no idea," I say. My mom was always smarter about that stuff than I was.

I watch my mom joke with the fish people and then pay. This fish store makes its own lox, and it is the best I've ever had. They give us samples of the lox to taste, and, of course, I am now craving more. We walk back to the car, and my mom directs me, "Now, let's go to cemetery."

I'm glad that I rented a car so I can help out. I know she likes having me take her around. A neighbor usually helps her out by driving her to the mall to shop, but it's not the same.

We get to the cemetery and first head over to my dad's tombstone.

I look down at the now familiar engraving on it. The image is of two hands that are close together, signifying the priestly blessing that is performed in synagogue. In the Jewish tradition, it is customary for Kohens to have this symbol on their tombstones. Kohen means *priest* in Hebrew, and the Kohen lineage has been passed on from generation to generation, from father to son, without interruption, for more than three thousand years. All Kohenim are supposedly direct descendants of the high priest Aaron, brother of Moses, a subset of the Levi tribe.

When a Kohen is born, they carry specific merits and special responsibilities. Kohens give the special blessing at Jewish festivals. At the synagogue, eight people are called to say the blessing over the Torah, and the

Kohen is the first to be called. The Kohen's special responsibility is that the special blessing must be given with love.

When a Kohen dies, the two hands are placed on the tombstone to signify the blessing they would do in the synagogue. The hands are together with their palms down, and the fingers are split so there are five spaces. One space is between the thumbs, one space is between the thumb and first finger of each hand and then there is a space between the second and third fingers of each hand. The Vulcan salute in Star Trek is based on the priestly blessing by the Jewish Kohen. Though I'm sure the Vulcans would say that the hand placement was taken from them!

The actual blessing is done with both arms held at shoulder level and the hands touching to form the Hebrew letter *shin*. *Shin* is the first letter of one of God's names, *Shadai*. The five spaces of the hand placement are there to allow the divine presence to shine into the world.

My mom stops at the graves of my grandmother and other relatives and friends, saying her own prayer and leaving a stone for each of them. It is Jewish tradition to leave stones at gravesites to remember the deceased.

I stay put and am mesmerized by the Kohen hands on my dad's tombstone. I stare at the hands and think of my dad. *Dad,* I think, *you were always a healer, and you always said it was because of your good blood. I inherited the healing hands. But the truth is, good blood allows the healing hands to have their magical powers. When I was little and asked you if I had good blood, you would always answer with a laugh. You may not have been able to put it in concrete terms because it came so naturally to you, but you knew. You knew that good blood is a mindset, a state of being, and we all have the potential to access it.*

I glance over at my mom. She is about 50 feet away at a different site, but I just can't seem to move from my dad to join her. I turn back to the tombstone and reflect.

Believing in the possibility of healing is the most important aspect of good blood. My dad had shown me that from the time I was little with all of his stories about how the body can heal in ways most people don't understand, but good blood is about healing more than the body. Good blood allowed my dad to always have a twinkle in his eyes and to still believe in the good of mankind after all he had been through.

He also understood how to tap into a light, a calmness, and a peace that always helped him better understand his circumstances and know what to do. That ability was always with him, even in the war. That's probably why he was able to beat the Russian officer in chess even though his body was so deprived. It is still impossible for me to understand how he could be so sharp in the mind with all that he had to endure, but he was.

Dad, I think, *when I am at work, I can tap into that light, just like you could for yourself. All fear disappears, and then I can just listen to what the body needs. I let go of all preconceived notions, all judgments, all beliefs, and I just listen.*

Dad always told me if I were nervous, I would never find an answer, and if I would try to make a decision when I am not thinking clearly, it would always be a bad decision. So he always would say, "don't try to figure it out or make a decision unless you're in a good place in your head."

He also always showed me how important it is to listen to your inner voice and to listen to your body. If he was tired, he stopped. If he had a headache, he went to bed and when he woke up it would be gone. If he didn't feel well, he would go to bed, and once again, he would be fine by the morning. If he was upset about something, he would say, "I'll go to sleep, and the answer will come to me," and it always did.

We know our own bodies better than anyone else. We just need to learn how to listen. A doctor once thought my dad had lung cancer, but Dad knew it was just an old rib injury. The doctor didn't believe him, but my dad knew he was right.

When I put my hands on patients, I can hear, see and feel things that the wisdom and inner voice of the body wants me to know. I know how to do for others what my dad did for himself. The body never lies. It always gives me information I need to help my patient. I find and release blocks so the body can take over and heal itself.

I take a deep breath, trying to hold back tears as I remember, for what feels like the millionth time, the last time I talked to my dad in that silver Malibu. He had said there was a positive in everything, that it was important to *focus on the positive,* and that many times people give up too quickly. When I work, I can help people see the positive, the bigger picture of what's happening, and many times, I tell them exactly what my dad had told me. It helps them every time.

"We better get home. Everyone will be arriving in two hours," my mom says, interrupting my thoughts. I look at my mom as I come back to the present. I know that she, too, has the important qualities of good blood. She is amazingly independent and always finds a way to figure things out. If she can't do it one way, she will persist until she achieves success. Yet, when she realizes it is not possible, she goes into immediate surrender and accepts what is. She doesn't waste any time being upset over what isn't or being angry over what is no longer possible.

Someone once asked her if she longs to be back in Israel or to go back to the roots of her childhood, and I loved her response. "I just accept what is. If I can't change it, I don't think about it." It's that same mindset that probably helped her survive and rise above her experiences during the holocaust. It's probably why she, too, healed so quickly from any health issues she encountered during the war.

I discover more in her each time I learn something new about her. I go to put a stone on my bubby's grave, and we head out.

We reach home, and no sooner does my mom have everything ready than the arrivals begin. Edna, my sister, is the first to arrive.

As usual, the yummy food comes out, and we all indulge. As we eat, my mom looks at Edna and says, "Edna, since the last time I saw you, you have gained about ten pounds. Now you're like me. I also have to lose ten pounds, and my stomach is too big. Are you sure you are alright?"

I'm shocked. That is the first time I have seen her pick on my sister about weight.

"Mom, I'm fine," Edna sighs. Usually I am the one who gets all of those comments because I am skinny. I think that is the Jewish way, at least in the circle I grew up in. Suddenly, it dawns on me for the first time that my mom worries about my sister because she believes she is too fat, and my mom worries about me because she thinks I'm too skinny. I always took it so personally, but the truth is, she just worries regardless. It's just the way our mom is. It's how she expresses herself when she worries.

I smile at this realization and have to hold back a laugh as my mom turns to me. "Every time I see Irit she gets skinnier and skinnier," she says, starting in. "She needs to gain ten pounds. I would give her my ten pounds, but these pounds are too old so it wouldn't be good for her."

I look at my mom, and we both crack up. This is the teasing side of my mom that I rarely got to see when I was younger.

The doorbell rings.

"Hi, Bubs," Ryan says as he leans over to kiss her.

"Hi, Bubby," Michelle, Ryan's wife, says next, leaning in to give her a kiss.

"Hi, Bubs," Marc says, and Robyn leans over to give her a kiss.

"Bubby, can I have chocolate cake?" little Zach asks, breaking the chain of hellos and kisses.

"You taught him that?" my mom asks, smiling.

"No," Marc says as he laughs. "Zach has been talking about your chocolate nut roll cake since the plane ride. He remembers it from when you visited us three months ago."

~~~~~~~~~~~~~~

At 8:30 p.m, my sister and my mom decide to babysit while the rest of us head to the movies. Within forty-five minutes, we're back.

"What happened?" Edna asks, "You're back so early."

"There was a fire alarm 20 minutes into the movie, and they shut down the theatre. No one would tell us why it went off," Ryan says.

Now that we are all back, we start putting everything away and setting up the sleeping arrangements. Ryan's son, Ben, is taking a nap in his crib in the den, but since I need more space for the fold-out bed I will be sleeping on, Edna heads into the den to move it out of the way.

Before she can get very far, Ryan says, "Mom, I told you I'd do it."

"Ok, but be careful," my mom says.

Ryan heads into the den and closes the door. Not long after, I hear a crashing sound. A dead silence follows, and then the door slowly opens. "Bubby," Ryan says awkwardly, "I need a broom and tray."

"Why?" she asks as she and my sister make their way into the room.

"*Yoi eeshtanam*," they both say in unison as they see my mom's old plant on the floor. The dirt is spread all over the area rug that covers most of the floor. I look at the overturned plant in shock.

"*Yoi eeshtanam*," I hear again. "The carpet is ruined."

"Bubby, I'll fix it," Ryan says apologetically.

"Everyone, get out," my mom says in that gruff voice she is so famous for, the one that years of smoking gave her.

"Bubby, I'll do it."

Instead of responding, my mom pushes Ryan out of the way. She turns the plant upright, puts it into the flimsy holder, and then sweeps as much of the dirt from the hardwood floor as she can before vacuuming the rest. Somehow, as she sweeps, the broom nudges the plant and it falls over once again as we all watch in tense silence.

"*Yoi eeshtanam*," my sister says.

My mom picks up the plant again, and Ryan, in a calm voice, says, "I'll do it."

"No, leave me alone," she says.

"Ryan, she is going to hurt her back," I say with some trepidation.

"I just had the cleaning lady here today," my mom says loudly, "so we were ready for Passover, and now look. *Yoi eeshtanam.* The whole place is a mess."

"Mom," my sister says in a similar tone to my mom's, "keep your voice down, the kids will wake up." This just gets my mom even more riled up.

"Mom," I say, "you will hurt your back. Let Ryan help."

"No," she says in her stern tone. I can't believe she is not letting her grandson help. He was always the one who could do no wrong in her eyes. None of her grandsons could for that matter.

"Irit," Ryan whispers, "she doesn't want help. We'll just have to leave her alone. She's upset, and if she's upset, the best thing to do is leave her alone until she calms down."

"You mean you're not upset?" I say, surprised at how calm he seems under these circumstances.

"She doesn't want my help, and there is no stopping her. When you're upset, does it help when someone tries to reason with you?"

"But how do you not let it get to you?"

"Eear, my dad yells when he is upset, too, but he is just blowing off steam, and after he yells, he forgets it. Bubby does the same thing. When we were little, my brothers and I realized that it was just my dad being my dad, and we always knew that his bark was worse than his bite. We just knew if we stayed calm, it would pass, and if we reacted, it would fuel the anger."

My mom carries the plant into the kitchen to fix it up. She puts the earth back into the pot, and as she leans to grab more dirt, there is another crash as the plant turns over again. At this point, I find it comical in some crazy way.

"*Yoi eeshtanam,*" Edna says in shock.

"Bubby, I'll do it for you," Ryan says in one last attempt, but my mom just silences him.

"No, leave me alone," she says harshly, cleaning the dirt from the kitchen floor.

Ten minutes later, the tension eases up in the room as she finally gets everything together, until, once again, crash, the plant turns over as she tries to move it. The anger is like smoke around my mom's body this time, and nothing can penetrate it.

"Watch, Eear. Stay calm, and it will pass. Get upset, and you will fuel it," Ryan says quietly to me.

"Everyone out of the room," my mom shouts.

The vacuum cleaner comes out, and Edna says, once again, "Mom, the babies will wake up."

"Leave me alone," my mom says in a tone that told us not to mess with her. The vacuum cleaner quickly removes any sign of dirt from the floor, and fortunately, the babies somehow sleep through it.

After retreating to another room, I turn to Ryan, who is looking as composed as ever, and say, "Ryan, I still can't believe you didn't get upset, even in the moment."

"Why would I? Bubby was upset, and she probably was upset because she was afraid the dirt wouldn't come out and the place would not be clean for Passover. She wanted everything to be perfect for us. At that point, there was no way to talk to her."

"But, you weren't upset?"

"No," he says, laughing at my persistence. "She didn't want my help, and that was her choice," he says, shrugging.

You mean there was another way I could have handled these situations all these years? I want to say, but I refrain. Instead, I start to imagine how different my life would have been if I hadn't taken things so personally my whole life.

~~~~~~~~~~~~~

The next afternoon, everything is quiet, as if nothing had happened.

Zach takes my hand, and says, "Watch me play the drums."

Bang, bang, bang, I hear as he sits on the little stool in front of the drum set I bought him.

In the dining room, Michelle, Ryan's wife is sitting at the table and talking with my mom. Michelle is not Jewish, but from the moment they met, she and my mom bonded in a warm and loving way, which is something I never would have imagined growing up. From the get-go, Michelle called her 'Bubby', the same name her grandkids used, and my mom treated her as if she were the granddaughter she had never had.

Michelle is a nurse practitioner, and she loves to work with the elder population, so they start talking about my mom's health routines.

"Here are my drugs," she says, showing the bottles to Michelle. "This is for my high blood pressure; this is for my heart; and this is for stomach problems."

Michelle looks at all the meds and says, "Bubby, these look good."

My mom and Michelle are talking quietly, in soft tones. It is a complete contrast to last night. Finally, as the subject changes I hear Michelle timidly say, "Bubby, I'm sorry about the plant."

My mom takes a deep breath and sighs, "I've had that plant for over 20 years. Last night I got so angry that I threw it out. I'm sorry I got so angry. It was a mistake to get so angry and to throw out the plant."

My head turns almost a full 180 degrees as I listen to this reply. I cannot believe what I am hearing. My mom is calm, and she is expressing herself. I seldom have heard her apologize for outbursts like that, but then again, I have always done what Ryan advised me not to do last night. My whole life, I had always tried to reason with her when she was upset, when there was no way she would be able to hear me. I always tried to get her to see my point of view, when, in reality, that was not something she could do.

"Bubby, you have so many beautiful possessions in this house," Michelle continues. "Which of your possessions is the most precious to you?"

"That's an easy one to answer. It's the gold chain I am wearing around my neck," she says with the utmost pride.

"Why is it so valuable to you?" Michelle asks.

"It is the only possession I have from before the war. When the Gestapo took us, I had hidden it in one of my shoes. When we got to the camps, they let me keep my shoes. The day we were liberated in 1945, I took it out of my shoe, where it was hidden, and I have worn it every day since. I love it. I love it. My daddy gave it to me before the war. It was his gift to me. He died on the day of liberation. This is what I have to remember him by. I wouldn't trade it for all the money in the world, but when I'm gone, you can sell it, because then it doesn't matter."

"Bubby," Michelle says with so much warmth in her voice, "we would never sell it."

I am stunned. In all these years I didn't understand the true meaning of that necklace for my mother. I flash back to last year when I came to visit. My mom had scheduled an MRI for her back while I was visiting so I could take her. After she was done, she asked me to untangle the knot in her gold chain. I did, and then I helped her put it back on because she was having trouble with the clasp. As soon as it was back around her neck, she said "I wouldn't trade this gold chain for a million dollars."

Of course, I had thought to myself. *This is her gold chain. It is her reminder of everything she overcame,* but I never really got it until now. I didn't realize until this moment that it represented her strong bond of love with her dad. It was her constant reminder of him and her connection to his unconditional love.

My mom had recently asked me if I still had the gold bracelet from my dad. I had told her, "of course," and that I would always cherish it. I don't wear it to Montréal because when I work on her and other relatives, I have to take it off, and I don't want to risk losing or forgetting it.

I look at my mom and she is beaming, then Michelle and she share a long hug.

I am so grateful to Michelle for allowing my mom the ability to just express herself in that softness and vulnerability. I have never been able to really talk to my mom like that.

"Michelle, tonight we should go out to eat. No more food in the house until tomorrow night for Passover. I don't want to clean anymore."

"Bubby, that sounds good. Let's go early."

"How about Chinese?"

"Sure."

"Mom," I say, "I don't like Chinese. The MSG additive gives me a headache."

"Fine, you choose. I'll stay home."

"Mom," Edna interjects, "let's go to the Greek restaurant. We went there last time I was here. You liked it."

"Ok," she says reluctantly. I smile, over the years I have started to see a different, softer, and more awe-inspiring side to my mom. The bickering is still there. It's part of our family dynamic, but it never really escalates to anything more than that.

Later that night, it takes three cars to get everyone to the restaurant. We arrive, and I ask for a table for nine adults and three little ones.

We end up being seated in the back room, which works out perfectly. It is as if it is our own private party.

About ten minutes after we arrive, my 87-year-old Auntie Rose comes in with her daughter, Beth, supporting her by the arm. She is still sharp as a fiddle, and she likes having people to lean on.

The waiter comes over and looks at my mom, waiting for her order.

"I will have the shrimp and deep fried calamari," she says. Those are the non-kosher foods she loves to eat most when she goes out. I can see the delight in her face whenever she eats foods that are forbidden to her not only because of the Jewish laws but also because of her high blood pressure and cholesterol.

Everything is running smoothly, which is rare with all of the babies and toddlers running around these days. Robyn brought a video player to the restaurant, so Zach is watching his videos while we eat, and Ben and Jake are asleep.

"Mommy, I need to go potty," Zach says.

"Ok, Zach, I'll take you. Order tiramisu for me," Robyn says.

In the midst of the four conversations that are going on at the same time, which is the norm in the Jewish tradition, Zach suddenly comes running back to us, crying. A silence falls across the table as we see blood on his face, on his sweater, and on Robyn. Robyn is crying hysterically.

"His finger got caught in the bathroom door," she says between sobs. "Oh, my God, I didn't see his finger. Oh, my God!"

Ryan, the Emergency Room doctor in the family, calmly says, "Let me see." I cringe as I see the damage, and Ryan says, "It doesn't look good. We need to go to the hospital."

Beth, who lives in Montréal, tells us, "The Children's Hospital is the best hospital to go to." Her voice is quivering and loud, and I am sure that the whole restaurant hears her.

"I'm not sure what the best way to get there is."

"We should call an ambulance," Ryan says. "He will get seen faster that way."

"*Yoi eeshtanam*," my mom says.

Edna looks at Zach's finger.

"*Yoi eeshtanam*," she echoes my mom. "His finger is horrible; it is hanging by a thread."

Marc, Zach's dad, is white as a ghost, taking in the scene around him. I sit quietly. I am calm. I know Zach will be fine. Besides, Ryan and Michelle look calm, so I know everything is under control.

The ambulance arrives, and Ryan, Marc, Zach, and Robyn go in. Edna, Michelle and my mom go home with the other kids, and I am delegated to drive Marc's car to the hospital. This is perfect for me because it is a chance to get away from all the hysteria and still be of some help.

Somehow, I find my way to the hospital. I don't think I have the navigational genes my mom has, but my internal radar still guides me as usual. It is 8:30 p.m. when I walk through the door and see the waiting area. It is full of parents and their kids. The hallways are littered with paper, and there is even a Kleenex on the floor. It reminds me of the hospital in Prague where I had my appendix out. I go through another door and am in the Emergency Room.

Ryan is talking to the ER doctor, and Zach is in Robyn's arms. Marc is still quiet as he stands beside Zach and Robyn.

"What's going on?" I ask.

"Thanks to Ryan's connections as an Emergency Room doctor, we got into the ER quickly, bypassing the long list of patients waiting to be seen. It was a good time to use pull. Now we just have to wait to get an x-ray to see if Zach's finger is broken."

"Robyn, how are you doing?" I ask.

"I just can't stop playing the tape over in my head."

"Robyn, it was a freak accident."

"I keep thinking it is my fault."

"Robyn, if it was going to happen, at least it happened with you there," I say reassuringly. "Imagine what would have happened had it been Bubby, or Edna ... or me for that matter."

"I know. I thought the same thing, but his finger ..."

"Robyn, he'll be fine. Look at him. He is already better, and his hand is bandaged. He's not crying."

Finally, they move us to the x-ray waiting room. There is a big machine by us in the waiting area.

"Zach, look at this. What do you think it is?" Robyn says, trying to keep him entertained.

"I don't know, Mommy."

"Is it Bob the Builder?" she sings to the tune of the song from the show.

"No."

"Is it a house?" she sings again.

"Nooo."

"Is it a dinosaur?"

"Nooo."

"Is it a vacuum cleaner?"

"Nooo."

"Is it a camera?" Ryan interjects.

"Yes."

"Do you think it is a fire truck," Robyn continues.

"No, Mommy. It's a camera."

We all laugh. He is a smart kid. It is a kind of camera; it's an x-ray machine.

"Zach, you are right," Ryan says. "You're going to go inside a machine just like this, and they are going to take a picture of your finger with the camera. You're so lucky. You can tell everyone that you had a big camera take a picture of your finger."

Just then, a little girl of four and her mother sit beside us. The little girl had fallen, and the mother thinks she may have broken her arm.

I watch as the mom asks her little girl, "Do you want to sing the ABC song?"

The little girl starts, "A B C D E F G..." and then she stops. After a few seconds, Zach pipes in with "H I J K" and then finishes the song with a smile of accomplishment on his face.

Finally, Zach goes inside and we wait.

"Ryan, what kind of pain meds did they give Zach?" I ask.

"They gave him kids' Tylenol."

"That's all? How come he stopped crying?" I say, surprised. "He was just singing and smiling as if he was in no pain at all. I wouldn't think one Tylenol would do that."

"I guess he stopped being scared."

"What about the pain?"

"Kids are good that way. They seem to cope better than us."

Finally, Zach comes out of the room and excitedly says, "They took a picture! Can you read to me now, Mommy?"

We get the results, and Zach has no broken bones. Next, we just have to get a doctor to repair the damage to the finger, which, unfortunately, the ER doctor tells Ryan, "will probably still be at least three hours from now."

The time passes slowly. I look at Zach. His mom is reading to him. I can't believe he is not screaming from the pain and complaining. He needs a plastic surgeon to reinsert part of his finger. That is no small cut. I look from Zach to his father, Marc. I have never seen Marc so white and so non-responsive. He has gone through a lot, but he has always found the positive in everything. Even when he was in the ICU after he got shot and the doctor said, "Marc, you are a lucky guy. One inch to the left, and you would have been paralyzed. One inch down, you would have been dead." Marc responded, "Yeah, and one inch to the right, it would have hit a tree."

I remember visiting Marc shortly after he got home from the hospital. He was in bed most of the time or in a wheelchair when he had to get around. He had a bandage on his lower abdomen that had to be changed frequently, and he would not let anyone do it for him. The tape was sticky and would pull on his hair. It looked miserable, but I watched him do everything himself with the utmost care and patience. He had an amazing ability to give himself that tender loving care that most people need to get from others. That always stayed embedded in my brain. Not once did he wince. Was that what it was like for my dad when he had the bullets taken out? Did he have the same calmness, the same acceptance, and the same sheer determination?

That was when I knew Marc had the same healing abilities as my dad. They were both so gentle and kind to themselves. They didn't spend time second-guessing themselves, and playing the "what if," "should have," "could have," and "if only" tapes over and over in their heads. Gentleness and kindness to oneself is a very important ingredient for good blood.

Yet now, with his son, I can see he is at a loss. I've never seen him like this. He is so quiet it is as if he has shut down. Could it be because he feels helpless? Or maybe the memory of being in the ER when he got shot is coming back to haunt him? Or maybe it's a little bit of both?

Zach is in the hospital with his first injury, his first surgery, and Marc is scared, but it has already become clear that Zach inherited the ability to heal.

Zach was partially named after my dad. They decided to name him something that started with the letter Z, like Zoli, and they wound up choosing Zach. Marc had talked about his grandfather, Zoli, at Zach's Briss; the circumcision ceremony performed on every Jewish male on the eighth day of his life.

"My grandfather was a giant, and he was very calm," Marc had said. "He taught me how to play chess when I was six. He was a genius in my eyes, and he was my hero. He died two weeks before my ninth birthday, and I was crushed." Tears welled up in Marc's eyes. "We are naming Zach after my grandpa."

I smile at that memory as Zach is wheeled into a room and they prepare to put an IV in him so they can sedate him for the surgery.

"Zach, do you want to sing the ABC song?" The nurse asks, trying to distract him from the needle. She sings with Zach, but then, the needle misses the vein and Zach starts to cry. There is one more attempt and one more miss. Now Zach is screaming loudly.

"Pick me up, Mommy, I want to go home. Take me away."

Zach can't stop crying, so Robyn picks him up and calms him down. Another nurse comes in to try. She is supposed to be the "magic hands" nurse who always finds the vein.

When his mom tries to set him down again, Zach screams. "I don't want to go on the table!"

Marc and Robyn keep Zach down, and finally, the nurse is successful. The IV tube is in.

Zach is hysterically crying, but his mom tries to comfort him, "Zach, this will help fix the booboo. We can go outside now."

Once out of the room, Zach quickly stops crying.

"Read to me, Mommy," he says.

Marc and Robyn take turns reading to him.

"Irit," Robyn says to me as Marc reads. "Thank you for coming, for being here. I was so hysterical, and you calmed me down. You just have to put your hands on Zach, and he calms down. I remember that happened at his Briss, too. You held him before and after the Briss, and he just calmed down with you."

I think of Zach. He had one children's Tylenol. It was almost five hours later, and he still wasn't complaining apart from his tears over the IV. How did my father get the bullets out without anesthetics? How did Marc heal so well from his close encounter with death? Somehow they weren't afraid. Maybe that's the key ingredient to life. *I'm not afraid to die, Irit.* The words pass through my head for the zillionth time. He wasn't afraid. Fear is a major block to healing. Letting go or overcoming fear is the major key to allowing healing.

"Thanks for being here and for your healing ways," I hear again.

After the initial shock and pain of hurting himself, Zach calmed down. After the nurse missed so often with the IV needle, he once again calmed down and was read to while waiting for surgery.

I'm amazed at how resilient Zach is. Kids have a natural ability to be in the moment. The past or future is not in their makeup. They don't worry about what if, about the potential loss, about the pain never going away. They don't let fear or limiting beliefs take over. They just know everything is possible. Their bodies can heal faster because of their age, but they live in joy, playfulness and love—love for themselves and others—and they have an ability to be gentle with themselves, qualities which have been shown time and again to enhance healing for anyone at any age.

Dolphins live in that same space of joy, playfulness, and love that kids live in. When we swam with the dolphins, we were taught how to be more like them so that they would want to play with us, but children match that dolphin energy naturally.

Healing is a lifelong journey. One of my patients once asked me, since I have such strong role models, why I still get scared, why I am not just in my good blood mode all the time, and why I have had so many injuries that took so long to heal.

I laughed. "It's not about being perfect. No one is perfect," I said. "If you have pain over and over again, it doesn't mean you are doing anything wrong. We don't know what problems our genes have given us, and we don't know what lessons we are meant to learn so everyone may have a different journey. The important thing is how we focus to help ourselves access the inner healer within each of us."

"The key is awareness," I said. "My dad could recognize when he was stuck, but he had different comparisons to pull from, like his war experiences, that taught him about light and perspective in the deepest way. For most of us, when we get stuck, it's hard to recognize. It's easy for me to see it in my patients. I can help them see it and help them with letting it go, but it's often hard for me to see it in myself.

When we get stuck, it's hard for us to recognize it, so we need someone to help us become aware and to help us to let go of our blocks, our stuckness, and our limiting beliefs that stop us from accessing our good blood. If we are stuck in pain or painful thoughts, we make different choices than if we realize we are stuck. That's why it is so important to be aware. Then we can choose to create our lives rather than live out everything through our reactions. We can have the choice of redirecting and correcting our paths, just like I did on the skid pad at the BMW course.

~~~~~~~~~~~~~~

Finally, at 3 a.m., Zach goes in for surgery, and they put the anesthetics in the IV tube. It is the first medicine he has gotten since coming to the hospital besides the Tylenol, and it puts him to sleep right away.

~~~~~~~~~~~~~~

At about 1 p.m. the next day, Zach comes in the door. It's the eve of Passover.

"Look at my cast, Bubby. Can I have chocolate cake?" He says cheerfully.

Everyone laughs, and my mom serves him up a big slice. He eats his cake happily and then heads to his drum set.

Bang! Bang! Bang! His injury doesn't seem to be slowing him down.

I smile, and think back to when Marc was staying with me. He would always joke around with me and say he was the lucky one in the family.

"Why?" I had asked.

"It's easy," he explained adamantly. "In school we learned about survival of the fittest. Grandma and Grandpa were the fittest because only those with incredible strength could survive such hardships. You and my mom were born, but you both inherited the aftermath of all the suffering, so you still had to struggle. We're third generation, though, so everything got worked out, and we're left with the good traits."

Now it's fourth generation for Zach, and looking at that content little boy banging away on the drums, I think Marc may have been onto something, but I'll never tell him that.

By 6 p.m., it's time for another goodbye. Marc has to be at an important meeting in the morning so the family has to fly out at 8 p.m.. They are going to miss Seder. I give them all hugs and kisses, and Edna and my mom walk downstairs with them.

Ben is sleeping, and the place seems much quieter now that there are fewer of us here.

I look at the table with the special Passover tablecloth already on it, and the Passover Seder plate, with space for the five special foods that will be placed on it when the Seder begins. The five symbolic foods are displayed on this plate and eaten in remembrance of the exodus of the Israelites and the beginning of their freedom.

We have bitter herbs (*maror*), to signify the bitterness of slavery.

We have *haroset*, a brownish, unappetizing dish made from a mixture of apples, nuts, cinnamon, and wine, which looks like the mortar used to build the cities in Egypt but with a sweetness to represent the promise of a better world.

Then we have lamb shank (*z'roah*), which represents the blood of the lamb that was put on the doorposts of the homes of the Israelites so they would not be harmed with the tenth plague before the exodus, the killing of the firstborn male children.

Next is the roasted egg (*betzah*), which represents the animal sacrifice brought to the temple for each festival and is also a symbol of life.

The last item placed on the plate is fresh greens (*karpas*), to represent the new life of the Israelites in freedom. There are prayers for each of these dishes, and each one is presented in a specific order.

There are also four glasses of wine, or grape juice for the kids, which we drink throughout the night as a part of the special ceremony. We have a separate glass of wine for Elijah, the prophet. This glass is set in the middle of the table. I always loved that part. If Elijah drank from his glass, then we knew that he showed up.

Elijah showing up means there will be better times ahead in the world, or at least, that has always been my interpretation. There is a special section in the ceremony for Elijah, where the door is opened to allow him in, and we sing a special song for him, *Elijah Hanavi*. When I was younger, I always opened the door, and then a few minutes later, we would close the door with another tribute to him.

Every year when I was little, I would say in an excited tone, "Elijah was here! See, the glass of wine is less full now."

The door opens, and my mom comes into the kitchen. "Ednooka," she says to my sister, "set the table. We will start in ten minutes."

We have been through so many Seders in this family, and even after all these years and my mom's back, neck and hand pains, her strong independence remains the same. Once again, she creates magic with the food.

When the table is set, Edna goes back into the kitchen and offers to help with the food.

"Get out of the kitchen. I will do it," I hear Mom say in her loud voice.

Michelle and I smile. For my mom, food preparation is like meditation. She is the master of her kitchen, and she shows her love through the food she prepares in it. When someone tries to help, it creates havoc for her because she has everything organized in her mind; "help" breaks her flow. Besides, the fact that she still doesn't want help means her body and mind are doing well, and we're grateful and thrilled for that.

The aroma of the matzo ball soup, roasted chicken, potatoes, greens and flourless Passover chocolate cake, which had been in the oven earlier in the day, makes me even hungrier than I am. The foods are placed on the Passover plate, and all the wine glasses are filled.

My brother-in-law, Al, was at the head of the table in previous years, but he is not feeling well this year so he stayed home. Ryan is taking the seat at the head of the table today, in the reclined position to symbolize freedom.

I open the *Hagaddah,* and we begin. As I look through the book, I smile. Passover is the symbol of freedom, and I can still hear my dad saying, '*Iritka, every day I am free, I am happy.*'

~~~~~~~~~~~~~~

The night ends, and we all go to sleep. At 5:45 a.m., I slowly crawl out of bed and get ready to leave for California. I don't want to wake anyone up, but when my mom does awaken, she goes into a flurry, getting me ready.

"Don't forget the food I prepared for you," she says as she hands it to me.

I head to the door and lean over to kiss her on the left cheek.

"Call me when you get home," she says.

I head to the elevator, which is about 200 feet away, and when I turn around, she is following me with her eyes. I wave goodbye, and the doors close. When I reach my car, I look up. I can't see my mom because she is on the ninth floor, but I know she is watching. It makes me feel warm inside, and I smile as I look up.

My trip home is uneventful. I arrive home, unpack, and call my mom. It's 9:35 p.m. her time.

"How was your trip?" she asks.

"It was good."

"Did you have trouble bringing the food through the checkpoint?"

"No, it smelled so good I think the officers got hungry, but they let me go through with the food."

"The kids all left this afternoon. I'm tired."

"Well, you should go to bed early. You've worked really hard. Thanks for everything, and thanks for all the delicious food. I love you."

"I love you, too."

~~~~~~~~~~~~~~

The next morning, I'm in bed when the phone rings. "Irit, my cousin, how are you?"

"Hey Susan, I'm good. A little tired from my trip. How are you doing?"

"Good. I found a box of pictures and letters that I thought you might find interesting. The letters are in Hungarian."

"Yeah! That sounds awesome. I'll have to visit soon and check them out."

After Aunt Ersie's death, Susan and I had kept in contact for a few months, but we eventually lost touch.

After five years had passed, I was trying to gather some information about Aunt Ersie. I looked for Susan's number in the phone book, but it was unlisted. Fortunately, my cousin George in Holland, to whom I never speak, emailed me the next day because he wanted some historical information, too. I asked him for Susan's email, and he sent it to me. He also told me that, coincidently, Susan had just asked for my email.

I emailed Susan about a week later, and within a few minutes, I saw an email from her in my inbox. I could tell from her message that she had not read my email. We just happened to write each other at the same time. I decided to call her shortly after. She still had not checked her inbox.

When we both realized we had written each other at the same time, we both exclaimed in unison, "It is like our grandmother, she always knew. She always knew things before they happened."

"Irit, it is amazing how the years go by so quickly," she had said. "Uncle Zoli and my mom were so close. They wanted us to be close. It was so important, especially to my mom. I bet they are smiling down at us now that we are back in touch."

"I bet they are."

"Irit, how is your mom doing?" she asks, bringing me back to the present.

"She's amazing. She is definitely an example of the impossible being possible. Can you believe she is getting sharper and sharper as the years go by?"

"I remember the first time I met her, but for me, the main event was meeting your father. One of the most beautiful moments in my life was when I met Uncle Zoli for the first time. Do you remember that time?"

"I was too little to remember."

"We were living in Aruba, and my mom, for a reason I don't remember, had to wait for a long time to get the passport to travel. I was twelve, and I was supposed to write a book report about my visit to Montréal. No one in my class had been to Canada before so that was exciting in itself.

"I remember the most important thing for me was seeing how my mother would react when she saw Uncle Zoli. It had been almost 25 years since they had last seen each other. That would have been almost twice my age at the time. I remember wondering, *What would that feel like?* I knew it would be huge. I had never seen my mom cry. She never cried in front of us, and I kind of wanted to see if she would cry. I knew all the stories, especially the ones where they were little and cried themselves to sleep when their mom had to leave them. It was as if they were a team against the world. My mom said that Zoli was gentle and that he always protected her."

"I heard those stories, too. I always wanted my dad to tell me the stories about our family over and over again when I was a kid. So, what happened next?"

"The doorbell rang, and I remember this moment perfectly. I saw this very gentle man with an aura of light around him. I noticed his thin, big, pointed nose and his big hands. His mouth was puckered. It was less like a smile and more like he was going to kiss you. When my mom saw Uncle

Zoli, she was breathless. She did not go crazy. She was reserved, but somehow, I knew it was monumental. I saw you and your sister at the top of the stairs. I had never met any cousins before, so that was exciting for me. Does your sister remember?"

"I don't think so because she never said anything. I never asked your mom or my dad what it was like. I just made my own assumptions in my head. It is so cool hearing it now from your perspective. Please go on."

"We started coming up the stairs, and Uncle Zoli was coming down. It was quiet. My mom and your dad held each other for a long time. They wouldn't let go. Neither Zoli nor Ersie cried, but I could see tears rolling down my dad's face and your mom's face. I was hoping to see my mom cry for the first time, but it ended up being the first time I saw that from my father.

"How did you end up communicating with my dad? Did he speak any English?"

"Uncle Zoli spoke to us in Hungarian even though he knew we wouldn't understand, and it did not matter. Somehow, I understood. He loved me. He was so happy for his sister and her children. He was happy to know his sister was well provided for. I could feel it.

"They stayed up late and talked, and my mom could not be distracted. Julie and I could always get her attention, but not now, with Uncle Zoli. She was drinking in all the things she had missed.

"Your father, with his gentleness, was how I always wished my dad was, but that was never to be."

"Susan," I finally interrupt, "my dad and your mom chose partners who were very similar. I guess it's an interesting coincidence, but then again are there any coincidences?"

We both laugh.

"I can't wait to have you visit. I hope the pictures and letters will be helpful."

"Maybe I'll come in a few weeks. I'll check my schedule and let you know soon."

"That would be great. Let's connect soon. Love you!"

"Love you, too. Bye."

I hang up the phone, and I think of my Aunt Ersie and how her voice called my dad back into the world. I can hear my dad's voice as it always sounded when he would first say hello to me, '*Eareeeatka*'. I can hear the first six words of the Shema. '*Sh'ma Yisrael Adonai Eloheinu Adonai Echad*.' (Hear, O Israel: the Lord is our God, the Lord is One.)

I can feel my ancestors in the room. I can see the blue-blue eyes of Ari Ben Canaan, and I can feel that familiar tingling in my body that those eyes always gave me. I can see my angel in Prague, with her soft brown eyes as she held my hand.

I can taste the chicken that Jofie and Barna brought to the hospital on my birthday.

I can hear *Chariots of Fire* playing in my head, and I can feel the energy of all of my students in every cell of my body.

I can see my aunt Ersie, with that beautiful smile. She is surrounded by her favorite color, purple, the same color that my client, Barbara, told me was the most powerful color for her healing.

I can smell the aroma of delicious food, the food my mom prepares with "a little bit of this and a little bit of that," the food she has prepared for me so many times.

I can see my mom's gold chain, her connection to her dad's love. I can see her amazing fortitude, resilience, and resourcefulness, which I never even recognized as a child. I can feel her love as she gives me the food she always spends hours preparing.

I can feel the effortlessness of my motion through the air toward a trapeze, and the strength with which I held on. I can feel exhilaration as I land right in the bull's eye after skydiving without any help.

I can see the eyes of that dolphin, embodying kindness, joy and playfulness and changing my life forever. I watch my Ellinani as she climbs those fifty four stairs, and I can see the smile on her face as she is the first to reach the top.

I can hear Marika's voice say, "Everything I say is true," as I look at the numbers on her left forearm. I can hear Ellinani's voice say, "The greatest gift of life is the gift of love." And then I hear my dad's voice: "There is a positive in everything; you just have to plant the seed and keep watering every day and not give up."

The human spirit is resilient. Love is the common thread. It allows us to heal our wounds, forgive, and transform.

"Thank you," I say, and I hear an ocean of voices call back. I see my dolphin friend jumping out of the water, with that special dolphin squeal, saying "*Lechaim*" (to life).

~~~~~~~~~~~~~~

Irit Schaffer

2014: Conclusion

On Christmas Eve of 2014, Alise passed away. In the four months of her illness, I was inspired by my mom's ability to surrender, be grateful, keep her amazing sense of humor, and still care deeply about those around her. Our relationship deepened, and I was in awe of her. I was inspired by her ability to be in her light.

At the funeral service, Ryan took the podium and began his eulogy. It was clear there was no better way to conclude this story:

Bubby was my hero. Today we are here to celebrate the life of my hero. Although I am extremely sad that Bubby is no longer with us, I am also truly honored that I got to spend 42 years of my life with this amazing woman. To me, she was more than a grandma. She was my superhero. In my opinion, she was bulletproof. No matter how many times she said my face was fat, called me a stinker, or pinched my *tuchas* (bum), she was the one person who, in my eyes, could do no wrong.

The qualities I admired most about her were her humility, her inner strength, her independence, and most important, her sense of family.

Humility: Bubby has accomplished so many unbelievable feats in her life, and the irony is that the only time that she would let us honor her is at her funeral. Not once in her life would she ever let us celebrate her life and its many accomplishments. Not once in her life did I ever hear her complain, and let me tell you, she had a lot she could have complained about.

Inner Strength: One word. Survivor.

Independence: She lived for almost 30 years by herself and not once did she ever ask for help from anyone. At age 92, she was still cooking unbelievable meals and would never let me in the kitchen to help her cook or clean.

Family: Her family, above all else, was her biggest accomplishment and sense of pride. As I grew up, I always had to take the Bubby tour, which gave her the ability to brag to her friends about her grandkids. This lasted until we had kids, at which point I quickly became chopped liver and her great-grandchildren were her objects of greatest pride. Her pictures of family that completely encompassed her apartment were the true trophies of her life.

There are many stories that I could tell about Bubs, and the one I will remember most occurred when I was trying to learn how to cook her famed chocolate cake. I was looking for a spoon and picked one out of the drawer. It had an engraving on it, and she said I could not use that one. I then asked her what was special about that spoon. She said as she was leaving Bergen Belsen Concentration Camp, she grabbed that spoon so she would never forget.

As I live my life, I imagine the days that she spent at Bergen Belsen and how every day she stayed alive because of the optimism that tomorrow would be the day of liberation, and I think to myself, *Bubs, I will miss your cake. I will miss your chicken soup. I will miss you speaking your mind as only a 92 year old Jewish woman can, and as long as I live, I will carry your humility, your optimism, your inner strength and your family values to pass on to my children, but there is one thing I will never do. I will never forget my hero!*

I love you,
Ryan

Select MSI Books

Self-Help Books

57 Steps to Paradise (Lorenz)

A Woman's Guide to Self-Nurturing (Romer)

Creative Aging: A Baby Boomer's Guide to Successful Living (Vassiliadis & Romer)

Divorced! Survival Techniques for Singles over Forty (Romer)

Living Well with Chronic Illness (Charnas)

Publishing for Smarties: Finding a Publisher (Ham)

Survival of the Caregiver (Snyder)

The Rose and the Sword: How to Balance Your Feminine and Masculine Energies (Bach & Hucknall)

The Widower's Guide to a New Life (Romer)

Widow: A Survival Guide for the First Year (Romer)

Inspirational and Religious Books

A Believer-Waiting's First Encounters with God (Mahlou)

A Guide to Bliss: Transforming Your Life through Mind Expansion (Tubali)

El Poder de lo Transpersonal (Ustman)

Everybody's Little Book of Everyday Prayers (MacGregor)

How to Get Happy and Stay That Way: Practical Techniques for Putting Joy into Your Life (Romer)

Joshuanism (Tosto)

Living in Blue Sky Mind: Basic Buddhist Teachings for a Happy Life (Diedrichs)

Puertas a la Eternidad (Ustman)

Surviving Cancer, Healing People: One Cat's Story (Sula)

The Gospel of Damascus (O. Imady)

The Seven Wisdoms of Life: A Journey into the Chakras (Tubali)

When You're Shoved from the Right, Look to Your Left: Metaphors of Islamic Humanism (O. Imady)

Memoirs

Blest Atheist (Mahlou)

Forget the Goal, the Journey Counts . . . 71 Jobs Later (Stites)

Healing from Incest: Intimate Conversations with My Therapist (Henderson & Emerton)

It Only Hurts When I Can't Run: One Girl's Story (Parker)

Las Historias de Mi Vida (Ustman)

Losing My Voice and Finding Another (C. Thompson)

Of God, Rattlesnakes, and Okra (Easterling)

Road to Damascus (E. Imady)

Foreign Culture

Syrian Folktales (M. Imady)

The Rise and Fall of Muslim Civil Society (O. Imady)

The Subversive Utopia: Louis Kahn and the Question of National Jewish Style in Jerusalem (Sakr)

Thoughts without a Title (Henderson)

Psychology & Philosophy

Anxiety Anonymous: The Big Book on Anxiety Addiction (Ortman)

Road Map to Power (Husain & Husain)

The Marriage Whisperer: How to Improve Your Relationship Overnight (Pickett)

Understanding the Critic: Socionics in Everyday Life (Quinelle)

Understanding the Entrepreneur: Socionics in Everyday Life (Quinelle)

Understanding the People around You: An Introduction to Socionics (Filatova)

Understanding the Seeker: Socionics in Everyday Life (Quinelle)

Humor

How My Cat Made Me a Better Man (Feig)

Mommy Poisoned Our House Guest (C. B. Leaver)

The Musings of a Carolina Yankee (Amidon)

Parenting

365 Teacher Secrets for Parents: Fun Ways to Help Your Child in Elementary School (McKinley & Trombly)

How to Be a Good Mommy When You're Sick (Graves)

Lessons of Labor (Aziz)

CPSIA information can be obtained
at www.ICGtesting.com
Printed in the USA
LVHW011329170319
610956LV00018B/745